The Ancient World

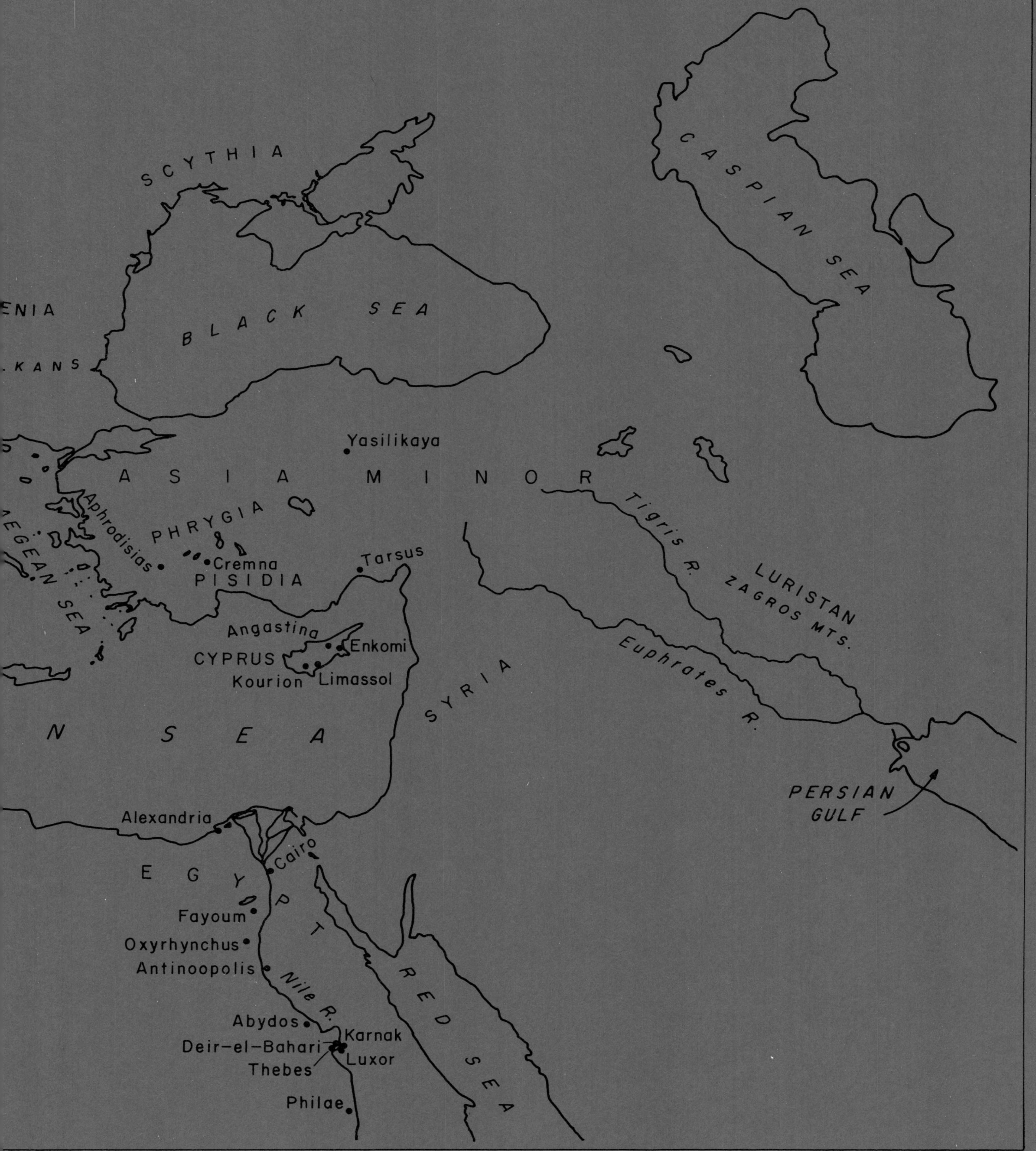

SCYTHIA
ENIA
BLACK SEA
CASPIAN SEA
KANS
Yasilikaya
ASIA MINOR
Aphrodisias
PHRYGIA
AEGEAN SEA
Cremna
PISIDIA
Tarsus
Tigris R.
LURISTAN
ZAGROS MTS.
Angastina
Enkomi
CYPRUS
Kourion
Limassol
SYRIA
Euphrates R.
N SEA
PERSIAN GULF
Alexandria
Cairo
EGYPT
Fayoum
Oxyrhynchus
Antinoopolis
Nile R.
RED SEA
Abydos
Karnak
Deir-el-Bahari
Luxor
Thebes
Philae

The ARCHAEOLOGICAL COLLECTION of the Johns Hopkins University

The ARCHAEOLOGICAL COLLECTION of the Johns Hopkins University

ELLEN REEDER WILLIAMS

The Johns Hopkins University Press

Baltimore and London

This volume has been brought to publication with the generous assistance of the Middendorf Foundation.

© 1984 by The Johns Hopkins University Press
All rights reserved
Printed in the United States of America

The Johns Hopkins University Press, Baltimore, Maryland 21218
The Johns Hopkins Press Ltd., London

LIBRARY OF CONGRESS CATALOGING IN PUBLICATION DATA

Williams, Ellen Reeder.
The archaeological collection of the Johns Hopkins University.

1. Classical antiquities—Catalogs. 2. Near East—Antiquities—Catalogs. 3. Johns Hopkins University—Archaeological collections—Catalogs. I. Johns Hopkins University. II. Title.
DE46.5.B344W54 1984 930 83-18699
ISBN 0-8018-3050-8

Frontispiece: See pages 32–33 in this volume.

DE
46.5
.B344
J64
1984

For Terry Weisser

and the

Department of Conservation and Technical Research

of the

Walters Art Gallery

DEC 6 '84
223173

Contents

Acknowledgments

This publication could not have materialized without the support of the Middendorf Foundation, which made possible both the conservation of the objects and the publication itself. I am most grateful to the Foundation's officers, E. Phillips Hathaway, Roger B. Hopkins, Jr., Craig Lewis, and Robert B. Russell II. The conservation project was also funded by the National Endowment for the Arts; the George Washington University provided grants for the photography and the drawings.

Numerous individuals participated in the many aspects of this project. Foremost among these are Terry Weisser and her assistants in the Department of Conservation and Technical Research of the Walters Art Gallery: Meg Craft, Christine Del Re, Ellen Howe, Paul Jett, Judith Levinson, Henry Lie, Linda Scheifler, Linda Sirkis, Carol Snow, Donna Strahan, Shelley Sturman, and especially Shelley Reisman, who worked solely on the Hopkins material during 1978 and 1979. I would also like to thank Janet Macht for her drawings, Dean Pendleton for the maps, Virginia Greene of the University Museum in Philadelphia for the vase profiles, William Seim of Service Photo Supply in Baltimore for most of the photographs, and Theresa Morrison for skillfully transferring the manuscript to a word processor.

It is also a pleasure to acknowledge the assistance of the many people who generously contributed their expertise on individual objects: Carolyn Beecheno, Simone Besques, Larissa Bonfante, Bernard Bothmer, Dietrich von Bothmer, Diana Buitron, H. W. Catling, Mario del Chiaro, Diskin Clay, Raymond Cunningham, Richard DePuma, Katherine Dunbabin, William V. Elder III, Sally Freeman, Ingrid Gantz, Hans Goedicke, Claireve Grandjouan, Dorothy Hill, N. Himmelmann, Lilian Jeffrey, Alan Johnston, Frances F. Jones, Guntram Koch, Gunther Kopcke, Deena Kurtz, Frederick Matz, David Mitten, Julie Morgan, William Needle, Richard Nicholls, Joseph Noble, Andrew Oliver, Jr., Karl Parlasca, Kyle Phillips, John Pollini, Betty Poucher, James Poultney, Richard Randall, Emeline Richardson, Sally Roberts, Diana Schramm, Peter Siewert, Peter van Slyke, Penny Small, Patricia Spencer, Jürgen Thimme, Dorothy Burr Thompson, Homer Thompson, Susan Tripp, Lucy Turnbull, Cornelius C. Vermeule III, and Gary Vikan.

The volume owes its final appearance to production editor Mary Lou Kenney and designer Gerard Valerio. I am most appreciative of their patience and thoughtfulness.

Finally, I thank my husband, Charles, for his willingness to carry out time-consuming chores associated with the project, and for his unending support.

Abbreviations

AA: *Archäologischer Anzeiger.*
ABL: C. H. E. Haspels, *Attic Black-figured Lekythoi* (Paris, 1936).
ABV: J. D. Beazley, *Attic Black-Figure Vase-Painters* (Oxford, 1956).
ActaA: *Acta Archaeologica.*
AJA: *American Journal of Archaeology.*
AJP: *American Journal of Philology.*
AntK: *Antike Kunst.*
AntK Beiheft: *Antike Kunst Beiheft.*
ArchEph: *Archaiologike Ephemeris.*
ArtB: *Art Bulletin.*
ARV[2]: J. D. Beazley, *Attic Red-Figure Vase-Painters*, 2d ed. (Oxford, 1963).
AthMitt: *Mitteilungen des deutschen archäologischen Instituts, Athenische Abteilung.*
AthMitt Beiheft: *Mitteilungen des deutschen archäologischen Instituts, Athenische Abteilung, Beiheft.*
AZ: *Archäologische Zeitung.*
BABesch: *Bulletin van de Vereeniging tot Bevordering der Kennis van de Antike Beschaving.*
BCH: *Bulletin de correspondance hellénique.*
Beazley, *AttV*: J. D. Beazley, *Attische Vasenmaler des rotfigurigen Stils* (Tübingen, 1925).
Beazley, *VA*: J. D. Beazley, *Attic Red-figured Vases in American Museums* (Cambridge, 1918).
Besques: S. Besques, *Catalogue raisonné des figurines et reliefs en terre-cuite grecs étrusques et romains. Museé du Louvre et collections des universités de France.* 3 vols. (Paris, 1954–72).
Bieber, *Sculpture*: M. Bieber, *The Sculpture of the Hellenistic Age* (New York, 1955).
Bieber, *Theater*: M. Bieber, *The History of the Greek and Roman Theater*, 2d ed. rev. (Princeton, 1961).
Bloesch: H. Bloesch, *Formen Attischen Schalen* (Bern, 1940).
BMusArt: *Bulletin des Musées r. d'art et d'histoire.*
Boardman, *Black Figure*: J. Boardman, *Athenian Black Figure Vases* (New York, 1974).
Boardman, *GGFR*: J. Boardman, *Greek Gems and Finger Rings* (New York, 1972).
Boardman, *Red Figure*: J. Boardman, *Athenian Red Figure Vases: The Archaic Period* (London, 1975).
Boucher, *Bronzes grecs*: S. Boucher, *Bronzes grecs, hellénistiques et étrusque des musées de Lyon* (Lyon, 1970).
Boucher, *Bronzes romains*: S. Boucher, *Bronzes romains figurés du musée des beaux-arts de Lyon* (Lyon, 1973).
Breitenstein: N. Breitenstein, *Catalogue of Terracottas Cypriote, Greek, Etrusco-Italian and Roman* (Copenhagen, 1941).
Brendel: O. Brendel, *Etruscan Art* (New York, 1948).
BSA: *British School at Athens, Annual.*
BSR: *British School of Archaeology at Rome, Papers.*
Carter: J. C. Carter, *The Sculpture of Taras. Transactions of the American Philological Association*, New Series, vol. 65, pt. 7 (1975).
CIL: *Corpus Inscriptionum Latinarum.*
Comstock-Vermeule: M. Comstock and C. Vermeule, *Greek Etruscan and Roman Bronzes in the Museum of Fine Arts Boston* (Greenwich, 1971).
CVA: *Corpus Vasorum Antiquorum.*
DarSag: C. V. Daremberg and E. Saglio, eds. *Dictionnaire des antiquités grecques et romaines d'après les textes et les monuments* (Paris, 1875–1919).
Deltion: *Archaiologikon deltion.*
de Ridder: A. de Ridder, *Les bronzes antiques du Louvre*, 2 vols. (Paris, 1913–15).
Dohan: E. H. Dohan, *Italic Tomb-Groups in the University Museum* (Philadelphia, 1942).
Dörig: J. Dörig, ed., *Art antique. Collections privées de la suisse romande* (Geneva, 1975).
EAA: *Enciclopedia dell'arte antica, classica e orientale* (Rome, 1958–66).
EEF: *Egypt Exploration Fund.*
EES: *Egypt Exploration Society.*
EVP: J. D. Beazley, *Etruscan Vase-Painting* (Cambridge, 1947).
FdD: *Fouilles de Delphes, École Française d'Athènes* (Paris, 1902).
FR: A. Furtwängler and K. Reichhold, *Griechische Vasenmalerei*, 3 vols. (Munich, 1904–32).
Furtwängler, *ND*: A. Furtwängler, *Neue Denkmäler antiker Kunst*, vol. 3 (Munich, 1905).
Gerhard: E. Gerhard, *Etruskische Spiegel*, 5 vols. (Berlin, 1840–97).
GettyMusJ: *J. P. Getty Museum Journal.*
Hartwig, *Meisterschalen*: P. Hartwig, *Die griechischen Meisterschalen* (Stuttgart and Berlin, 1893).
Heldensage[3]: F. Brommer, *Vasenlisten zur griechischen Heldensage*, 3d. ed. (Marburg, 1973).
Hencken, *Peabody*: H. Hencken, "Tarquinia,Villlanovans and Early Etruscans," *Peabody Museum Bulletin* 23 (1968).
Hencken, *Tarquinia*: H. Hencken, *Tarquinia and Etruscan Origins* (New York, 1968).
Higgins: R. A. Higgins, *Catalogue of the Terracottas in the Department of Greek and Roman Antiquities, British Museum* (London, 1954).
Hill, *Bronzes*: D. K. Hill, *Catalogue of Classical Bronze Sculpture in the Walters Art Gallery* (Baltimore, 1949).
Hoppin, *I and II*: J. C. Hoppin, *A Handbook of Attic Red-figured Vases*, 2 vols. (Cambridge, 1919).
Hornbostel: W. Hornbostel, *Kunst der Antike* (Mainz, 1977).
HSCP: *Harvard Studies in Classical Philology.*
JARCE: *Journal of the American Research Center in Egypt.*

JdI: *Jahrbuch des (k.) deutschen archäologischen Instituts.*

JdI Bilderheft: *Jahrbuch des (k.) deutschen archäologischen Instituts, Bilderheft.*

JdI-EH: *Jahrbuch des (k.) deutschen archäologischen Instituts, Ergänzungsheft.*

JHS: *Journal of Hellenic Studies.*

JRS: *Journal of Roman Studies.*

JWalt: *Journal of the Walters Art Gallery.*

Klein, *LI*: W. Klein, *Die griechischen Vasen mit Lieblingsinschriften*, 2nd ed. (Leipzig, 1898).

Klumbach: H. Klumbach, *Tarentiner Grabkunst* (Reutlingen, 1937).

MAAR: *Memoirs of the American Academy in Rome.*

Mitten, *Master Bronzes*: D. G. Mitten and S. I. Doehringer, *Master Bronzes from the Classical World* (Mainz, 1967).

Mitten, *RISD*: D. G. Mitten, *Classical Bronzes, Catalogue of the Classical Collection, Museum of Art, Rhode Island School of Design* (Providence, 1975).

MJb: Münchener Jahrbuch der bildenden Kunst.

MonAnt: *Monumenti Antichi.*

MonPiot: *Monuments et mémoires publ. par l'Académie des inscriptions et belles lettres, Fondation Piot.*

Naville, 1: E. Naville, "The Eleventh Dynasty Temple at Deir el-Bahari," pt. 1. *EEF* 28 (1907).

Naville, 2: E. Naville, "The Eleventh Dynasty Temple at Deir el-Bahari," pt. 2. *EEF* 30 (1910).

Naville, 3: E. Naville, "The Eleventh Dynasty Temple at Deir el-Bahari," pt. 3. *EEF* 32 (1913).

NSc: *Notizie degli Scavi di Antichità.*

OCD: N. G. L. Hammond and H. H. Scullard, eds. *Oxford Classical Dictionary*, 2d ed. (Oxford, 1970).

ÖJh: *Jahreshefte des österreichischen archäologischen Instituts.*

OlBer: *Bericht über die Ausgrabungen in Olympia*, 1936–).

OpusArch: Opuscula Archaeologica.

OpusAth: *Opuscula Atheniensia.*

OpusRom: *Opuscula Romana.*

PAAR: *American Academy in Rome, Papers and Monographs.*

Paralipomena: J. D. Beazley, *Paralipomena*, 2d ed. (Oxford, 1971).

Pernice: E. Pernice, *Die hellenistische Kunst in Pompeji*, Vols. 4–5 (Berlin and Leipzig, 1925, 1932).

Philippart: H. Philippart, *Collections d'antiquités classiques aux états-unis* (Brussels, 1928).

Pohl: I. Pohl, *The Iron Age Necropolis of Sorba. Skrifter utgivna av Svenska Institute I Rom* ser. 4, vol. 32, 1972.

Poulsen: V. Poulsen, *Catalogue des terres cuites grecques et romaines. Publications de la Glyptothèque Ny Carlsberg*, no. 2 (Copenhagen, 1949).

RA: *Revue archéologique.*

RDAC: *Report of the Department of Antiquities, Cyprus.*

RE: A. Pauly, G. Wissowa and W. Kroll, eds. *Real-Encyclopädie der klassischen Altertumswissenschaft* (Stuttgart, 1894–1919).

Rebuffat-Emmanuel: D. Rebuffat-Emmanuel, *Le miroir étrusque d'après la collection du Cabinet des Médailles. Collection de l'école français de Rome*, vol. 20 (Rome, 1973).

RendPontAcc: *Atti della Pontificia Accademia Romana di Archeologia, Rendiconti.*

RGKomm: *Römisch-germanische Kommission d. arch. Inst. d. deutschen Reichs, Berichte.*

RGZM: *Römisch-germanische Zentralmuseum, Mainz, Jb.*

Richter, *Bronzes*: G. M. A. Richter, *Greek, Etruscan and Roman Bronzes, The Metropolitan Museum of Art* (New York, 1915).

RömMitt: Mitteilungen des deutschen archäologischen Instituts, Römische Abteilung.

RömMitt-EH: *Mitteilungen des deutschen archäologischen Instituts, Römische Abteilung, Ergänzungsheft.*

Sculpture BMFA: M. B. Comstock and C. C. Vermeule, *Sculpture in Stone. The Greek, Roman and Etruscan Collections of the Museum of Fine Arts Boston* (Boston, n.d.).

Simon: E. Simon, *Die griechische Vasen* (Munich, 1976).

Spinazzola: V. Spinazzola, *Le arti decorative in Pompeii e nel Museo Nazionale di Napoli* (Florence, 1928).

StEtr: *Studi Etruschi.*

Sundwall: J. Sundwall, *Die älteren italischen Fibeln* (Berlin, 1943).

TAPA: *Transactions of the American Philological Association.*

Thompson, *Troy*: D. B. Thompson, *Troy. The Terracotta Figurines of the Hellenistic Period. Supplementary Monograph 3* (Princeton, 1963).

Ward-Perkins and Claridge: J. Ward-Perkins and A. Claridge, *Pompeii A.D. 79* (Boston, 1978).

The ARCHAEOLOGICAL COLLECTION of the Johns Hopkins University

No. 5. Basalt Group of Bak and Ruiw

Introduction

Established in 1882, the Archaeological Collection of the Johns Hopkins University is one of the oldest university collections of archaeological material in the United States. It is of special significance because it is linked both with the history of classics at Johns Hopkins and with distinguished scholars and collectors who have figured prominently in the growth of the discipline of classical archaeology.

The Archaeological Collection comprises thousands of objects from Egyptian, Near Eastern, Greek, and Roman civilizations. Although a few items have been the subject of individual studies,[1] no catalogue of the collection has ever been published. The volume in hand is necessarily selective, inasmuch as it presents only as many of the finest objects as could be studied and receive conservation treatment within the parameters of the grants received for these purposes. The pieces included were chosen on the basis of their quality and their ability to represent both the breadth of the collection and the variety of contributing sources. In view of the nonspecialized background of visitors to the collection and of individuals interested in the university, the entries are intended to be comprehensible and useful to the layman as well as the scholar and student.

History of the Collection

Soon after the Johns Hopkins University had been established, in 1876, farsighted members of the Latin and Greek Seminaries, the Department of History and Politics, and the Oriental Seminary envisioned a historical museum for the university.[2] Among these individuals was Herbert Baxter Adams, who taught in the Department of History and Politics from 1876 to 1900 and who was a co-founder of the American Historical Association in 1884. Through Adams's efforts, the first historical material was acquired in 1882: an Indian axe from Joppa, Maryland, and a brick from the first courthouse in Baltimore County.[3] These items were displayed in the Seminary Library of Historical and Political Science, and in the Bluntschli Library in McCoy Hall, buildings located on the old campus.[4]

The first major group of objects arrived in 1884, when the Egyptian collection of Colonel Mendes Israel Cohen was purchased by the university.[5] Colonel Cohen was a Baltimorean who fought in the War of 1812 and then briefly engaged in a family banking operation before departing for Europe in 1829. His travels took him to Egypt in 1832, when he sailed up the Nile as far as the second cataract at Wadi Halfa near the Sudanese border, an area that had been visited by few western travelers since Burckhardt first explored the region in 1813. With the help of his Arab servant, Cohen purchased fabric in a local town and constructed an American flag that is still in the possession of the university and that is believed to have been the first American flag ever flown upon the Nile. Cohen's engaging letters home to his family recount colorful incidents, such as his encounter at Luxor with the French officers who were removing the obelisk that would become the celebrated focal point of the Place de la Concorde.[6] Throughout his journey, and particularly at Memphis and Thebes, Cohen acquired small statuettes, some larger sculpture, jewelry, and animal mummies. This material was supplemented in 1835 by purchases Cohen made in London at the auction of the collection of Consul General Salt (see no. 5). Eventually, Cohen's holdings included 689 objects, most of whose provenances and dimensions he admirably recorded in a catalogue that is now in the possession of the Maryland Historical Society. Cohen's collection was the first private collection of Egyptian antiquities in the United States, and in 1845 was used by George

No. 14. Marble Theater Relief, Side B

R. Gliddon, a former U.S. vice-consul at Cairo, to illustrate what were some of the earliest lectures on Egyptology ever presented in this country.[7]

In the same year in which the Cohen Collection arrived at Johns Hopkins, 1884, Arthur L. Frothingham, Jr., a Fellow in Greek from 1882 to 1885, presented the university with its first classical material, in the form of several clay lamps and Etruscan vases.[8] Frothingham would play a key role in the growth of the Archaeological Institute of America; in this same year he and Alfred Emerson, also a Fellow in Greek, established the Baltimore Society of the Archaeological Institute of America,[9] and in 1885 Frothingham and his colleague Allan Marquand initiated the publication, in Baltimore, of the *American Journal of Archaeology*.

In 1887, Frothingham and Emerson conceived a plan to conduct an archaeological expedition to Eretria, and they successfully sought funding for the project from members of the Baltimore Society of the Archaeological Institute of America. The expedition did not materialize, however, so Frothingham and Emerson decided to use the money to acquire archaeological objects for the Baltimore Society. While in Rome in 1887, they purchased a collection of vases that the German archaeologist Hartwig had intended to sell to the Antiquarium, the archaeological museum in Berlin, but agreed to turn over to the Baltimoreans when the German funds were delayed.[10] These red-figure vases are of exceptional quality and are probably the objects for which the Johns Hopkins collection is best known today (nos. 101–5, 107, 109, 111–15). In addition to these vases, Frothingham and Emerson obtained several items from the German archaeologist K. F. Helbig; this material included the amphora by Nikosthenes (no. 100) and the architectural terracottas from Capua and Tarentum (nos. 73, 74, 81–85). The remaining monies were spent in acquiring a variety of items, including a fragment from one of the archaic buildings on the Acropolis (no. 67). All this material was purchased as the property of the Baltimore Society of the Archaeological Institute of America, but the objects have been at Johns Hopkins since their arrival in the United States.

During that same visit to Rome, Frothingham and Emerson inspected Professor Helbig's coin collection, which included about twelve hundred Greek and Roman coins. In the following year, 1888, a number of Baltimoreans submitted contributions that enabled the Helbig collection to be acquired by the University.[11]

Several years later, in 1900, Theodore Marburg, a well-known benefactor of the university, presented a collection of one hundred Cypriot objects, mostly seals.[12] These items had been assembled by his wife's cousin, Colonel Falkland Warren, who was Government Secretary for Cyprus between 1879 and 1891 and who had acquired the material through purchase and excavation. A year later, in 1901, the holdings of the university expanded yet again, as Paul Haupt, Professor of the Oriental Seminary from 1883 to 1926, persuaded Henry Sonneborn to donate a collection of seventy-three Jewish ceremonial implements.[13]

During the first decades of this century there were great opportunities to purchase antiquities in Italy, and Harry Langford Wilson, professor of Roman archaeology and epigraphy, was eager to take advantage of this situation during his sabbatical year in Rome. Before leaving for Italy in 1906, Wilson obtained $300 from the university[14] and $2,800 from several prominent Baltimoreans.[15] These funds enabled him to make substantial purchases in Rome and Naples during 1906 and 1907.[16] Wilson's letters enthusiastically describe the vast amounts of material on the market at this time and specifically mention the strainer (no. 48), the figurine of Hephaestos (no. 62), the savings bank (no. 96), and the cinerary urns (nos. 88, 89).[17] The material Wilson acquired encompassed bronzes, marbles, terracottas, and coins, and it was especially rich in Etruscan and Italic bronzes and pottery. Wilson also obtained more than one hundred Latin inscriptions, many of which he published in the following years.[18] After his return to Baltimore in 1907, Wilson solicited additional contributions, which he sent to Italy for further purchases in 1909.[19] In all, Wilson acquired more than a thousand objects for the university.

No. 62. Bronze Statuette of Hephaestos

At the same time that Wilson was obtaining material in Italy, more Egyptian objects were arriving on campus. In 1905/6, and again in 1906/7, a Baltimorean, James Teackle Dennis, volunteered his services to the Egypt Exploration Fund, which was then beginning its third and fourth seasons of excavation of the Eleventh Dynasty temple of Mentuhotep at Deir el-Bahari. Dennis provided photographs and drawings and also directed the excavation for a brief time in December, 1906. Dennis's letters to his family describe both the delights of Luxor, which was then a fashionable social resort, and the excitement of the archaeological discoveries, especially the day in February, 1906, when the chapel of Tuthmosis III was uncovered and Dennis and the excavation's director, Naville, were the first of the expedition members to investigate the structure. During this period Dennis contributed funds to the excavation and persuaded the university to lend its support as well. As a result, the university shared in the distribution of material for the season of 1905/6 and received, among other objects, two reliefs, one from the Mentuhotep temple, the other from the adjacent Eighteenth-Dynasty temple of Hatshepsut (nos. 1, 3).[20] In 1907 Dennis secured subscriptions to the Egypt Exploration Fund from a number of Baltimoreans and he encouraged the university to submit another contribution. In return, a second shipment was sent to the university from the finds of what was to be the last season's expedition to Deir el-Bahari (1906–7). In this lot was probably relief no. 2 as well as various fragmentary inscriptions.[21] The Egypt Exploration Society then turned to the predynastic sites of Abydos and El Mahasna, and from these expeditions several more shipments arrived at Johns Hopkins in 1909, 1911, and 1913.[22] Dennis's abiding support of the university's archaeological interests was demonstrated once again at his death, in 1918, when he bequeathed to the university his own collection of Egyptian material, including a number of objects from Deir el-Bahari.[23]

No. 1. Detail of Limestone Relief from Deir el-Bahari

No. 79. Terracotta Female Head

Yet another important addition to the collection was made during the first decades of this century through the efforts of William Buckler, a respected archaeologist who helped initiate the excavations of Sardis in 1910, and who served as a trustee of the university and a generous contributor to the fund that had supported Wilson's purchases in Italy. In 1909, Buckler purchased and donated to the university a large collection of almost four thousand Roman and Spanish coins.[24] Several years later, in 1920, he presented to Johns Hopkins a collection of thirty-seven Roman surgical instruments dating from the first or second century A.D. These objects had belonged to Alfred O. von Lennep, Dutch Vice-Consul at Smyrna, and were said to have come from Colophon.[25]

The first major acquisition of Near Eastern material was officially received in 1926, at the death of Professor Paul Haupt, who bequeathed to the university his collection of cylinder seals and cuneiform tablets. Among these items was a tablet Haupt had written in cuneiform to Professor Gildersleeve; the text included the pronouncement that the "Assyrians were not mad." Another cuneiform tablet, which is now in Special Collections of the Eisenhower Library, is a congratulatory letter from Haupt to President Gilman written on December 30, 1899, on the occasion of Gilman's twenty-fifth anniversary as president of the university.[26]

The growth of the collection during the first part of this century can be attributed largely to the efforts of Professor David M. Robinson, who arrived at Johns Hopkins in 1905, soon after the establishment of the Department of Archaeology. Robinson first served as associate professor, then as professor of Greek archaeology, and finally as professor of classical archaeology and Greek epigraphy.[27] During his forty-three years at Hopkins, Robinson was instrumental in initiating an expedition to Sardis in 1910 and in conducting the excavations of Olynthos (1928–38), the results of which were published in a monograph series, *The Johns Hopkins Studies in Archaeology,* which Robinson initiated in 1924. Robinson enriched the Archaeological Collection by actively seeking contributions, one of which was the collection of Helen Tanzer, who received her doctorate under Robinson in 1929 and whose dissertation, *The Common People of Pompeii,* was published in 1939 as monograph 29 in the above-mentioned series. In 1939, Tanzer officially donated to the university her extensive collection of over one thousand Greek and Roman objects, which she had assembled during the years that she was a student at Johns Hopkins and then a professor at Hunter College and Brooklyn College.[28]

No. 61. Bronze Matrix for Cuirass Pteryx

No. 116. Bell Krater by the Christie Painter

In 1942, through Robinson's efforts, the Brooklyn Museum presented the university with about a hundred objects, mostly Greek and Roman pottery and terracottas. Among these pieces were the Capenate vase carrier (no. 124), the bucchero vases (nos. 125–27), and the terracotta head from Smyrna (no. 79).[29]

During his years at Hopkins, Robinson expanded his own collection of objects, which was displayed and housed with the Johns Hopkins material. Between 1934 and 1938 Robinson published his own vases in three fascicules of the *Corpus Vasorum Antiquorum,* and also included in these volumes vases that belonged both to the university and to the Baltimore Society of the Archaeological Institute of America.[30] Substantial contributions to this publication were made by Mary McGehee, who prepared an inventory of the collection in 1933, and by Sarah Elizabeth Freeman, who served for many years as Curator of Fine Arts at Johns Hopkins and who completed a survey of the collection in 1942.[31]

Robinson retired in 1947, and in the following year he moved his collection to the University of Mississippi, where he taught until his death in 1960. During the transfer of material there was confusion about the ownership of several

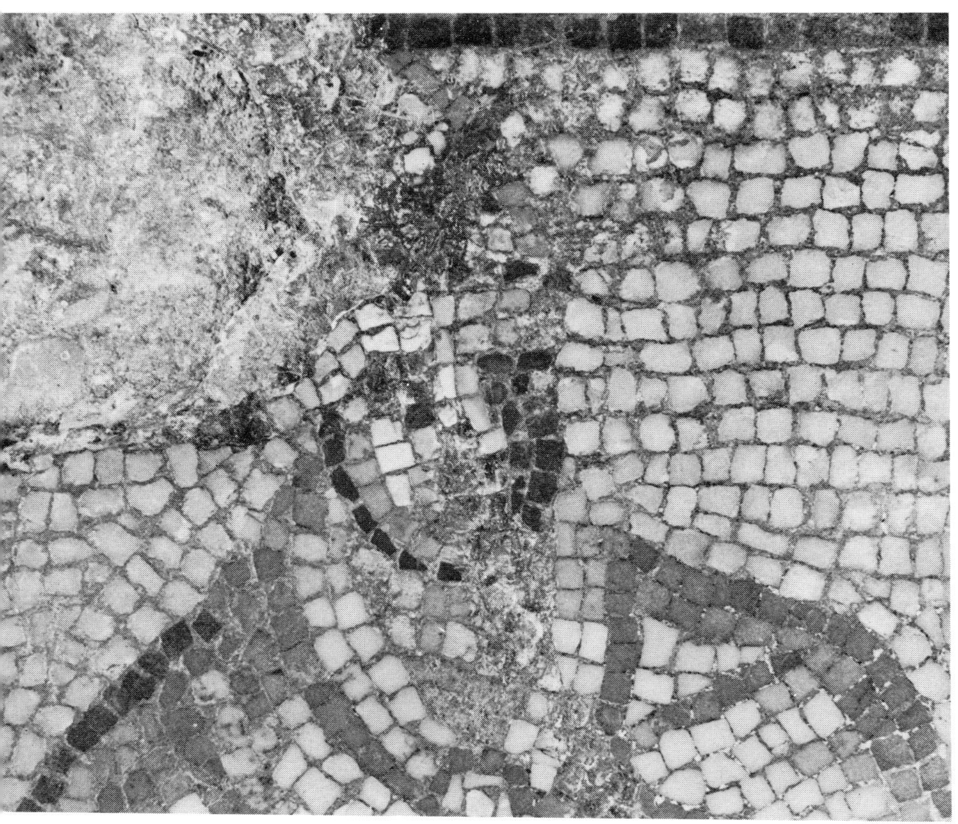

No. 137. Detail from Emblema Mosaic with Rural Scene

objects, and in some cases these mistakes were never rectified. Thus, remaining in the Johns Hopkins collection is a bronze matrix (no. 61), which originally formed part of Robinson's collection, while still at Mississippi is an alien lid, which was acquired together with the amphora by the Harrow Painter (no. 113). Today, Robinson's collection is principally divided between the University of Mississippi and the Fogg Museum. A few items are elsewhere; for example, several vases from the Robinson collection were acquired by the Baltimore Museum of Art and are now back at Johns Hopkins on extended loan (nos. 96, 116, 119).

In recent decades the collection has been augmented by two major additions.[32] In 1964, Kemper Simpson (B.A. 1914, Ph.D. 1917) donated to the university his collection of about one hundred examples of Greek and Roman decorative arts. Although his collection is exceptional, Simpson was not an archaeologist, but a distinguished economist who played a key role in the drafting of the Stock Exchange Act of 1932, which created the Securities and Exchange Commission.[33]

Finally, in 1977, the Baltimore Museum of Art generously placed on extended loan at Johns Hopkins a number of Greek vases (nos. 99, 109, 116–18), three of which once formed part of Robinson's collection, while two white-ground lekythoi are published here for the first time.

Through the years the university has also received groups of objects that do not pertain to the ancient world, such as oriental fabrics, Mayan pottery, and medieval armor. For a time this material was housed with the Archaeological Collection and responsibility for it was shared with the history department.[34] Gradually, however, these items were detached, and today are no longer part of the collection. Similarly, practically all of the coins from the Buckler and Helbig collections have been separated from the Archaeological Collection and are now part of the Johns Hopkins University Collection, together with the ancient coin collection of John Work Garrett, which was acquired in 1942.

Almost all of the material that now comprises the Archaeological Collection is located in 129–131 Gilman Hall.[35] The remaining objects are a few inscriptions and amphorae that are at Evergreen House and animal mummies from the Cohen Collection that are in storage in Ames Hall. The Sonneborn Collection of Jewish ceremonial implements is on extended loan to Baltimore Hebrew College, and the Buckler Col-

No. 24. Bronze Corinthian Helmet

lection of Greek and Roman surgical instruments is on display in Welch Library at the Johns Hopkins Medical School.

A final mention should be made of the ancient material that belongs to the university but that was never associated with the Archaeological Collection. This group includes fragments of Oxyrhynchus papyri that were acquired by the university in 1901, 1904, 1907, and 1922 in return for donations made to the Graeco-Roman section of the Egypt Exploration Fund. These items are largely published and are housed in Special Collections of the Eisenhower Library.[36]

Conservation of the Collection

Until the inception of this catalogue, the Archaeological Collection had never received conservation treatment, and, as a result, the relatively few objects included in this volume required extensive attention. Conservation of these items was made possible through grants received from 1978 to 1980 from the National Endowment for the Arts and the Middendorf Foundation. The project consisted of a survey of the conservation needs of the entire collection and the treatment of almost all the objects included in this catalogue, with the exception of the vases belonging to the Baltimore Museum of Art. The grants also made possible the purchase of a high-kilovoltage x-ray machine (300 KV) to facilitate both conservation treatment and technical studies on bronze manufacture. Also purchased was an airbrasive unit to remove heavy corrosion from bronze objects. Both instruments are now on extended loan to the Walters Art Gallery.

The conservation work was carried out in the laboratory of the Walters Art Gallery under the direction of Terry Weisser, Director of Conservation and Technical Research. For one year, a conservator hired specifically for the project worked exclusively on Johns Hopkins material. Subsequently it was agreed that all the conservators in the department would benefit from exposure to the variety and complexity of the problems. Accordingly, the objects were thereafter apportioned among the conservation staff, which included both recipients of postgraduate Mellon Fellowships in conservation and interns from the conservation training programs of Winterthur, New York University, Cooperstown, Queens University, and the Institute of Archaeology of the University of London. The students from Winterthur were already familiar with Johns Hopkins material since the collection had previously supplied objects for the in-house training of the second-year conservation students. As the Hopkins conservation project progressed, the conservators were encouraged to pursue their own technical studies, such as pigment analysis, consolidated reduction of silver, and quantitative analysis of several bronze objects, using equipment in the laboratories of Winterthur and the National Bureau of Standards.

No. 56. Radiograph of Beaked Oinochoe with Griffin Handle

The conservation process served to stabilize and to restore the objects and to reveal additional information about their fabric, technique, and decoration. Not unsuspected were the findings of extensive bronze disease and of salts in the terracottas and pottery. Several items, such as the mosaic (no. 137) and the mirrors (nos.

Plate A. No. 106, Lekythos in Six Technique

Plate C. No. 113, Amphora by the Harrow Painter

Plate B. No. 49, Etruscan Mirror, Annealing Twins

49–51), were especially difficult to repair, while the restoration of objects like the oinophoros (no. 129) and the stemmed plate (no. 123) was complicated and time-consuming.

Most rewarding, however, were the unexpected dicoveries. The cleansing of many terracottas recovered much remaining pigment, especially on the Boeotian maiden (no. 68), the cinerary urn (no. 89), and the antefixes (nos. 82–85). Removal of the corrosion on the bronzes revealed more engraved design than had been expected, particularly on the fibulae (nos. 26–28, 33) and the mirrors (nos. 49–51). Conservation treatment also determined that, before it entered the collection, the lekythos in Six technique (no. 106) (see plate A) had been overpainted with a scene that deliberately modified the lascivious original picture by altering the gesture of the maenad and by increasing the distance between the figures.

Microscopic examination of the bronzes was helpful in determining manufacturing techniques, and in some instances detected annealing twins, which are crystalline structures that result when a bronze is annealed, or heated, to make the metal malleable enough to be reworked without cracking. The presence of annealing twins on mirrors 49 and 51 (see plate B) indicated that these objects had been more carefully treated than mirror 50, which apparently was never annealed after the engraved scene was completed. In contrast, the Corinthian helmet (no. 24) displayed extensive annealing twins, thereby confirming the assumption that the helmet had been hammered and annealed.

The x-ray machine also proved most useful, clarifying, for example, the engraved inscription on the inside of the cheekpiece of the Corinthian helmet (no. 24). Radiographs also established the fact that the body and neck of the griffin jug (no. 56) had been cast in one piece, evidence that suggested that the jug was made in Italy, where one-piece casting was customary. Experimental radiographs provided fairly clear representations of the engraved scenes on the mirrors (nos. 49–51).

The red-figure vases proved particularly challenging. Prior to their acquisition in 1887, almost all of them had been mended by the filing down of the edges of the pieces and the application of a clinging adhesive that resisted removal. Since the limited resources of our project did not allow time for what would be a laborious disassembly and reassembly of every vase, it was decided that only the overpainting would be removed and those elements that were modern additions, such as foot and neck, detached. In the case of the figural scenes, the decision was made to restore only those details with absolutely clear contours. Otherwise, an orange or black matte paint was applied that could be easily distinguished from the original fabric.

During treatment of the vases, unpleasant surprises inevitably occurred. The foot and stem of the Antiphon kylix (no. 111) proved to have been so filed down that it was impossible to determine if the two units had ever belonged together. Removal of overpainting left the cups by Epiktetos (no. 103), Makron (no. 112), and Douris (no. 114) discouragingly incomplete. The amphora by the Harrow Painter (no. 113) (see plate C) was more heavily restored than had been suspected and incorporated an alien foot and rim and modern handles. The rim and handles were detached and replaced by others that replicated those on an intact amphora of this shape decorated by the same artist. Also removed was the extensive overpainting, under which emerged, as somewhat of a consolation, a trademark on the shoulder.

Notes

1. The published objects not included in this catalogue are: medical instruments from Colophon [R. Caton, *JHS* 34 (1914):114–18], lead curse tablets [W. S. Fox, *The Johns Hopkins Tabellae Defixionum, Supplement to AJP* 33.1 (1912)], copper dagger [S. E. Freeman, *Bulletin of the American Schools of Oriental Research* 90 (1943):28–30], and Latin inscriptions [R. V. D. Magoffin, *AJA* 14 (1910):51–59; H. L. Wilson, *AJP* 30 (1909):61–71, 153–70; ibid., 31 (1910):25–42, 251–64; ibid., 32 (1911):166–87; ibid., 33 (1912):168–85; ibid., 35 (1914):421–34].

2. Several articles on the history of the collection have appeared over the years: Ralph Van Deman Magoffin, *Alumni Magazine* 4 (1915–1916):27–33, and *Classical Weekly* 9 (1915–1916):99–101; D. M. Robinson, *Art and Archaeology* 19 (1925):265–67, and *Alumni Magazine* 14 (1925):25–33; W. G. Dinsmoor, *Proceedings of the American Philosophical Society*, Philadelphia, 87, no. 1 (1943):70–104; C. Carlson, *Johns Hopkins Magazine*, January 1974:6–11; F. P. Moeckel, *Forecast FM*, October 1974:54–55; and P. Gray, *Johns Hopkins Magazine*, April 1979:8–13.

Over the years, several inventories of the collection have been compiled. A brief list appeared in *A List of the Gifts and Bequests Received by The Johns Hopkins University, 1876–1891 (A Supplement to the Sixteenth Annual Report of the President, 1892)*, 30. *A Catalogue of the Historical Museum, 1887–1899* (present whereabouts unknown), compiled by Dr. Vincent, is mentioned in letters from President Bowman to S. Freeman dated November 3, 1943, and from Freeman to Bowman in a letter of November 13, 1943. A letter to President Ames from Mary McGehee, dated January 5, 1933, mentions an inventory being prepared by McGehee based upon previous records of 1908–9 (present whereabouts unknown). A letter from D. M. Robinson to President Bowman, dated February 21, 1942, summarizes McGehee's inventory. A report prepared by S. Freeman in June, 1943, gives an overview of the holdings. All the above-mentioned letters and the Freeman report are in the JHU archives, box 51, Office of the President.

3. H. B. Adams, *Methods of Historical Study: JHU Studies of Historical and Political Science*, 2d ser., nos. 1–2 (1884):125, 137. R. Cunningham, *The History Teacher* 9 (1976):244–57. *A List of the Gifts* (see note 2), 30. *Baltimore Sun*, February 5 and 6, 1901.

In 1884, William Ellinger presented a collection of Stone and Bronze Age material from Switzerland. The material is mentioned in *A List of the Gifts* (see note 2), 30, and in the *President's Report* 9 (1884):55, and is noted as an official gift in the *President's Report* 28 (1903):14.

In the same year, Stone Age objects from Virginia and Maryland were acquired from Rev. Dr. Randolph of Virginia and Col. Benjamin Taylor of Maryland [*President's Report* 9 (1884):56, and Adams, *Methods of Historical Study*, 125; *A List of the Gifts* (see note 2), 30].

4. J. M. Vincent, "An Example of a Seminar: The Department of History and Politics," *The Johns Hopkins University: Retrospect of Twenty Years, 1876–1896 (President's Report for 1896)*, 34–36. Articles in the *Baltimore American*, February 1 and 8, 1891. See Adams (note 3), 137.

5. *President's Report* 9 (1884):14, 55, 83; *A List of the Gifts* (see note 2), 4; *University Circulars* 35 (1884):21–23. Cohen was featured in an exhibition organized by Andrew Oliver, Jr., for the December 1979 meetings of the Archaeological Institute of America in Boston. The exhibition was entitled "Beyond the Shores of Tripoli." See also W. R. Dawson, *Who Was Who in Egyptology, EES* (1972):67; *Baltimore Sun*, January 18, 1976, and January 4, 1980.

6. Cohen's letters and catalogue are in the Maryland Historical Society. The flag is in Evergreen House.

7. Dinsmoor (see note 2), 96–97.

8. *A List of the Gifts* (see note 2), 30; *President's Report* 9 (1884):55; *President's Report* 10 (1885):21. This gift was supplemented by a group of Etruscan and Roman pottery and coins that had been in the possession of Mrs. Langdon Williams. See the *President's Report* 9 (1884):55; *President's Report* 10 (1885):21. *A List of the Gifts* (see note 2), 30; letter to President Bowman from S. Freeman dated November 13, 1943, in JHU archives, box 51, Office of the President.

9. *President's Report* 9 (1884):14, 81–83; *President's Report* 10 (1885):20; letter from Frothingham to President Gilman dated May 19, 1887, in Special Collections, Eisenhower Library.

10. Vincent, *Retrospect*, 27. For more on Frothingham, see *Archaeology* 29 (1976):221.

11. Letter from Frothingham to President Gilman dated May 19, 1887, in Special Collections, Eisenhower Library; *President's Report* 13 (1888):49; *University Circulars* n. 64

(1888):45; *A List of the Gifts* (see note 2), 16; *Trustees Minutes* of March 5, 1888; Vincent, *Retrospect*, 26. The donors were Christian Ax, Jr., D. L. Bartlett, Mendes Cohen, G. W. Gail, Robert Garrett, T. Harrison Garrett, Daniel C. Gilman, Hodges brothers, Reverdy Johnson, Francis T. King, J. W. McCoy, W. W. Spence, and Francis White. Letter from H. B. Adams to President Gilman dated November 1, 1887, in Daniel Coit Gilman Papers, Special Collections, Eisenhower Library.

12. *Trustees Minutes* of December 3, 1900; *President's Report* 26 (1901):27. The *Baltimore Sun*, December 19, 1900, includes an inventory of the collection.

13. *President's Report* 26 (1901):26. Additions were made in 1903 [*President's Report* 28 (1903):15] and 1906 [*President's Report* (1906):13]. An article appeared in the *Sun*, February 6, 1901.

14. *Trustees Minutes* of June 4, 1906.

15. Donors are listed in the *President's Report* (1907):13, as R. B. Keyser, Robert Garrett, Waldo Newcomer, William H. Buckler, Julian LeRoy White, Richard J. White, and Howard A. Kelly.

16. Wilson letter to President Remsen dated April 15, 1907, in JHU archives, box 51, Office of the President.

17. Letter from Wilson to William Buckler dated March 17, 1907, from box 51, Office of the President. Wilson also mentions curse tablets and antefixes (Wilson's letter to President Gildersleeve, January 26, 1907 in Special Collections, Eisenhower Library). A more complete list of objects appears in the *President's Report* (1907):97–98. A few purchases were made by Ralph Van Deman Magoffin (Ph.D. 1908), who acquired terracottas and bronzes at Praeneste (letter from Magoffin to President Gildersleeve, April 4, 1907 in Special Collections, Eisenhower Library).

18. See note 1.

19. $1,260 (*Trustees Minutes* of May 3, 1909). The contributors were listed as Keyser, Buckler, White, Garrett, Roger, Spence, Dennis, Levering, Miller, Jacobs, Acer (see note 1). *President's Report* (1909):12. Letter from Wilson to President Remsen dated April 27, 1909, in JHU archives, box 51, Office of the President.

20. *EEF Report* 24 (1905–6):10, 16, 23. *EEF Report* 25 (1906–7):18. Letter from Dennis to his aunt dated February 12, 1906, in possession of his great-niece, Mrs. Allen Poucher. Letter from Dennis to President Remsen dated December 26, 1906, in JHU archives, file 322, Office of the President. Letter from secretary of EEF dated August 16, 1906, in JHU archives, file 322, Office of the President. *Trustees Minutes* of November 5, 1906. Dawson (see note 5), 83.

21. *Trustees Minutes* of October 7, 1907. Letter from secretary of EEF dated September 18, 1907, in JHU archives, file 322, Office of the President. *President's Report* (1907):14.

22. Letters from secretary of EEF dated August 3, 1909, and June 30, 1911, in JHU archives, file 322, Office of the President. *Trustees Minutes* of October 2, 1911. *President's Report* (1912):9.

23. *President's Report* (1920):32. Dennis's will, dated October 24, 1918, in JHU archives, box 51, Office of the President.

24. *President's Report* (1909):12. Letter from Buckler to W. Brent Keyser dated November 2, 1918, in JHU archives, box 51, Office of the President. D. M. Robinson, *Alumni Magazine*, 14 (1925):31.

25. Letter from D. M. Robinson to President Goodnow dated May 15, 1920, in JHU archives, box 51, Office of the President. D. M. Robinson, *Art and Archaeology* 19 (1925):266–67, illus. on p. 273. R. Caton, *JHS* 34 (1914):114–18. H. E. Sigerist, *History of Medicine*, vol. 2 (Oxford, 1961), 314, figs. 3, 4.

26. *President's Report* (1926–27):17. Magoffin, *Alumni Magazine*, 4 (1915–16):28.

By this date several other noteworthy gifts had entered the collection. Among these was the Edgar Miller collection of Egyptian statuettes, Roman glass, cylinder seals, and Greek coins [*President's Report* (1911):11; *President's Report* (1912):9; letter from Wilson to Remsen dated May 20, 1911, in JHU archives, box 51, Office of the President]. Another gift was the collection of ancient marble samples belonging to Ralph Van Deman Magoffin, who taught in the Department of Archaeology for many years and served as president of the Archaeological Institute of America [Robinson, *Alumni Magazine* 14 (1925):29].

27. Notice in the *President's Papers* for June, 1913. D. M. Robinson, *Alumni Magazine* 14 (1925):25, 30, 31.

28. *Trustees Minutes* (Executive Committee) for March 6, 1939, wherein is filed letter from Tanzer to President Bowman dated March 5, 1939; *Baltimore Sun*, June 17, 1939; *New York Times*, December 24, 1961; *Washington Post* and *Times Herald*, December 25, 1961. A report to the President from D. M. Robinson dated February 20, 1942, states that the material had been at Hopkins since 1930–31. (Report is in JHU archives, box 51, Office of the President.)

Tanzer also played a role in securing part of the Olcott Collection of the University of Illinois, although there is no evidence that Olcott material entered her own collection. See Ingrid Edlund, "The Iron Age and Etruscan Vases in the Olcott Collection of Columbia University, New York." *TAPA* 70, pt. 1 (1980):7, and *California Studies in Classical Antiquity* 12 (1979):105 n. 2. Tanzer was also the author of *The Villas of Pliny The Younger* (New York, 1924).

29. Letters from D. Robinson to President Bowman dated May 27, 1942, and July 13, 1942, in JHU archives, box 51, Office of the President.

30. *CVA USA fasc. 4, Robinson fasc. 1*, 1934; *CVA fasc. 6, Robinson fasc 2*, 1937; *CVA USA fasc. 7, Robinson fasc. 3*, 1938. The descriptions of the red-figure vases in this volume are based upon the entries in *CVA USA fasc. 6, Robinson fasc. 2.*

The items published in *CVA Robinson fasc. 3* that belong to the archaeological collection and that are entered as such occur therein on: 40, pl. XXIX.4; 42, pl. XXX.1; 43, pl. XXXI.8; 46, pl. XXXIII.5; 48, pl. XXXV.4–7; 49, pl. XXXVI.3–4; 50, pl. XXXVII.5; 50, pl. XXXVIII.1; 51, pl. XXXVIII.5; 53–54, pl. XL.2–7; 54–55, pl. XLI.1–9; 55, pl. XLII.1, 3; 55–56, pl. XLIII.1–4; 56–67, pl. XLIV.1–5.

Items that belong to the archaeological collection but that are not indicated as such occur on: 39, pl. XXIX.1; 44, pls. XXXII.1, XXXII.3.

31. Freeman report to the President, 1942. See note 2.

32. In 1953–54, several objects from the excavation of Nippur entered the collection through the efforts of Dr. William Albright.

33. *Washington Post*, July 2, 1970.

34. Freeman report to the President, June 1943. See note 2.

35. After the move to Homewood in 1916, the collection was located in 109–10 and 112 Gilman Hall (letter from D. M. Robinson to President Bowman, January 9, 1942, in JHU archives, box 51, Office of the President).

36. R. A. Coles, *Location and List of the Oxyrhynchus Papyri and of Other Greek Papyri published by the EE Society*. Vol. 59 of *EES Graeco-Roman Memoirs*, no. 2 (London, 1974), 20.

CATALOGUE

Each entry is discussed individually. Exceptions are items 1–2 and 7–12, which, in each case, belong to a single monument that is discussed in an introductory essay preceding the entries.

Each entry has the following format:

ITEM NO.—ITEM TITLE (DATE)

The first paragraph gives the inventory number, the original collection, the reputed provenance (if any), the material, the preserved dimensions, and the present condition of the piece. The abbreviations employed for giving dimensions, which are metric measurements, are: diam = diameter, l = length, w = width, ht = height, th = thickness, depth = depth, max = greatest, av = average.

The second paragraph describes the representation.

The third paragraph, under the heading "Bibliography," lists all previous publications of the object, in chronological order.

These paragraphs are followed by a general discussion of the item and, finally, by numbered notes.

This format is a master plan; minor variations of this format occur in individual entries where information is not available or where the information is particularly extensive.

Sculpture

EGYPTIAN

1–2. Limestone Reliefs from the Temple of Mentuhotep II at Deir el-Bahari

(ca. 2000 B.C.)

These two reliefs come from the funerary temple of Mentuhotep II, the Eleventh-Dynasty king who reunited Egypt and launched the prosperity of the Middle Kingdom. Mentuhotep built his funerary temple at Deir el-Bahari, on the west bank of the Nile across from his capital at Thebes. This complex later served as the model for the Eighteenth-Dynasty temple of Hatshepsut, which was constructed alongside it.

The Mentuhotep temple was excavated by the Egypt Exploration Society from 1903 to 1907. During the last two seasons, a Baltimorean, James Teackle Dennis, assisted in directing the excavation and contributed drawings and photographs.[1] At his suggestion, the Johns Hopkins University made a contribution to the Egypt Exploration Fund and shared in the distribution of finds for the seasons of 1906 and 1907.[2]

The funerary temple has been extensively restudied in recent years, although the fragmentary evidence permits only a hypothetical restoration of certain key features.[3] The structure was partially carved from the limestone cliffs, with columns and walls of sandstone and the wall facing and most of the reliefs of fine limestone.

The temple consisted of a lower courtyard with two porticoes flanking a ramp to an upper terrace, which was partially carved out of the rock. This terrace was organized in concentric rectangles. On the north, east, and south sides, two rows of pillars enclosed a square-walled area, within which there was a columned ambulatory surrounding a solid mass of masonry. The precise appearance of this core is uncertain, but we can assume that the core symbolized the mythical primeval mound upon which civilization was believed to have arisen when the Nile flood waters first receded.[4] To the west of the terrace was a colonnaded court, in the center of which was an underground corridor leading to Mentuhotep's tomb. Beyond the courtyard lay a colonnaded hypostyle hall that gave access to a rockcut sanctuary.

The temple complex differs from Old Kingdom funerary complexes in several ways. Most noticeable is the absence of a pyramid, although the solid core was related in form and probably in meaning. Also significant is the fact that, unlike the Old Kingdom complexes, which were dedicated only to the king, the worship of Mentuhotep is here combined with the cults of Amon, Hathor, and possibly Osiris, an association of king and deity that became customary in funerary temples of the Eighteenth Dynasty.[5]

1. Dennis served as honorary secretary for the fund in Baltimore in 1903–4 [*EEF Report* (1903–4):6] and 1904–5 [*EEF Report* (1904–5):7]. During the season of 1905–6, he volunteered his assistance to the excavations [*EEF Report* (1905–6):10, 16; Naville, 1:VII]. During the fourth season, 1906–7, Dennis assisted in the direction of the excavation [Naville, 1:VII, Naville, 2:preface; *EEF Report* (1906–7):18]. Dennis's drawings and photographs appear in Naville, 1:pls. XXVI, XXVIII.

2. The temple exploration was published in three volumes (Naville, 1–3). The south court was cleared during the latter part of the second season, 1904–5, and the first part of the third season, 1905–6 (Naville, 1:36, 38, 57).

3. D. Arnold, *Der Tempel des königs Mentuhotep von Deir el-Bahari*. Bd. 1. *Architektur und Deutung* (Mainz, 1974); Bd. 2, *Die Wandreliefs des Sanktuares* (1974); Bd. 3, *Die königlichen Beigaben* (1981).

4. Ibid., Bd. 1, 77.

5. Ibid., 75–83.

1. Relief of Crocodile from Deir el-Bahari

(ca. 2000 B.C.)

9211. EEF from Deir el-Bahari. Limestone. L, 75.3 cm; ht, 30.2 cm; th, 7 cm. Broken into three pieces and chipped along all sides and over surfaces. Back smooth. Blue on water; red on horizontal band along lower edge.

Crouching on a smooth band 3 cm high is a crocodile in right profile gripping a fish in its teeth. Crocodile rendered in low relief, with little interior modeling but much incised detail: diamond and grid patterns describe torso, legs, neck; chain pattern behind rear leg; row of ellipses behind right leg and ear. Back and tail have serrated edges. Fish has smooth body with grooved tail. Watery background indicated by vertically incised zigzags, evenly spaced. Swimming in front of crocodile is second fish with wedge-shaped tail. Beneath band serving as groundline is another band, painted red.

Bibliography: Naville, 1:69, pl. XVI.D.

This relief was recovered at the end of the second season (1904–5) or the beginning of the third season (1905–6), and was discovered in the court south of the upper terrace. The piece probably fell to that spot from its original position on the wall at the back of the south colonnade.[1] Since adjacent passages depict other animals, it is likely that the wall bore a representation of the king hunting along the Nile and in the desert.[2] The reliefs surmounted a 60 cm dado painted with bands of red and blue and were themselves crowned by a frieze of stars, stripes, and kheker ornament, also in red and blue.[3]

The Hopkins relief is characteristic of Middle Kingdom sculpture in the crisp contours and absence of interior modeling. The contrasting zigzags for the water and the schematic handling of the crocodile's body are happily counterbalanced by the smooth surfaces of the animal's face, the fish's body, and the groundline.

In ancient times the Nile crocodile (*Crocodylus niloticus*) averaged about 10 m in length and was prevalent along the Nile Valley. Today the crocodile ranges just over 3 m long and is predominantly found in central, eastern, and southern Africa.[4]

1. Naville, 1:39–40, 69.

2. Ibid., 25, 39; D. Arnold, *Der Tempel des königs Mentuhotep von Deir el-Bahari*. Bd. 1, *Architektur und Deutung* (Mainz, 1974), 77.

3. Naville, 1:25, 40.

4. See "Crocodilia" in the *New Encyclopedia Britannica*, 15th ed. (Chicago, 1974), 5:286–89, and *Encyclopedia Britannica* (Chicago, 1972), 6:791–93.

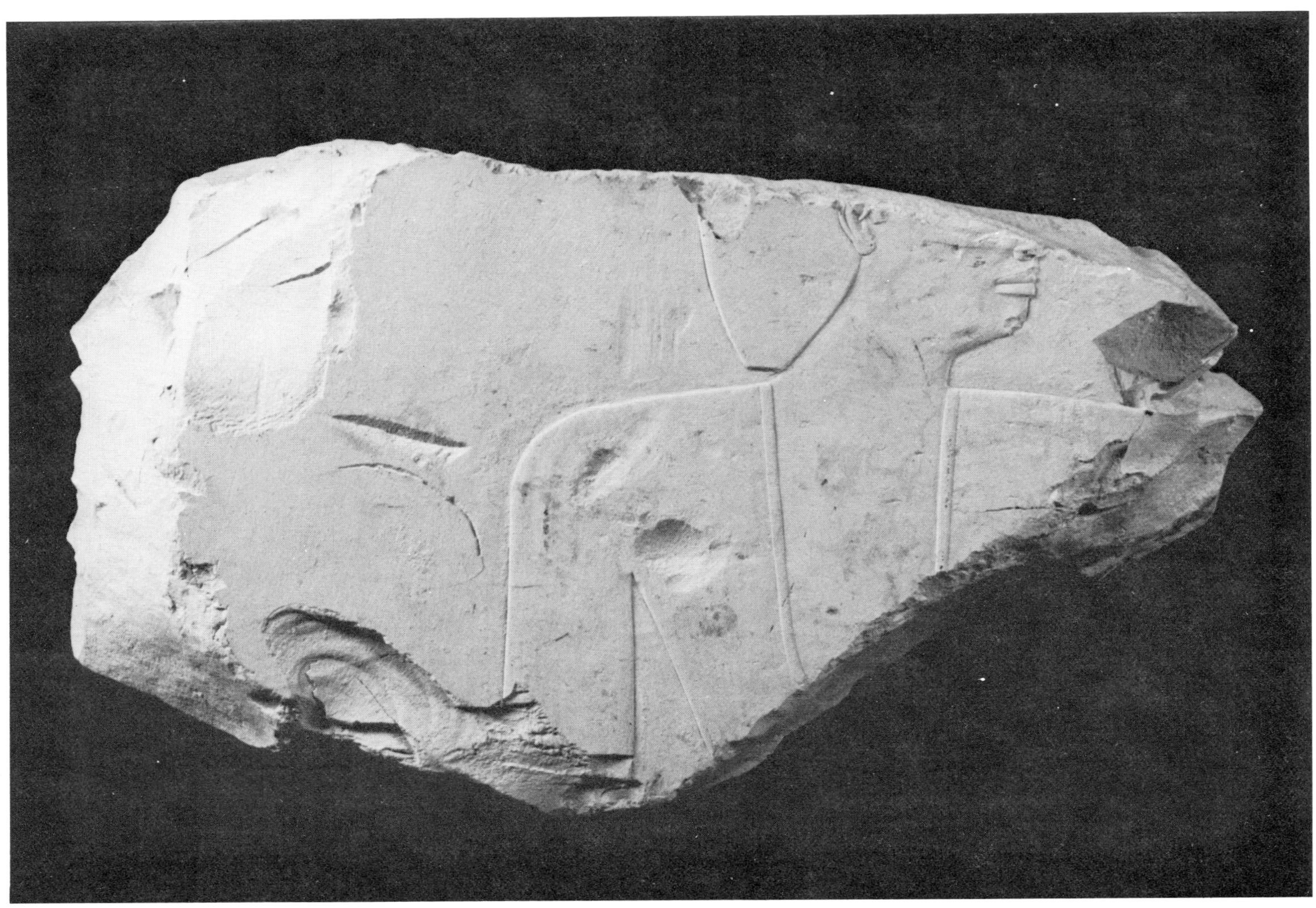

2. Relief of Man from Deir el-Bahari

(ca. 2000 B.C.)

2939. EEF from Deir el-Bahari. Limestone. L, 34 cm; ht, 17 cm; th, 6.3 cm. Entire figure would have been about 60 cm high. Part of original edge survives on top; other sides and back broken. Chips missing from surface. Blue on background; red on left shoulder, right upper arm, right ear, right nipple.

Lower half of face, left shoulder, right shoulder, and upper arm of frontal male torso. Head in right profile wearing wig with blunt tip at nape. Torso nude except for long necklace, 0.4 cm wide.

Like the preceding fragment, this relief comes from the Middle Kingdom temple of Mentuhotep at Deir el-Bahari.[1] The low relief, as well as the absence of color, indicates that the fragment cannot have come from the chapels or shrine, where the relief was higher and the color is better preserved.[2] The quiet pose suggests that the figure formed part of a ceremonial scene, perhaps one celebrating the foundation of the temple or depicting processions of priests, foreigners, and dignitaries bearing gifts.[3]

Characteristic of the Middle Kingdom is the short wig with a blunt tip at the nape of the neck and a small extension directly in front of the ear.[4] Also distinctive are the flaring nostrils and the small stylized ear.[5] The broad lips are of even thickness throughout and have a vertical groove at the corners.[6] The vertical profile of the chin is commonly found in sculpture of this period, as is the oblique contour of the jawline.

The execution is extremely fine and can be compared with the best reliefs from this temple.[7] Noteworthy are the exceptionally crisp edges and the absence of interior modeling.

1. *EEF*, Neg. No. DB 1907/234.
2. Naville, 1:40–41.
3. Ibid., 40.
4. Ibid., 68, pl. XII.D.
5. Naville, 3:23, pl. XIII.2.
6. Compare the sarcophagi of Ashayet and Kawit from this temple in C. Aldred, *Middle Kingdom Art in Ancient Egypt* (London, 1950), 35, nos. 8–9, and W. S. Smith, *The Art and Architecture of Ancient Egypt*, 2d ed. rev. (New York, 1981), 164, fig. 155.
7. D. Arnold, *Der Tempel des königs Mentuhotep von Deir el-Bahari*. Bd. 2, *Die Wandreliefs des Sanktuares* (Mainz, 1974), frontispiece.

3. Fragment of Hieroglyphic Inscription from Temple of Hatshepsut at Deir el-Bahari

(ca. 1500 B.C.)

9193. EEF from Deir el-Bahari. Limestone. Ht, 19.2. cm; w, 20.3 cm; max th, 7 cm; max depth of relief, 1 cm. Broken all around and across back. Horizontal groove 4 cm long above head. Yellow over entire face and on beginning of motif to viewer's right.

Facing male head in sunk relief. Smooth band over forehead, elongated almond eyes, large jutting ears, flaring nostrils. Short mouth, square chin with beard. Part of motif to his left also deeply incised and painted. Delicate undulating modeling over entire face.

This relief belongs to the Eighteenth-Dynasty temple of Hatshepsut, which was inspired by the immediately adjacent complex of Mentuhotep, where our fragment was recovered. The piece was acquired in 1906 from the Egypt Exploration Fund and was probably found at the end of the 1904–5 season or during the excavations of 1905–6.[1] The relief formed part of a monumental hieroglyphic inscription and bears the sign *hr*, which is the determinative for face. This sign can also carry the meaning of the preposition "upon," and, rarely, can signify the Egyptian god Horos. The sign has the same phonetic value as that of the sign of the falcon-Horos.[2]

The fundamental characteristics of the sign are the facing head, the beard, and the yellow color of the skin. The short hair is usually shown as a cap of tight curls with an irregular hairline. Often the face has flaring nostrils and thick lips reminiscent of African and Asian peoples. Occasionally, the face bears the individual features of an Egyptian king.[3]

The sign is an intriguing composite of what appear at first to be irreconcilable elements. The foreign appearance of the nose and lips seems incompatible with a sign that can designate Horos. Moreover, yellow is the color traditionally reserved for female skin, while males were painted a reddish hue. Finally, the beard, although an attribute of royalty and of deities, also denotes peoples from the land of Punt.[4] All these incongruities, however, can be explained through the association of the sign with the god Horos, a deity envisioned as a celestial face whose eyes were the sun and the moon.[5] At the apogee of his cycle, Horos was regarded as a goddess and hence could logically be painted yellow, which is also the color of the moon and of gold.[6] Both the non-Egyptian facial features and the beard allude to the legendary home of Horos in Punt and the international character of his daily travels.[7] As Myśliwiec points out, the association of the sign *hr* with the god Horos also explains why the sign can mean "upon" and why many of the words in which the sign appears carry meanings that describe Horos himself, i.e., to dominate, to be in front, to be far away.[8]

The Hopkins fragment exemplifies the handling of the sign in the reliefs from the Hatshepsut temple, where the foreign features of the face are exaggerated, the eyes elongated, and the ears enlarged.[9] The smooth raised band along the hairline has parallels on several other signs from the temple,[10] where the cap of curls is also missing. The quality of our relief is especially high, with admirably crisp edges and a delicate undulation of the surface.

1. See entries for nos. 1 and 2.
2. E. Budge, *An Egyptian Hieroglyphic Dictionary*, vol. 1 (New York, 1978), cv.
3. K. Myśliwiec, *Zeitschrift fur ägyptische Sprache und Altertumskunde* 98 (1970–72):85, 96. I thank Bernard Bothmer for directing me to this study.
4. Ibid., 85–86.
5. Ibid., 86.
6. Ibid., 90–91, 94.
7. Ibid., 86.
8. Ibid., 95.
9. Ibid., 87, figs. 2, 5; 88, fig. 7; 89, fig. 12.
10. Ibid., 87, fig. 5; 88, fig. 7.

4. Wooden Statuette of Maiden, Middle Kingdom

(ca. 2134–1991 B.C.)

9213. Cohen Collection. "Thebes." Wood. Ht, 33 cm. Base: l, 14 cm; w, 5.5 cm; ht, 3.3 cm. Right arm missing. Each arm was carved separately and fitted onto a dowel that passes completely through arm and into shoulder. Under each foot is 2.5-cm cubical tang, which was inserted into base. Front half of each foot carved separately, attached to base, and slipped into back half of foot by horizontal tang. Eyes have bronze lids, inlaid whites, and black pupils. Black paint on eyebrows and on cosmetic lines at outer corners of eyes. Red paint over right half of face. Label on side of base reads: no. 157.

Slim maiden with attenuated proportions stands frontally, feet together, left arm at side with fingers extended. She wears a thin, clinging halter dress that extends to mid-calf and that reveals navel, median line, genital area, and vertical division between legs. Shoulder straps described by two vertical grooves between breasts and a groove circling torso beneath breasts. Necklace consists of three or four rows of long cylindrical beads. Bracelet on left wrist. Hair of wig, indicated by regularly spaced grooves, is center-parted and brushed to sides behind ears, with locks hanging to middle of back and top of breasts.

The Hopkins maiden is one of the many wooden figurines that have come from Middle Kingdom burials. The composite construction is fairly typical, although on less fine examples the feet are modeled separately in gesso.[1] On many pieces, as here, the paint is applied directly upon the wood, but on some figurines there is an intervening layer of gesso on the wig or offerings.[2]

Our maiden displays the characteristic proportions of Middle Kingdom figurines, having a slim, elongated body with increased length between waist and knees and strikingly long hands and feet.[3] Also typical are the form of her wig, the elongated eyes, and the thick lips of even width, which form awkward transitions to the cheeks.[4] Her clinging garment was probably painted with a scale or net pattern like those found on contemporary statuettes.[5]

Because no inscription can be discerned on the base and because the right arm is missing, it is not clear whether our maiden represents a noblewoman or a servant girl. On statuettes of tomb owners, the arms usually hang at the sides and there is an identifying inscription.[6] Servant figurines, on the other hand, may have one arm upraised to steady an offering carried on the head.[7] Excellent examples of the latter type are the two large statuettes from the tomb of Meket-Rē of the Eleventh Dynasty that are now in Cairo and New York.[8]

The tradition of placing figurines of servants with the dead can be traced back to predynastic times. The custom was revived in the Fourth Dynasty, for which examples average about 30 cm tall and are carved from limestone and wood.[9] In the less prosperous economy of the Middle Kingdom, most of the figurines were of wood, and they were placed in the burial chamber or in a side chamber or niche made specifically for that purpose.[10] In addition to single figurines, in the Middle Kingdom there can be found an increased number of miniature farmyards, granaries, bakeries, and breweries.

1. H. E. Winlock, *Models of Daily Life in Ancient Egypt from the Tomb of Meket-Rē at Thebes* (Cambridge, 1955), 74, 90.

2. Ibid., 91.

3. C. Aldred, *Middle Kingdom Art in Ancient Egypt* (London, 1950), 44, no. 38; I. Woldering, *The Art of Egypt* (New York, 1963), 87, pl. 23; J. H. Breasted, Jr., *Egyptian Servant Statues* (Washington, D.C., 1948), 94, no. 4, pl. 87.

4. Compare the sarcophagi of Kawit and Ashayet, in Aldred, *Middle Kingdom Art*, 35, nos. 8–9.

5. Ibid., 35, no. 7; Winlock, *Models of Daily Life*, 9–13, 40, 90–91, pl. 30.

6. Woldering, *Art of Egypt*, 87, 130, pl. 23; Aldred, *Middle Kingdom Art*, 35, no. 6.

7. Breasted, *Egyptian Servant Statues*, 60–62 (see also p. 94, concubine-type figurine, no. 4, pl. 87, a and b). M. Mogensen, *La Glyptothèque Ny Carlsberg, La collection égyptienne* (Copenhagen, 1930), 69, pl. 67.

8. See note 5.

9. Breasted, *Egyptian Servant Statues*, 2–3.

10. Winlock, *Models of Daily Life*, 12–13. See also tomb of Meket-Rē in H. E. Winlock, *Excavations at Deir el-Bahari 1911–1931* (New York, 1942), 22.

5. Basalt Group of Bak and Ruiw

(late Eighteenth Dynasty, ca. 1325 B.C.)

9212. Cohen Collection from Salt Collection. "Thebes." Basalt. Ht, 35.4 cm; w, 17.4 cm; depth, 22.2 cm. Cracked from fire. Section between couple's feet missing; her right foot restored; his beard broken off.

Seated couple with woman on man's right. Both figures sit with legs together; inside arms omitted. Her outside arm rests on right thigh, palm down and fingers extended. His left arm rests on left thigh, palm down and fingers closed except for extended thumb and fourth finger. Each wears a long garment reaching to ankles and with sleeves that just cover elbows. Straps of her dress indicated by two vertically incised grooves between the breasts and a horizontal incision under the breasts. She wears a wig cover completely covering her ears, with a narrow lock of hair extending across forehead and below each ear. He is bearded, with wig cover passing behind ears. On both faces the upper contour of the upper eyelid is accented by an incised line, and both contours of the cosmetic lines and eyebrows are delineated by incisions. Chair has curving top that reaches just beneath figures' heads; base extends beyond feet. Hieroglyphs over base and back, and additional bands down skirt of each garment.

During the New Kingdom it was fashionable for privileged subjects to seek permission from the pharaoh to dedicate statue groups in the temple to Amon at Karnak;[1] the inscription on our piece tells us that Bak and Ruiw commissioned this portrait of themselves. The couple is represented in a traditional manner, although it is more common for the woman to be seated on the man's left side. The inside arms are not indicated, but are to be understood as passing behind the other's waist.[2] This composition is only one of several formulaic poses that appear among contemporary statue groups; on other examples, one of the man's arms is bent to his chest, the other at his waist.[3] Occasionally, a child stands between the couple.[4]

The figures of the Hopkins group exemplify the New Kingdom ideal of beauty, especially the elongation, the slimness, and the man's broad shoulders and fleshy breasts.[5] Our group probably dates from the end of the Eighteenth Dynasty, since the fleshy round faces with their sweet, bland smiles find counterparts in work of this period.[6] The woman's hairstyle, with locks overlying the wig cover, is paralleled in a portrait of the wife of Nakht-Min from the end of the reign of Tutankhamen.[7]

1. C. Aldred, *New Kingdom Art in Ancient Egypt* (London, 1972), 5.
2. Ibid., 62, no. 68 (see the statue of Sen-nefer and wife). See also E. Terrace and H. Fischer, *Treasures of Egyptian Art from the Cairo Museum* (Boston, 1970), 113, no. 24.
3. Aldred, *New Kingdom Art*, 53, no. 40; M. Mogensen, *La Glyptothèque Ny Carlsberg, La collection égyptienne* (Copenhagen, 1930), 17–18, no. A68, pl. 16.
4. Terrace and Fischer, *Treasures of Egyptian Art*, 113, no. 24.
5. Ibid., 105, no. 22.
6. Aldred, *New Kingdom Art*, 93, no. 175.
7. Terrace and Fischer, *Treasures of Egyptian Art*, 137, no. 31.

Sculpture

GREEK

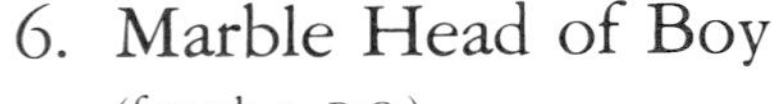

6. Marble Head of Boy

(fourth c. B.C.)

9096. Ht, 13.4 cm; max diam, 12.7 cm. White, fine-grained marble. Broken across neck, with nose and chin chipped.

Head inclined to right and downward. Short, curly hair extends below ears; short braid extends from forehead to crown. Delicate modeling of features, with rough unfinished surface of hair at back of head.

This head belonged to a statuette that was just under life size. The boy has a chubby face and short, thin lips that are set in a gentle smile. Reminiscent of sculpture from the second half of the fifth century are the accented eyelids, with the upper lid overlapping the lower lid at the outer corners. Especially noteworthy is the unfinished state of the sides and back of the head suggesting that the statuette was intended only for a frontal view.

Both the unfinished back and the treatment of the face find close parallels among the statues of children who served as *arctoi*, or little bears, in attendance upon Artemis in her sanctuary at Brauron.[1] These figures, which date largely to the fourth century, stood within the fifth-century stoa and were probably aligned against the wall so that only the front could be seen. Those dating from the end of the series are portrayed as blind.[2] Contemporary heads of the same style and with similarly unworked backs come from other sites, including the Ilissos[3] and Delphi.[4]

In the fourth century there was an enormous interest in children and a consequent demand for representations of them, to which the many terracotta figurines from this period bear witness.[5] Probably not many years after the Hopkins head was made, Lysippos created his famous Eros with a bow.[6] The Lysippan child had a similarly detailed hairstyle, but an expression of concentration that contrasts with the cheerily smiling countenances of the Brauron and Hopkins sculptures.

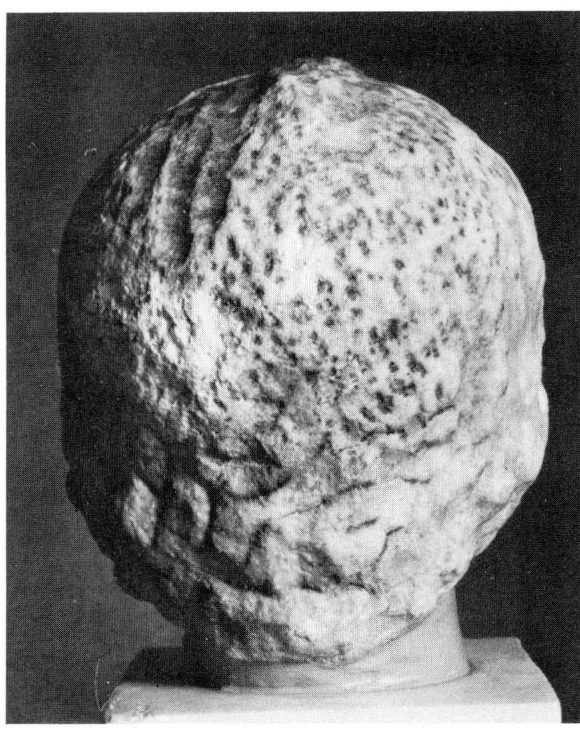

1. M. A. Zagdoun, *BCH* 103 (1979):399–401, figs. 13–20. Also, *BCH* 102 (1978):307–9, no. 17, fig. 21; and P. Themelis, *Brauron: Guide to the Site and Museum* (Athens, 1971). See also G. Daux, *BCH* 84 (1960):665, fig. 6.

2. *Antiken aus dem Akademischen Kunstmuseum Bonn* (Düsseldorf, 1971), 16, no. 10, pl. 7; Themelis, *Brauron*, 26; and S. Papaspyridi-Karousou, *ArchEph* (1957):68–83.

3. Papaspyridi-Karousou, *ArchEph* (1957):78, fig. 8, pls. 20–21.

4. *Antiken Bonn*, 16, no. 10, pl. 7.

5. M. Trumpf-Lyritzaki, *Griechische Figurenvasen* (Bonn, 1969), 132–35; D. B. Thompson, *Hesperia* 21 (1952):138; S. Miller, *Hesperia* 43 (1974):212–17.

6. A. F. Stewart, *AJA* 82 (1978):480, fig. 9; Bieber, *Sculpture*, 38; H. Döhl, *Der Eros des Lysipp; Frühhellenistische Eroten* (Göttingen, 1968), 15–35.

7–12. Limestone Reliefs from Tarentum

(ca. 330–250 B.C.)

The following six fragments come from funerary naiskoi, or shrines, which were set up in Tarentum between about 330 and 250 B.C.[1] These naiskoi were relatively small, about 2 m high, and contained a smaller than life-size statue of the deceased. Architectural sculpture consisted of a triglyph-metope or continuous frieze, a pedimental relief, and akroteria. Occasionally there was a frieze on the base. The naiskoi were made of stuccoed sedimentary stone, with finer limestone used for the sculpture and such features as column capitals, bases, and moldings. Paint was applied to details of the capital, and, on the reliefs, to the background, facial features, and garments, with the flesh left uncolored.[2]

The reliefs from the naiskoi are extremely important because they date from the otherwise poorly documented years between the middle of the fourth century B.C. and the Altar of Pergamon (ca. 180–160 B.C.). The sculptures represent everyday scenes, Dionysiac themes, or heroic combats. Both iconography and style are derived from mainland tradition and compare closely with monuments like the frieze from the temple of Apollo at Bassae (ca. 390 B.C.). The style of the sculptures has been recently re-examined by J. C. Carter, who has recognized a progressive development toward greater three-dimensionality, freer movement in space, and the emancipation of the figure from the background.[3] Especially significant is the increasing emotional content, which, in its contorted forms, windblown drapery, and vigorous facial expressions, foreshadows the Pergamene baroque.

1. The basic study is Carter. Dating is based on pottery (pp. 103–11). See also Klumbach. The Hopkins reliefs are noted in Furtwängler, *ND* 252, no. 7.

2. Carter, 15–16, 29–30, 32.

3. Ibid., 26–27.

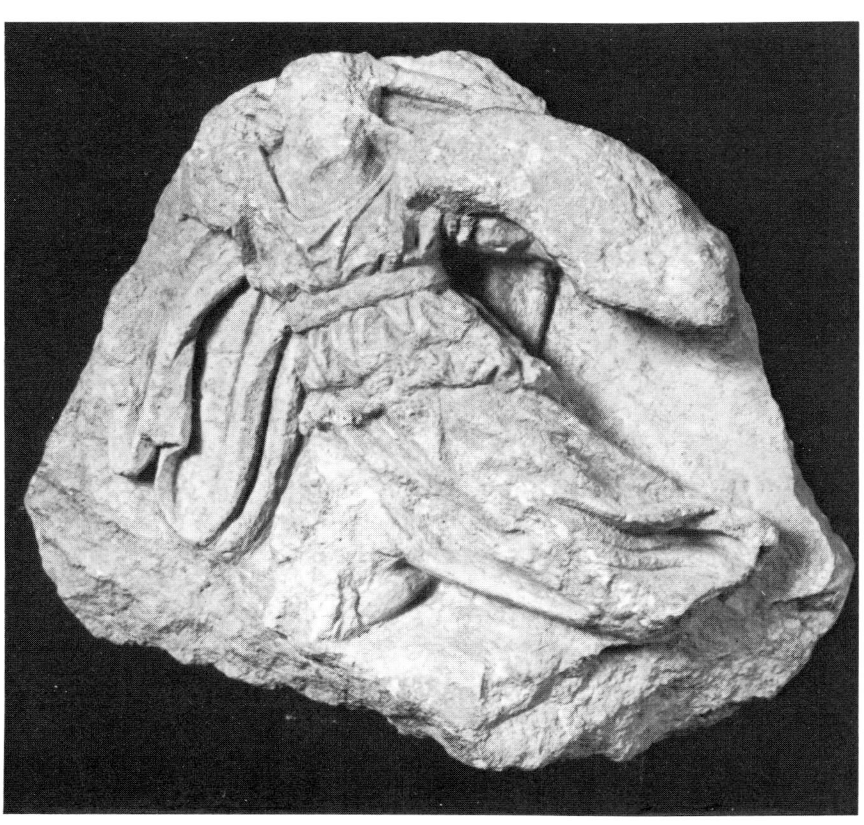

7. Amazon from Pediment

(ca. 330–275 B.C.)

1801. Baltimore Society AIA. Limestone. L, 17.5 cm; ht, 14.5 cm; th background, 3 cm. Smooth back and part of smoothed underside survive; other edges broken. Head and right arm missing; right breast chipped.

Upon a rocky terrain, an Amazon lunges forward on right knee, barely supported by her left leg, which is extended out behind her. Her left arm holds pelta shield; her extended right hand grasps a spear, which is visible behind head. Her chiton with overfold is girded beneath breast and again at waist. Himation billows out behind.

Bibliography: Klumbach, 2, no. 6, pl. 2; Carter, 78, no. 246.

8. Cuirassed Male Warrior from Pediment

(ca. 330–275 B.C.)

1802. Baltimore Society AIA. Limestone. Ht, 17.5 cm; w, 13 cm; th background, 3 cm. Mended from two pieces. Smooth back and part of smooth underside survive; other edges broken.

Male in left profile lunges forward on right leg; left leg extended behind him; head gazing back. His right arm was uplifted and held a weapon that is now missing. Foreshortened shield over left arm. He wears a cuirass that has shoulder lappets and two rows of tongue-shaped pteryges; beneath is a chiton that extends to mid-thigh. Between his legs is a shrub. Drapery to his right belongs to another figure. Beneath is a smooth band 2 cm high that serves as groundline.

Bibliography: Klumbach, 2, no. 5, pl. 2; Carter, 78, no. 245.

9. Reclining Figure from Pediment
(ca. 330–275 B.C.)

1806. Baltimore Society AIA. Limestone. L, 12.2 cm; ht, 12.5 cm; th background, 3 cm. Smooth back, underside, and sloping upper edge survive; other edges broken. Feet and upper half of figure broken away.

Supine maiden seen in left profile lies on back with clinging drapery wrapped around legs and beneath her. Tree in background; uneven terrain indicated by ledge 2 cm high.

Bibliography: Klumbach, 1, no. 4, pl. 2; Carter, 78, no. 244.

These three fragments (nos. 7–9) belong to a pedimental relief, of which the sloping upper edge survives on item no. 9. Characteristic of the Tarentine school are the uneven terrain and the interest in landscape elements, such as the tree behind the supine female and the stylized shrub between the feet of the cuirassed male.

The theme of the Greeks versus the Amazons was a popular one in naiskos sculpture, probably because the subject served as a mythical parallel for Tarentum's conflicts with its neighbors.[1] The treatment of the theme on our relief shows a more advanced approach than that found at Bassae (ca. 390 B.C.)[2] or on the Mausoleum of Halicarnassus (ca. 350 B.C.).[3] On our reliefs the figures either stride forth vigorously with legs widespread or lunge forward on bended knee, with little weight borne by the leg that is extended behind the body. Despite such overtones of urgency, however, the reliefs probably still date within the fourth century,[4] since the figures are rendered with frontal torsos and profile legs. Furthermore, the handling of the drapery can be compared with that on the Alexander sarcophagus (ca. 311 B.C.),[5] especially the opaque fabric, which falls in continuous ridges over the thighs and forms wide, flat panels in the himation. Foreshadowing the third century and the Pergamon Altar[6] of the second century are the heavy upper arms and the double girding beneath the breasts.

1. Carter, 17.
2. C. Hofkes-Brukker and A. Mallwitz, *Der Bassai-Fries* (Munich, 1975), 69–91.
3. W. Fuchs, *Die Skulptur der Griechen* (Munich, 1969), 450–51, nos. 520–25.
4. Carter, 78, dates the pieces in Group L (dated on p. 34, 330–275 B.C.), but suggests that the reliefs could belong in Group E, dated ca. 325 B.C.
5. J. Charbonneaux et al., *Hellenistic Art* (New York, 1973), 234–36, figs. 248–50.
6. Ibid., 267, fig. 288.

10. Wounded Centaur from a Frieze
(late fourth–early third c. B.C.)

1803. Baltimore Society AIA. Limestone. L, 9.6 cm; ht, 11.8 cm; th, 3 cm. Back smooth; otherwise broken all around. Male torso and half of equine barrel survive.

Centaur, seen from behind, clasps his left shoulder blade with his left hand. Right arm was extended out to side. Locks of hair, evenly grooved, extend to shoulders.

Bibliography: Klumbach, 3, no. 11, pl. 2; Carter, 49, no. 58.

The Centauromachy is not a common subject on the Tarentine reliefs.[1] The figure on our fragment is derived from an Attic prototype and can be compared with the wounded centaur from the Bassae frieze;[2] the gesture was probably inspired by the figure of the so-called Capaneus from the Amazonomachy on the shield of Athena Parthenos.[3]

The strictly profile equine body and the moderate torsion of the human back suggest a date still early in the series.[4] The projecting fascia of the top of the fragment is typical of many of the frieze slabs, which may have similar borders along the base and sides.[5]

1. Carter, 55, no. 97; 44, no. 26.
2. C. Hofkes-Brukker and A. Mallwitz, *Der Bassai-Fries* (Munich, 1975), 57–58.
3. E. B. Harrison, *Hesperia* 35 (1966): 115, 116, 123, 129–30.
4. Carter, 49, assigns this piece to his Group D, dated (on p. 34) to ca. 325–280 B.C.
5. Ibid., 29.

11. Lunging Amazon from a Frieze

(early third c. B.C.)

1800. Baltimore Society AIA. Limestone. L, 11.8 cm; ht, 10.5 cm; th, 4 cm. Smooth underside; back and left edge preserved; other edges broken away. Right forearm missing. Lower part of torso worn.

Amazon in sleeveless, belted chiton lunges forward on right knee, left leg extended behind. Pelta shield with gorgon emblem over left shoulder. Right arm uplifted with hand holding sword brought behind head. Torso in three-quarter view.

Bibliography: Klumbach, 3, no. 10, pl. 2; Carter, 78, no. 248.

The figure is in the same pose as no. 7 and exhibits a similar absence of torsion. The thin, clinging fabric and the continuous ridges of drapery indicate a date not long after the end of the fourth century. Carter places the piece in his Group L, before 275 B.C.[1]

1. Carter, 78, no. 248.

12. Male Warrior from a Frieze

(ca. 290 B.C.)

1799. Baltimore Society AIA. Limestone. L, 11.6 cm; ht, 15.2 cm; th background, 3 cm. Smooth back and part of upper edge survive; other edges broken. Torso missing below hips.

Nude male seen frontally turns to his left, head in right profile. Left arm was extended, right arm uplifted with spear in right hand. Chlamys brought over left shoulder with end blowing out behind. Sword belt over right shoulder. Short curly hair. Behind figure are forelegs of horse and drapery of its rider. Above head is projecting ledge 2 cm high.

Bibliography: Klumbach, 3, no. 12, pl. 2; Carter, 69, no. 193.

This fragment is the latest of the series and illustrates the most developed phase of the naiskos sculpture; the figure moves freely in space and is well separated from the horse behind him. The agitation of the drapery ends and the tightly coiled locks of hair foreshadow the Pergamon Altar and compare closely with a fragmentary naiskos frieze in Cleveland.[1] Carter assigns the Hopkins piece to his Group J, which he dates about 290 B.C.[2] The scene probably illustrates an Amazonomachy or a struggle against barbarians.

1. Carter, 68, no. 188, pl. 31A.
2. Ibid., 34, 69, no. 193.

Sculpture

ROMAN

13. Marble Head of Herm

(first c. B.C.–first c. A.D.)

9189. Probably purchased in Rome or Naples in 1906–9. Marble. Ht, 18.3 cm; w, 14.3 cm. Nose and top of fillet chipped. Back cut flat. Modern dowel hole beneath. Three rows of corkscrew curls frame face; fillet behind; rest of hair finely striated. Mustache, goatee, and beard similarly handled, with wavy locks of beard terminating in corkscrew curls.

A Herm is composed of a head, traditionally of Hermes, surmounting a pillar with male genitals. Because Hermes was the patron god of athletes, travelers, and those engaged in commerce, Herms were usually located in the palaestra, the agora, or at road crossings.

Herms were first made during the archaic period,[1] but they received what would be their conventional treatment during the fifth century B.C. in the Hermes Propylaeos by Alcamenes. This lost work is reflected in one or both of the well-known and similar ancient Herm types, which are named for the sites where they were recovered, Pergamon and Ephesos.[2] Both heads combine mid–fifth century features with an archaic treatment of hair and beard, consisting of three rows of corkscrewlike curls at the forehead and a jutting beard of wavy, striated locks with curly tips. The archaic treatment of the hair identifies the Alcamenoid Herm as one of the earliest known works in an archaizing style.[3]

Before the end of the fifth century, non-archaizing Herms were being sculpted,[4] and during the Hellenistic period beardless Herms came into fashion.[5] The archaizing bearded Herm returns to prominence about 100 B.C., when neo-Attic workshops began to produce examples for the villas of wealthy Romans, including Cicero.[6] The impetus for this demand lay in both the resurgence of interest in the archaizing style and the cosmopolitan aspirations of Romans living in the first century B.C. Our piece is a typical example of these small-scale eclectic works. The beard is shorter and less wavy than the Alcamenoid type and the strands of the goatee are in high relief. Betraying influence from the Praxitelean school are the deep-set eyes and minimal lower lid.

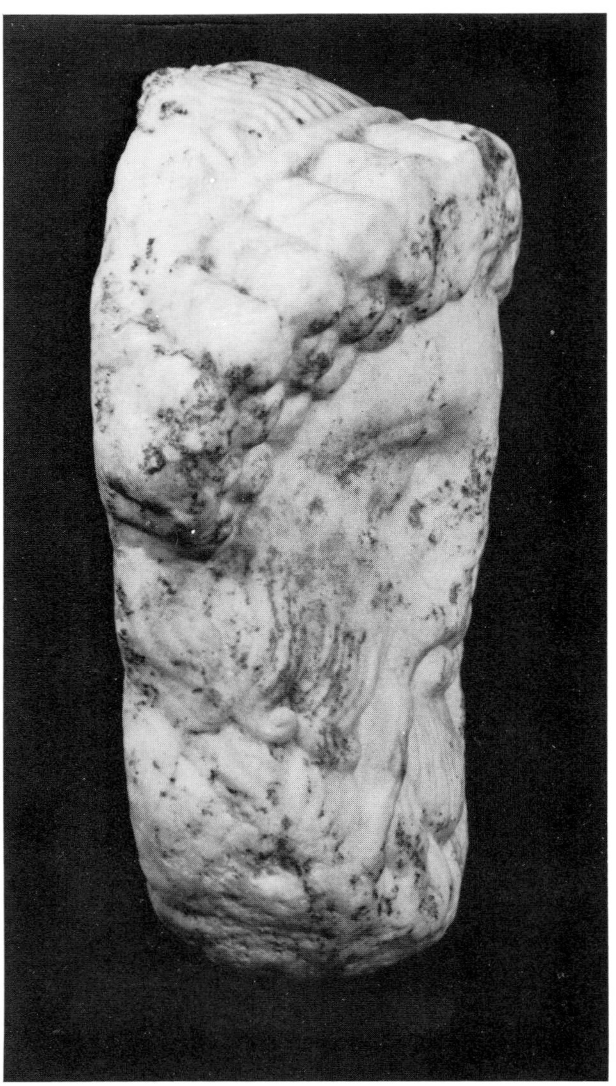

If the flat back is original, it is likely that this Herm was intended to be displayed against a wall. On the other hand, it is possible that the head originally formed part of a double herm, like those that occupied the center of a peristyle garden; these, however, usually paired Dionysos with Ariadne or with Dionysiac beings, such as Silenos or a Bacchante.[7]

1. E. Harrison, *Archaic and Archaistic Sculpture. The Athenian Agora XI* (Princeton, 1965), 112, 122.

2. Ibid., 122–24, 130–34; B. S. Ridgway, *The Archaic Style in Greek Sculpture* (Princeton, 1977), 311, 318, and *Fifth Century Styles in Greek Sculpture* (Princeton, 1981), 174, 190; B. Schlörb-Vierneisel, *Klassische Skulpturen des 5 und 4 Jahrhunderts v. Chr., Glyptothek München, Katalog der Skulpturen*, Bd. II (Munich, 1979), 49; D. Willers, *Zu den Anfängen der archaistischen Plastik in Griechenland, AthMitt Beiheft* 4 (1975), 33–47.

3. Ridgway, *The Archaic Style*, 318. See Harrison, *Archaic and Archaistic Sculpture*, 129–30.

4. Harrision, 132.

5. Ibid., 127.

6. Ibid., 127. Cicero, *Epistulae ad Atticum*, I.6.2 / I.4.3 / I.8.2 / I.9.2 / I.10.3.

7. W. Jashemski, *The Gardens of Pompeii* (New Rochelle, 1979), 35, fig. 54; 37, fig. 59; 38, fig. 60; 39, fig. 63; 44, fig. 74.

14. Marble Theater Relief

(ca. A.D.. 50–75)

1160. Probably purchased in Rome or Naples in 1906–9. Marble. Ht, 21.4 cm; w, 24.6 cm; th background, 1.5 cm. Broken down each side and across bottom. Small (1.5-cm diam.) hole in center of upper edge is probably modern.

Rectangular relief carved on both sides.

Side A

On side A there are two comic masks turned three-quarters to right. On mask at viewer's left, hair is brushed back from forehead. Other mask has curly mustache and beard, hair brushed back from face with curly locks beneath ears. Lying along hairline is wreath wrapped with fabric and surmounted by bunches of fruit. Undulating eyebrows. Drill holes in wreath and in locks of hair and beard. On both masks irises are pierced and mouths open.

Side B

Seen in right profile is face of bearded elderly Papposilenos, rendered in low relief. Bald except for wisps of hair behind ears. Frowning brows and grooved forehead, bulbous nose, open mouth.

Bibliography: E. R. Williams, *AntK* 21 (1978):32–39.

This relief is one of several reliefs with theatrical subject matter that were made in the first centuries B.C. and A.D. for the decoration of private villas located around the Bay of Naples and in Rome.[1] Some examples, such as our own, are carved on both sides and were placed in gardens on top of pillars or columns.[2] Reliefs that were carved only on one side were set into the walls at the back of the peristyle.

Our relief was made in the same workshop as several other examples that have been found in Rome, Pompeii, and probably Ostia.[3] All of the reliefs display the same repertory of theatrical masks and the same style. These masks were inspired from those used in Hellenistic and contemporary performances of Greek and Latin comedy and can be approximately identified through examination of the descriptions of Pollux, a Roman writer of the second century A.D. who drew upon Hellenistic sources that are now lost. The masks on side A of our relief belong to a youth, perhaps the *neaniskos melas* or *apalos*. The other mask is that of a slave, probably Pollux's wavy-haired slave.

Side B does not depict a mask, but rather the aged Papposilenos, who was a mythical being, part animal, part man, associated with Dionysos. As late as the fifth century B.C., the Papposilenos was distinguished by his pointed ears as well as his snub nose, but during the fourth century and Hellenistic period he underwent a humanization, so that occasionally, as here, he can be recognized only by the context or the exaggerated expression.

The style of our relief and of those that were made in the same workshop dates the group in the third

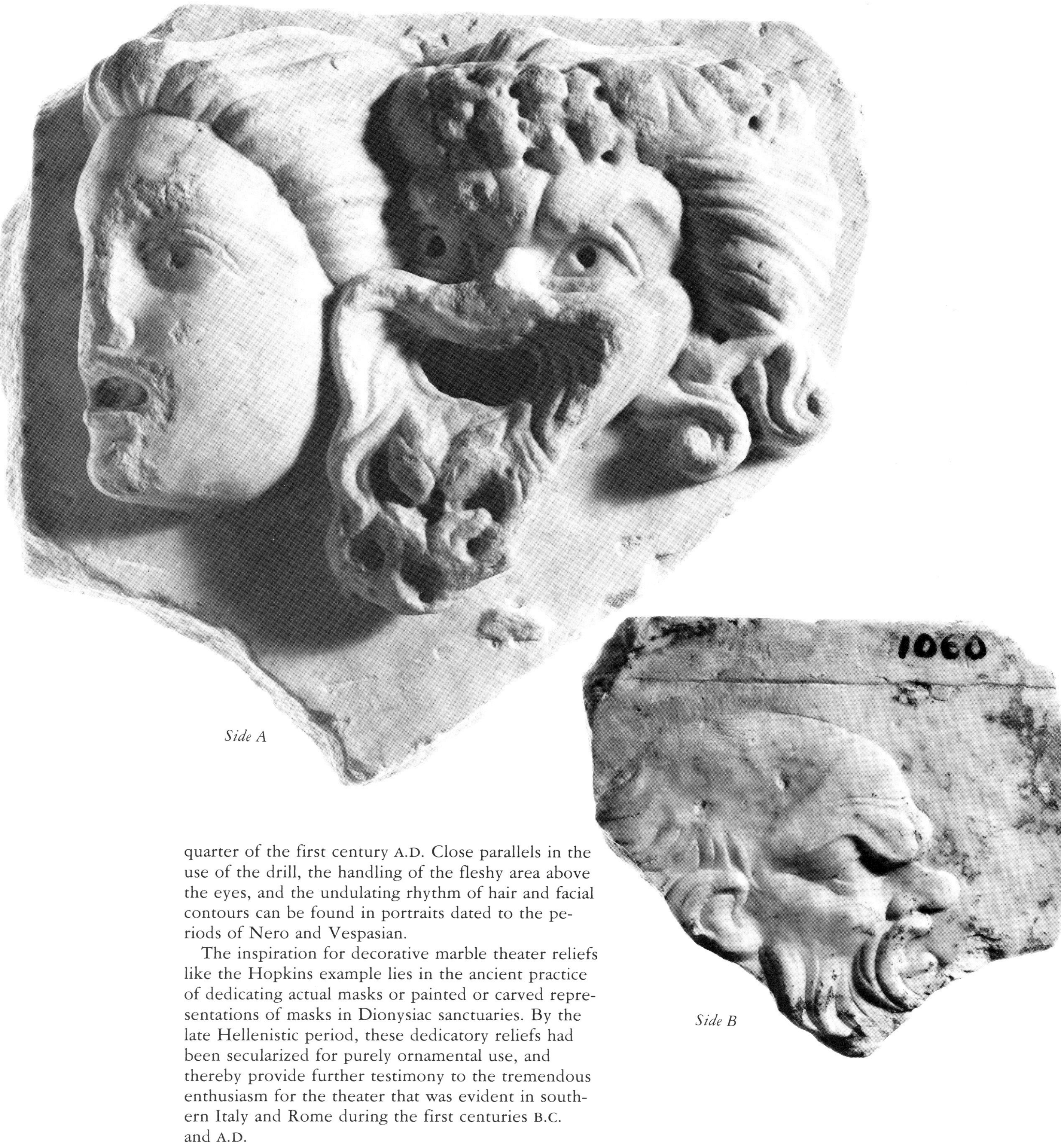

Side A

Side B

quarter of the first century A.D. Close parallels in the use of the drill, the handling of the fleshy area above the eyes, and the undulating rhythm of hair and facial contours can be found in portraits dated to the periods of Nero and Vespasian.

The inspiration for decorative marble theater reliefs like the Hopkins example lies in the ancient practice of dedicating actual masks or painted or carved representations of masks in Dionysiac sanctuaries. By the late Hellenistic period, these dedicatory reliefs had been secularized for purely ornamental use, and thereby provide further testimony to the tremendous enthusiasm for the theater that was evident in southern Italy and Rome during the first centuries B.C. and A.D.

1. See full publication in E. R. Williams, *AntK* 21 (1978):32–39.

2. For good photographs of the reliefs in the House of the Gilded Cupids, see W. Jashemski, *The Gardens of Pompeii* (New Rochelle, 1979), 39–40, fig. 64; and E. Dwyer, *RömMitt* 88 (1981):255–56.

3. Add *Sculpture BMFA*, 189, no. 302.

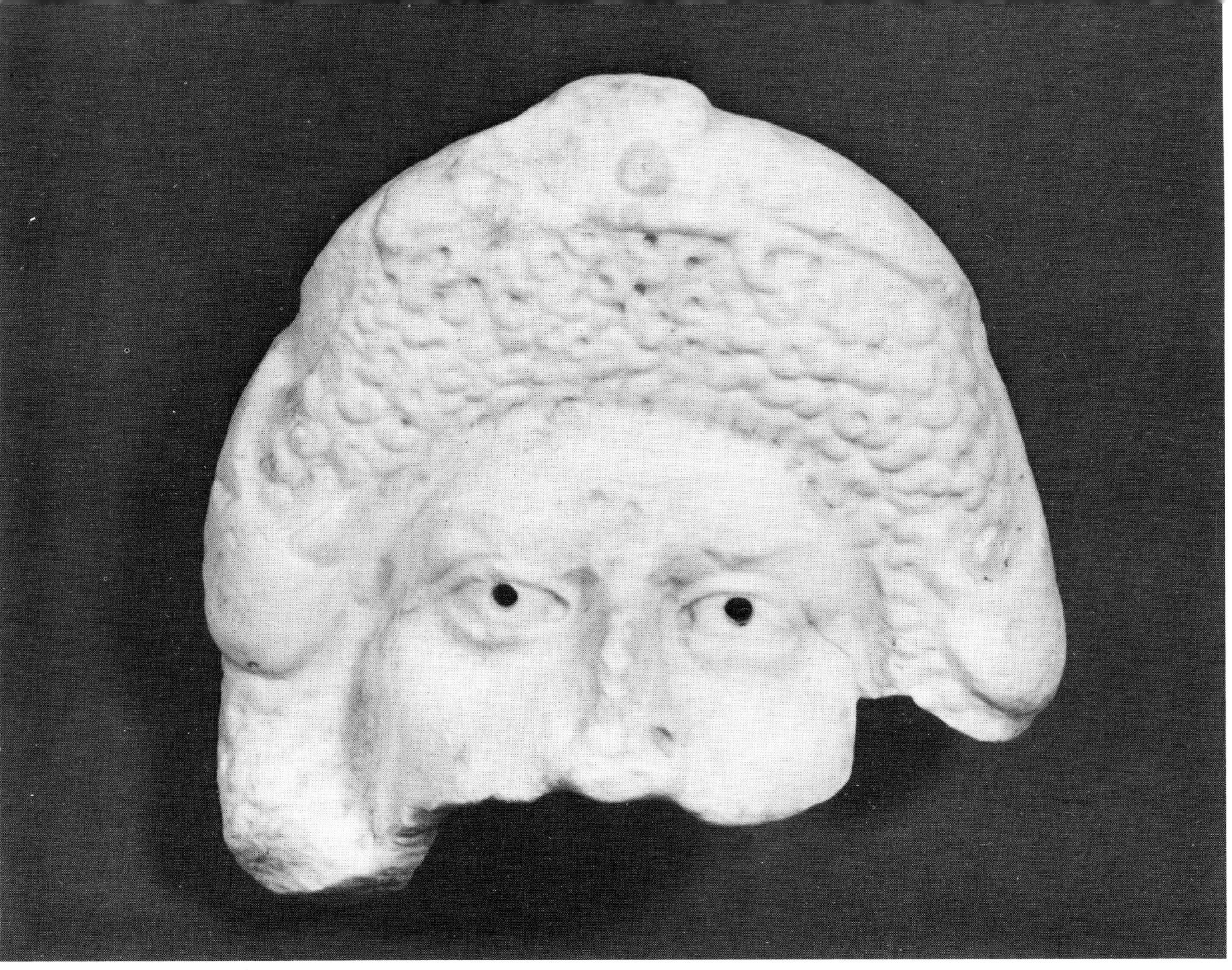

15. Marble Tragic Mask of Herakles

(ca. A.D. 75–90)

154. Purchased in Rome or Naples in 1906–9. "Capua." Marble. Ht, 21.5 cm; w, 23.5 cm; max th, 10 cm. Missing lower part of face beneath nose. Remains of two iron dowels through crown. Surface stained. Back hollow.

Mask wearing lion-scalp above curly locks with drilled centers. Pupils are pierced and irises incised.

Marble friezes of tragic and comic masks were used in the Hellenistic period as ornaments for theaters, as in the one in Pergamon.[1] In the Roman world, individual marble masks were acquired for private villas, where they were suspended between columns of a peristyle[2] or were attached to garden walls, often in the vicinity of fountains.[3] Several of these masks, usually termed *oscilla*, survive from Herculaneum and Pompeii,[4] thereby testifying to the enormous popularity of the theater in southern Italy during the first century A.D.

The lion-scalp identifies our mask as that of Herakles, wearing the Nemean lion-skin. This type of mask is found on Hellenistic monuments,[5] but often without the high hairstyle and extremely wrinkled brow that identify our example as a Roman adaptation.[6] A similar mask of Herakles decorates the fountain in the House of the Large Fountain in Pompeii.[7]

Our mask has spongelike hair rendered as tiny shell curls with drilled centers. A similar handling of the hair appears on portraits of Domitia, the wife of Domitian, dating about A.D. 80.[8] On these heads we also find a comparable treatment of the eye area, with a curving lower eyelid, deep groove at the base of the upper eyelid, and fleshy underbrow area. Further comparison can be made with portraits of Julia Titis, daughter of Titus (ca. A.D. 81),[9] of Domitian (ca. A.D. 73),[10] and with several heads on the Cancelleria reliefs (A.D. 85–96).[11] Our mask, therefore, must have been made in the last quarter of the first century A.D., when numerous masks were appearing in wall paintings of the Fourth style. It is interesting to note that at this time the paintings of tragic and comic masks far outnumber those of Dionysiac masks, which had been more popular in the preceding decades.[12]

Our mask probably accurately reproduces the actual masks of Herakles that were being used on the contemporary stage. Although Greek tragedies were presented in Italy as late as the second century B.C.,[13] it was surely more common in the latter part of the first century A.D. to encounter a Latin version of Sophocles' *Trachinian Women*,[14] or Accius's *Amphitryo*, which was a reworking of Euripides' *Madness of Herakles*.[15] Not long before our mask was made, Seneca completed his *Herakles Furens*, which Nero himself performed.[16]

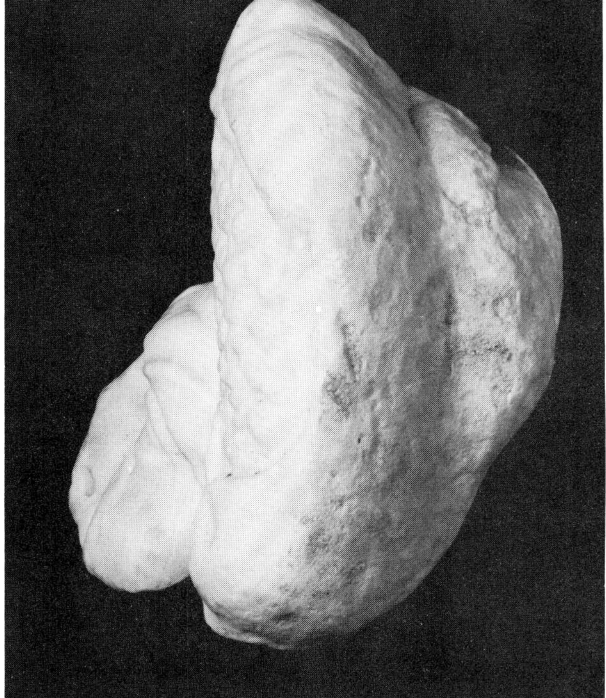

Although decorative marble masks fell out of fashion by the second century A.D., we continue to encounter representations of masks of Herakles, both on Muse sarcophagi, where an example may be held by Melpomene,[17] and on Season sarcophagi, where the mask is coupled with one of Deianira.[18]

1. Bieber, *Theater*, 85, fig. 311.
2. E. Dwyer, in *Pompeii and the Vesuvian Landscape* (Washington, D.C., 1979), 67 n. 85, points out that originally *oscilla* were masks of Dionysos that were hung from pine trees. Eventually an *oscillum* became any ornament that was suspended from the architrave of a peristyle (see Ward-Perkins and Claridge, 141). For other masks, see Spinazzola, pl. 57; *Sculpture BMFA*, 188, no. 301; and W. Jashemski, *The Gardens of Pompeii* (New Rochelle, 1979), 38, fig. 60; 40, fig. 65; 82, fig. 132. For the House of the Gilded Cupids, see *NSc* 4 (1907):583, fig. 32.
3. M. Brion, *Pompeii and Herculaneum* (London, 1960), 21 (House of Neptune and Amphitrite).
4. Ward-Perkins and Claridge, 140, nos. 64, 65; E. Dwyer, *RömMitt* 88 (1981):248.
5. Bieber, *Theater*, 30, fig. 109; 83, fig. 305.
6. Ibid., 85, fig. 311; 157, fig. 569.
7. Ibid., 243, fig. 800. Jashemski, *The Gardens of Pompeii*, 42, figs. 69–70; 121–23. Spinazzola, pl. 194. E. Dwyer, *RömMitt* 88 (1981), 279, no. 88, pl. 116.2.
8. V. Poulsen, *Les portraits romains II* (Copenhagen, 1974), 47, no. 12, pl. XXII. A Hekler, *Greek and Roman Portraits* (London, 1912), xxxv, 239A. G. Daltrop et al., *Das römische Herrscherbild, II.1. Die Flavier* (Berlin, 1966), 66, 123, pl. 53. See also a head from the Domitianic period in H. von Heintze, *Die antiken Porträts in Schloss Fasanerie bei Fulda* (Mainz, 1968), 43, no. 29, pls. 50, 51, 120b,d.
9. Daltrop et al., *Das römische Herrscherbild*, 54, 118, pl. 42.
10. Ibid., 33, 104, pl. 24A.
11. F. Magi, *I rilievi flavi del Palazzo della Cancelleria* (Rome, 1945), pls. IX, X, XI.
12. A. Allrogen-Bedel, *Maskendarstellungen in der römisch-kampanischen Wandmalerei* (Munich, 1974), 62–63; Jashemski, *The Gardens of Pompeii*, 63, fig. 102.
13. Bieber, *Theater*, 152.
14. Ibid., 157, and fig. 569.
15. Ibid., 229.
16. Ibid., 233, 235.
17. C. Vermeule and N. Neuerburg, *Catalogue of the Ancient Art in the J. Paul Getty Museum* (Malibu, 1973), 40, no. 90.
18. Bieber, *Theater*, 244, fig. 806.

16. Marble Flavian Head of Man from a Relief

(ca. A.D. 69–79)

9194. Probably purchased in Rome or Naples in 1906–9. Marble. Ht, 19.6 cm; w, 11.5 cm. Nose largely chipped away. Chips missing from forehead and chin. Back cut smoothly in modern times. Modern dowel hole beneath.

Very short, stippled hair. Deeply grooved and undulating features.

The surface of the face is a constantly changing terrain marked by jowls, sags, and furrows. The restlessness is heightened by the frowning forehead and the quivering corners of the slightly open mouth.

In many respects the portraits of the Flavian period resemble the Republican heads of the previous century. Specific individual features are rendered and the geography of the sitter's face, complete with lines and furrows, is respectfully recorded as the badge of experience.[1] Flavian portrait sculpture, however, is distinctive in its sense of immediacy. On our head the arched brows and open mouth express a momentary concern that mirrors a pensive mind.

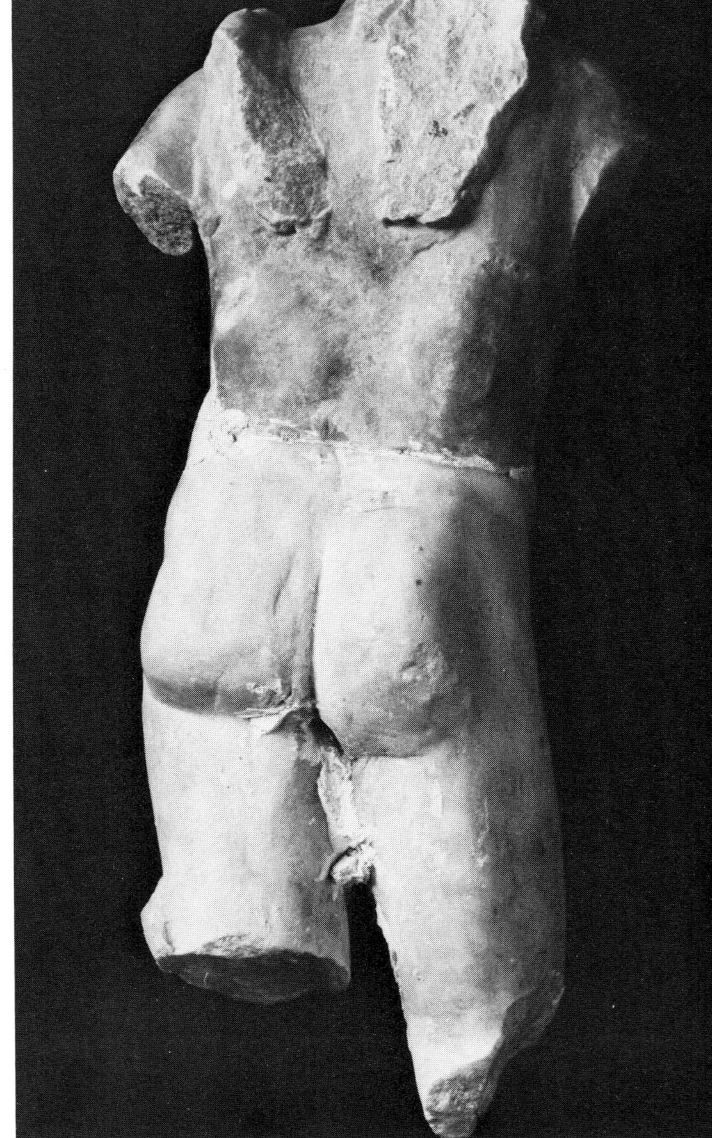

Our work finds its closest parallels among the portraits of Vespasian that were executed during the later years of his rule. On these and contemporary heads we find the same juxtaposition of shallow incisions for the hair with deep channels running above the eyebrow and from nose to mouth.[2]

Especially interesting is the treatment of the eye area. On our head the groove at the base of the upper eyelid continues beyond the corner of the eye in the manner of Pheidian and Augustan sculpture. Distinctive on our example, however, is the additional groove that curves upward from the outer corner of the eye to the overhanging brows, thereby enclosing the fleshy underbrow area in a treatment reminiscent of the Pergamene baroque. In sculpture that postdates the Hopkins piece, such as the Cancelleria reliefs (A.D. 85–96), there is a return to a less protruding brow and to a single grooved eyelid, although the fleshy expanse beneath the brow remains.[3]

1. G. Hanfmann, *Latomus* 11 (1952):457–58.

2. G. Daltrop et al., *Das römische Herrscherbild, II.1. Die Flavier* (Berlin, 1966), 10, 13, 15–16, 75, pl. 3 (a head of Vespasian in Copenhagen); V. Poulsen, *Les portraits romains II* (Copenhagen, 1974), 52, no. 18, pl. XXXII.

3. F. Magi, *I rilievi flavi del Palazzo della Cancelleria* (Rome, 1945), pls. IX, X, XI.

17. Marble Statue of Eros

(second c. A.D.)

9187. Marble. Ht, 52.5 cm; w, 22 cm. Missing head, arms, wings, legs below knees. Mended across waist from two pieces. Stains over surface.

Slim youth stands with weight on left leg, right leg relaxed. Left hip elevated; arms were lowered. On each shoulder are ends of long curls. Remains of strut on outside of left thigh just above knee. Back summarily worked with concavity on outside of right buttock.

The distinctive features of our statue—the slender, delicately muscled torso; the pose, with left supporting leg and upraised hip; the lowered arms; and the shoulder-length hair—find their closest parallels among terracotta figurines of Eros and Dionysos dating from the first half of the fourth century B.C.[1] These figurines carry drinking vessels and jugs, attributes that can be tentatively restored here, since the strut on the outside of the left thigh indicates that the arm was held away from the body, and perhaps held a drinking vessel.

The terracotta figurines and the Hopkins youth are probably ultimately derived from a statue in the major

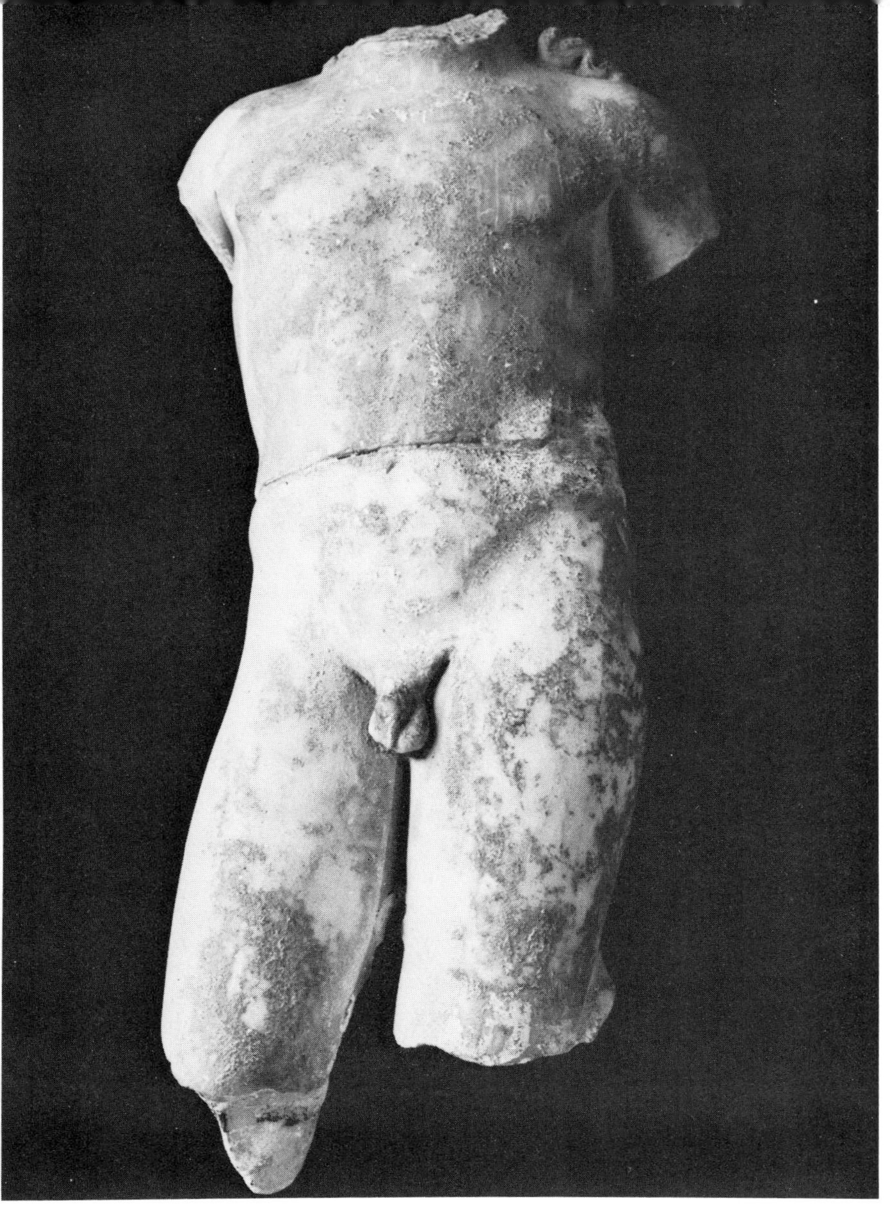

arts, but the identity and appearance of that prototype remain unclear. Certainly the pose and the handling of the body agree with the well-known types of the Palatine Eros and the Palermo Satyr. This latter figure (as probably did the Palatine Eros) holds a jug in his upraised right hand and a vessel in his outstretched left hand, but since this composition is yet to be attested for the fourth century, it must remain questionable whether these statues are accurate copies of bronzes by Praxiteles or merely reflect later adaptations of a Praxitelean work.[2]

The deeply drilled locks of hair date our piece in the second century A.D. The superficial treatment of the back of the figure suggests that the statue was intended to be displayed against a wall.

1. M. Trumpf-Lyritzaki, *Griechische Figurenvasen* (Bonn, 1969), 12–15, nos. 24–32 for Eros, and 15, nos. 33–35 for Dionysos.

2. M. Pfrommer [*AA* (1980):532–44, particularly 536–37, figs. 1–3] believes that the Palatine Eros reproduces the statue seen by Kallistratos, but since the ancient writer tells us that Eros carried a bow and arrow, either the Palatine Eros does not reflect the lost work or is only a loose adaptation of it. On the bronze handle from Myrina of the mid-fourth century B.C. (Pfrommer, 538–41), the right hand does not hold a vessel, but strokes the hair.

18. Marble Head of Tuxe-Fortuna

(ca. A.D. 150–200)

9196. Fine-grained marble, highly polished. Ht, 14.5 cm; w, base of neck, 5.3 cm; depth, 4.2 cm. Face chipped. Cut smoothly across neck, probably in modern times.

Hair is center-parted, with wavy locks brushed back over ears to top of head. Rest of hair is gathered in a knot at nape, with a long lock hanging down each side of neck. Maiden wears city crown with five turrets, on each of which is a portal in high relief. Pupils are pierced and irises incised. Drill holes at corners of mouth and in tear ducts of eyes.

The turreted city crown first appears in the Hittite rock sculptures at Yasilikaya (ca. 1260 B.C.)[1] and is later adopted by the Phrygian mother goddess, Cybele, whose cult was established in Athens by the fifth century and in Rome by 204 B.C.[2] By the fourth century B.C., the turreted crown was assumed by Greek deities with protective functions, such as Demeter,[3] and in the early third century the crown was bestowed upon Tuxe, the deity of fortune, in the famous work by Eutychides of Sicyon.[4] Henceforth the turreted

crown was as much at home with Tuxe as with its former proprietess Cybele.[5]

Our head is noteworthy in its highly polished surface with minimal modeling, the feathering of the brow, the thick eyelids, and the short mouth with thin, compressed lips. This style is paralleled on Antonine portraits, especially those of the younger Faustina of ca. A.D. 160.[6]

The style of our head, and most notably its size and Praxitelean hairstyle, can also be compared with the head of a statuette in Boston depicting Tuxe-Fortuna and dated about A.D. 200.[7] That piece was found in Cremna, Pisidia, together with several other statuettes of Tuxe, one of Hermes, and a group of Muses, three of which are now in Malibu.[8] Vermeule postulates that all the sculpture was made for a single building, probably a Sebasteion; it is possible that our head belonged to a similar sculptural program.

1. V. Müller, *Der Polos, Die griechische Götterkrone* (Berlin, 1915), 46.

2. M. Bieber, *Collection Latomus* 103 (1969), vol. 3, 29–40. See also Thompson, *Troy*, 77–78.

3. Müller, *Der Polos*, 47.

4. W. Fuchs, *Die Skulptur der Griechen* (Munich, 1969), 277, fig. 306; Bieber, *Sculpture*, 40.

5. Bieber, *Collection Latomus* 103 (1969), vol. 3, 30–33.

6. V. Poulsen, *Les portraits romains II* (Copenhagen, 1974), 116, no. 110, pl. CLXXXIV; 100, no. 85, pls. CXL–CXLI.

7. *Sculpture BMFA*, 123, no. 190.

8. C. Vermeule and N. Neuerburg, *Catalogue of the Ancient Art in the J. Paul Getty Museum* (Malibu, 1973), 20, nos. 39–41.

19. Marble Sarcophagus Fragment

(ca A.D. 250 or late third c. A.D.)

1175. White, fine-grained marble. Ht, 33 cm; max w representation, 27 cm; max th, 13 cm; av th, 8.5 cm. Broken all around. Back roughly flat.

A portion of two registers, separated by a narrow uneven ledge from which an olive tree grows. The upper register depicts an outdoor banquet scene. At the left is a woman who gazes to her right, her right hand brought to her chin. She wears a long-sleeved tunic with an overfall to the top of her thigh. Her hair is center-parted, with tight waves drawn back over the ear. Hair at nape is plaited, with the braids bent upward and secured at the back of the head. To her left is a male with close-cropped hair who wears a tunica exomis. He gazes to his left at a man in a sleeved tunic and pallium who carries a staff in his left hand. In the foreground are two nude reclining males, one of whom cradles the ankle of the other. In the lower register are two figures, one of whom holds a flabellum in her right hand. At the viewer's far left is part of a much larger figure who draws back his sleeved right arm; in his hand is the hilt of a thrusting dagger or sword.

The stocky bodies, the deep drilling with summary modeling, and the man's close-cropped hairstyle date this relief in the mid- to late third century A.D.[1] The woman wears the "scheitelzopf" hairstyle, in which the hair at the nape is braided and brought up the back of the head or over the crown. This hairstyle first appeared in its developed form on portraits of

Julia Paula (ca. 223)[2] and it remained popular through the third century. Close parallels to the Hopkins version are found on portraits of Tranquillina (241–244)[3] and Otacilia (244–248).[4]

The scene on our fragment cannot be identified with certainty. A banquet in a bucolic setting was a common theme on Christian and pagan sarcophagi of the third century,[5] although the armed warrior suggests a more traditional subject, such as the triumph of Dionysos, Endymion and Selene, Achilles and Penthesilea, or Meleager.

1. I thank N. Himmelmann and G. Koch for their suggestions concerning this piece.

2. K. Wessel, *AA* (1946–47):66.

3. S. Wood, *AJA* 85 (1981):61, and fig. 1; Wessel, *AA* (1946–47): 67.

4. Wood, *AJA* 85 (1981):61, and fig. 2; Wessel, *AA* (1946–47):67.

5. K. Weitzmann, ed., *Age of Spirituality* (New York, 1979), 254, no. 236.

Metalwork

LURISTAN

20. Luristan Horse Bit

(ninth–eighth c. B.C.)

K 69. Kemper Simpson Collection. Bronze. L, 18.5 cm; l each cheekpiece, 13 cm. Intact.

Rigid tubular mouthpiece, the ends of which are coiled in opposite directions. Each cheekpiece has shape of two openwork triangles joined at apexes, with extensions in form of horse neck and head. Each horse wears necklace with spherical ornament; mane in five or six clumps with projecting forelock. Upraised ears, accentuated curve of jawline, circular ridge for eyelids, eyeballs in high relief. Indentations for nostrils and mouth. Prong on inside of each of four corners of cheekpiece with another prong at mid-section either above or below mouthpiece.

The Luristan bronzes come from an area in the central Zagros mountains that is today inhabited by the Lurs. The bronzes were unknown before 1928, when they were looted by nomads from necropolises, and subsequently were sold on the art markets in Teheran and Paris. Unfortunately, there have been few, if any, controlled excavations since that time.[1] Today it is believed that the objects were made by descendants of the Elamites[2] or Kassites,[3] who fled into the mountains in the thirteenth century B.C. and worked first for Babylonian patrons and then, between the ninth and seventh centuries, for the peoples of the plains to the west, particularly the Assyrians. Most scholars date the bronzes between the ninth and seventh centuries B.C. and believe that their production was arrested by the arrival of the Medes around 600 B.C.[4]

Luristan horse bits are characterized by rigid mouthpieces, the ends of which pass through the flanking cheekpieces. On our example the reins would have slipped through either the curved end of the mouthpiece or an intervening ring. The ends of the

cheekstraps passed through the adjoining openings in the cheekpiece. The spikes on the inside of the cheekpieces are common and noticeably increase the severity of the bit.

Our example belongs to Type I of Potratz's classification,[5] as does a variant that substitutes a goat head for that of the horse.[6] Almost exact parallels to the Hopkins bit appear on the reliefs of Assurnasirpal of about 875 B.C.[7] Later Assyrian monarchs preferred a different type of horse bit, although our type continued to be made in the Zagros area into the early seventh century.[8]

The horse is not a common motif on the Luristan bronzes, nor is its treatment conventional. Whereas many of the bronzes depict imaginary hybrids and fantastic forms of the native wild goat,[9] the horse is always represented realistically, with head in profile and with actual features of the animal's appearance carefully recorded, such as the bell around the neck and the ornamental knots of mane. It has been suggested that the Assyrians, who relied heavily upon the horse, encouraged horse breeding in the Zagros area.[10] Here the people must have attained some familiarity with the animal, because in several graves from this area a horse bit had been placed beneath the head of the deceased.[11] Some of these bits show no wear and thus must have been made specifically for burial.

1. For summary of the recent excavations, see P. Amiet, *Art of the Ancient Near East* (New York, 1980), 554–55.

2. P. R. S. Moorey, *Catalogue of the Ancient Persian Bronzes in the Ashmolean Museum* (Oxford, 1971), 288–89.

3. T. Arne, *Medelhausmuseet, Bulletin* 2 (1962):17.

4. Moorey, *Catalogue*, 289.

5. J. Potratz, *Die Pferdetrensen des alten Orient* (Rome, 1966), 103–10. J. Potratz, *Luristanbronzen: Die einstmalige Sammlung Professor Sarre* (Berlin and Istanbul, 1968), 18. Moorey, *Catalogue*, 106–9.

6. Potratz, *Pferdetrensen*, 107, no. 19, pl. XLVIII, fig. 112.

7. Moorey, *Catalogue*, 108.

8. Ibid., 108, 110. The type of bit in use under Sennacherib is discussed on p. 115.

9. See discussion of item no. 21.

10. Potratz, *Pferdetrensen*, 160, 179.

11. Moorey, *Catalogue*, 107.

21. Luristan Whetstone

(ninth–seventh c. B.C.)

K 68. Kemper Simpson Collection. Bronze. L, 22 cm; l of goat without whetstone, 11.1 cm. Tip of whetstone broken off.

Protome of recumbent goat, whose slim forelegs are tucked up under chest. Shoulder in low relief. Long circular horns arch back to neck. Upright ears, thick projecting triangular eyelids, long protruding eye, beard indicated by strap attached between chin and neck. Area under jaw concave. Socket terminates in ring molding that has two holes pierced through one side, one hole in opposite side. Part of sandstone whetstone still in place.

The caprid or gazelle is a common subject in Luristan whetstones, although one also encounters horses, panthers, and birds perched on animals' backs.[1] Within the goat type, variations exist in the position of the horns and forelegs, and in the presence of a beard or of knobs on the horns.[2]

The treatment of the goat in this whetstone exemplifies the zoomorphic character of Luristan art. The form of the animal emerges from the shape of the utensil, and prominent features, such as neck and horns, are exaggerated, while other elements, such as the forelegs, are abbreviated. Also noteworthy are the general absence of organic handling in the shoulder, the inclination for geometric shapes—especially curves—and the predilection for openwork.

Because many whetstones are known, it is believed that the objects were made over most of the period of Luristan production, but particularly during the eighth century B.C.[3]

This whetstone was suspended by means of a chain attached to a ring that passed through the holes at the base of the socket.[4]

1. P. R. S. Moorey, *Catalogue of the Ancient Persian Bronzes in the Ashmolean Museum* (Oxford, 1971), 100, nos. 106–7; J. Potratz, *Luristanbronzen: Die Einstmalige Sammlung Professor Sarre* (Istanbul and Leipzig, 1968), 15–16.

2. Potratz, *Luristanbronzen*, 15; *Ancient Bronzes: A Selection from the Heckett Collection* (Pittsburgh, 1964), nos. 18, 23.

3. Moorey, *Catalogue*, 99.

4. For an intact example see Potratz, *Luristanbronzen*, 15, fig. 58, pl. XII.

Metalwork

GREEK

22. Geometric Horse

(ca. 700 B.C.)

K 37. Kemper Simpson Collection. Bronze. Ht, 5.7 cm; base l, 3.5 cm; w, 0.9 cm. Intact.

Horse with tubular barrel and thin, straplike legs stands on rectangular base comprised of a bar connecting each foot. Tubular tail attached to base. Thin neck arches into cylindrical head with upright ears. Incised on outside of each leg below knee or hock is column of inverted V's. On sides of base are groups of oblique incisions that alternate direction. Cast in one piece.

This horse compares closely with examples from Thessaly, especially Pherae.[1] The Thessalian horses can be distinguished from those made in Corinth, Laconia, and Argos[2] by the cylindrical body, the thin, flat legs, the horizontal, tubular muzzle with arching ears continuing the curve of the neck, the continuous curving contour of forelegs and neck, the hollow rectangular base, and the diagonal incisions on base and legs.

Our example clearly belongs to the late mannered phase of geometric art, when horses in vasepainting also display attenuated forms and an exaggerated curve of neck and head.[3]

Small horses like the Hopkins one were made as votive offerings and have often been recovered from sanctuaries,[4] especially in Thessaly, which was renowned for its horse breeding. The figurines also served another function, one appropriate to the funerary connotation the horse had acquired in Mycenaean times:[5] in burials uncovered in Macedonia, Akarnania, and Messenia, horse statuettes had been placed on the breast of the deceased as amuletic pendants.[6]

1. Y. Béquignon, *Recherches archéologiques à Phères de Thessalie* (Paris, 1937), 67–68, nos. 1–4, pl. 19. H. W. Biesantz, *Die thessalischen Grabreliefs* (Mainz, 1965), 32, nos. L 64–67, pls. 51–52; 159. Other Thessalian characteristics are the circle-and-dot motif on the flanks (see item no. 23 and Mitten, *Master Bronzes*, 38, nos. 19–20, and 40, no. 22). Comstock-Vermeule, 8, no. 6. Dörig, no. 103, attributed to Thessaly. I. Kilian-Dirlmeier, *Getty MusJ* 6–7 (1978–79):128–30.

2. H. Herrmann, *JdI* 79 (1964):2–46; Mitten, *RISD*, 24, no. 6.

3. S. Benton, *BSA* 35 (1934–35):102–8 and *JHS* 70 (1950):21, class III. See also D. K. Hill, *AJA* (1955):41–43.

4. C. Rolley, *Fouilles de Delphes V. Les statuettes de bronze* (Paris, 1969), 57–76.

5. J. L. Benson, *Horse, Bird and Man. The Origins of Greek Painting* (Amherst, 1970), 25, 29, 46, 49, 96.

6. Kilian-Dirlmeier, *Getty MusJ* 6–7 (1978–79):130.

23. Bronze Horse on Wheels

(ca. 700 B.C.)

K 36. Kemper Simpson Collection. Bronze. Ht, 7.8 cm; ht horse, 2.4 cm; w across circles, 3.2 cm. Very thin. Intact.

Horse surmounts two tangential columns, each comprised of three stacked perforated discs. A short tang protrudes from the base of each column. Horse has pelleted eyes, a tubular, tapering muzzle, and high curving ears that touch at tips. Unarticulated stumps for legs; long tail. Incised on each side is motif of punched dot within two concentric circles decorating shoulder, haunch, center of each disc, and point of contact between discs and between discs and tangs.

An identical object in Cambridge is said to come from Thessaly,[1] and certainly the tapering muzzle and the dot-and-circle ornament are best paralleled on north-

ern Greek bronzes.[2] The elegant contours of our horse indicate a late geometric date,[3] when the wheel was an especially popular motif in vasepainting and bronzes.

There are many late geometric bronze statuettes of animals, especially horses and birds, surmounting wheels. The wheels may be openwork spheres[4] or thin, solid, or openwork discs that stand upright, as on our example,[5] or lie beneath the figures as a base.[6] The wheels may appear singly or in pairs. Occasionally, two spheres are connected by a horizontal bar to suggest a two-wheeled wagon.[7] The wheel motif is especially popular in bronzes from Thessaly and northern Greece,[8] although the type with openwork spheres may have originated in the Peloponnesos.[9]

Benson has convincingly shown that the wheel is an abbreviation for the chariot, which in geometric times was still very much in use and carried funerary connotations as a legacy of the Mycenaean world.[10] Our piece can be compared with a terracotta horse from a protogeometric grave in Athens; each of the legs is supported by a wheel, in an undoubted allusion to the four-wheeled funerary wagon.[11]

The bird was closely linked with the horse in Mycenaean vasepainting and, like the horse, also signified the world of the dead.[12] The association of bird and wheel in geometric bronzes is thus logical, as is the appearance in Greek sanctuaries of bronze wheels, which had already served as isolated symbols in Mycenaean vasepainting.[13] Less easy to explain is the relationship of the wheel to the stag or doe[14] and to the fox.[15] These couplings may simply be ornamental.

The Hopkins horse, like the other figurines that pair wheels and animals, may have been intended for suspension as an amulet or votive decoration.

1. J. Bouzek, *Graeco-Macedonian Bronzes* (Prague, 1974), 141, pl. 10.

2. Mitten, *Master Bronzes,* 38, no. 20, and 39, no. 21.

3. See discussion of item no. 22 and S. Benton, *JHS* 70 (1950):21–22.

4. C. Rolley, *Fouilles de Delphes V: Les statuettes de bronze* (Paris, 1969), 83, no. 129; 86, no. 143, pl. XXII.

5. P. Amandry, *Collection Hélène Stathatos I* (Strasbourg, 1953), 59, no. 8, fig. 33; Dörig, no. 106.

6. D. K. Hill, *AJA* 84 (1980):90–91.

7. J. Bouzek, *Eirene* 6 (1967):118–19, fig. 2; Rolley, *Fouilles,* 86, no. 145, pl. XXIII.

8. Amandry, *Collection Hélène Stathatos I,* 59, no. 8, fig. 33. Bouzek, *Graeco-Macedonian Bronzes,* 140, no. 3, fig. 43.8. J. Bouzek, *Eirene* 6 (1967):122; 126, fig. 5; 135. Mitten, *Master Bronzes,* 38, no. 20.

9. Rolley, *Fouilles,* 88–89.

10. J. L. Benson, *Horse, Bird and Man. The Origins of Greek Painting* (Amherst, 1970), 23–25, 46, 49, 68. The motif was formerly considered a solar emblem. See Bouzek, *Eirene* 6 (1967):133–35.

11. Benson, *Horse, Bird and Man,* 25, 46, 49, 53, pl. VIII, fig. 2.

12. Ibid., 29, 30, 46, 67; and see item no. 34.

13. D. K. Hill, *AJA* 60 (1956):41, no. 8, pl. 28. Benson, *Horse, Bird and Man,* 67.

14. Mitten, *Master Bronzes,* 39, no. 21.

15. Bouzek, *Graeco-Macedonian Bronzes,* 140, no. 2, fig. 43.9.

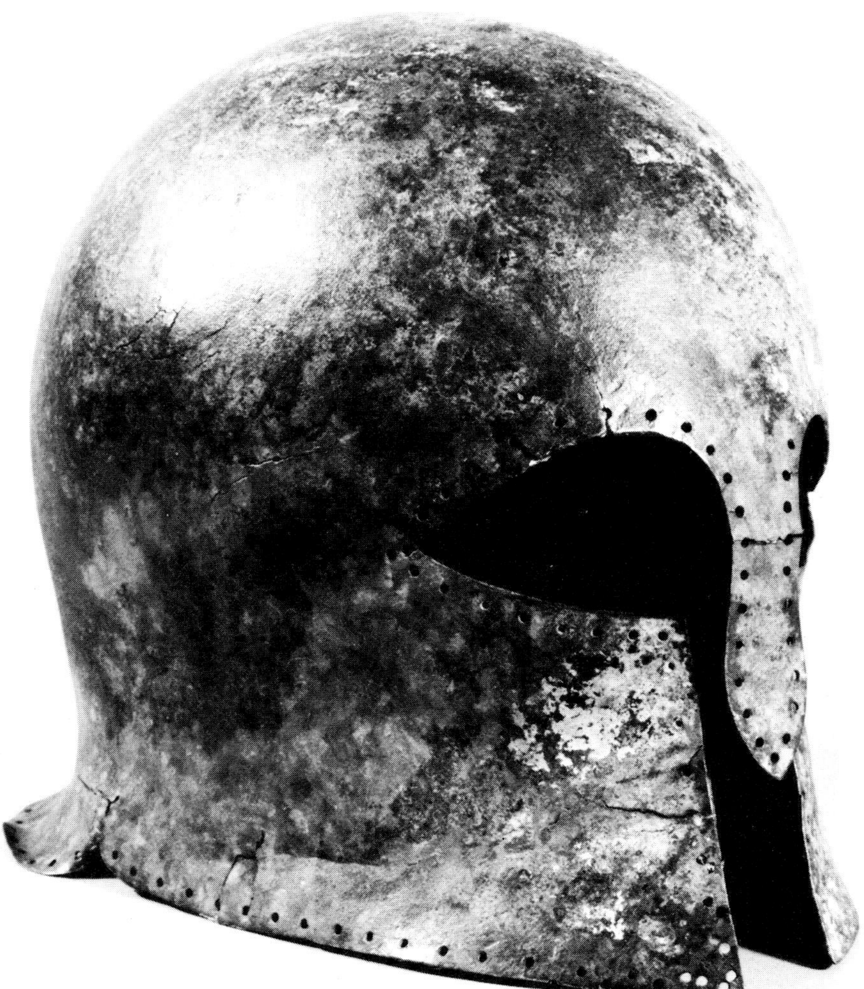

24. Corinthian Helmet

(700–650 B.C.)

K 59. Kemper Simpson Collection. "Olympia." Bronze. Ht, 22.2 cm; w, 17 cm; l, 26.5 cm. Long crack down back. Minor cracks over rest of surface. Bottom half of nosepiece reattached in ancient times with plate and rivets. Two other ancient plates with rivets reinforce outer corners of eyes. Rows of holes around entire perimeter.

Back curves out smoothly below as neckguard. Sides also curve out slightly. Inside edges of cheekpiece angled to mouth. Outer corners of eyes elongated; noseguard tapers to point. Inscription on inside of proper right cheekpiece running retrograde.

Bibliography: J. Young, *AJA* 69 (1965):179.

This helmet was raised from a single sheet of bronze and was then lined with leather or cloth, which was sewn or riveted through the holes around the edges.[1]

The Corinthian type of helmet developed in the later eighth century B.C. concurrently with the introduction of the hoplite phalanx and the growing sophistication of metalworking techniques.[2] Our example belongs to the phase designated by Snodgrass as Group II (690–650) and by Kunze as Group I (700–ca. 640).[3] Distinguishing features are the soft outward curve at the nape, the shaping of the bowl to the skull (thereby losing the earlier stovepipe appearance), the angling of the inside edges of the cheekpiece, and the arched and elongated eye openings. The absence of a crest is typical of Corinthian helmets of this date.

Helmets of the next, more developed phase (Snodgrass III and Kunze II) were in use between ca. 650 and 570–550 B.C.[4] These are recognized by their more concave profile at the neckguard, the more strongly marked notch beneath each ear, the continuously curving contour from the nose to the cheekpiece, which is now shorter, and the sloping, rather than horizontal, rim edging the lower eyelid. Later versions of the Corinthian helmet continued to be made throughout the fifth century in many metalworking centers in mainland Greece and in Italy. Gradually, however, the lighter pilos attained greater favor, so that by the end of the fifth century, the Corinthian helmet is not often encountered.[5]

The inscription is in the Achaean script and in lettering of the first half of the seventh century.[6] The reading should probably be Krataimenes, a name documented in Thucydides (6.4), who tells us that an individual of that name (probably only a contemporary of the owner of our helmet) left Chalkis in Euboea to establish the city of Zancle in Sicily, which we know was founded during the seventh century.[7]

Our inscription is curiously placed on the inside of the cheekpiece, where it would have been concealed by the lining, in contrast to the customary position on the exterior of the cheekpiece. It would thus seem

that the inscription was added before the helmet was completed or when the piece needed repair and the lining had torn away. If the reputed provenance of Olympia is correct, it is possible that the inscription was added before the owner dedicated a helmet that had served him well.

In the Greek world, a helmet was an emotionally significant and expensive possession of a warrior.[8] The helmet was a necessary accouterment of the hoplite phalanx, and its acquisition proclaimed that a youth had crossed over the threshold into manhood. Since the helmet had to be custom fitted, it was an expensive purchase, and thus care was understandably taken to repair or reinforce it, as our example testifies.[9] Between engagements, the helmet was hung proudly on the wall of a man's home, and in early times a man's helmet was buried with him when he died.[10] Hoplites also dedicated their helmets in sanctuaries in appreciation of its safe protection; in this case the cheekpieces were often bent backward, to signify that the object would never be worn again.[11]

When a man wore his helmet, he could barely hear and he could scarcely see his flanking colleagues. He was also difficult to recognize, and for this reason he usually attached an identifying emblem to his shield.[12] When a warrior assembled beside his compatriots, their uniform and impersonal row of Corinthian helmets gave the phalanx a formidable appearance. The power of these anonymous masks was not lost on sixth-century vase painters, among whose work that of Exekias is especially chilling.[13]

1. See G. Chase, *Bulletin of the Museum of Fine Arts* (1950):80–83 for a late sixth-century helmet in which the pins driven from the outside are still preserved. It is clear that the leather was brought around to the outside and then fastened.

2. A. M. Snodgrass, *Arms and Armour of the Greeks* (Ithaca, 1967), 51; A. M. Snodgrass, *Early Greek Armour and Weapons* (Edinburgh, 1964), 20–28.

3. E. Kunze, *OlBer* 7 (Berlin, 1961):72; Snodgrass, *Early Greek Armour*, 23, 26–27.

4. Snodgrass, *Early Greek Armor*, 23, 27, 220, no. 95; Kunze, *OlBer* 7 (1961):77, the "Myros" group.

5. Snodgrass, *Arms and Armour*, 94.

6. I thank L. Jeffrey and P. Siewert for looking at this inscription for me.

7. I thank J. Poultney for calling my attention to passage by Thucydides. A. G. Woodhead, *The Greeks in the West* (London, 1962), 55. Zancle was founded in the late eighth century by Cumae and subsequently resettled by oikistai from Euboea led by Perieres and Krataimenes.

8. I owe this observation to H. A. Thompson. For inscriptions on helmets, see E. Kunze, *OlBer* 5 (Berlin, 1956):69–74; *OlBer* 6 (Berlin, 1958):145–46; *OlBer* 7 (Berlin, 1961):129–37. See also Comstock-Vermeule, 408, no. 583.

9. Another example of ancient helmet repair is discussed by C. Weiss, *California Studies in Classical Antiquity* 10 (1977):197–99.

10. Snodgrass, *Arms and Armour*, 71–73, 89. The practice died out around 700 B.C.

11. Ibid., 93; Richter, *Bronzes*, 411, no. 1530.

12. Snodgrass, *Arms and Armour*, 54–55.

13. Ajax and Achilles playing dice: G. M. A. Richter, *Handbook of Greek Art*, 7th ed. (New York, 1974), 333, fig. 446; and Achilles and Penthesilea, J. Boardman, *Greek Art*, rev. ed. (Oxford, 1973), 86, fig. 82.

25. Bronze Oinochoe

(late sixth c. B.C.)

K 54. Kemper Simpson Collection. Bronze. Ht, 18.5 cm; ht without handles, 14.8 cm; diam foot, 4.6 cm. Foot and handle cast separately; body hammered. Section of body restored.

Footed trefoil oinochoe with handle curving high above mouth. Rim encircled by beading inside tongue. At base of neck are three horizontal grooves. On shoulder is a tongue ornament above double guilloche, enclosed above and below by three horizontal grooves. Undecorated foot consists of cyma reversa above toros. Strap handle with slight ridge down center, raised flange at each side. Handle broadens at mouth to horizontal strip that is attached beneath rim by two rivets. Base of handle widens to plaque engraved with inverted nine-petal palmette beneath two volutes, the centers of which are linked by a horizontal band. Underside of handle flat and smooth.

Bibliography: D. K. Hill, *Greek and Roman Metalware, Walters Art Gallery* (Baltimore, 1976), no. 20.

During the sixth and fifth centuries, Greek metalworkers attained an admirable mastery of their medium. This facility is well illustrated by the Hopkins oinochoe, which combines the techniques of hammering (for the body) with casting (of handle and foot). Since the hammered part of a vessel is necessarily much thinner than the cast sections, the body of a vase is often corroded or otherwise damaged, while the cast elements survive intact.

The horizontal shoulder and the severe taper to the foot date our jug to the end of the sixth century, when oinochoai of approximately comparable shape were being made in pottery.[1]

The ornament of our vessel links it with a contemporary group of large oinochoai[2] and hydriai.[3] These elaborate vessels were used as prizes in athletic contests and, in the case of the hydriai, as cinerary urns or ballot receptacles.[4] These vases also have beading and tongue ornament around the rim and often a band of tongue and guilloche around the shoulder and body. The technique of the vertical handles differs from that on our vessel in that the handles were not riveted beneath the rim, but fitted onto the top of it; nonetheless, the engraved palmette at the base of these handles compares closely with that of our example.[5] Identical palmettes appear on the attachments to the horizontal handles of the hydriai.

The place of manufacture of these large bronze oinochoai and hydriai has been variously identified as Corinth, the Argolid, or Tarentum,[6] although it is certainly possible that more than one center shared in the production of what became a popular type of vessel. Evidence provided by a clustering of findspots suggests that examples with elaborate tongue and guilloche patterns, like our own, were made in southern Italy.[7] Further support for the attribution of our vase is provided by parallels with the handles on footless trefoil jugs from southern Italy and Etruria.[8] On these vessels we also find strap handles without beading, elongated attachments riveted beneath the rim, and an engraved palmette at the base of the handle.

1. L. Talcott and B. Sparkes, *The Athenian Agora XII: Black and Plain Pottery* (Princeton, 1970), 59, no. 100; 243, pl. 5 (shape 1).

2. D. von Bothmer, *Studies in Classical Art and Archaeology Presented to Peter H. von Blanckenhagen* (Locust Valley, 1979), 63–67. K. A. Neugebauer, *RömMitt* 38 (1923):341–56.

3. Neugebauer, *RömMitt* 38 (1923):371–83. E. Diehl, *Die Hydria* (Mainz, 1964), 216, nos. B75–85. D. von Bothmer, *Gnomon* 37 (1965):601, and *Getty MusJ* I (1974):15–16.

4. von Bothmer, *Getty MusJ* I (1974):15.

5. At the top of the oinochoe handle is a female bust flanked by rotelles or a siren above a palmette [von Bothmer, *Getty MusJ* I (1974):15–16; 19, figs. 3, 4, 7]. von Bothmer's no. 2 (p. 16) from Ankara is Diehl's (see note 3) no. B77 (216, pl. 5). See the engraved palmette beneath the handle of a long-beaked bronze jug [I. Vokotopoulou, *Chalkai Korinthiourgeis Prochoi* (Athens, 1975), 16, 86–90].

6. D. M. Robinson, *AJA* 46 (1942):188–89. See also K. A. Neugebauer, *RömMitt* 38 (1923):415–40, and Vokotopoulou, *Chalkai*, 170.

7. Mitten, *Master Bronzes*, 83, no. 77. See E. Langlotz, *Die Kunst der Westgriechen* (Munich, 1963), 78, pl. 93. U. Liepmann, *Niederdeutsches Beiträge zur Kunstgeschichte* 15 (1976), 19–20.

8. K. A. Neugebauer, *RömMitt* 38 (1923):356–62. His no. 14 (360) is Comstock-Vermeule no. 436 (311), attributed to southern Italy by D. K. Hill [*Greek and Roman Metalware* (Baltimore, 1976), no. 20]. Neugebauer's no. 9 (357) is U. Liepmann's [*Griechische Terrakotten, Bronzen, Skulpturen, Kestner-Museums, Hannover* (Hannover, 1975), 115] no. B19, from Capua. See also Liepmann (note 7), 24 n. 17. Other sources are: R. Blatter, *AA* (1966), 48–58, for an example from Padula; *EVP* 266, no. 15; L. Pernier, *NSc* 5, 4 (1907):326–27, fig. 61, example from Tarquinia; G. delli Ponti, *I Bronzi del museo provinciale di Lecce* (Lecce, 1973), 28, no. 29, pl. 23, example from Rudiae. See also U. Höckmann, *Antike Bronzen* (Kassel, 1972), 26, nos. 42–43, pl. 14, for a related type of vessel.

Metalwork

ETRUSCAN AND ITALIC

26. Bow Fibula with Disc Foot

(ninth–early eighth c. B.C.)

1283. Probably purchased in Rome or Naples in 1906–9 Bronze. L, 10.6 cm; max diam disc, 4.8 cm. Intact.

Center of bow thickened. Bow entirely threaded except for smooth band at center and each end. Spring has three turns. Engraved ornament on spiral disc foot; around edge is band of zigzag, flanked on each side by concentric circles and terminating at foot in columns of inverted V's. In center of disc is circle enclosing ring of supine V's. Rest of field occupied by three squares, each enclosing cross and two concentric squares.

The bow fibula developed from the violin fibula in the pre- or proto-Villanovan settlements of central and southern Italy about 1100 B.C.[1] Early bow fibulae have a simple catchplate bent up to secure the pin,[2] but in central Italy that form soon admitted a spiral disc foot, incised with elaborate patterns.[3] Gradually the bow was thickened in the center, the disc became larger, and the spiral was hammered out. The dates of these developments vary regionally, but in Tarquinia the spiral had largely disappeared from the disc foot by 800 B.C.[4]

Because the Hopkins example lacks a provenance, it cannot be precisely dated. However, it compares closely with several bow fibulae from Tarquinia dated by Hencken to I B or the ninth century.[5] Our fibula also finds close parallels in form among Sundwall's class B III b[6] and in ornament with examples of classes B III c[7] and C I d b.[8]

Since most bow fibulae have been found in female burials, it appears that this type was primarily used by women,[9] who occasionally strung amber beads and bone discs along the bow.[10] The fibula was fastened by passing the pin through a bronze ring attached to the edge of the garment;[11] signs of fire on many examples indicate that both fibula and garments were burned with the body.

1. Sundwall, 20–21. Useful summaries of this period and its problems are discussed by R. Peroni in *Italy Before the Romans*, ed. D. Ridgway (New York, 1979), 7–30, and in the same volume by M. Delpino, 31–51.
2. Sundwall, 21, 33, 38, 97, class B II a c.
3. Ibid., 26, 40, 112, class B III b.
4. Hencken, *Peabody*, 83.
5. Ibid., 67, 70, fig. 56A from grave 76; 66, 69, fig. 55 from grave 72.
6. Sundwall, 40, 112–13, especially 113, no. 11, fig. 140.
7. Ibid., 40, 113–14, especially 113, no. 1, fig. 141.
8. Ibid., 40, 127–28, especially 128, nos. 1, 3, figs. 167, 168.
9. Hencken, *Peabody*, 431.
10. Pohl, 279.
11. Sundwall, 113, no. 1, fig. 141.

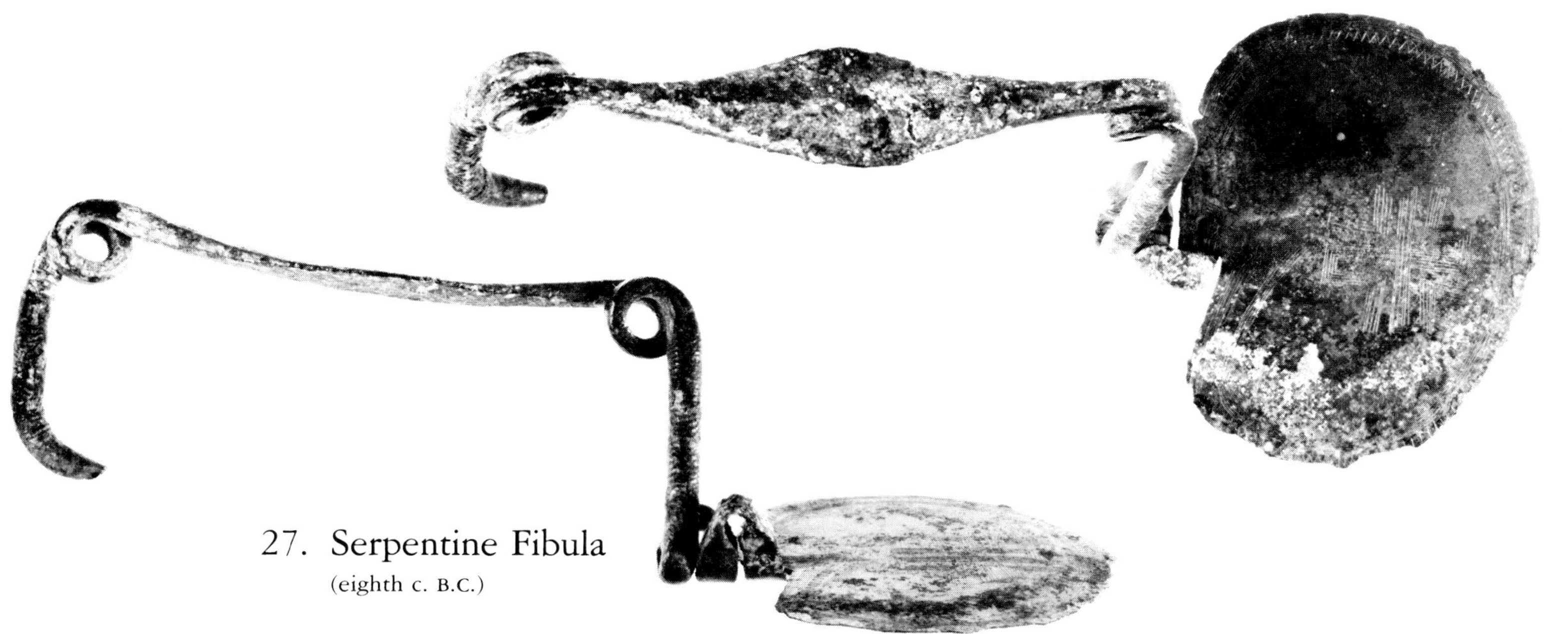

27. Serpentine Fibula

(eighth c. B.C.)

9136. Probably purchased in Rome or Naples in 1906–9. Bronze. L, 19 cm; diam disc, 8.2 cm. Pin broken away but seems to have continued to foot without winding into spring.

Diamond-shaped back with central longitudinal ridge terminating in coil at each end. Vertical sides are threaded. Disc made separately and attached by two rivets. No interior spiral to foot, which has incised ornament; around edge is band of zigzag flanked on each side by five or six incised circles. Within is swastika described by series of six or seven parallel lines.

The coil at each end of the back identifies this fibula as a member of the serpentine type, which developed from a late stage of the violin fibula.[1] Our example is unusual in that the pin was not separately attached, but formed a single piece with the back and sides. The form of the missing pin cannot be restored with certainty, but the minimal curvature of the surviving stump suggests that the pin continued directly from this point to the catchplate without winding into a third coil. Sundwall did not have a classification for fibulae of this type; his closest parallel is a two-part fibula with a separate pin attached to the vertical arm without intervening coil.[2] He did, however, know of a one-piece version from the Balkan area,[3] and it is logical that a corresponding Italian type existed.

As noted for item no. 26, the spiral disc with incised patterns was popular in central Italy, where by 800 B.C. the spiral had been almost completely hammered out. The swastika on our disc may be compared with ornament on hut urns of the eighth century.[4]

Most serpentine fibulae have been found in male graves,[5] and the unwieldy size of this example certainly supports that association.

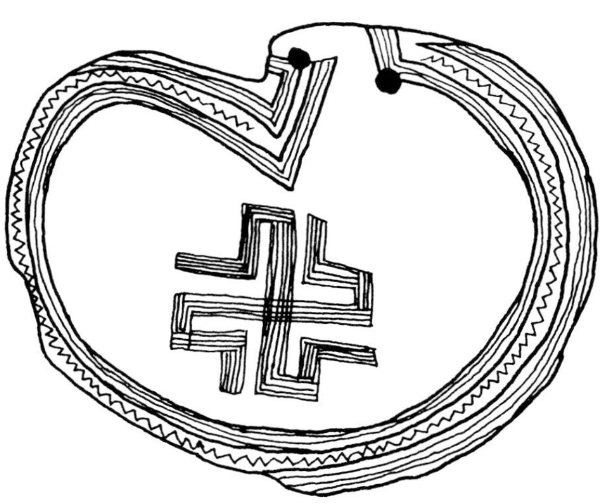

1. Sundwall, 18, 46, 72, class A III a 1. Earliest serpentine type is class D II a a (45, 142). Immediate predecessors to our type are classes D II a d and D II a f (26, 46–48, 143, 145).

2. Ibid., 28, 48, 160, class D IV a c, fig. 247.

3. Ibid., 47, fig. 23a.

4. Brendel, 25, figs. 3, 4.

5. Sundwall, 44; Pohl, 279.

28. Navicella Fibula

(ca. 700 B.C.)

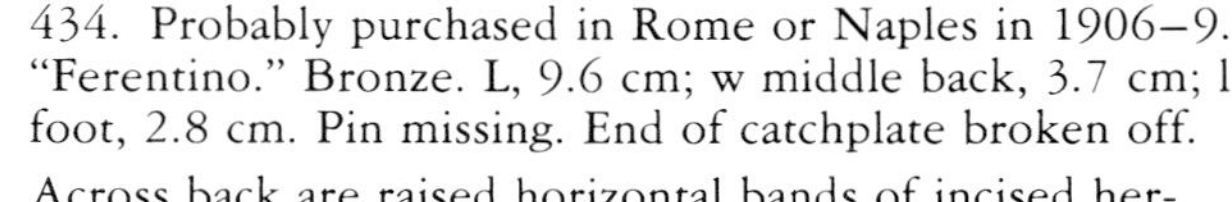

434. Probably purchased in Rome or Naples in 1906–9. "Ferentino." Bronze. L, 9.6 cm; w middle back, 3.7 cm; l foot, 2.8 cm. Pin missing. End of catchplate broken off.

Across back are raised horizontal bands of incised herringbone alternating with smooth bands. A third of the distance from each end is a wider band stamped with row of four dot-and-circle motifs.

The navicella fibula is characterized by a wide, curving bow that is open on the side toward the pin, in contrast to the sanguisuga-leech type of fibula, whose back is solid.[1] The navicella type developed from the bow fibula, possibly first in Greece.[2] Between 775 and 750 B.C. in Pithecusa (Ischia) and after 750 B.C. in Cumae, the bow became wider and the catchplate longer.[3] These innovations first appeared on leech fibulae from Veii (period II B), around 760–720 B.C.,[4] and soon afterward in Tarquinia (period II B) (725–700 B.C.),[5] and Caere (720 B.C.).[6]

On our example the foot is elongated, but not extremely, since the tapering is evident even before the break. Thus our example should certainly be dated before the fibula with extremely elongated foot from the Regolini-Galassi tomb of ca. 650–630 B.C.[7] Since the dot-and-circle ornament on our piece was especially popular on bronze hut urns and helmets of the later eighth century,[8] it is likely that our fibula was made around that date.

The navicella fibula is usually found in women's graves.[9] Occasionally, bracelets[10] or amber beads[11] are strung upon the pin.

1. Hencken, *Peabody*, 2.
2. H. Hencken, *AJA* 62 (1958): 271. S. Benton, *BSA* 48 (1953):350. Early examples are Sundwall, 54–55, 177–82, classes F I a a to F I a b.
3. Hencken, *AJA* 62 (1958):270.
4. J. Close-Brooks and D. Ridgway, in *Italy Before the Romans*, ed. D. Ridgway (New York, 1979), 103–4, fig. 5; *NSc* 8, 17 (1963):57, fig. 5.
5. Hencken, *Peabody*, 562; Hencken, *AJA* 62 (1958):271.
6. Pohl, 300; see also 208, fig. 184, and 209, fig. 185.
7. L. Pareti, *La tomba Regolini-Galassi* (Rome, 1947), 175, no. 1, pl. VII. Brendel, 71, fig. 41.
8. Brendel, 29, fig. 8. H. Hencken, *The Earliest European Helmets*, *Peabody Museum Bulletin* 28 (1971):91, fig. 61; 92, fig. 62; 96, fig. 67.
9. E. Richardson, *MAAR* 27 (1962):166. M. Pallottino, *MonAnt* 36 (1937):156–81.
10. E. Stefani, *NSc* 5, 8 (1911):434, figs. 1, 2, from Nazzano.
11. Sundwall, 55.

Detail from helmet urn in Karlsruhe

29. Figurine of Man

(ca. 700 B.C.)

2492. Purchased in Rome or Naples in 1906–9. Bronze. Ht, 6.4 cm; max w, 4.8 cm. Stands with feet together, left hand on head, right arm outstretched with palm held vertically, but most of fingers missing. Long-sleeved tunic to mid-thigh over trousers; peaked cap. Head tipped upward, with bulbous eyes, broad nose, gashed mouth, and short beard.

This figure's distinctive face as well as his unmodeled and rubbery limbs find their closest parallels among the figurines on a bronze amphora from Bisenzio dated ca. 710 B.C.[1] Around the shoulder of the Bisenzio amphora stands a ring of warriors who are poised for attack with spear and shield. Encircling the lid are helmeted warriors with arms extended, and, in one instance, with both hands clasping the ends of a sword held horizontally.

Also similar to our figure are the three male figurines that surmount a bronze helmet urn in Karlsruhe (see above).[2] One figure holds both ends of a sword horizontally in front of him, while the others lift their arms upward, grasping objects that are unidentifiable or missing. The urn has been dated to the late eighth century and attributed to southern Etruria, possibly Tarquinia, where a similar bell helmet was found.

Our figure can also be compared with the figurines that encircle the rim of a late seventh-century clay basin from Poggio Buco.[3] Three standing women with both hands held to their heads alternate with three mounted males who rest their right hands on top of their heads, their left hands on the horses' manes. Comparable to our figurine are the tilted heads, the pointed beards, and the broad noses. Also notable is the gesture of hand to head, which is believed to have originated in the eastern Mediterranean.[4]

Our figure's outstretched arm with extended fingers and palm held inward foreshadows Etruscan bronzes of the seventh and sixth centuries. Richardson has shown that the horizontal position of the arms is found in Hittite and Syrian art and that outstretched fingers with palm facing upward signify prayer.[5] It is likely, then, that our figurine surmounted the lid of a dedicatory vessel made in southern Etruria at the end of the eighth century.

1. R. Bianchi Bandinelli, *Etruschi e Italici prima del dominio di Roma* (Rome, 1972), 44, fig. 46; M. Pallottino et al., *Le Museo Nazionale etrusco di Villa Giulia* (Rome, 1980), 84–85, pls. 96–97.

2. Badisches Landesmuseum. Inv. no. 65/85. H. Hencken, "The Earliest European Helmets," *Peabody Museum Bulletin* 28 (1971):47–49, figs. 24–25; L. A. Forest, *AA* (1981):21–43.

3. Bandinelli, *Etruschi e Italici*, 35, fig. 35, in Florence; E. Scamuzzi, *NSc* 7, 1 (1940):20, from Pitigliano.

4. E. Richardson, *MAAR* 27 (1962):165.

5. Ibid., 191, 194; E. Richardson, *The Etruscans* (Chicago, 1964), 60–62. See also entry for item no. 39.

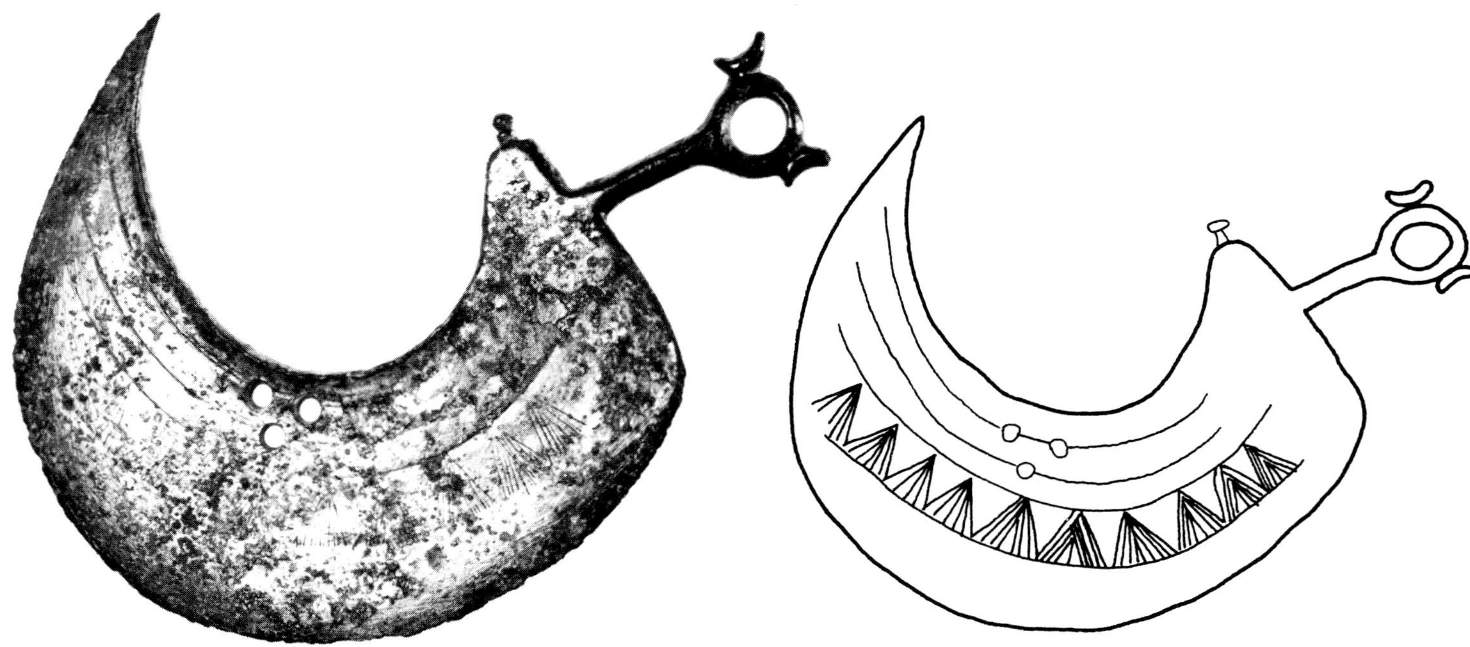

30. Lunate Razor

(ca. 750–seventh c. B.C.)

9107. Probably purchased in Rome or Naples in 1906–9. Bronze. Max l, 7.6 cm; max ht, 6.8 cm; distance between tips of arc, 4.4 cm. Very thin. Intact.

Razor with sharply curving profile has knob at tip nearest handle, which consists of shaft terminating in ring flanked by two crescents. Adjacent to midpoint of inner contour of blade are three small holes. Engraved design on each side consists of three concentric arcs echoing inside contour; beneath is row of triangles suspended from apex. Each triangle has third side open and interior filled with lines radiating from apex. Base of triangles bounded by another arc.

Because razors are almost exclusively found in male burials, it is assumed that these objects were used for shaving or beard trimming.[1] The holes were probably for suspension.

It is likely that the lunate razor originated in the Balkan area, where examples of elongated, rectangular form have been found dating from the eleventh century.[2] Shortly afterward, but still within the eleventh century, the razor appeared in the pre-Villanovan urn fields of Etruria and Apulia.[3]

By about 800 B.C., or the Villanovan I C period in Tarquinia, the razor had taken on a more curved profile[4] and was often decorated with pendant triangles, probably of European origin.[5] In this same time the ring handle was flanked by bird heads, a motif that is surely derived from the sun disc flanked by bird heads on Middle Bronze age pottery from Otenia and Banat (1400–1200 B.C.).[6] The crescents on the Hopkins handle are descendants of those bird heads.

Still later are the lunate razors with an extremely curved profile and a knob at the end of the arc. Examples similar to our piece were found in Tarquinia in contexts of period III C (750–seventh c. B.C.).[7] Approximately contemporary parallels come from Veii,[8] Caere,[9] and Narce.[10]

1. Hencken, *Tarquinia*, 31. At least one example was found in a female burial (Hencken, *Peabody*, 431).
2. Hencken, *Tarquinia*, 89; Hencken, *Peabody*, 469.
3. Hencken, *Tarquinia*, 42, 89; Hencken, *Peabody*, 49.
4. Hencken, *Tarquinia*, 42; Hencken, *Peabody*, 113, 115, fig. 104.
5. Hencken, *Peabody*, 530, 546.
6. Brendel, 37; Hencken, *Tarquinia*, 110; Hencken, *Peabody*, 514–17.
7. Hencken, *Peabody*, 353, fig. 351.
8. J. Palm, *OpusArch* 7 (1952):70, pl. XXVII from tomb XVIII. Hencken, "The Earliest European Helmets," *Peabody Bulletin* 28 (1971):152, fig. 119, dated late ninth to eighth century.
9. Pohl, 202–3, fig. 179.2, from tomb of ca. 700 B.C.
10. Dohan, 71, no. 31, pl. XXXVII, from tomb 7 F, dated (on p. 108) to the first half of the seventh century.

31. Pectoral Discs

(ca. 700–650 B.C.)

701 and 702. Purchased in Rome or Naples in 1906–9. "Province of Aquila." Bronze.

701. Diam, 16.8 cm.

Slightly convex surface. Stamped dot-and-circle motif in center surrounded by two concentric punched circles flanking a ring of stamped dot-and-circle ornament. Outside are three unevenly spaced punched circles on either side of circle of dot-and-circle motifs. Interrupting these circles are eight spokes in form of bands delineated by incised lines and alternately decorated with stamped dot-and-circle or cross motifs. Opposite sides of rim pierced with four large holes; along rest of circumference are three pairs of smaller holes evenly spaced. Several smaller holes are irregularly located around edge or near center. Rivets still remain in a few holes.

702. Diam, 11 cm.

Convex surface. Pierced center. Incised decoration consists of concentric bands of hatched zigzags and z's separated by groups of concentric circles.

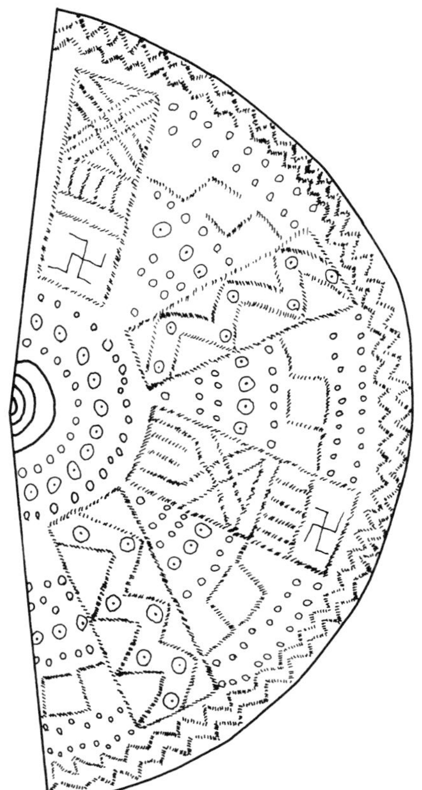

701

These discs formed part of a set of armor. The larger disc, riveted to a leather backing, was attached to a metal or leather belt that passed from right shoulder to left underarm with the disc centered over the chest. It is possible that the other holes around the edge of the disc were for the attachment of a sword. The smaller disc, characteristically pierced only through its midpoint, would have been attached to the same belt, but positioned over the middle of the person's back.[1] This form of armor is worn by the Capestrano warrior of ca. 550 B.C., although his disc is set within a frame that may be imitating an iron frame on actual examples.[2]

Armor discs like the Hopkins set were in use in Italy from the seventh century to the Hellenistic period and were worn by the Picenes, Umbri, Vestini, Paeligni, Sabines, Aequi, and Marsi.[3] Although examples have been found in many sites throughout central and southern Italy,[4] discs most similar to the Hopkins pair come from the Umbrian region around Perugia.[5]

The punched geometric ornament on our pieces is best paralleled on discs dating shortly after 700 B.C.[6] By the end of the century, the fashion was for discs worked in repoussé with orientalizing motifs.[7] Later examples from the fifth century inspired Celtic ornament.[8]

1. A. Andrén, *Medelhaussmuseet Bulletin* 4 (1964):41.
2. Brendel, 100–2; R. Bloch, *MonPiot* 59 (1974):67, fig. 23.
3. Andrén, *Medelhaussmuseet Bulletin* 4 (1964):38; E. Richardson, *Art Bulletin* 60 (1978):356.
4. Andrén, *Medelhaussmuseet Bulletin* 4 (1964):39; Richardson, *Art Bulletin* 60 (1978):356; Bloch, *MonPiot* 59 (1974):68.
5. Brendel, 437 n. 12; Richardson, *Art Bulletin* 60 (1978):356.
6. Richardson, *Art Bulletin* 60 (1978):356.
7. Mitten, *RISD*, 87, no. 27.
8. P. Jacobsthal, *Early Celtic Art* (Oxford, 1944), 82.

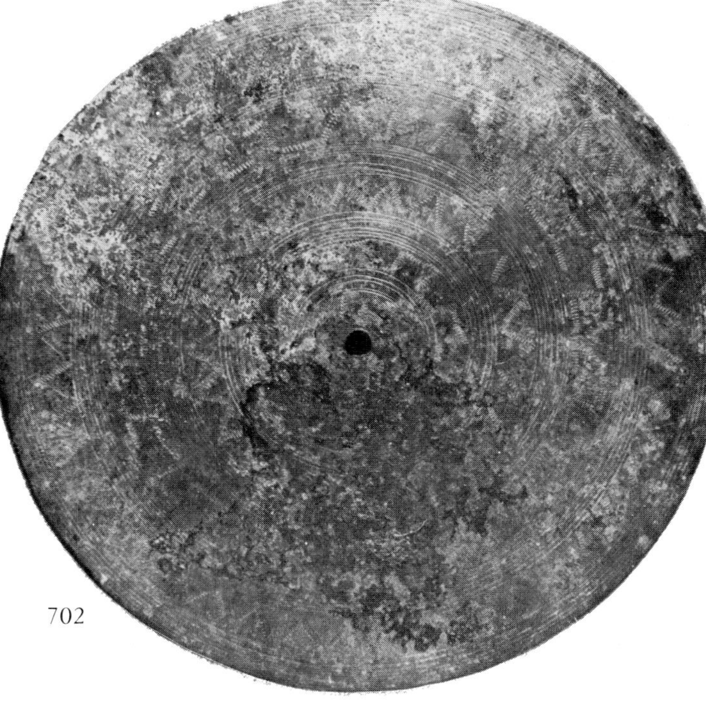

702

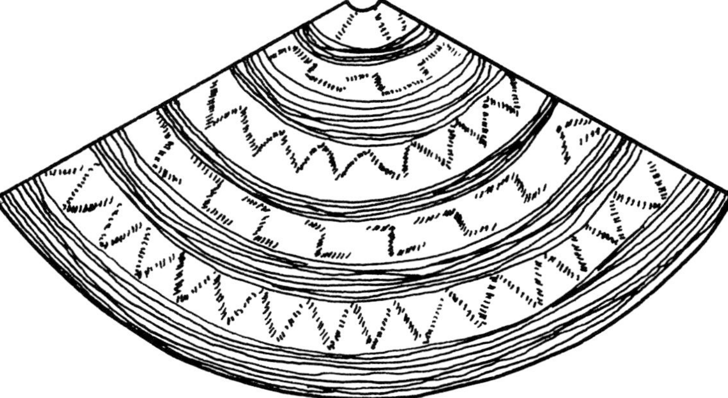

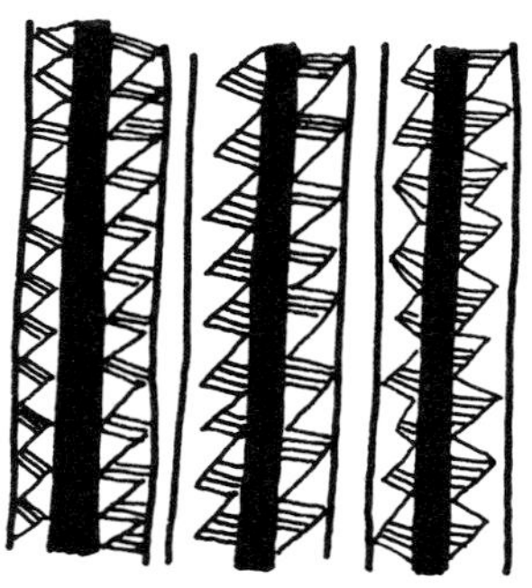

32. Spiral Bracelet

(700–650 B.C.)

546. Purchased in Naples in 1906–9. "Naples." Bronze. L, 15 cm; diam, 6.5 cm. Individual coils vary in width from 1 to 1.5 cm. Chipped near one end.

A strip of bronze is wound into twelve coils with a spiral at each end. Each coil has a raised central ridge flanked on each side by a row of incised wolf's teeth with hatched interiors.

Similar bracelets, some with as many as twenty coils, have been found in Ancona,[1] Verucchio near Rimini,[2] Chiusi,[3] Cumae,[4] and Nocera.[5] Miniature versions, only ca. 4 cm in diameter, have been identified as hair ornaments and come from Veii,[6] Narce,[7] and Nocera.[8] On large and small versions, the coils may end in rings from which additional rings are suspended. The striated wolf-tooth motif dates our piece to the seventh century, when the ornament was also applied to pottery from the Warrior's tomb (ca. 680 B.C.)[9] and a sword from the Regolini-Galassi tomb (ca. 650–630 B.C.).[10]

The origin of these spiral coils may be Greece, since miniature examples have been found in the Kerameikos in a Submycenaean context.[11] Bracelets with as many as thirteen coils were found in Vergina[12] in contexts of the tenth to eighth centuries.

1. G. Pellegrini, *NSc* 5, 7 (1910):335, fig. 2.
2. E. Brizio, *NSc* (1894):300, fig. 9.
3. Boucher, *Bronzes grecs*, 112, no. 109.
4. *MonAnt* 22 (1913), 146, nos. 57, 73, pl. 19.1.
5. de Ridder, vol. 2, 78, no. 2104, pl. 90.
6. F. Healey, *NSc* 8, 26 (1972):235, fig. 28.8; 241.
7. Dohan, 17, 108, no. 19, pl. VI from tomb no. 71 M.
8. E. Stefani, *NSc* 5, 15 (1918):105, fig. 3.
9. A. Åkerström, *Der geometrische Stil in Italien, Svensker Institutet I Rom Skrifter IX* (Uppsala, 1943), 78, no. 2, pl. 20.2.
10. Ibid., 107, pl. 31.5.
11. Mitten, *RISD*, 78, no. 21, H. Müller-Karpe, *JdI* 77 (1962):119, 128; 83, fig. 4.4; fig. 33.10, opposite p. 114.
12. C. Rolley, *Monumenta graeca et romana V: Les arts mineurs grecs* (Leiden, 1967), 19, no. 179, pl. 61; M. Andronikos, *Studies in Mediterranean Archaeology* 13 (1964):5; 9, fig. 5.

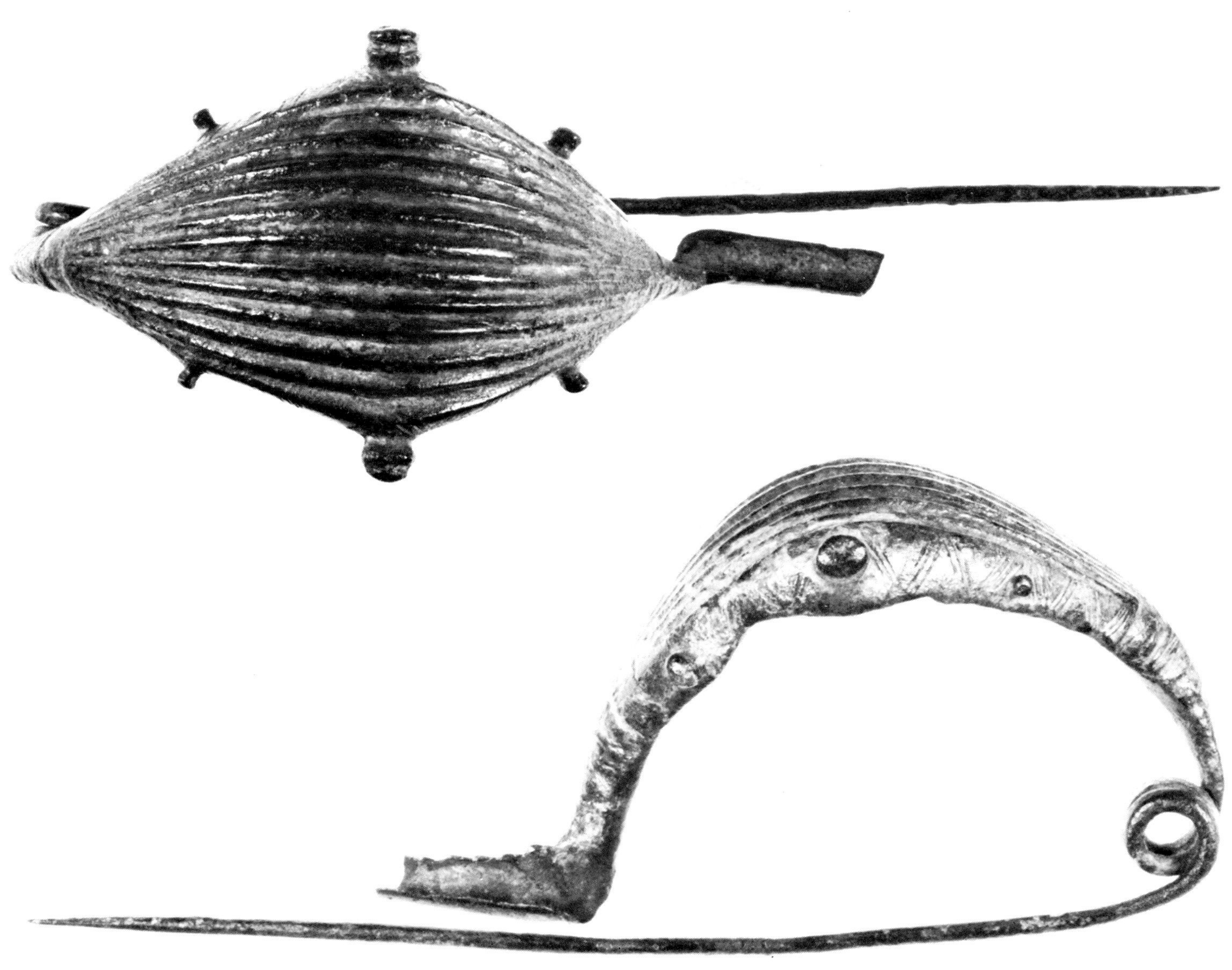

33. Navicella Fibula

(ca. 600 B.C.)

HT 609. Helen Tanzer Collection. Bronze. L with pin, 14.3 cm; to end of foot, 10 cm; l of foot, 2.6 cm; w back, 3.8 cm. Tip of foot broken away.

Nine deep grooves run longitudinally over back and are bounded at either end by short horizontal incisions. Back drawn out at midpoint of sides in points surmounted by double knobs. Between these knobs and extremities of back are four single knobs rising above band of incised zigzag. Spring has two turns; elongated foot.

During the eighth century B.C., the navicella fibula acquired an enlarged back and an elongated foot.[1] At the end of the eighth century knobs were added along the sides.[2] Around 600 B.C., the foot became even more elongated[3] and a knob appeared at its tip.[4] Because the end of our fibula's foot is missing, we cannot be certain to which stage of this later development the Hopkins piece belongs. However, the length of the pin, which was normally enclosed by the foot, indicates a correspondingly long foot, which was characteristic in the sixth century. Furthermore, the closest parallels for our ornament are among fibulae of this later date.[5] Ribbing was popular in Etruria during the seventh century, and appears, for example, on a bucchero vase from the time of the Bocchoris tomb (ca. 670 B.C.).[6] The zigzag pattern is also familiar on contemporary metalwork, such as a bracelet from the Regolini-Galassi tomb of ca. 650–630 B.C.[7]

1. See discussion of item no. 28.
2. Hencken, *Peabody*, 346; 350, fig. 348; 352, fig. 350. Sundwall, 224, Class G III a; 56, 58, 225–28, Class G III B a and b.
3. J. Close-Brooks, *NSc* 8, 19 (1965):57, fig. 5; 60–61, fig. 7, of Veii (period II B).
4. Sundwall, 58, 228–29, Class G III B c; G. Viegi, *StEtr* 23 (1954):432, fig. 43.
5. Sundwall, 228, Class G III B c, no. 1, from Bologna; 229, no. 11, from Belmonte in Picenum.
6. R. Hampe, *Neuerwerbungen, 1957–1970*, vol. 2 (Heidelberg, 1971), 38, no. 60.
7. Brendel, 69, fig. 39.

34. Bull with Bird on Back

(ca. 670–630 B.C.)

1178. Purchased in Rome or Naples in 1906–9. Bronze. L, 6.2 cm; ht, 7 cm; max w, 2.4 cm. Intact. Iron deposits on back, perhaps from an adjacent burial.

Bull has tubular barrel, unmodeled legs, upraised tailbone, long tubular neck, conical projecting ears, and snub muzzle with two raised ridges around tip. Head reversed, with gaze directed at haunches, where a bird with punched eyes and mouth is perched.

Bibliography: Mitten, *Master Bronzes*, 36, no. 16.

An almost exact counterpart in Amsterdam has the same oblique angle of the front legs, large cylindrical muzzle, and punched eyes similar to those of the bird on our figure's rump.[1] A smaller version in Brussels, which is provided with a ring for suspension, differs from our example only in slightly longer ears.[2] All three animals have the projecting ears, wrinkled muzzle, and upraised tailbone of a bull.

It is likely that the composition has been derived from the more common motif of a horse with head reversed. On fibulae from Tomb 1 at Narce,[3] of about 670 B.C., animals whose long muzzles and legs identify them as horses gaze back at apes perched on their rumps. Another horse with head reversed serves as a finial on an approximately contemporary vase from Civita Castellana.[4]

The origin of this composition ultimately may have been Mesopotamia,[5] but the image surely came to Italy from the Greek world, where horses with inverted heads had been associated with bulls in Mycenaean vasepainting.[6] On many vases from the eighth century, horses[7] are depicted with heads reversed; occasionally, a bird stands beside a horse[8] or alights upon his back, but I know of no Greek vase or geometric bronze figurine where a horse or other quadruped gazes back at a bird on his rump.[9]

In Mycenaean and Greek geometric vasepainting the horse and bird were closely associated and probably carried a funerary connotation.[10] In the orientalizing spirit of Villanovan art, the image was probably simply ornamental and hence susceptible to substitutions, such as the bull of our example, or the Phoenician apes perched upon horses on fibulae from the Bocchoris tomb (ca. 670 B.C.).[11]

1. H. van Gulik, *Catalogue of the Bronzes in the Allard Pierson Museum* (Amsterdam, 1940), 59, no. 84, pl. XX.
2. A. Roes, *Greek Geometric Art* (Oxford, 1933), 102, fig. 84.
3. Dohan, 58, no. 43, pl. XXXII.
4. R. Bianchi Bandinelli, *Etruschi e Italici prima del dominio di Roma* (Rome, 1972), 36, fig. 38.
5. Brendel, 37–38; 437 n. 18.
6. J. L. Benson, *Horse, Bird and Man. The Origins of Greek Painting* (Amherst, 1970), 34, pl. VIII, fig. 3; 29, pl. VII, fig. 2.
7. Also bucks. Ibid., 34, pl. 21.
8. Ibid., 62, 70, pl. 80; 69, pl. 82.
9. There are a number of bronze figurines representing birds on the rumps of horses that gaze forward. See Roes, *Greek Geometric Art*, 24, fig. 15A; C. Rolley, *Fouilles de Delphes V: Les statuettes de bronzes* (Paris, 1969), 58, no. 49, pl. XIII. See also an incised fibula in B. Schweitzer, *Greek Geometric Art* (London, 1971), 208, fig. 120.
10. Benson, *Horse, Bird and Man*, 25, 28–30, 34, 46. See also Schweitzer, *Greek Geometric Art*, 54.
11. Hencken, *Tarquinia*, 139, pl. 163.

35. Figurine of Woman

(ca. 630–600 B.C.)

412. Purchased in Rome or Naples in 1906–9. Bronze. Ht, 5.7 cm; base l, 2.5 cm; w, 1.6 cm; depth hands to back, 3.1 cm. Intact.

Figure stands with feet together, arms outstretched with palms upward, extended fingers individually incised. Small sphere on right palm. Pointed head, center-parted hair, with incised strands of hair evenly separated and extending to jawline. Sloping forehead, punched eyes, bulbous protruding nose, wide groove for mouth. Cylindrical shoulders and arms, indented waist, rounded hips. Horizontal incision around waist. Vertical incision between legs on front and back. Garment obscures feet and curves into flat, rectangular base.

Our figure's punched eyes and slit mouth, as well as the pointed head, sloping profile of the forehead, prominent nose, and fleshy cheeks are reminiscent of a figurine from Vizzini.[1] Her outstretched hands and upturned palms have been identified as a gesture of prayer inspired by Hittite prototypes.[2] Comparable figurines with this gesture come from Etruria and southern Italy[3] and date from the late seventh century, when votive bronzes outnumbered the formerly popular decorative bronzes.[4]

Also typical of late seventh-century figurines is the foldless chiton girded by an ornamental belt, which is indicated here by incisions around the waist.[5] On our figurine and on several others, the division between the legs is demarcated by a vertical incision, but on many examples the groove bifurcates to a V over the genitals.[6]

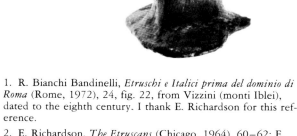

1. R. Bianchi Bandinelli, *Etruschi e Italici prima del dominio di Roma* (Rome, 1972), 24, fig. 22, from Vizzini (monti Iblei), dated to the eighth century. I thank E. Richardson for this reference.

2. E. Richardson, *The Etruscans* (Chicago, 1964), 60–62; E. Richardson, *MAAR* 27 (1962):191. See also J. Balty, *Bulletin de l'institut historique belge de Rome* 33 (1961), 5, 38; M. A. Hus, *Mélanges d'archéologie et d'histoire* 71 (1959):15.

3. Richardson, *MAAR* 27 (1962):191–92, figs. 87–91.

4. Ibid., 191.

5. L. Bonfante, *Etruscan Dress* (Baltimore, 1975), 32.

6. Ibid., 32.

36. Handle from Etruscan Jug

(fifth c. B.C.)

653. Purchased in Rome or Naples in 1906–9. Bronze. Ht, 14.3 cm; w between tips of arms, 10.5 cm. Corroded. Intact.

Broad, flat grip has a vertical row of beading flanked on each side by two ridges. At top is lion head between two reclining lions. Underside of lions is grooved for attachment. At base of grip is horizontal row of beading enclosed by two ridges. Beneath are two volutes that wind into snakes whose heads rise vertically. Beneath volutes is inverted palmette consisting of four petals on each side of two larger central ones. All petals have convex surfaces and pointed tips.

In a novel fashion, this handle combines motifs that first appeared in Greek metalwork during the sixth century. A pair of reclining lions along the rim can be found as early as the first half of the sixth century on a hydria handle from Nîmes that is probably of Spartan manufacture.[1] At the base of that handle there is a female head between rotelles. Not long afterward, the pair of lions was combined with the palmette-snake motif on two hydria handles now in Pesaro and Brussels.[2] Hill, who has extensively studied the history of the palmette-snake motif, believes that the handles were made in Sparta, since the site has yielded contemporary counterparts in pottery.[3]

A lion head gazing into a vessel appeared on handles of archaic Greek oinochoai, where it was enclosed by arms terminating in ape heads; at the base of the handle there was either a palmette[4] or, between 550 and 500 B.C., the palmette-snake motif of our example.[5] All these motifs were adapted and recombined by the Etruscans, who in late archaic years introduced an oinochoe handle on which the lion head is flanked by reclining lions along the rim,[6] while the attachment is decorated with hippocamps flanking a palmette, a composition that was replaced by the palmette-snake motif in the early fifth century.[7]

About six examples of the Hopkins type are known, all varying sightly in the shape and number of the palmette petals. Every one is detached from its vessel, but the similarity to Etruscan handles of the lion/ape type suggests that the original vessel was also a trefoil-mouthed oinochoe.

Variations of handles of the Hopkins type modify the palmette-snake motif by substituting anchors for the snakes[8] or by inverting the snakes so that the heads are directed downward.[9]

1. W. Brown, *The Etruscan Lion* (Oxford, 1960), 118–19. E. Diehl, *Die Hydria* (Mainz, 1964), 11–12, 214, no. B24; pl. 3. See D. von Bothmer, *Gnomon* 37 (1965):600; H. Hoffmann, *AJA* 68 1964):187 n. 26. See also L. Polite, *ArchEph* (1936), 152, no. 1, fig. 5.

2. D. K. Hill, *AntK* 10 (1967):39–40; Hoffmann, *AJA* 68 (1964):185–86.

3. Hill, *AntK* 10 (1967):40.

4. Brown, *Etruscan Lion*, 125–26; Diehl, *Die Hydria*, 213, no. B3, pl. 1. von Bothmer [*Gnomon* 37 (1965):600] believes the vessel is in oinochoe.

5. Hill, *AntK* 10 (1967):43, Type IVA, nos. 1–7, 13. Other examples are discussed by F. Gino Lo Porto, *MonAnt* 48 (1973):208, pl. LVI, from Matera; M. Squaitamatti, *AntK* 25 (1982):81–87. The Etruscans produced their own version in the early fifth century [Hill, *AntK* 10 (1967):43, Type IVA, nos. 8–12, 14–20].

6. Brown, *Etruscan Lion*, 129.

7. Ibid., 129–30. Hill, *AntK* 10 (1967):44, Type IVB.

8. Brown, *Etruscan Lion*, 129, nos, 6, 7, 9, 13.

9. Hill, *AntK* 10 (1967):44, Type IVC.

37. Handle from Etruscan Schnabelkanne

(fifth c. B.C.)

HT 1239. Helen Tanzer Collection. Bronze. Ht, 17.3 cm; w between arms, 9.7 cm; ht palmette, 6.5 cm; max w palmette, 3.7 cm. Left arm of handle broken away at rivet.

On grip are two vertical channels enclosed by beading. Arms, which extended along vessel's rim, terminate in animal heads, of which one survives. Rivet passes through tip of each arm. At base of grip are two beads above two leaves, which surmount two pairs of double volutes. Beneath is a volute, from which is suspended an inverted palmette with seven convex petals. Rivet driven through base of palmette.

This handle belongs to a distinctive Etruscan form of jug, the schnabelkanne, which is primarily characterized by its long, beaked spout.[1] More than one hundred handles belonging to these jugs are known, some still attached to their vessels. Most have been found in Etruria, but others come from Carthage and sites in Europe, thereby testifying to the far-reaching demand for these products of the Etruscan metalworking industry. Findspots have led scholars to suggest that Vulci manufactured most of these jugs during the late sixth and fifth centuries, but that local versions were also produced in Umbria and Picenum.[2]

A schnabelkanne can bear any one of several types of handles, of which that of the Hopkins example is the most common.[3] The type to which our handle belongs admits a number of variants: in the number of channels in the handle, the number and arrangement of the volutes, and the number of petals in the palmette. The base of the palmette may be closed,[4] as in our example, or *à jour*,[5] and the arms that lie along the rim may terminate in a complete animal or only an animal head.

1. The main studies are P. Jacobsthal and A. Langsdorf, *Die Bronzeschnabelkannen* (Berlin, 1929) and B. Bouloumié, *Les oenochoés en bronze du type "schnabelkanne" en Italie*, in *Collection de l'École française de Rome* 15 (Rome, 1973). As early as the seventh century, the beaked jug was produced in Etruria, probably after a Cypriot prototype (see Brendel, 50, fig. 24). A related form of beaked jug, a prochoos, was made in Italy and Greece during the sixth and fifth centuries [see L. Vokotopoulou, *Chalkai Korinthiourgeis Prochoi* (Athens, 1975); D. K. Hill, *AJA* 66 (1962):57–63, and *AJA* 82 (1978):418–19].

2. Bouloumié, *Les oenochoés*, 6, and *Mélanges d'archéologie et d'histoire* 80 (1968):401–2.

3. A second type has a female at the base of the handle (Hornbostel, 87, no. 57). On a third type, the attachment has a palmette beneath volutes that wind into snake heads. This type has been studied by D. K. Hill [*AntK* 10 (1967)], who recognizes two variants: a plain channeled grip, as here, but with the snake heads pointing downward (41–42, IIIB, dated fifth century), and a backward-leaning youth forming the grip and holding the tails of two lions that lie along the rim (42, IIIC, also of the fifth century, but not from Vulci).

4. S. Boucher, *Vienne, Bronzes antiques* (Paris, 1971), 143, no. 271).

5. Comstock-Vermeule, 369, no. 515; M. Guarducci, *StEtr* 10 (1936):34–35, pl. X.3.

38. Etruscan Handle

(late fifth c. B.C.)

HT 1215. Helen Tanzer Collection. Bronze. L, 11.3 cm; ht, 8.3 cm; w grip, 1 cm. Intact.

Grip was cast in one piece together with decorative attachment, which is curved for attachment to convex surface. Grip forms three sides of rectangle and has central channel enclosed on each side by row of beading, edged beneath by incised groove. Across base of each arm are five horizontal grooves. Beneath grip are two lion-scalps above inverted nine-petal palmette suspended from volutes. Additional volute on outside of each lion head. Between heads are two volutes with inverted nine-petal palmette suspended from midpoint. Buds above, between, and beneath volutes.

Our handle belonged to a low, round basin or bowl. Its type is descended from that of an archaic pair of handles now in New York.[1] The New York handles differ from our own in that the grip is curved, the eyes of the lion are open, and the lion head is flanked by paws. Also distinctive are the two eyes, which lie just under the rim and which have counterparts in black-figure cups of the sixth century. Beneath the eyes is the decorative scheme of our handles: two volutes above an inverted palmette. Beneath the lion heads is a supine volute flanked on the outside by a supine palmette.

A later development of the scheme depicted on the New York handle is now in Lyons;[2] here the lion heads are again flanked by paws, but now each surmounts the back of a fallen stag. Between the two stags is a large lotus and beneath the lotus and stags is the same volute and palmette pattern from the New York handle except that here the outer supine palmette has been suspended beneath the outer volute under the lion head. Also similar to the New York handle is the curved grip, which is now channeled throughout. Langlotz attributes the Lyons handle to southern Italy, citing the comparable facing lion heads on coins from Rhegion and the similar lotuses on late fifth-century mirrors from Locri.[3] Since the lion heads on the Lyons handle resemble those on the New York examples, it is possible that the New York pair were also made in southern Italy.

Our handle presents a simplified version of the decorative scheme on the Lyons example. On our piece, the lion protomes have become scalps and the palmette and volute patterns have been placed directly under the rim. To accommodate the lion-scalp, half of the outer volute has been removed and the inverted palmette springs from small volutes beneath the lion-scalp. Close parallels to our handle have been found in Vulci[4] and at Falerii Veteres.[5] Another similar example is in New York.[6] Our handle is thus almost certainly of Etruscan manufacture and therewith provides further evidence for the close relationship between south Italian and Etruscan metalworking centers during the sixth and fifth centuries B.C.

1. Richter, *Bronzes,* 33, nos. 52–53.

2. Boucher, *Bronzes grecs,* 39, nos. 19–20; K. A. Neugebauer, *RömMitt* 38 (1923):368, fig. 9; E. Langlotz, *Ancient Greek Sculpture of South Italy and Sicily* (New York, 1965), 288, pl. 128.

3. Langlotz, *Ancient Greek Sculpture,* 288.

4. M. Guarducci, *StEtr* 10 (1936), pl. X.6.

5. Villa Giulia Museum, from corridor to burial chamber in Tomb L 84.

6. Acquired in 1966, Rogers Fund 66.11.3, a,b.

39. Etruscan Maiden

(ca. 400 B.C.)

409. Purchased in Rome or Naples in 1906–9. Bronze. Ht, 9.2 cm; max w, 5.6 cm; l tang, 1 cm. Intact.

Maiden stands with weight on right foot, left knee bent, with left foot flat on ground. Forearms extended, with pomegranate in left hand, bird in right hand. She wears a chiton, the folds of which are indicated by vertical incisions over chest and at ankles. Above is a himation, which is wrapped around her body from waist to calf with ends thrown over left shoulder. Broad border between breasts and down left side is decorated with stamped circles; folds indicated by diagonal grooves. Hair center-parted with vertical incisions for locks, which are rolled up around nape. Cylindrical diadem with vertical incisions. Beneath feet are two tangs, which meet at tips.

This votive statuette bears the traditional dedicatory gifts, a bird and a pomegranate, and wears the characteristic dress for Etruscan women of the fifth century—chiton, himation, and unpointed boots.[1] Also typical is her speira hairstyle whereby the hair is rolled around a metal headband.[2] Her pose has been influenced by the work of Polykleitos, but the foot of the relaxed leg is still firmly planted on the ground, thereby imparting a rubbery effect to the body. Her inorganic structure is further emphasized by the lack of volume as well as by the absence of modeling.[3] Typically Etruscan[4] is the exaggerated size of the hands and of the bird, whose extra mass necessitated thickening the maiden's right shoulder and enlarging her right hand, which was then bent upward to support the bird. Also characteristic is the elaborate and often careless decorative treatment of the surface. Although the circles on the hem are carefully stamped, the folds of drapery, locks of hair, and facial features are crudely worked.

The figure was cast in one piece together with her offerings. The tangs by which the liquid wax escaped and the molten bronze entered were retained beneath the feet as a means of securing the figure to a base.

1. J. Keith, *The Pomerance Collection of Ancient Art, The Brooklyn Museum* (1966), 109, no. 125, from last half of fifth century or early fourth century. See similar examples in E. Babelon and J. A. Blanchet, *Catalogue des bronzes antiques de la Bibliothèque National* (Paris, 1895), 92, no. 203. For circle ornament, see *An Exhibition of Small Bronzes of the Ancient World* (Detroit Institute, 1947), no. 40, dated 500–450 B.C., and L. Bonfante, *Etruscan Dress* (Baltimore, 1975), 52–53, 76.

2. Bonfante, *Etruscan Dress*, 74.

3. Brendel, 308–9, 315.

4. A. Hus, *Les bronzes étrusques*, in *Collection Latomus*, 139 (1975), 151–56.

40. Etruscan Ladle

(late fifth c. B.C.)

620. Purchased in Rome or Naples in 1906–9. Bronze. L, 23 cm; diam. bowl, 8 cm. One bird protome completely broken away and head of other is missing. Handle reattached to bowl.

Strap handle with tapering midsection flares out with slight projections at end nearest bowl. Top of handle bifurcates into two cylindrical units. Engraved on the obverse at the base of the bifurcation are two bird heads above an inverted lotus bud. Shallow bowl was soldered to handle. Inscription engraved on rim of bowl adjoining handle.

The origin of the ladle probably is Phrygia, where examples have been found dating to the eighth century.[1] Early Etruscan ladles, such as an example from the Bernardini tomb (ca. 630–600 B.C.),[2] have a deeper bowl than our example and a much shorter handle, which also terminates in a bird head.

The Hopkins ladle best reflects the proportions favored in Greece[3] and Italy during the fifth century: a long handle, slightly curved at the top, and a wide, shallow bowl. The closest parallels have been found in tombs of the fifth century at Sasso Marconi (Bologna)[4] and Felsina.[5] Another example now in New York is said to be from Civita Castellana.[6] All of these ladles terminate in one or two bird heads, which we can thus confidently restore on our example. Similar handles appear on fifth-century Etruscan strainers.[7]

In the fourth century, Greek and Etruscan ladles took on deeper bowls and had shorter handles, with elaborate decorative flourishes at the juncture with the bowl; the bird heads were larger and the necks curved in a tighter arc, so that the ladles could be hooked over the edge of a vessel.[8] This form remained relatively unchanged throughout the Hellenistic and Roman periods.[9]

Although the bird on the handle is usually identified as a duck or swan, it has been suggested that the head might belong to a goose, a bird sacred to Dionysos and thus most suitable to a wine implement.[10]

1. E. Akurgal, *Die Kunst anatoliens* (Berlin, 1961), 101–2, pl. III,a,b.

2. C. D. Curtis, *MAAR* III (1919):49, no. 30, pl. 26, fig. 3.

3. See fifth-century ladle in D. M. Robinson, *Olynthus* 10 (1941):196–97, nos. 613, 614, pl. L.

4. G. Gentili, *StEtr* 38 (1970):244–49, figs. 4, 5.

5. G. Montanari, *StEtr* 21 (1950–1):309, 311, fig. 7b.

6. J. Keith, *The Pomerance Collection of Ancient Art, The Brooklyn Museum* (1966), 112, no. 131.

7. G. delli Ponti, *I Bronzi del Museo Provinciale di Lecce* (Lecce, 1973), 37, no. 57, pl. 38.

8. A. Oliver, *Silver for the Gods* (Toledo, 1977), 43, no. 13, from Kavalla of late fourth–third centuries; 46, no. 15, from Akarnania of ca. 300–250 B.C. See also *The Search for Alexander: An Exhibition* (New York, 1980), 167, no. 128, from Derveni.

9. Mitten, *RISD* 153, no. 41 (dated first c. B.C.–second c. A.D.); Oliver, *Silver,* 100, no. 58, dated to the mid-first c. B.C.

10. *The Search for Alexander* (see note 8), 167, no. 128.

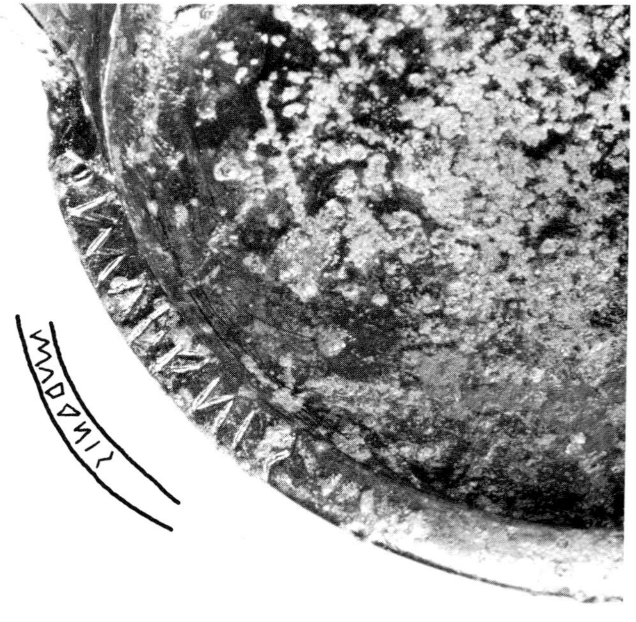

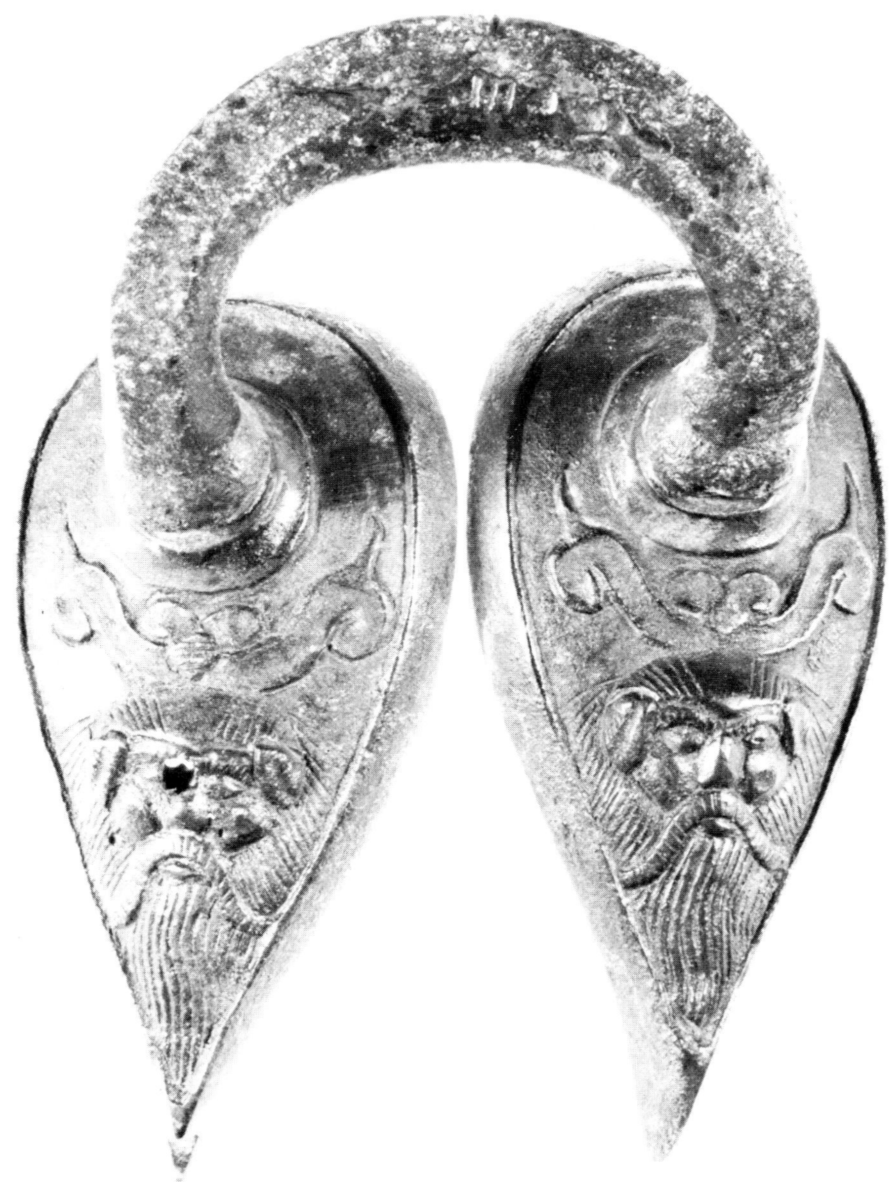

41. Etruscan Handle with Satyr Heads

(fifth–fourth c. B.C.)

K 58. Kemper Simpson Collection. Bronze. Ht, 16 cm; w, 12.2 cm; w each attachment, 6 cm; ht each attachment, 12.1 cm. Intact.

Polygonal grip with ring molding at roots curves down to contiguous attachments having convex surface and concave underside. Each attachment has a pointed oval shape and a raised border enclosing a facing satyr head with beard, mustache, pointed ears, and bald head. Above each satyr's head are two volutes linked by a crossband, then raised border around root of grip.

This handle and its lost mate were attached to an Etruscan stamnos, a large lidded wine container, which was made in the fifth or possibly fourth century. Our example belongs to a group of at least forty handles that are distinguished by their pointed oval attachments with raised borders.[1] Most of the handles have representations of a satyr head beneath floral motifs or eyes. On some examples the satyr head is replaced by a head of Acheloos,[2] and other handles omit the head completely.[3] A few attachments carry different motifs or are unadorned.[4] The scroll of our attachments admits several variations. The volutes may be well separated[5] or completely merged, with the inner volutes suppressed; sometimes the volutes are flanked by palmettes.[6]

Although many of these handles have been found in Etruscan tombs, others come from Celtic burials, which suggested to Jacobsthal that individual elements on the attachments served as prototypes for Celtic motifs.[7]

1. *EVP*, 248–50. Mitten, *Master Bronzes*, 196, no. 201. *Ars Antiqua* (December 1969), no. 12. G. Montanari, *StEtr* 21 (1950–1):309, 312–13, no. 7, fig. 9, tomb dated fifth century. Boucher, *Bronzes grecs*, 138, nos. 149–50. S. Boucher, *Vienne: Bronzes antiques* (Paris, 1971), 149, nos. 294–95.
2. *EVP*, 250, the Worcester Group.
3. Ibid., 249, no. 16.
4. Ibid., 250, Group D.
5. Boucher, *Bronzes grecs*, 138, nos. 149–50.
6. Richter, *Bronzes*, 32, nos. 50–51; Boucher, *Vienne*, 149, nos. 294–95.
7. P. Jacobsthal, *Early Celtic Art* (Oxford, 1944), 21, 88, 136–38.

420

421

42. Pair of Umbrian Votive Warriors

(fifth–fourth c. B.C.)

420, 421. Purchased in Rome or Naples in 1906–9. Bronze.

420. Ht, 9.3 cm; ht tang, 1.5 cm; w crest, 2.4 cm. Right lower leg broken off.

Nude male with semicircular crested helmet, hole in right hand for lance. Incised circles for eyes, nipples, navel; gash for mouth; gash and bump for genitals. Tang beneath left leg. Polygonal contours with signs of file.

421. Ht, 8.5 cm; w between hands, 3 cm; ht tang beneath legs, 1.5 cm. Right hand broken away.

Careless grooves for facial features; incised circles for navel and nipples; gash and bump for genitals. Tang beneath each foot.

These so-called yardstick figurines are characterized by their geometric forms and elongated proportions, especially their long necks, torsos, and legs.[1] The figurines are crudely made and often have irregular contours, suggesting that the wax was carved in sweeping strokes. The tangs beneath the feet are the channels by which the molten bronze entered the mold; these protrusions were retained after cooling for inserting statuettes into bases. Coldwork is evident in the pierced right hand (for a lance) and the stamped circles for features of face and body. The majority of the figurines are warriors, many of whom have a crested helmet and lance. A few examples are female.

Most of these yardstick figurines come from Umbria (to the east of Etruria), and especially from southern Umbria around Nocera Umbra.[2] The figurines are simplified, contemporary versions of similarly elongated but larger and more detailed statuettes of warriors that were made from the mid-fifth century into the fourth century in the Etruscan-Umbrian area around Perugia and as far north as the Po River. Richardson has shown that these statuettes were derived from an Etruscan version of a Greek hoplite type.[3] She traces the origin of the elongation that characterizes the Umbrian school back to the Villanovan period and suggests that this geometric tendency was suppressed with the transition to the orientalizing style, but reappeared in Umbria during the fifth century, perhaps as a result of influence from workshops in Spina.[4]

1. See G. Colonna, *Bronzi votivi umbro-sabellici a figura humana I: Periodo "arcaico"* (Florence, 1970), 100, nos. 285, 287, pls. LXXII, LXXIII.

2. Ibid., 85, 100; D. Mitten, *RISD*, 119, no. 34.

3. E. Richardson, in *Studies Presented to G. M. A. Hanfmann*, ed. D. Mitten (Mainz, 1971), 161–68.

4. E. Richardson, *MAAR* 27 (1962):159, 195–98. See also Brendel, 311–14.

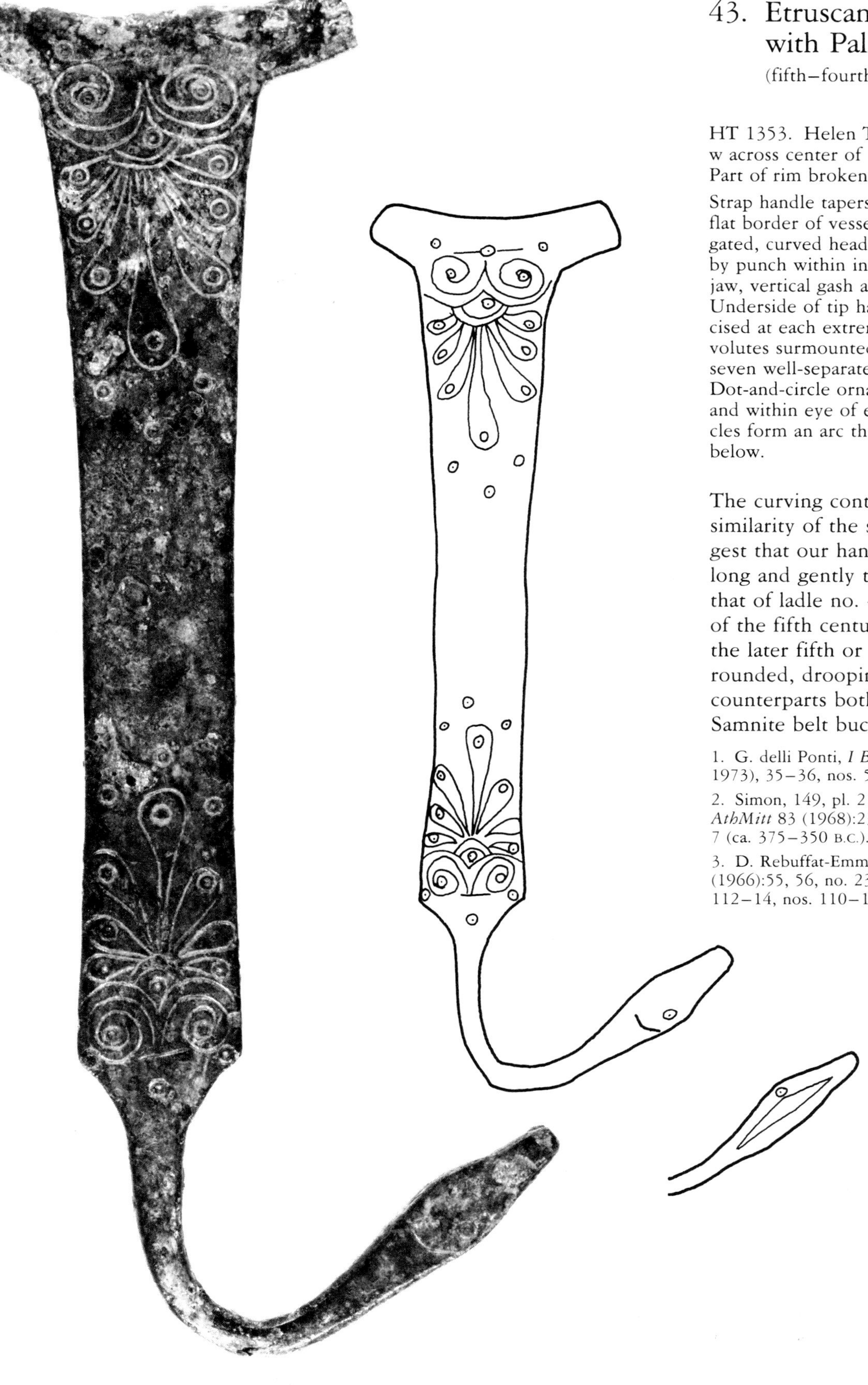

43. Etruscan Strainer Handle with Palmettes

(fifth–fourth c. B.C.)

HT 1353. Helen Tanzer Collection. Bronze. L, 17 cm; w across center of handle, 2 cm; w at rim end, 4.8 cm. Part of rim broken off with handle.

Strap handle tapers in center, then flares out to curved, flat border of vessel rim. Tip of handle becomes elongated, curved head of duck whose features are indicated by punch within incised circle for eye, incised arc for jaw, vertical gash and chevrons for nose and mouth. Underside of tip has misplaced dot and circle for eye. Incised at each extremity of upper side of strap are two volutes surmounted by two palmettes. Each palmette has seven well-separated petals with rounded, drooping tips. Dot-and-circle ornament at end of each petal, between and within eye of each volute. Three more dots and circles form an arc that encloses each palmette above and below.

The curving contour of the attachment end and the similarity of the shape to that of strainer no. 48 suggest that our handle also belonged to a strainer. The long and gently tapered strap handle is paralleled by that of ladle no. 40, and by Etruscan strainer handles of the fifth century.[1] Further evidence for a date of the later fifth or fourth century is provided by the rounded, drooping petals of the palmettes, which have counterparts both in Attic pottery of this date[2] and on Samnite belt buckles of the fourth century.[3]

1. G. delli Ponti, *I Bronzi del Museo Provinciale di Lecce* (Lecce, 1973), 35–36, nos. 52–53, pl. 36; 37, no. 57, pl. 38, of fifth c.

2. Simon, 149, pl. 219 (Meidias Painter). E. A. Zervoudaki, *AthMitt* 83 (1968):23, no. 26, pl. 6 (ca. 350 B.C.); 11, no. 1, pl. 7 (ca. 375–350 B.C.).

3. D. Rebuffat-Emmanuel, *Mélanges d'archéologie et d'histoire* 78 (1966):55, 56, no. 23054; 61, no. 23053. Boucher, *Bronzes grecs*, 112–14, nos. 110–11, 115–18.

684 685

44. Pair of Belt Buckles

(fourth–third c. B.C.)

684, 685. Purchased in Rome or Naples in 1906–9. Bronze. L, 10.5 cm each; max w, 2 cm. Intact.

684

Nude youth with weight on right leg, left relaxed, turns slightly to his left, head frontal. Wing visible outside right shoulder. Both hands at his side; right hand holds dagger. Greaves? Short skullcap hairstyle indicated by vertical incisions. Incised circular eye, horizontal gash for mouth. Beneath feet is head of a wolf, whose eyes and mouth are also incised. Rising from youth's head is channeled cylindrical extension that terminates in wolf head with hook under jaw. Two rivets are driven through center of youth's chest and another passes just above eye of wolf head beneath feet.

685

Nude winged youth with weight on left leg, right relaxed, hands at side with object in right hand. Otherwise identical to mate.

Surviving belts with buckles still in place are comprised of a 10-cm-wide metal strip lined with leather. The buckles were riveted to one end of the belt so that the hook could be slipped through either a ring or a hole at the belt's opposite end.

We know that many of these belts belonged to armor, both because belts were found in tombs together with Osco-Samnite cuirasses and because paintings from Lucania, Apulia, and Campania show these belts being worn by athletes, charioteers, and gladiators.[1] In several paintings, a triumphant soldier carries, on the tip of his lance, a belt that must have been taken from a conquered enemy, a custom that would explain why two belts have occasionally been found together with one cuirass. The belts were not exclusively for military wear, however, since in other paintings they are worn by infants, old men, and women.

Since most of the belts or buckles have been found in the Samnite area, it is believed that the objects were made there and then exported to Campania, Lucania, and Apulia.[2] The belt buckles can be dated to the fourth–third centuries on the basis of tomb contents and the paintings in which they appear.[3]

An example bearing the type of our pair has been found in Paestum[4] and another comparable buckle is in St. Germain.[5] Because the nude youths are winged and appear in a context of protection or propitiousness, it is logical to conclude that the figures are the luck-bringing Dioskouroi, whose cult flourished in southern Italy, especially Tarentum, around this time.[6] The Dioskouroi could also be the subject of a related type of buckle, which represents two nude unwinged youths standing on wolf heads and sharing a single channeled extension that terminates in a wolf head and hook.[7]

Other Samnite belt buckles of the same period depict different subjects, such as a cicado (see no. 45), a palmette, goats, Herakles, and a nike.[8]

1. D. Rebuffat-Emmanuel, *Mélanges d'archéologie et d'histoire* 74 (1962):353, 355.

2. Ibid., 356–60.

3. Ibid., 360–63; P. Jacobsthal, *Early Celtic Art* (Oxford, 1944), 147–48.

4. Rebuffat-Emmanuel, *Mélanges d'archéologie et d'histoire* 74 (1962):341.

5. Ibid., 78 (1966):49–52.

6. See discussion of item no. 50.

7. G. delli Ponti, *I Bronzi del Museo Provinciale di Lecce* (Lecce, 1973), 55, no. 79, pl. 49. Jacobsthal, *Early Celtic Art,* 148, pl. 260c. A variant shows two women [see Rebuffat-Emmanuel, *Mélanges d'archéologie et d'histoire* 74 (1962):340].

8. Rebuffat-Emmanuel, *Mélanges d'archéologie et d'histoire* 74 (1962):340–44; and ibid., 78 (1966):43–65.

45. Cicado Belt Buckle

(fourth c. B.C.)

9023. Probably purchased in Rome or Naples in 1906–9. Bronze. L, 10.9 cm; max w, 2.9 cm. Metal is very thin, with volutes in low relief and underside closely echoing contours of surface. Intact.

Back of cicado rendered as two volutes beneath elytra, which take form of a palmette with long central petal flanked on either side by fifteen petals. Stem beneath volutes is incised with two concentric semicircles and six horizontal ridges. Head of cicado has form of spearhead described by wide borders meeting in a V and enclosing a groove flanked by oblique incisions. Two rivets, one driven through middle of tip of central petal and other at base of elytra just above volutes. Hook beneath lance head.

This belt buckle was used in the same manner as the preceding pair (no. 44). It and a missing mate were riveted to one end of a metal belt; the hook slipped through either a hole or a corresponding attachment and eye at the other end of the belt.[1] Our example is in the form of a cicado whose head resembles a spearhead and whose elytra have obviously been inspired by treatments of palmette petals. On other buckles, the spearhead is replaced by the head of a horse, wolf, or serpent.[2]

The origin of the cicado belt buckle probably is Greece, since an example from the first half of the fifth century was found in Boeotia.[3] The cicado type was especially popular in Italy, where burial contexts indicate dates of the fourth century, particularly the first half. The objects may have been made in several centers, since examples have been found not only in southern Italy,[4] but also in Sicily,[5] Campania,[6] and even Turin.[7] Celtic imitations are also known.[8]

Since the underside of the wings is concave, with the windings clearly visible, it appears that this part of the buckle was made by hammering the metal into a matrix. It is possible that the entire buckle was first cast and then extensively reworked.

1. Buckle complete with belt in G. delli Ponti, *I Bronzi del Museo Provinciale di Lecce* (Lecce, 1973), 49, no. 71, pl. 45.

2. D. Rebuffat-Emmanuel [*Mélanges d'archéologie et d'histoire* 74 (1962):343 and 78 (1966):55] suggests that the spearhead is really a simplified protome.

3. C. Rolley, *Monumenta graeca et romana V: 1, Les bronzes* (Leiden, 1967), 19, no. 175.

4. delli Ponti, *Bronzi*, 49, no. 71, pl. 45, from Rudiae; 50, no. 73, pl. 47; 52, no. 78, pl. 48.

5. Boucher, *Bronzes grecs*, 113, nos 113–14, from Marsala.

6. Rebuffat-Emmanuel, *Mélanges d'archéologie et d'histoire* 78 (1966):55.

7. Ibid.

8. Mitten, *Master Bronzes*, 197, no. 202.

46. Etruscan Handle in Shape of Pair of Hands

(late fourth–third c. B.C.)

9030. Probably purchased in Rome or Naples in 1906–9. Bronze. L, 21.5 cm; w each hand, 7.5 cm; ht each hand (through thumb), 3.5 cm. Intact.

Grip is channeled, with three ring moldings at midpoint, the two outer ones beaded. Attachments are in the shape of a pair of hands, fingers extended and touching, thumbs pointing upward. Veins and joints indicated by grooves. Nails incised.

Like the satyr head handle (no. 41), this piece was one of a pair that belonged to a stamnos, in this instance one made in the late fourth or third century B.C.[1] The use of human hands on a vessel handle is, however, much older. The motif appears on a hydria from Paestum[2] of the third quarter of the sixth century and on a similarly dated hydria and handle from Trebenishte.[3] Detached handles have been found in Delphi[4] and on the Acropolis.[5]

Not surprisingly, the motif appealed to the Etruscans, whose liking for individual anatomical elements is also reflected in the human legs on the thymiaterion (no. 47). Predecessors to our handle can be found in the canopic clay funerary urns from Chiusi of the second half of the sixth century.[6] These urns take the form of a rotund individual with a modeled head surmounting the vessel and with handles resembling hands clasping the belly. By the end of the sixth century the Etruscans were applying the motif to metalware, such as a strainer.[7]

The motif has a certain popularity in metalwork of the Hellenistic period, although the hands become increasingly stumpy and less carefully incised. Examples from Pompeii include handles to a bowl of the third–second centuries B.C.,[8] and a large hot water heater dated to the second–first centuries B.C.[9] Detached handles of this period were found both in Pompeii[10] and on Delos.[11]

1. Mitten, *RISD*, 147, no. 39. Add to his list of detached handles (150, n. 9), M. Bieber, *Die antiken Skulpturen und Bronzen des könig. Museum Fridericianum in Cassel* (Marburg, 1915), 91, no. 408, pl. LIII.

2. L. Vokotopoulou, *Chalkai Korinthiourgeis Prochoi*, 130, no. 8, pl. 46; 170, 186, where vessel is attributed to Cumae. C. Picard, *Latomus* 19 (1960):422, pl. XIX. A. Van Buren, *AJA* 59 (1955):306, pl. 86, fig. 5.

3. Vokotopoulou, *Chalkai Korinthiourgeis Prochoi*, 129, nos. 2–3, and 186, attributed to Cumae. Picard, *Latomus* 19 (1960):424, pl. XXI.

4. P. Perdrizet, *Fouilles de Delphes V* (Paris, 1908) 74, no. 299, fig. 246.

5. A. de Ridder, *Bronzes trouvés sur l'acropole d'Athènes* (Paris, 1896), 52, no. 154.

6. Picard, *Latomus* 19 (1960):422.

7. D. Mitten, *HSCP* 69 (1965):163–67, pl. 1.

8. Pernice, vol. 4, 31, fig. 42; 32, fig. 43. Boucher, *Bronzes grecs*, 66, no. 44.

9. Pernice, vol. 4, 33, fig. 44, pl. VII.

10. Ward-Perkins and Claridge, 201, nos. 256, 257.

11. W. Deonna, *Exploration archéologique de Délos XVIII: Le mobilier délien* (Paris, 1938), 119–20, figs. 144–45.

47. Etruscan Thymiaterion or Incense Burner

(fourth–third c. B.C.)

9029. Probably purchased in Rome or Naples in 1906–9. Bronze. Ht, 39.5 cm; w between legs, 15.8 cm; l each side of bowl's rim, 6.7 cm.

Shaft divided by horizontal incisions into five sections that are alternately smooth and decorated. The two smooth bands are surmounted by a feline above a rooster. The decorated bands are filled with diagonal incisions that alternate direction between bands. Bottom of shaft terminates in roundel above a larger roundel decorated with tongues. Foot consists of three human legs (two left, one right), wearing short skirt to knee and soft shoes. Between each leg is ivy leaf with vertical incision down center and groove within hatching around contour. Shaft supports separately made bowl, which has a rectangular flat rim. At each corner is perched a small bird facing counterclockwise and secured by a rivet driven under rim into body.

Bibliography: Mitten, *Master Bronzes*, 217, no. 220.

This thymiaterion, or censor, was used in a domestic shrine to burn incense. The birds on the corners of the bowl probably allude to the birds used in augury and the haruspices, rituals of divination in which incense would also have been used.

The thymiaterion probably originated in the Near East in the eighth or seventh century B.C.[1] An Etruscan version was made in Vulci by the sixth century,[2] and until about 400 B.C. normally consisted of three feline legs supporting a shaft comprised of a figure surmounted by discs.[3]

The candelabrum was first made in Etruria in the seventh century,[4] but sometime in the fifth century acquired a new configuration, probably in Vulci. As on the contemporary form of the censor, the base consisted of feline or equine legs, but the shaft was a slender, smooth stem surmounted by a disc beneath a statuette that was enclosed by four vertical prongs for candles.[5]

The Hopkins thymiaterion represents a fourth-century refinement of the censors and candelabra of the fifth century. On this new type, which was probably conceived in Vulci,[6] the base consisted of three human legs, three equine legs,[7] or three feline legs springing from griffin beaks.[8] The shaft had the slender form of the fifth-century candelabra, but occasionally incorporated a human figure.[9] By the Hellenistic period, this new, simplified form of censor was being utilized for candelabra.[10]

Several censors survive that have the three-legged base of the Hopkins example and either a plain shaft or one that includes a human figure.[11] Multiple variations exist, i.e., a plaque base can appear beneath each shoe,[12] or a palmette[13] or pointed leaf[14] can be inserted between the legs. The shaft may have no animals,[15] may incorporate lotuses,[16] or may be entwined with serpents.[17] Rings or chains occasionally dangle from the corners of the bowl.[18]

The motif of three human legs is a curious one, but understandably attractive to the Etruscans, whose fascination with isolated human parts is well known. The inspiration may lie in tripods from the Near East,[19] but human legs are found on bronze tripods from Tarquinia as early as the seventh century B.C.[20] On our censor the short skirts and soft shoes identify the legs as those of dancers, whose connotations of festivity recall those evoked by figurines of jugglers on censors of the sixth century.[21] The appeal of the three human legs was probably reinforced, or the motif was possibly suggested, by its resemblance to the three-legged triskeles, a traditional symbol for human labor that appeared on archaic coins.[22] The three human legs live on in Roman metalwork, appearing on the base of a candelabrum from Pompeii[23] and another one from Belgium dating to the second century A.D.[24]

1. Brendel, 217; 461 n. 14.
2. Ibid., 216–17.
3. Ibid., 216–17, 298; Boucher, *Bronzes Lyons*, 116, no. 122.
4. T. Dohrn, *RömMitt* 66 (1959):57. For Greek candelabra, see B. Rutkowski, *JdI* 94 (1979):174–222; F. Messerschmidt, *StEtr* 5 (131):71–84.
5. Brendel, 299, 302. T. Dohrn, *RömMitt* 55 (1959):59.
6. Brendel, 332–34, fig. 256.
7. For equine or goat legs, see Boucher, *Bronzes grecs*, 121, no. 125; Hornbostel, 93, no. 64; Richter, *Bronzes*, 373, no. 1303; *Ars Antiqua* (June 1966), no. 45.
8. Brendel. 333. See unusual example on 334, fig. 258.
9. Boucher, *Bronzes grecs*, 119, no. 123.
10. An example with three human legs is shown in Spinazzola, pl. 295.
11. Brendel, 333, fig. 257; Boucher, *Bronzes grecs*, 119, no. 123.
12. Brendel, 333, fig. 257.
13. Hornbostel, 98, no. 68.
14. *Ars Antiqua* (June 1966), no. 46.
15. A. Emiliozzi, *La collezione Rossi Danielli nel Museo Civico di Viterbo* (Rome, 1974), 260, no. 613, pl. CXCIII.
16. G. Becatti, *StEtr* 9 (1935):298, no. 9, pl. XXXVIII.
17. R. Teitz, *Masterpieces of Etruscan Art* (Worcester, 1967), 96, no. 88.
18. Becatti, *StEtr* 9 (1935):292, no. 7, pl. XXXVIII; E. Fiumi, *StEtr* 25 (1957):485, fig. 10.
19. See a clay tripod from Azerbaijan (near the Caspian Sea) in A. U. Pope, *Masterpieces of Persian Art* (New York, 1945), pl. 38. See also C. Hopkins, in *Hommages à Marcel Renard*, vol. 3. *Collection Latomus* 103 (1969), 3, 308.
20. H. Hencken, *AJA* 61 (1957), 1–4; Hencken, "The Earliest European Helmets," *Peabody Bulletin* 28 (1971), 115, fig. 85; Hopkins, *Collection Latomus* 103 (1969), 308.
21. Brendel, 333.
22. C. Kraay, *Greek Coins* (New York, 1966), 325, no. 340, pl. 114; 329, no. 388, pl. 126.
23. Pernice, vol. 4, 21, fig. 33.
24. G. Faider-Feytmans, *Les bronzes romains de Belgique* (Mainz, 1979), 185, no. 381, pl. 161.

48. Etruscan Bronze Strainer

(fourth–third c. B.C.)

605. Purchased in Rome in 1906–7. "Near Cortona." Bronze. L, 30.8 cm; diam bowl over rim, 13.7 cm; depth bowl, 4.9 cm; w rim, 1.1 cm. Cracked across bowl; tip of handle broken away.

Strap handle with curved tip tapers to low bowl with broad, flat rim. Punched into interior of bowl are eleven concentric circles. Opposite handle is an extension formed by two tangs that meet to support a thin, rectangular, curved plaque. Inscribed on rim adjoining handle: sacro matre mursina.

Bibliography: H. Langford Wilson, *AJP* 28 (1907):450–55; Letter from Wilson to Gildersleeve, January 26, 1907, in Special Collections, Eisenhower Library; Letter from Wilson to Buckler, March 17, 1907, in JHU Archives, box 51, Office of the President; *CIL I*, pt. 2, fasc. 1, 434, no. 580.

Strainers like this one were primarily used for wine, but on occasion may have held snow to chill the wine, since Martial (*Liber Spectaculorum* 14.103–4) refers to a *colum nivarium*. The handle and extension rested on the wine container's rim, and the curved tip of the extension allowed the strainer to be hung out of the way when it was not needed.

Strainers similar to our own have been found in a number of Etruscan burials, several of which can be dated to the fourth or beginning of the third century.[1] The handles on undamaged examples terminate in a bird head like that on the handle of our similarly shaped but slightly earlier bronze ladle (no. 40).

Although this strainer is an Etruscan form of implement, it bears a Latin inscription, a reminder that by the fourth and third centuries Rome had gained control over most of Etruria. The name "mater mursina" is not otherwise attested, but it has been suggested that this may be an obscure title for one of the better-known divinities, who is here addressed by her association with a gens or town having the name Mursina.[2]

1. A. Emilozzi, *La Collezione Rossi Danielli nel Museo Civico di Viterbo* (Rome, 1974), 70, no. 28, pl. XXV (Musarno); H. L. Wilson, *AJP* 28 (1907):451 (Cortona); E. Scamuzzi, *StEtr* 16 (1942):472, no. 7, pl. XXV (Carmignano); A. Minto, *NSc* 6, 8 (1932):92, fig. 3 (Orvieto); G. M. A. Richter, *Handbook of the Etruscan Collection* (New York, 1940), 30, fig. 87.

2. H. L. Wilson, *AJP* 28 (1907):455.

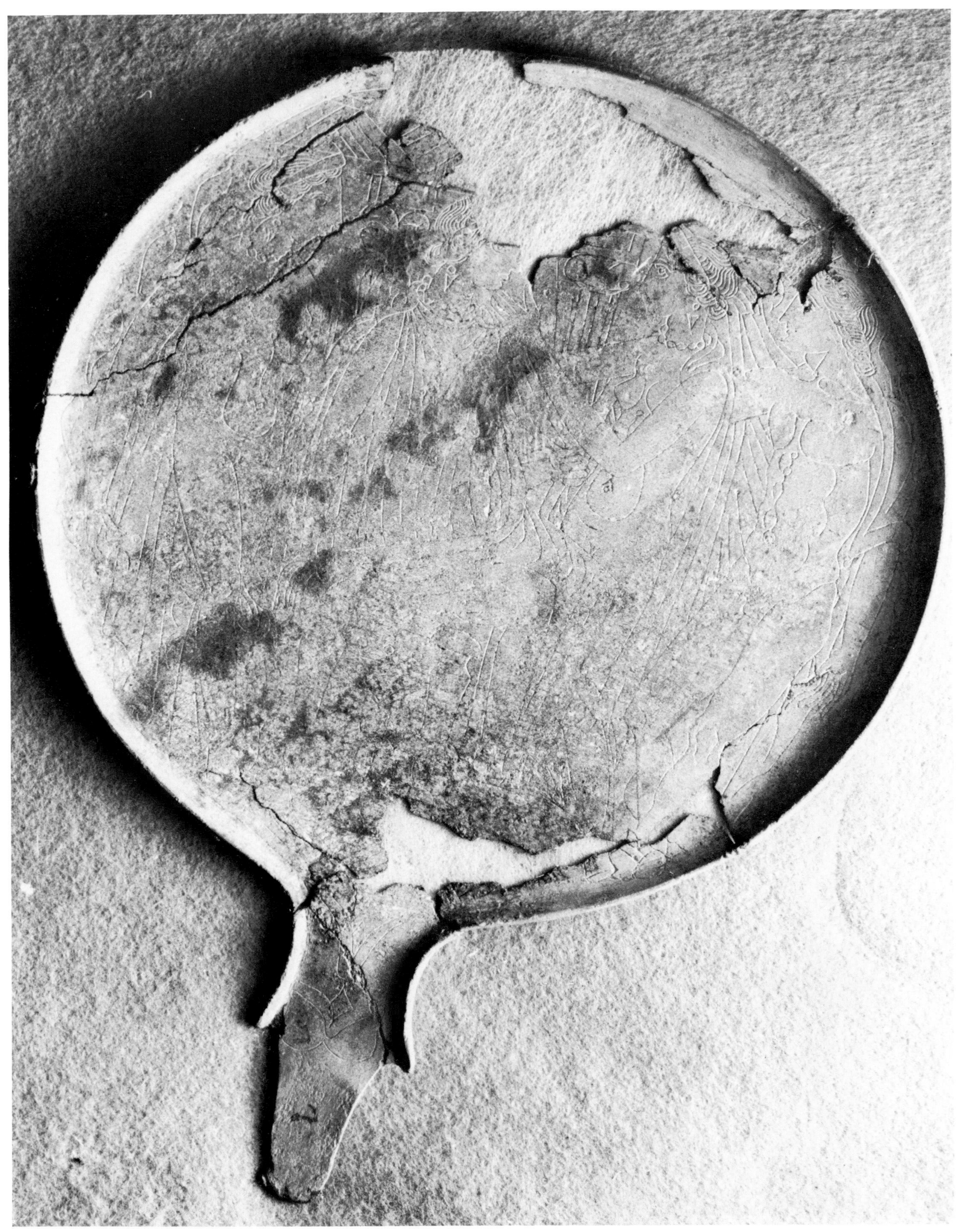

a

49. Etruscan Mirror with Toilette of Malavisx or Helen

(third c. B.C.)

9089. Probably purchased in Rome in 1906–9. Bronze. L, 24 cm; diam disc, 17.7 cm; l attachment without tang, 2.8 cm; w across center of attachment, 2.5 cm; l tang, 3.4 cm. Mended from several fragments.

Mirror has a round disc with flaring attachment and a broad tang with rounded tip. Obverse has a beaded border and an engraved volute-leaf design on the attachment (*e*). Reverse has an upturned edge and a lotus motif engraved on the attachment (*d*). The representation (*a, c*) shows four figures before an Ionic facade, of which two columns and part of a third are indicated. The entablature is rendered by oblique lines and there are similar lines in the exergue. A female sits to her left in a girded peplos with a himation draped behind her shoulders and across her waist and legs. She wears a diadem, earrings of ball-and-triangle shape, a beaded necklace, and a torque. Her right arm hangs at her side; her left hand, at her hip, holds the edge of her himation and a staff. She is seated on a stool that has a cushion and turned legs; the underside of the stool is indicated in faulty perspective. Her feet rest on a footstool.

Facing her is a nude female whose left hand is raised to the other's chin and whose right forearm disappears behind the other's mantle. This standing maiden wears a diadem, earrings, beaded necklace, and a mantle, which is draped behind her shoulders and across her left knee and lower leg. Behind her is a nude youth whose upraised right hand holds the edge of his mantle, which passes behind his back and over his left shoulder and elbow, where a tassel hangs from its tip. He wears boots with lotus-shaped tops. At the viewer's left is another nude standing female, whose upraised left hand holds a staff as well as the ends of her himation, which falls behind her back and over her left knee. A similar tassel hangs from the folds of her garment where it spills over the left elbow. She wears a diadem, earrings, a necklace, and boots with lotus-shaped tops. Along the rim of each side of the scene are teardrop-shaped motifs.

Radiographs (*g*) clearly revealed near the abdomen of the seated figure a central depression that is surely the centering point where the disc was lathe-turned.[1] Microscopic examination revealed slip lines from coldworking and annealing twins, evidence that the mirror had probably been cast, coldworked, annealed, and coldworked again.[2]

This mirror belongs to one of the two classes of mirrors that Beazley termed Group Z.[3] The class with which we are concerned is characterized by a large round disc (17–19 cm diam) with flaring attachment and tang, and a crowded composition consisting of four or more figures before an architectural facade. Other characteristics are the alternating bands of parallel oblique lines in pediment and exergue, the locks of hair rendered as concentric semicircles, and the treatment of the iris as a semicircle suspended from the upper eyelid.

Close examination of mirrors belonging to this class reveals an unevenness in quality among the members, an observation that prompted Haynes to divide the class into two subdivisions according to the complexity of the representations and the care with which they were executed.[4] Our mirror definitely belongs within the secondary group.

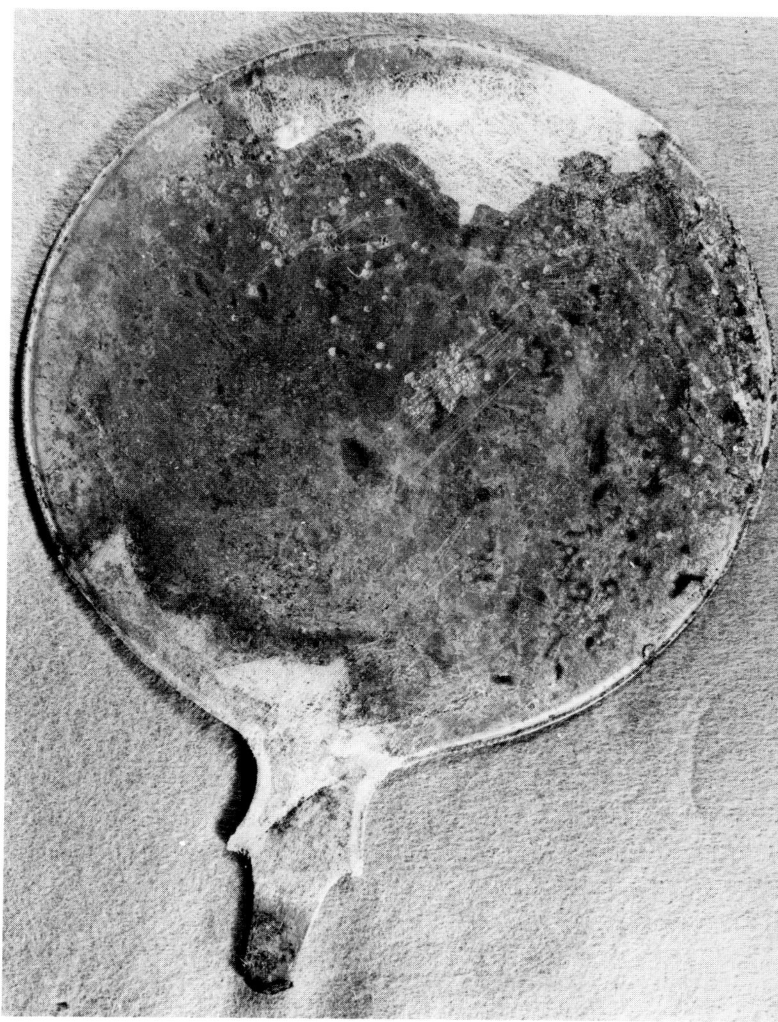

b

The Hopkins mirror can be contrasted with a mirror (Gerhard 212)[5] that displays those characteristics of the primary subdivision that are missing on our piece (see *f*): circles along the broad hem of the garments, fine dotting for the interior modeling, figures in the pediment and exergue, and a scalloped treatment of the rim.

The representation on the Hopkins mirror is in fact a very simplified version of the scene on Gerhard 212. On the Hopkins mirror, the lower halves of the columns have disappeared and the faces are all in profile. Elements in the Hopkins scene have also been confused: the standing figure behind the seated female holds her own mantle and staff, not the ends of the diadem, as on Gerhard 212, and the maiden in front of the seated figure no longer lifts her right hand to adjust the other's diadem—instead, her right forearm disappears behind her companion's mantle. Finally, the youth has lost the identifying attributes of wreath and staff and holds only the ends of his own mantle. Our mirror does, indeed, suffer when compared with Gerhard 212, but it fares better when placed beside a still weaker version of the same scene.[6]

c

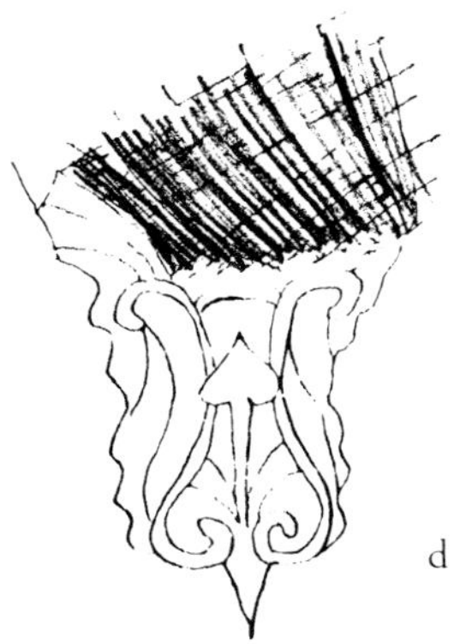

d

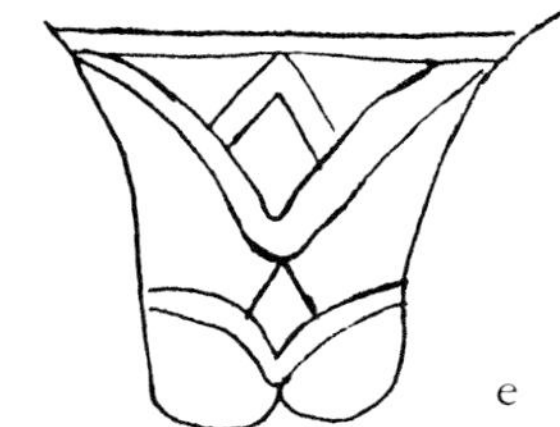

e

f

The subject depicted on the Hopkins mirror and on Gerhard 212 is the Toilette of Malavisx (Helen). Rebuffat-Emmanuel has shown that the basic elements of the scene are the seated Malavisx in right profile, a standing female who adjusts the diadem with one hand while the other is lifted to Malavisx's chin, and an assisting female who stands behind Malavisx holding the ends of the diadem.[7] Other figures may be present as onlookers.[8] Turan may assist[9] or she may only supervise.[10] Occasionally, the attending females are designated by such names as Epie/utile,[11] Munthux,[12] or Resxualc.[13]

The nude youth on our mirror and on Gerhard 212 has been borrowed from another representation, the Judgment of Paris, of which a mirror in Indiana is a good example. In her discussion of the latter piece, Bonfante[14] has shown how easily the two types could be conflated, so that the seated female may be labeled Malavisx or Turan, while the youth standing to the far left or right may be labeled Elcsntre (Alexander), referring to the Judgment of Paris, or he may be unlabeled, as here, in which case he may be intended to recall Apollo.[15]

The marked tendency toward conflation on mirrors of this class demonstrates how heavily the engravers relied upon pattern books, which provided scenes whose components could be variously combined. The Hopkins mirror is obviously closely related to several

g

other mirrors of this class, on which we find either the same flanking figures or the identical treatment of the architectural facade, with its unusual abaci of Ionic capitals and the bands of oblique lines in the pediment.[16] The representations in these books would have been derived from mirrors like Gerhard 212 and the Indiana mirror, but were probably more simplified, thereby providing figures who could be treated as interchangeable and anonymous units. Mirrors composed from these pattern books could thus simultaneously display the slender, nude bodies fashionable in Hellenistic times and the drapery styles and jewelry derived from fourth-century prototypes. On the Hopkins mirror the early details are the massive, draped torso of the seated figure, the beaded necklaces, low diadems, tasseled garments, and the bead-and-triangle earrings.[17]

Haynes convincingly argued that the finest mirrors of this class were made in the last half of the fourth century, while the more derivative, secondary mirrors, like our own, date from the third century and were probably not made in the same city that produced the primary mirrors.[18] Because the secondary mirrors vary far more between themselves in quality and style than do the primary mirrors, it is possible that there were a number of secondary manufacturing centers, the identity of which is still undetermined.[19]

1. Rebuffat-Emmanuel, 378–80.

2. See G. Panseri and M. Leoni, *StEtr* 25 (1957):310–13.

3. *EVP*, 130–32, and J. D. Beazley, *JHS* 69 (1949):16–17, where the group is dated to the third century.

4. S. Haynes, *Mitteilungen des deutschen archäologischen Instituts* 6 (1953):21–45, especially 29–30, where there are lists of the mirrors belonging to these classes.

5. Gerhard, vol. 2, pl. 212; vol. 3, 202.

6. Ibid., vol. 2, pl. 211; vol. 3, 201.

7. D. Rebuffat-Emmanuel, *MonPiot* 60 (1976):53–67. The mirrors inscribed with Malavisx are Gerhard pls. 213, 215. Another is illustrated in *Historia* 6 (1932):435–37, and A. Emiliozzi, *La Collezione Rossi Danielli nel Museo Civico di Viterbo* (Rome, 1974), 58, no. 1, pls. 20, 33.

8. Rebuffat-Emmanuel, *MonPiot* 60 (1976):fig. 22, also published in *StEtr* 9 (1935):pl. 37.

9. Gerhard, vol. 2, pl. 215.

10. Ibid., pl. 213.

11. Ibid., pl. 213.

12. Ibid., pl. 213.

13. Ibid., pl. 215.

14. L. Bonfante, *StEtr* 45 (1977):149–68.

15. Ibid., 166.

16. Gerhard, vol. 2, 228; vol. 3, pl. 247A; vol. 4, pls. 300.2 and 351.1.

17. See ibid., vol. 4, pl. 373.3. L. Bonfante, *Etruscan Dress* (Baltimore, 1975), 9.

18. Haynes, *Mitteilungen* 6 (1953):35–37. Our mirror is certainly later than a mirror of this class from a tomb dated to the end of the fourth century [see R. Lambrechts, *Bulletin de l'institut historique belge de Rome* 39 (1968):5–22].

19. Haynes believed that the primary mirrors might have been made in Chiusi. See especially the similarities to the pottery in C. Albizzati, *RömMitt* 30 (1915):129–57. Beazley suggested (*EVP*, 132) that all of Group Z might have been made in Chiusi or Cervetri. See Haynes, *Mitteilungen* 6 (1953):36–37.

50. Etruscan Mirror with Dioskouroi

(third–second c. B.C.)

9119. Probably purchased in Rome or Naples in 1906–9. Bronze. L, 23.2 cm; diam disc, 11.9 cm; ht attachment, 2.7 cm; w at base of attachment, 2.5 cm; l handle to base of attachment, 8.4 cm. Mended from eleven fragments.

Mirror has round disc with flaring attachment and narrow handle. Obverse: beading around disc. Handle (from tip) has ram's head, two bird heads, acanthos leaves. Reverse: flat, ribbonlike band around rim. Handle has a ram's head beneath acanthos leaves. The scene shows two standing youths turned three-quarters toward each other, with outer leg advanced. Each wears a Phrygian cap and a short, girded tunic. The hands of the outside arms are behind the hips; the inside arms are not indicated. Behind each figure is a shield; between the youths at chest and thigh level are two pairs of horizontal lines that enclose an X.

Metal samples revealed lines from coldworking but no annealing twins. This indicates that the mirror was cast and coldworked but probably never annealed afterward.

This mirror belongs to a large group of mirrors that represent the standing Dioskouroi turned toward each other and seen in a three-quarter view.[1] The outside, supporting leg is advanced and the hands of the outside arms rest on or behind the hip, while the inside arms are usually absent.[2] The figures wear girded tunics, occasionally with a broad belt, sometimes with a kolpos. The youths usually wear Phrygian caps, but they may also wear piloi. They may wear high, laced boots, ankle-high boots, or none at all. Occasionally one of the figures is winged.[3] Behind each figure may be a shield or an altar. The space between the figures is filled with various objects: an animal,[4] an amphora,[5] one or two stars,[6] from one to five circles, which are probably stars,[7] a nude female,[8] floral stalks with volutelike tips,[9] a tree with a bird at its tip,[10] a column supporting an arc filled with rows of X's,[11] or a treelike unit at the top of which are volutes beneath a floral unit which is possibly a lotus.[12]

Very often we find this space filled with horizontal beams, the dokana, which Plutarch tells us were symbolic representations of the Dioskouroi in Laconian and Tarentine cult.[13] On the mirrors the dokana may appear as one, two, or three horizontal beams placed anywhere from knee to head level.[14] Occasionally there is a pediment above the topmost beam.[15] The lowest beam may rest on an amphora,[16] a column that tapers downward,[17] or a giant lotus plant.[18] The space between the beams may be left vacant or may be filled with circles and stars,[19] a phiale,[20] eggs,[21] or stalks with volute tips flanking eggs.[22] On some mirrors the upper beam is supported in various ways: by an Ionic column,[23] by two volutes,[24] or by multiple beams,[25] which are set obliquely in an X. Occasionally, as on our own mirror, there is only a single X connecting the beams.[26]

Mirrors that bear these representations of the Dioskouroi can be divided into several classes according to the shape of their discs.[27]

1. A few mirrors have only an upturned rim. This shape is more commonly found on mirrors that represent Lasae.[28]

2. A number of mirrors are of the "stachelkranz" type, on which the scene is recessed within a band of guilloche, laurel, or stachelkranz;[29] here we find high, laced boots and V-necked tunics, with the folds of the skirt falling in four or more panels. Frequently there is a horizontal line across the skirt about one-third the distance between hem and waist.

3. Our mirror belongs with a large group of discs that do not exhibit an engraved ornamental band, but instead have a flat, ribbonlike border.[30] As on our mirror, the Dioskouroi wear high-girded tunics that are inflated over the chests and that do not have V-necks. The skirts usually fall in only three vertical panels and ordinarily there are no boots. On many of the poorest examples the figures are elongated and doll-like. The figures are usually shown with their shields behind them and with only the simplest of motifs between them. These mass-produced examples probably all stem from one workshop, perhaps of the second century B.C.

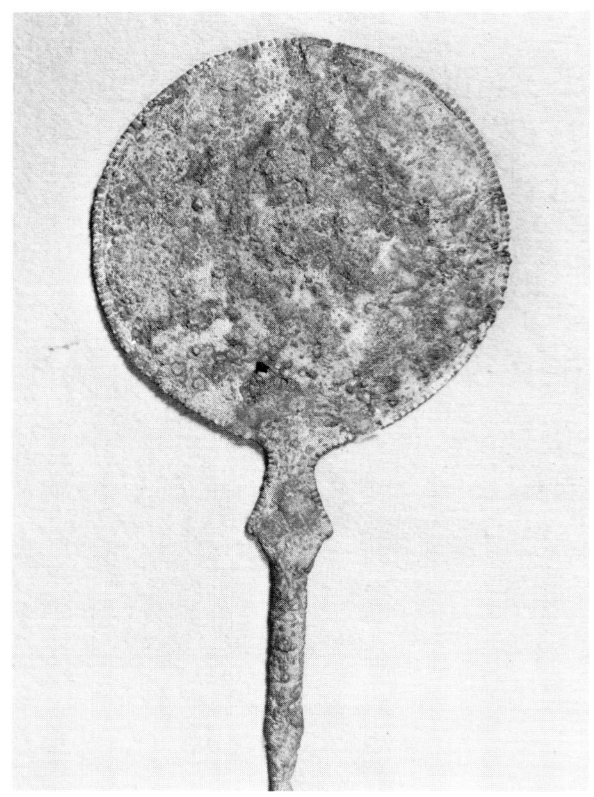

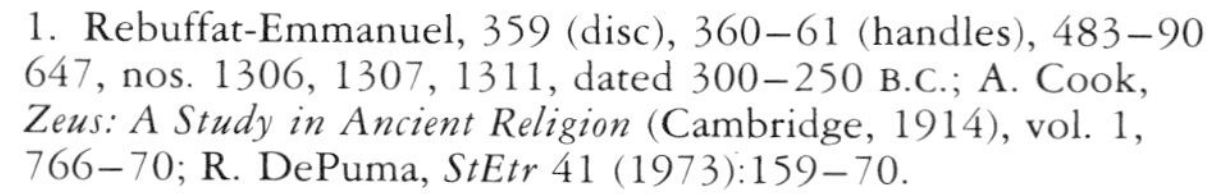

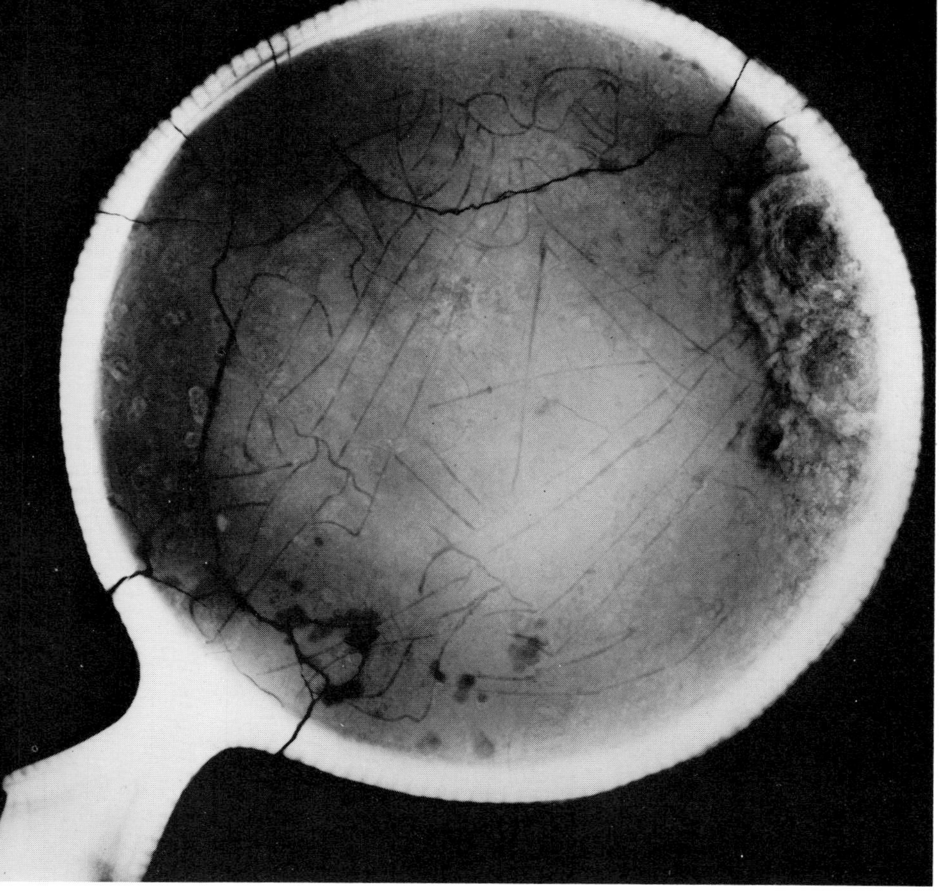

1. Rebuffat-Emmanuel, 359 (disc), 360–61 (handles), 483–90, 647, nos. 1306, 1307, 1311, dated 300–250 B.C.; A. Cook, *Zeus: A Study in Ancient Religion* (Cambridge, 1914), vol. 1, 766–70; R. DePuma, *StEtr* 41 (1973):159–70.

2. On some mirrors the tunic-clad Dioskouroi gesticulate with one or both arms (Gerhard, vol. 1, pl. 47.1.2.5; 48.1.2.3). Since all the other elements of the scene are identical to those of the Hopkins type, these mirrors are considered below where relevant. The gesticulating Dioskouroi have probably been influenced by another mirror type, on which two nude youths converse as they lean against their shields. In many cases these youths are certainly Dioskouroi. See the entry for item no. 51 and M. del Chiaro, *AJA* 59 (1955):277–86, especially 283. See also variants where one or both youths is winged: J. Szilagyi, *Acta Antiqua Academiae Scientiarum Hungarica* 10 (1962):250–58, no. 1; R. Noll, *ÖJh* 39 (1935):155–58.

3. Gerhard, vol. 1, pl. 52.2.

4. Ibid., pl. 48.7.

5. Ibid., pl. 48.6; F. Chapouthier, *Les dioscures au service d'une déesse* (Paris, 1935), 150 n. 1, 315–16; P. Wuilleumier, *Tarente*

(Paris, 1939), 439, 521; E. Peterson, *RömMitt* 15 (1900):7, fig. 1; 41–45.

6. Gerhard, vol. 1, pl. 46.2.4.5.8; Chapouthier, *Les dioscures,* 114, 268, 278, 281; E. Fiumi, *StEtr* 25 (1957):384, fig. 13; R. Noll, *ÖJh* 27 suppl. (1932):106, fig. 49; Richter, *Bronzes,* 284, no. 821; A. Emiliozzi, *La collezione Rossi Danielli nel Museo Civico di Viterbo* (Rome, 1974), 256, no. 589, pl. 189, and 257, no. 590, pl. 189; M. de Chiaro, *Re-exhumed Etruscan Bronzes: A Loan Exhibition at the University Art Museum* (Santa Barbara, 1981), 32, no. 27.

7. Gerhard, vol. 2, pl. 45, figs. 2, 3, 4, 7, 8; U. Ferraguti, *StEtr* 11 (1937):109, fig. 2; Richter, *Bronzes,* 284, no. 821. P. Lebel, *Catalogue des collections archéologiques de Besançon V: Les bronzes figurés* (Paris, 1959),73, no. 284, pl. 95; *Kunstwerke der Antike* (Luzern, June 1966), no. 33. L. Vanoni, *NSc* 8, 26 (1972):182, fig. 38.

8. Gerhard, vol. 5, pl. 81. The most plausible identification is Helen, who was traditionally associated with trees and pillars. See Chapouthier, *Les dioscures,* 148–49.

9. Gerhard, vol. 1, pl. 47.1; see Chapouthier, *Les dioscures,* 88–89, pls. IX, XIV, where similar representations are connected with silphium, which was sacred to the Dioskouroi (*RE* bd. 5, pt. 1, 1108).

10. Gerhard, vol. 1, pl. 46.8.

11. Ibid., vol. 3, pl. 253.3. This is probably a representation of a pillar supporting the heavens; for the Dioskouroi's connection with the hemispheres, see F. Cumont, *Recherches sur le symbolisme funéraire des romains* (Paris, 1942), 68–69.

12. Gerhard, vol. 1, 48.4.5; 52.2; Fiumi, *StEtr* 25 (1957):384, fig. 14; D. Carandini, *StEtr* 40 (1972), pl. 89c, where the volutes seem to end in eggs; Noll, *ÖJh* 27 (1932):107, fig. 50; D. Vaglieri *NSc* 5, 4 (1907):481, fig. 22, where the tree has a bulbous tip similar to the base of the column on the mirror of note 11. For the significance of the lotus, see *DarSag,* 255, and Cook, *Zeus,* 762–75.

13. Plutarch, *De frat, amor* 478a–b; M. Waites, *AJA* 23 (1919):1–18; DePuma, *StEtr* 41 (1973):164–65. Rebuffat-Emmanuel, 487–89; Wuilleumier, *Tarente,* 429–32; Peterson, *RömMitt* 15 (1900):3–61, especially 44.

14. Gerhard, vol. 1, pls. 46.2.3.4.6; 47.3.6.7.8, etc.; F. Magi, *La raccolta Benedetto Guglielmi nel Museo Gregoriano etrusco* (Rome, 1941), pt. II, 54, no. 9, and 182; R. Vighi, *NSc* 6, 12 (1936):419, fig. 6.

15. Gerhard, vol. 1, pls. 47.3.4.5.6, etc.

16. Ibid., pl. 48.8. See a relief in Sparta in M. N. Tod, *BSA* 13 (1906–7):213, no. 1.

17. Gerhard, vol. 1, pl. 46.4.

18. Ibid., pl. 46.9.

19. Ibid., pls. 45.9, 47.3.

20. Ibid., pl. 47.4.

21. Ibid., pls. 47.5, 48.6.8, etc. See Chapouthier, *Les dioscures,* 3; 54, no. 37, pl. III. *DarSag,* 250.

22. Gerhard, vol. 1, pl. 47.3.

23. Rebuffat-Emmanuel, no. 1311; Gerhard, vol. 3, pl. 253.A.3.

24. Gerhard, vol. 1, pls. 47.1.6.7, 48.6.8.

25. Ibid., pl. 47.2.3.

26. See J. M. Blasquez, *Archivo español de Arqueologia* 33 (1960), 149, no. VI, where there are two beams below the x unit. The x is above the upper beam in Gerhard, vol. 1, pl. 45.9.

27. Rebuffat-Emmanuel, 359, 483–90.

28. Ibid., 359 (disc), 490–93, dated to the third century; Gerhard, vol. 1, pls. 31–35.

29. For the "stachelkranz" mirrors, see the next entry. Gerhard, vol. 1, pls. 47.6, 48.5–8, 52.2; Carandini, *StEtr* 40 (1972):pl. 89.

30. Gerhard, vol. 1, pls. 45.2–5, 7–9; 46.1.3.6; 48.4. Magi, *Raccolta Benedetto Guglielmi,* 182, no. 9, pl. 54; Vighi, *NSc* 12 (1936):419, fig. 6; Blasquez, *Archivo,* 149, no. VI; Fiumi, *StEtr* 25 (1957):384, figs. 13–14; Ferraguti, *StEtr* 11 (1937):109, fig. 2; Noll, *ÖJh* 27 (1932):106, fig. 49.

51. Etruscan Mirror with Dioskouroi

(third–second c. B.C.)

K 61. Kemper Simpson Collection. Bronze. L, 23.9 cm; diam disc, 11.9 cm; l attachment, 3.1 cm; max w attachment, 3.1 cm; l handle to bottom of attachment, 9 cm. Label on obverse reads: C. Sangiorgi, Roma 2243.

The mirror has a circular bombé disc with flaring attachment. Obverse: convex handle is decorated (from tip) with ram's head, two beaked bird heads flanking a band of punched dots, acanthos leaves. A leaf-bud pattern is on the attachment. The disc is edged with beading outside of incised circles. Reverse: down center of handle is a concave groove in the center of which is a row of punched dots flanked on each side by a similar row of more widely spaced punchings. On the attachment is a lotus-volute design. Disc has a 0.6-cm-wide guilloche border encircling the indented field. Representation comprised of four figures who are standing in front of a beam, which is above their heads. At either side, standing before waist-high altars, are two youths wearing girded tunics with girded overfolds, laced boots, and Phrygian caps. The hands of the outside arms are behind their buttocks. Behind the youth at the viewer's right stands a long-haired nude youth in laced boots, his right elbow bent, head turned to his left. To his right is a draped woman in left profile, her right arm extended behind the youth to her right. She wears a Phrygian cap and a long girded tunic with girded overfold.

Bibliography: F. Brommer, *Denkmälerlisten zur griechischen Heldensage,* vol. 3 (Marburg, 1976), 353, no. 1.

The centering point for lathe-spinning is clearly visible on the right hip of the nude male. Metal samples revealed annealing twins and slip lines, evidence that the mirror was cast, coldworked, annealed, and coldworked again.

This mirror belongs to one of the two classes of mirrors that make up Beazley's Group Z.[1] One of these classes has already been discussed in relation to entry no. 49. The remaining class has been frequently studied, most notably by Herbig;[2] however, it is now clear that Herbig's "stachelkranz," the wreath of pointed leaves that appears on many of these mirrors, was only one of a number of border patterns available to the engraver and thus is not the hallmark of a distinct subdivision of this class.[3]

The scene on the Hopkins mirror is one of the more common representations on these mirrors. Several near duplicates exist,[4] as well as many mirrors depicting a variant scene in which a nude female appears in the place of the nude youth.[5] Both of these scenes are themselves related to another composition common to this class of mirrors, in which the maiden with the Phrygian cap and the nude male/female are flanked by two nude or semi-nude youths who are either seated or standing. On several inscribed mirrors, these two youths are identified as Dioskouroi.[6] Since the tunic-clad youths on our mirror represent a strong independent tradition as Dioskouroi (see item no. 50), it is likely that they are later substitutions for the nude/semi-nude youths.

Both the scenes with tunic-clad Dioskouroi and their immediate prototypes (with the nude/semi-nude youths) are at least partially derived from a Judgment of Paris. Our long-robed woman is clearly based upon figures of Minerva, although a Phrygian cap has been substituted in deference to the Dioskouroi.[7] The nude female (for whom the male was later substituted) is occasionally labeled Turan on mirrors where she appears with Minerva and the nude/semi-nude youths.[8] For most engravers, however, the prototype must have been all but forgotten. A comparison of mirrors having either the tunic-clad Dioskouroi or the nude/semi-nude youths shows how easily the third figure from our left would be adapted or substituted. The figure appears as a draped female,[9] a nude female with a mantle around her leg,[10] a nude female with boots only,[11] and finally, a booted male with a mantle[12] or without (our own). The facility and rapidity with which these units were combined are demonstrated by the way the triangle enclosed by the nude male/female's right arm is usually blank (as on our own mirror) and by the confusion of the nude female's drapery with that of Minerva behind her.[13]

Given such a collagelike method of composition, it is understandable that the identities of the figures are also interchangeable, a fact that is confirmed by the various combinations of inscriptions on mirrors that have a nude female flanked either by tunic-clad Dioskouroi or by the nude/semi-nude youths.[14] Phillips concluded that uninscribed examples of that scene probably represent Minerva and Turan flanked by the Dioskouroi.[15]

The nude male in the male variant scene on the Hopkins mirror is hard to identify, since there are fewer examples, a fact that is probably due to its later, derivative origin. On inscribed scenes where the flanking figures are nude/semi-nude youths, there is a great variety of labels[16] and in only three instances do the names of one or both of the Dioskouroi appear. On these latter mirrors the compositions are (viewer's left to right): Capaneus, Castra (?), Ajax, Castor; Atreus, Oenone, Pollux, Castor; Iolaos, Minerva, Pollux, Castor.[17] It is clear that, for the engravers, the identities of the figures were virtually interchangeable. It is also apparent that there were a great many mythological figures who could be linked with the Dioskouroi, and perhaps a few more whose relationships were largely in the imaginations of the engravers. Of mirrors of the Hopkins type, there is only a single inscribed example where the figures flanking the nude male are the tunic-clad Dioskouroi; on this piece the inscription can be read as Pollux, ______, ______, Menelaos.[18] The engraver may have regarded the nude male as Castor or, just as easily, any other Greek hero, although one associated with the Trojan War is more likely.

Gerhard was the first to suggest that mirrors with compositions of the Hopkins type depict the myth of the Three Kabiri.[19] It is certainly true that by the Hellenistic period the Dioskouroi had become very closely identified with the Kabiri;[20] however, it is highly significant that on the mirrors discussed above, the inscriptions identify the figures as well-known Greek heroes, particularly those connected with the Trojan War. Not one of the inscriptions refers to figures associated with the cult of the Kabiri. The myth of the third Kabiros was primarily based on Lemnos and in Macedonia, and neither in those areas nor else-

where do we find representations of the Three Kabiri comparable to those on the mirrors.[21] It is reasonable, therefore, to conclude that the mirrors of the Hopkins type, which group the Dioskouroi with so many different individuals, were not intended to suggest any specific mythological event, but simply reflect the contemporary ecumenical handling of Greek mythology.[22]

Mirrors like the Hopkins example, which depict the tunic-clad Dioskouroi, must be approximately contemporary with those mirrors upon which the tunic-clad Dioskouroi comprise the total composition (see preceding entry). Thus our mirror probably dates to the later third or second century B.C.

1. J. D. Beazley, *JHS* 69 (1949):16–17, dated to the third century; also *EVP*, 130–32; *Numismatic Chronicle* I (1942):1–7.

2. R. Herbig, *StEtr* 24 (1955–56):183–205; Rebuffat-Emmanuel, 359 (discs), 360–61 (handles), 462–69, 597, dated 300–250 B.C. L. Warren *AJA* 68 (1964):39–40] supports Herbig's dating of the first century B.C.; DePuma, *StEtr* 41 (1973):167–70.

3. M. Renard, *Latomus* 28 (1957):411–17. The stachelkranz can be found in Greek metalwork from the fourth and third centuries B.C. See a bowl and pyxis from Asia Minor in A. Oliver, *Silver for the Gods* (Toledo, 1977), 40, no. 10, and 53, no. 21; a silver strainer from Derveni in M. Andronikos, *The Greek Museums* (Athens, 1975), 282, no. 17; also a silver gilt harness ornament of the first century B.C. in X. Gorbunova and I. Saverkina, *Greek and Roman Antiquities in the Hermitage* (Leningrad, 1975), no. 101.

4. Rebuffat-Emmanuel, nos. 1305, 1315 (Gerhard, vol. 3, pl. 263.6); 1318, 914, "inedit," and 464ff. See also Gerhard, vol. 3, pls. 263.2, 264.2, 266, 267, and pls. 259.3 and 263.1, where the nude male is the second figure from our left. P. Lebel, *Catalogue des collections archéologiques de Besançon V. Les bronzes figurés* (Paris, 1959), 74, no. 286, pl. 97.

5. Most recently studied by K. Phillips, *StEtr* 36 (1968), 165–68; DePuma, *StEtr* 41 (1973):167–70.

6. See note 17.

7. Gerhard, vol. 3, 272, pl. 255B; 273, pl. 255C; 332, pl. 257C; Rebuffat-Emmanuel, no. 1291 (Gerhard, vol. 3, pl. 257C.1); R. Noll, *ÖJh* 29 (1935):159–63, no. 3, fig. 60.

8. Rebuffat-Emmanuel, no. 1291. See Renard, *Latomus* 28 (1957):411–17, where an uninscribed scene is identified as a Judgment of Paris, although Renard admits that "Turan" is a male.

9. Label, *Catalogue*, 73, no. 285, pl. 96.

10. Rebuffat-Emmanuel, no. 1317 (Gerhard, vol. 3, pl. 277.5). See also Gerhard, vol. 3, pl. 273.A.2. Phillips, *StEtr* 36 (1968):166–68 and bibliography; DePuma, *StEtr* 41 (1973):162–63, nos. 2, 3, pls. LII, LIII; R. Thouvenot, *Catalogue des figurines et objets de bronze du musée archéologique de Madrid* (Paris, 1927), 109, no. 561, pl. 23.

11. Rebuffat-Emmanuel, no. 1291.

12. Gerhard, vol. 3, 284, pl. 263.1.

13. DePuma, *StEtr* 41 (1973):162 n. 7, and no. 2, pl. 52.

14. Phillips, *StEtr* 36 (1968):165.

15. Ibid., 167.

16. Gerhard, vol. 5, 108. The other combinations are: Palamedes, Clytemnestra, Odysseos, Menelaos; Iolaos, Minerva, Herakles, Caran; Palamedes, Ajax, Menelaos, Diomedes; Menelaos, Agamemnon, Eliraic, Alexander. See also Noll, *ÖJh* 29 (1935):159–63, no. 3, fig. 60: Chryseis, Menelaos, Minerva, Diomedes. See also L. Bonfante, *GettyMusJ* 8 (1980):147–55.

17. Gerhard, vol. 5, 108.

18. Ibid., vol. 3, pl. 260.A.

19. Gerhard, vol. 3, 282, 294; D. Levi, *NSc* 6, 4 (1928):57–59; *NSc* 6, 7 (1931):209–11; S. Marstrander, *Symbolae Osloenses Supplement* 11 (1942):101–11; *DarSag*, 260, and 769ff.

20. B. Hemberg, *Die Kabiren* (Uppsala, 1950), 98–99, 144–45, 268. For their identification in Alexandria, see P. Fraser, *Ptolemaic Alexandria* (Oxford, 1972), 207.

21. Hemberg, *Die Kabiren*, 166, 207, 275. We know too little about the date or appearance of the images Pausanias (3.24.5) saw at Brasiae; see Roscher, *Ausführlichen Lexikon der griechischen und römischen Mythologie* (Leipzig, 1884–86), I.1.1163.

22. See O. Vessberg [*Medelhausmuseet Bulletin* 4 (1964):54–56.], who discusses an inscribed stachelkranz mirror that illustrates a mythological episode including Diomedes and Odysseos. Since this mirror constitutes the only example of this composition labeled in this specific manner, Vessberg suggests that the inscription came from the Italian theater, perhaps a comedy or mime.

Metalwork

ROMAN

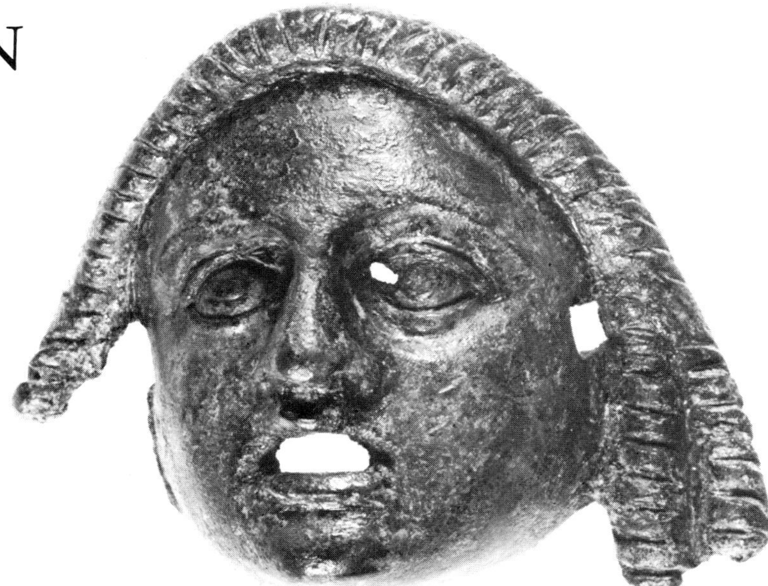

52. Mask Appliqué

(first c. B.C.—first c. A.D.)

428. Purchased in Rome or Naples in 1906–9. Bronze. Ht, 5.6 cm; w, 7.8 cm; depth at top, 2.6 cm. Two square holes at each ear and a small round hole at crown for attachment. Chip missing from inside corner of left eye. Lock of hair at right side broken way. Back hollow.

Hair brushed back from face, forming roll at forehead and two twisted ringlets at each ear. Regularly spaced grooves over hair. Eyes gaze upward, with contour of iris incised. Open mouth.

The size and placement of the holes indicate that the mask was a decorative appliqué. It was probably attached to a large wood and bronze chest or heating unit similar to those that have been recovered from Pompeii.[1]

This appliqué reproduces one of the masks used in Greek New Comedy, the form that developed in the late fourth century B.C. and continued into the first century A.D. The New Comedy plays were comedies of manners, often dealing with romantic dilemmas and based on a few stock themes and conventional characters. The comedies, especially those of Menander (290–240), were popular in Italy from the second century B.C. and inspired Latin versions, such as those of Terence.[2]

Since the characters of New Comedy and of their Latin counterparts were fairly standardized, the actors needed only a limited range of masks, which were probably made of linen and stucco on a wood or cork framework. None of these have survived, and so our information about them is primarily derived from the writings of Pollux (iv.15.143–54), who lived under Commodus (ca. A.D. 190) but who had available to him Hellenistic commentaries that are now lost. Pollux lists eleven masks for beardless young men, of which *apalos,* or delicate youth with soft effeminate features, seems best to describe our example.[3] Whatever the classification of our specific mask, the type was clearly popular, since it appears on a number of reliefs and oscilla from Pompeii.[4]

During the late Hellenistic period, the theater enjoyed particular popularity in the cities around the Bay of Naples. In 44 B.C., for example, Brutus commented on the large number of traveling companies in this area, many of which were performing both Greek New Comedy and Latin plays.[5] It is not surprising, therefore, that the excavations at Pompeii and Herculaneum have yielded abundant objects with theatrical subject matter. In addition to mask appliqués on furniture, we find masks in wallpainting and on marble reliefs that were set up in gardens[6] or suspended between the columns of a peristyle.[7]

1. de Ridder, vol. 1, 112, no. 830, pl. 56; Ward-Perkins and Claridge, 172, no. 154, and 177, no. 167; Boucher, *Bronzes romains,* 14, no. 26; Pernice, vol. 5, pls. 52–56; E. Dwyer, in *Pompeii and the Vesuvian Landscape* (Washington, D.C., 1979), 60.
2. Bieber, *Theater,* 148–56.
3. A. Pickard Cambridge, *The Dramatic Festivals of Athens,* 2d ed. (Oxford, 1968), 224–26; M. Bieber, *RE* XIV.2 (1930), 2097.
4. Our mask is similar to a mask on the Lateran Menander relief that has been variously identified as the *melas* or *apalos.* See T. B. L. Webster, *Greek Theater Production* (London, 1956), 75, 78; Bieber, *Theater,* 89, fig. 317. See Naples comedy relief in Bieber, *Theater,* 92, fig. 324; Ward-Perkins and Claridge, 145, no. 78; A. Sogliano, *NSc* 5, 4 (1907), 588, fig. 37.
5. Plutarch, *Brutus* 21.5; Pickard-Cambridge, *Dramatic Festivals,* 296.
6. See discussion of item no. 14.
7. Ward-Perkins and Claridge, 145, no. 78; A. Sogliano, *NSc* 5, 4 (1907), 588, fig. 37, and 591; Spinazzola, pl. 57; and see entry no. 15.

53. Dolphin Handle

(first c. B.C.–first c. A.D.)

HT 410. Helen Tanzer Collection. Bronze. L, 12.1 cm; max ht, 5.5 cm. Cracked across right dolphin's body.

Two dolphins kiss, their open beaks separated by a ring molding. The eyes are punched; the lids, beaks, and body scales incised. Each tail terminates in a lotus with hatched leaves. The handle surface is convex, except for two concave channels across the beaks. The underside is hollow.

The design is attractive and functional, since the second and third fingers slide comfortably along the grooves of the beaks. On a number of similar handles, bronze rings have been slipped through the loops formed by the dolphins' tails, thereby providing a means of attachment that is best suited for the handle of a small chest.[1]

The closest parallels to our handle come from Pompeii, together with a variation on which heads of satyrs appear at the base of the tails.[2] This type of handle continued to be made with little change, but with decreasing quality of execution, into the second and third centuries A.D. On many of these later examples from Gallo-Roman workshops,[3] the ring molding becomes a round object[4] or a bust of Minerva.[5]

The Greeks traditionally regarded the dolphin as man's special friend,[6] and for this reason and because of the animal's appealing habits and appearance, it was always a favorite artistic motif. The dolphin was depicted both on water jugs and on wine vessels, a logical association since Dionysos was traditionally linked with the sea.[7] Despite the frequency of its appearance, however, the dolphin was rarely depicted with accuracy. The mistakes on our handle are typical: the dorsal fin is placed on top of the head instead of in the center of the back; the flippers are missing; the body has an exaggerated curve; and the tail flukes are placed vertically rather than horizontally.[8] Although in actuality the dolphin's tail continues the almost uncurving line of the body, until the late fourth century artists regularly showed the tail pointing downward;[9] after this time the tail usually was turned upward, and in the Hellenistic period it was occasionally transformed into an acanthos or lotus blossom.[10] At this time, too, scales were added to the body.

With the blossoming of decorative metalwork in the Hellenistic and Roman periods, the dolphin enjoyed tremendous popularity. At Pompeii the dolphin appears on lamp handles[11] and on the feet of candelabra[12] and lampstands.[13] The dolphin also appears with other animals, hybrid beings, and floral designs on the handles of phialai,[14] jugs,[15] and lamps.[16]

1. G. Faider-Feytmans, *Les bronzes romains de Belgique* (Mainz, 1979), 120, nos. 192–94, pl. 79.
2. Ward-Perkins and Claridge, 198–99, no. 248.
3. Faider-Feytmans, *Les bronzes*, 120–24, nos. 192–214, pls. 79–85.
4. P. Lebel, *Catalogue des collections archéologiques de Besançon V: Les bronzes figurés* (Paris, 1959 and 1961), 72, no. 258, pl. XCIII.4.
5. H. Menzel, *Die römische Bronzen aus Deutschland I: Speyer* (Mainz, 1960), 51, nos. 87–88, pl. 55; Menzel, *Die römische Bronzen aus Deutschland II: Trier* (Mainz, 1966), 123, nos. 302–4, pl. 96.
6. K. Shepherd, *The Fish-Tailed Monster in Greek and Etruscan Art* (New York, 1940), 85–91; and full discussion in E. Stebbins, *The Dolphin in the Literature and Art of Greece and Rome* (Menasha, Wisconsin, 1927), 59–96.
7. M. Davies, in *Athens Comes of Age: From Solon to Salamis* (Princeton, 1978), 72–81.
8. Stebbins, *Dolphin*, 9–18.
9. B. S. Ridgway, *Classical Sculpture: Museum of Art, Rhode Island School of Design* (Providence, 1972), 58–59, no. 21.
10. Stebbins, *Dolphin*, 12.
11. Spinazzola, pl. 293.
12. Pernice, vol. 4, 20, fig. 31; 56, fig. 74.
13. Ibid., 20, fig. 30.
14. U. Höckmann, *Antike Bronzen* (Kassel, 1972), 39, no. 90, pl. 27.
15. J. Balty, *BMusArt*, 4, 37 (1965):13–16.
16. H. Menzel, *Antike Lampen* (Mainz, 1969), 121, no. 715, fig. 102.

54. Duck Hasp

(first c. B.C.–A.D.)

HT 1217. Helen Tanzer Collection. Bronze. L, 9.9 cm; w, 2.3 cm; ht projection beneath head, 1.2 cm. Iron deposit on hinge.

Flat, rectangular hasp with hinge partly broken away. End terminates in duck head turned back onto neck. Beneath head is open rectangular projection. Incisions for details of duck's bill and for feathers, which are arranged over back of hasp in four rows of three feathers each.

The hinge on this hasp was attached to the lid of a small chest. To secure the lid, the projection on the underside of the hasp was aligned between matching units on the chest, and a pin was then slipped through all three elements.

The turned-back bird head was in use in the Near East from the third millennium.[1] The motif appears in Minoan art beginning in Middle Minoan times and is familiar from the crystal vase of Shaft Grave VI,[2] as well as from Mycenaean ivories[3] and vasepainting.[4] The motif reappears in Greek metalwork of the sixth century, on the horizontal handle of a hydria (ca. 520 B.C.) whose vertical handle belongs to a well-known type, representing a youth between rams and lions.[5] Subsequently, the motif is used at the base of handles on Apulian kraters and their bronze counterparts.[6] In Pompeii the turned-back bird head appears both as a couch appliqué[7] and on a dipper.[8]

1. See A. Kozloff, ed., *Animals in Ancient Art from the Leo Mildenberg Collection* (Cleveland, 1980), 27, no. 12 bis.

2. S. Hood, *The Arts in Prehistoric Greece* (New York, 1978), 142, fig. 34.

3. Ibid., 127.

4. J. L. Benson, *Horse, Bird and Man. The Origins of Greek Painting* (Amherst, 1970), 61, pl. XVII, fig. 1. See also item no. 132.

5. D. K. Hill, *AJA* 62 (1958):194, 198, 201, no. 8, pl. 51.

6. H. Sichtermann, *Griechische Vasen in Unteritalien: JdI Bilderhefte 3 and 4* (Tübingen, 1966), 33–35, nos. K36–38, pls. 52–57.

7. Ward-Perkins and Claridge, 178, no. 172.

8. Ibid., 213, no. 323.

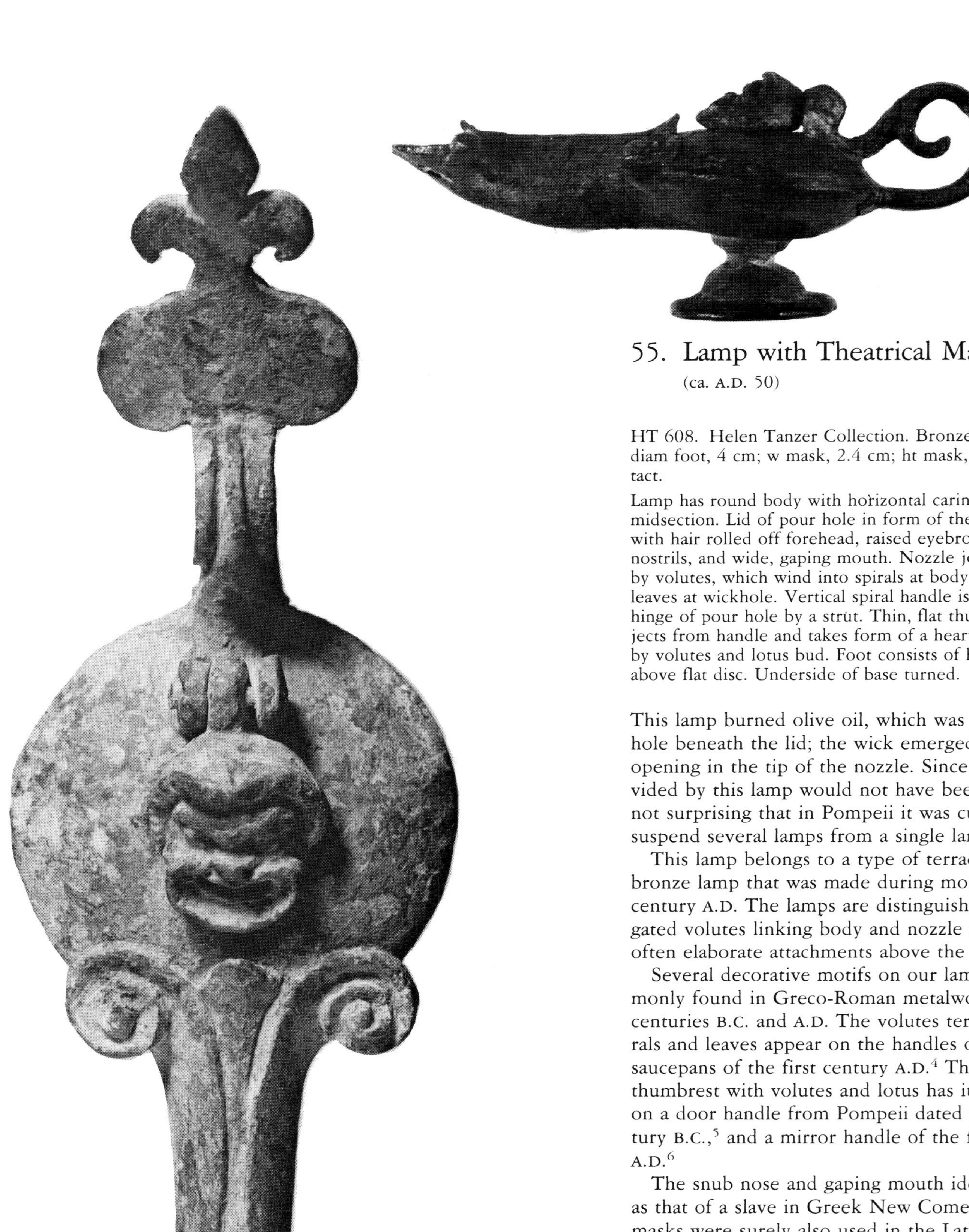

55. Lamp with Theatrical Mask

(ca. A.D. 50)

HT 608. Helen Tanzer Collection. Bronze. L, 17.7 cm; diam foot, 4 cm; w mask, 2.4 cm; ht mask, 2.6 cm. Intact.

Lamp has round body with horizontal carination around midsection. Lid of pour hole in form of theatrical mask with hair rolled off forehead, raised eyebrows, flaring nostrils, and wide, gaping mouth. Nozzle joined to body by volutes, which wind into spirals at body and into leaves at wickhole. Vertical spiral handle is connected to hinge of pour hole by a strut. Thin, flat thumbrest projects from handle and takes form of a heart surmounted by volutes and lotus bud. Foot consists of half round above flat disc. Underside of base turned.

This lamp burned olive oil, which was poured into the hole beneath the lid; the wick emerged from the opening in the tip of the nozzle. Since the light provided by this lamp would not have been great, it is not surprising that in Pompeii it was customary to suspend several lamps from a single lampstand.[1]

This lamp belongs to a type of terracotta and bronze lamp that was made during most of the first century A.D. The lamps are distinguished by the elongated volutes linking body and nozzle and by the often elaborate attachments above the handle.[2]

Several decorative motifs on our lamp are commonly found in Greco-Roman metalwork of the first centuries B.C. and A.D. The volutes terminating in spirals and leaves appear on the handles of ladles[3] and saucepans of the first century A.D.[4] The heart-shaped thumbrest with volutes and lotus has its counterpart on a door handle from Pompeii dated to the first century B.C.,[5] and a mirror handle of the first century A.D.[6]

The snub nose and gaping mouth identify our mask as that of a slave in Greek New Comedy. The same masks were surely also used in the Latin comedies, which were especially popular in southern Italy between the second century B.C. and first century A.D.[7]

1. Spinazzola, pl. 293.
2. H. B. Walters, *Catalogue of the Lamps in the British Museum* (London, 1914), 122, no. 808, pl. XXVI; Ward-Perkins and Claridge, 175, nos. 159–60; H. Menzel, *Antike Lampen* (Mainz, 1969), 25–28, 106.
3. A. Oliver, *Silver for the Gods* (Toledo, 1977), 138, no. 91
4 Ibid., 141, nos 93–94.
5 Ward-Perkins and Claridge, 176, no. 166.
6. Oliver, *Silver for the Gods*, 139, no. 92.
7. See discussion of items nos. 14 and 52.

56. Beaked Oinochoe with Griffin Handle

(first c. A.D.)

9242. Brooklyn Museum Gift. Bronze. Ht with handle, 17.4 cm; ht without handle, 15 cm; diam foot, 3.9 cm. Foot and handle cast separately. Intact.

Spouted jug with slight bulge between incised grooves at juncture of neck and shoulder. Body has horizontal shoulder and marked taper to foot. Foot, comprised of cyma recta over toros, was separately cast and turned and has a raised collar that fits onto pear-shaped tip of body. Handle ornament, rendered in relief, consists of clusters of acanthos leaves. At top of handle is protome of winged griffin, whose forearms lie along rim. At base of handle is gorgon head with silvered eyes; palmette beneath.

Bibliography: D. K. Hill, *Greek and Roman Metalwork, Walters Art Gallery* (Baltimore, 1976), no. 34.

The bronze beaked jug with elaborate handle, and occasionally with tongue ornament on the body, was popular over much of the Roman Empire between the first and third centuries A.D. The vessels are primarily distinguished by their handles, which usually have a floral pattern on the back and figural motifs at rim and base. A handle in the Walters Art Gallery has a griffin, as on our rim, coupled with a child's head at the base.[1] The Medusa head at the base of our handle has been paired with a variety of motifs at the rim: a griffin,[2] a triton and dolphins,[3] a horse,[4] swan's head,[5] and eagle.[6] Other combinations are known.[7]

The Hopkins vase was cast in three pieces (body, handle, base; see radiograph), a method of manufacture that identifies the jug as Italian; in Gallic workshops the neck and body were cast separately.[8] The bulge at the base of the neck, the horizontal shoulder,

and the marked taper of the body find their closest parallels among the jugs from Pompeii that were classified by Nuber as examples of Type G (Canterbury).[9] This type is possibly of Egyptian origin and was manufactured in Italy and Gaul from the time of the Flavians. The type continued to be made in the Danubean region into the third century A.D.

In many parts of the Roman Empire the long-beaked jug is found in tombs together with long-handled pateras of the type represented by item no. 58.[10] Votive reliefs pair these two vessels with a phiale, an association that suggests that the vessels were for religious use, perhaps for washing the hands before sacrificing or dining.[11] In Italy the jugs have been found in dining areas without accompanying pateras and thus could have served a secular function as wine or water containers.[12]

1. D. K. Hill, *Greek and Roman Metalware, Walters Art Gallery* (Baltimore, 1976), no. 32; J. Balty, *BMusArt* 4, 37 (1965):16, no. 1.

2. E. Babelon and J. Blanchet, *Catalogue de bronzes antiques de la Bibliothèque Nationale* (Paris, 1895), 569, no. 1390.

3. Balty, *BMusArt* 4, 37 (1965):14–16.

4. Babelon-Blanchet, *Catalogue*, 569, no. 1391.

5. de Ridder, vol. 2, 116, no. 2766, pl. 99.

6. S. Tassinari, *Gallia Supplement* 29 (1975):60, no. 152, pl. 29.

7. Ibid., 61, pl. 30; de Ridder, vol. 2, 115, no. 2765, pl. 99; Spinnazola, pl. 272; Balty, *BMusArt* 4, 137 (1965):19, no. 6, with Dionysos, satyr; see also entry no. 57.

8. H. U. Nuber, *RGKomm* 53 (1972):60–61.

9. Ibid., 60–73.

10. Ibid., 10–28; A. Radnoti, *Die römischen Bronzegefäss von Pannonien* (Budapest, 1938), 137–44, and nos. 69, 71, pls 13, 47, 48. See also entry for item no. 58.

11. Nuber, *RGKomm* 53 (1972):92–95, 99, 104, 118.

12. Ibid., 85.

83 METALWORK: ROMAN

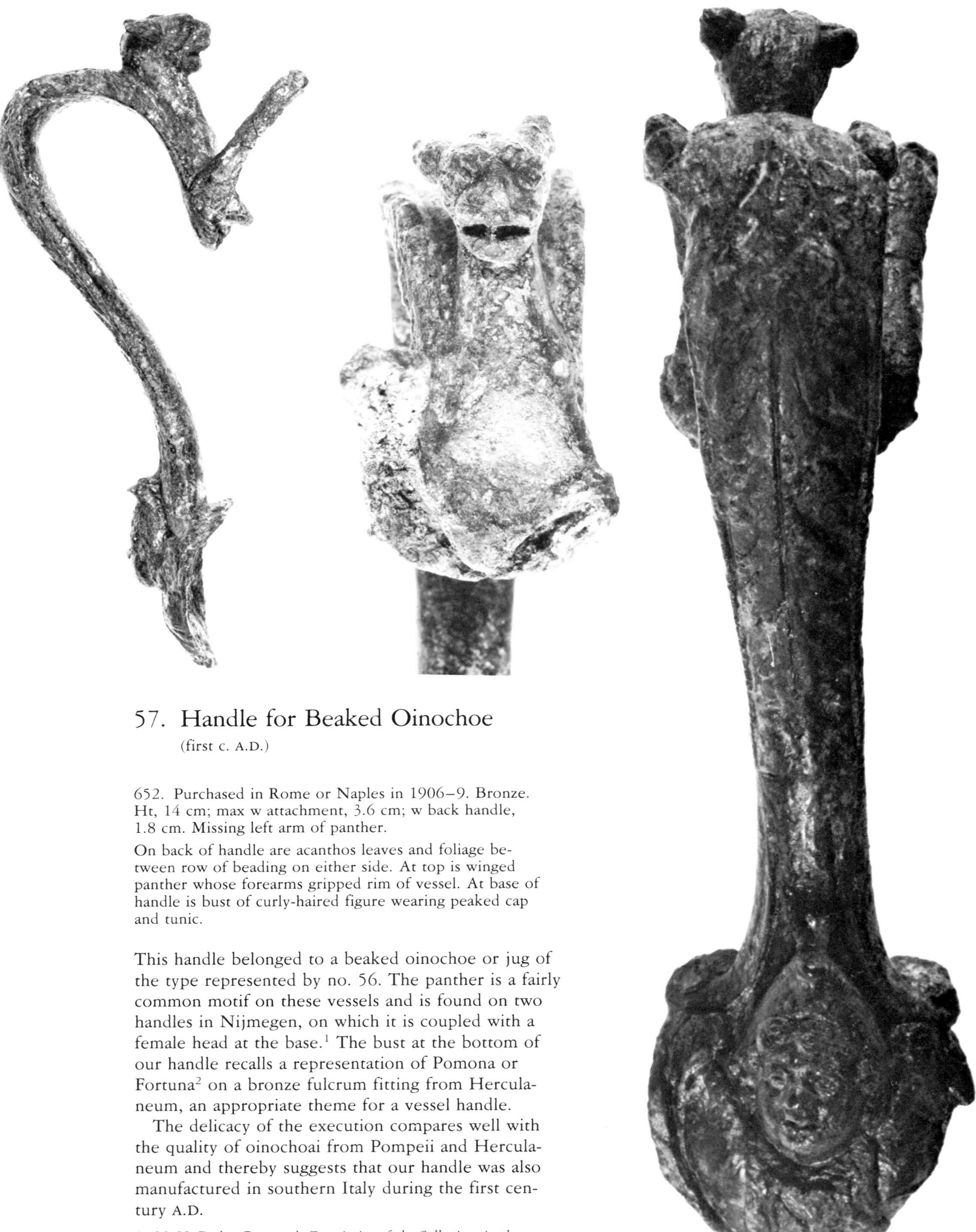

57. Handle for Beaked Oinochoe

(first c. A.D.)

652. Purchased in Rome or Naples in 1906–9. Bronze. Ht, 14 cm; max w attachment, 3.6 cm; w back handle, 1.8 cm. Missing left arm of panther.

On back of handle are acanthos leaves and foliage between row of beading on either side. At top is winged panther whose forearms gripped rim of vessel. At base of handle is bust of curly-haired figure wearing peaked cap and tunic.

This handle belonged to a beaked oinochoe or jug of the type represented by no. 56. The panther is a fairly common motif on these vessels and is found on two handles in Nijmegen, on which it is coupled with a female head at the base.[1] The bust at the bottom of our handle recalls a representation of Pomona or Fortuna[2] on a bronze fulcrum fitting from Herculaneum, an appropriate theme for a vessel handle.

The delicacy of the execution compares well with the quality of oinochoai from Pompeii and Herculaneum and thereby suggests that our handle was also manufactured in southern Italy during the first century A.D.

1. M. H. P. den Boesterd, *Description of the Collections in the Rijksmuseum GM.KAM at Nijmegen. Vol. 5, The Bronze Vessels* (Nijmegen, 1956), 65, nos. 225–26, pls. X, XVI, attributed to southern Italy.

2. Ward-Perkins and Claridge, 178, no. 173.

58. Ram Handle from Patera

(first C. A.D.)

9111. Probably purchased in Rome or Naples in 1906–9. Bronze. L, 15.3 cm; diam handle, 2.7 cm; max w curving end, 6.9 cm. Hollow cast. End adjoining bowl chipped.

Tubular handle with seven channels. At one end is ring molding with flanged edges adjacent to ram's head. Other end flares into curving extension, which was attached to side of bowl. Incised on top of handle is wavy line flanked by groups of punch marks and short, oblique grooves. Incised on underside of handle is word *aphos,* followed by horizontal line with curved tip, two oblique lines, and horizontal line flanked by four oblique lines on each side.

The curved end of this handle was soldered to the side of a low cast bowl. Examples of these phialai or paterae have been found all over the Roman Empire,[1] often in tombs, where the paterae are paired with beaked oinochoai of the type of nos. 56 and 57.[2] The use of these two vessels may have varied regionally, but it is thought that in Italy the oinochoe and patera were used in domestic cult for ritual ablutions before eating.[3]

The ram's head and the incised garland identify our handle as an example of Nuber's Type G (Canterbury), which Nuber believes was introduced into Italy from Egypt around A.D. 50.[4] Comparable examples from Pompeii[5] as well as the Greek inscription on the underside of our piece suggest that the Hopkins handle was made in Italy during the latter half of the first century A.D.

The ram's head is a traditional Greek ornamental motif that appears on vessels from the archaic period.[6] Its first appearance on a phiale handle comes from Derveni and is dated to the last half of the fourth century.[7]

1. See discussion of no. 56, especially H. U. Nuber, *RGKomm* 53 (1972):10–28. See also C. C. Edgar, *Catalogue général des antiquités égyptiennes du Musée du Caire: Greek Moulds* (Cairo, 1903), 65, nos. 32, 276, pl. XIX, for plaster mold probably from Memphis.

2. A. Radnoti, *Die römischen Bronzegefäss von Pannonien* (Budapest, 1938), 81–88.

3. Nuber, *RGKomm* 53 (1972):90–96.

4. Ibid., 72. M. H. P. den Boesterd, *Description of the Collections in the Rijksmuseum GM. KAM at Nijmegen.* vol. 5, *The Bronze Vessels* (Nijmegen, 1956), 25–26, no. 68, pl. IV.

5. A. Maiuri, *La casa del Menandro e il suo tesoro di argenteria* (Rome, 1936), 446, figs. 173–74.

6. U. Höckmann, *Antike Bronzen* (Kassel, 1972), 21, no. 25, pl. 6, on handle of ca. 500–475 B.C.

7. Nuber, *RGKomm* 53 (1972):35, pl. 1. See also a ram's head on the handle of a fire shovel from Palestrina of 350–325 B.C. See also Brendel, 336, fig. 260.

59. Statuette of Attis

(first c. A.D.)

1146. Probably purchased in Rome or Naples in 1906–9. Bronze. Ht, 9.5 cm; w between arms, 6.8 cm. Tips of toes broken off or miscast. Face gashed.

Chubby boy steps forward on right foot, right arm extended, holding penis in right hand; left hand holds lagobolon at side. Belted long-sleeved tunic flares open to expose stomach. Trousers fastened with row of four buttons down each leg. Curly hair beneath Phrygian cap.

Attis was a mythical Phrygian shepherd boy who castrated himself in frenzied devotion to the Anatolian mother goddess Cybele. Ovid relates that the boy was transformed into a pine tree,[1] but other traditions tell us that he was reborn.[2]

Attis and Cybele were very popular in Hellenistic Anatolia, where Attis was often represented as a seminude child and was frequently conflated with Eros and Dionysos.[3] The cult was introduced into Rome before 191 B.C., when a temple to Cybele or Magna Mater was constructed on the Palatine.[4] The divinities enjoyed tremendous popularity in Italy during the first century A.D. and there are numerous depictions of Attis on candelabras, handles, appliqués, table supports, and statuettes of that time from Pompeii and Herculaneum.[5]

Our figure alludes to the festival of the Tristia, which Claudius introduced to coincide with the March equinox and hence the symbolic revival of vegetation.[6] In the first days of the festival, the death of Attis was mourned with the deposit of a pine tree on the Palatine, the flagellation of the galli or priests, and, in early years, with the castration of new devotees. March 25th was a day of celebration, surely of the rebirth of Attis, and by the second century A.D., if not earlier, was called the Hilaria. The celebratory rites were accompanied by feasting, dancing, and probably theatrical performances of legends associated with Cybele and Attis.[7]

A type of bronze figurine that represents Attis as an animated boy has been called Attis hilaris, because the figure probably alludes to the festivities of the Hilaria. Typically, the figure wears the garments of the Hopkins figurine: the Phrygian cap, laced anaxurides, and a tunica manicata that blows open to reveal torso and genitals.[8] One foot is usually advanced or he

dances vigorously on tiptoe in a manner reminiscent of, and probably influenced by, the pose of the dancing Lar.[9] Attis's right hand is usually upraised and may hold the lagobolon (or staff), cornucopia, or grapes. The left hand is normally lowered but is upraised in examples where Attis holds a mask above his head in allusion to his association with Dionysos.[10] The Hopkins example is unusual in that Attis is shown castrated, with the penis in the right hand, while the lowered left hand holds the lagobolon.

Although statuettes of Attis hilaris have been found in Anatolia,[11] most examples are Roman bronze figurines, which may have been attachments to candelabra or, in the cases of the small versions, souvenirs purchased during the festival.[12]

The cult of Cybele and Attis spread over most of the Roman Empire and was especially popular in Gaul, where several bronze statuettes of Attis hilaris have been found in second-century (A.D.) contexts.[13]

1. Ovid, *Fast.* 4. lines 221–44; *Met.* 10. lines 103ff.; *Ibis* lines 505ff.

2. M. J. Vermaseren, *The Legend of Attis in Greek and Roman Art* (London, 1966), 45.

3. C. Picard, *ArchEph* (1953–54): 1–18, pt. 1; E. Töpperwein, *Terrakotten von Pergamon: Pergamenische Forschungen,* 3 (1976): 87, no. 390, pl. 55; A. Laumonier, *Exploration archéologique de Délos 23: Les figurines de terre cuite* (Paris, 1956), 137–38, nos. 364–69, pl. 40.

4. J. A. Hanson, *Roman Theater Temples* (Princeton, 1959), 14; M. J. Vermaseren, *Cybele and Attis* (London, 1977), 41.

5. Vespasian rebuilt the temple destroyed in 62 [see V. Tran Tam Tinh, *Le cult des divinités orientales à Herculanum* (Leiden, 1971), 25; Tran Tam Tinh, *Neue Forschungen in Pompeii* (Recklinghausen, 1975), 279–83].

6. F. Cumont, *Les religions orientales dans le paganisme romain* (Paris, 1929), 89; Vermaseren, *Legend of Attis,* 39–40.

7. See F. Cumont, *Les religions orientales,* 94; Vermaseren, *Cybele and Attis,* 114–16, 119, 123; Vermaseren, *Legend of Attis,* 43–44; Hanson, *Roman Theater Temples,* 15–16.

8. de Ridder, vol. 1, 12, no. 35, pl. 6; Vermaseren, *Legend of Attis,* 46–53.

9. Vermaseren, *Legend of Attis,* 55.

10. Ibid., 55–57; de Ridder, vol. 1, 96, no. 694, pl. 48; E. Babelon and J. Blanchet, *Catalogue des bronzes antiques de la Bibliothèque Nationale* (Paris, 1895), 432, no. 980; Tran Tam Tinh, *Forschungen,* 281.

11. Vermaseren, *Legend of Attis,* 48, 57.

12. U. Höckmann, *Antike Bronzen in Kassel* (Mainz, 1972), 34, no. 73, pl. 21.

13. H. Menzel, *Die römische Bronzen aus Deutschland II: Trier* (Mainz, 1966) 28, no. 58 a, pl. 99.

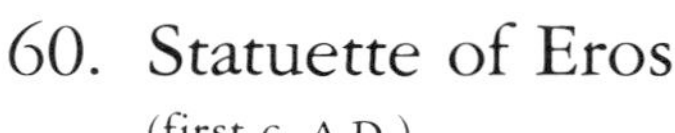

60. Statuette of Eros

(first c. A.D.)

K 24. Kemper Simpson Collection. Bronze. Ht, 14.5 cm; ht head, 3.2 cm; depth (wingtips to breast), 5.8 cm. Torso hollow cast. Missing right hand, left arm from elbow, left leg below knee, left wing. Modern tenon under right heel. Inlay missing from pupils and nipples.

Nude baby Eros alights on toes of right foot; left leg was extended behind him. Head gazes upward in direction of uplifted right arm; left arm was at side and slightly behind torso. Plump body with protruding belly and incised nipples, originally inlaid. Round fleshy face with thin ridges for eyebrows, indented pupils, snub nose, jowly cheeks, and short, thick lips. Hair on crown of head braided and tied at forehead in top knot. On brow is curl in low relief; locks at side and back fall to shoulders in individually striated ringlets. Short wing has long primaries, single row of semicircular binaries, irregular rows of tertiaries. Edges of wing hatched; inside smooth.

The running or alighting Eros is first encountered in the later Hellenistic period, when he appeared, for example, among the Myrina terracottas.[1] The subject became popular for bronze figurines of late Hellenistic and Roman date, and examples have been found in Italy, Britain,[2] Germany,[3] Gaul,[4] and Switzerland.[5] The smaller statuettes, which are only a few centimeters high, hold torches or vessels and were probably votives or souvenirs. The larger examples have the size of the Hopkins Eros, but can also be as large as a meter.[6] It is thought that the latter figurines served as table lampstands or candelabra, since at least one intact example from Boscoreale holds in his uplifted hand a torch upon which a candle could have been impaled.[7] The lowered arm of another figurine holds a vine branch that could have supported a lampstand.[8]

The chubby body of our example, and especially the hairstyle, fleshy cheeks, and short lips, are all paralleled on figurines of Eros and other children from Pompeii and Herculaneum.[9] Particularly noteworthy is the delicate treatment of the hair and the eyes, which, in the manner of better-preserved contemporary figurines, would have been silvered.

Dancing figures with uplifted arms, such as the Erotes, satyrs, and fauns,[10] may have inspired representations of the dancing Lar or Lar compitalis,[11] who was a protective deity of the crossroads. It is thought that, as part of Augustus's revival of domestic cults, a type of dancing Lar was introduced that consisted of a tunic-clad youth bearing a rhyton in his uplifted right hand and a phiale in his lowered left hand.

1. E. Pottier and S. Reinach, *La nécropole de Myrina* (Paris, 1887), 323–28, pls. XI–XVII; J. Charbonneaux, *Les terres cuites grecques* (Paris, 1963), 87, pl. XXVII.

2. J. Toynbee, *Art in Roman Britain* (London, 1962), 130, no. 13, pl. 32, perhaps from a workshop in Italy or southern Gaul.

3. H. Menzel, *Die römische Bronzen aus Deutschland II: Trier* (Mainz, 1966), 24, no. 51, pls. 22–23.

4. H. Rolland, *Gallia* 34 (1976): 406, fig. 26, and 459, fig. 25; H. Rolland, *Gallia Supplement* 18 (Paris, 1965), 74, no. 115; Mitten, *RISD*, 184, no. 62 (Mitten suggests it may have been made in Germany); Boucher, *Bronzes romains*, 4–6, nos. 7–10. See also F. Braemer, *Actes du IVe colloque international sur les bronzes antiques* (Lyons, 1977), 41–52.

5. A. Leibendgut, *Die römische Bronzen der Schweiz, III: Bern, West Schweiz und Wallis* (Mainz, 1980), 35–37, no. 29, pl. 34.

6. J. Sieveking, *Die Bronzen der Sammlung Loeb* (Munich, 1913), 59, pl. 24; *Sotheby catalogue*, May 19, 1979, no. 200 (49.5 cm); Hill, *Bronzes*, 34, no. 64, pl. 17.

7. Richter, *Bronzes* 85, no. 131, from Boscoreale. See also Toynbee, *Art in Roman Britain*, 130, no. 13, pl. 32.

8. Richter, *Bronzes*, 119, no. 228.

9. Spinazzola, pl. 250; V. Spinazzola, *Pompeii alla luce degli scavi nuovi di Via dell' Abbondanza I* (Rome, 1953), 400, fig. 456.

10. Pernice, vol. 4, 3, fig. 2.

11. Mitten, *RISD*, 190, no. 67; *OCD*, s. v. "Lares."

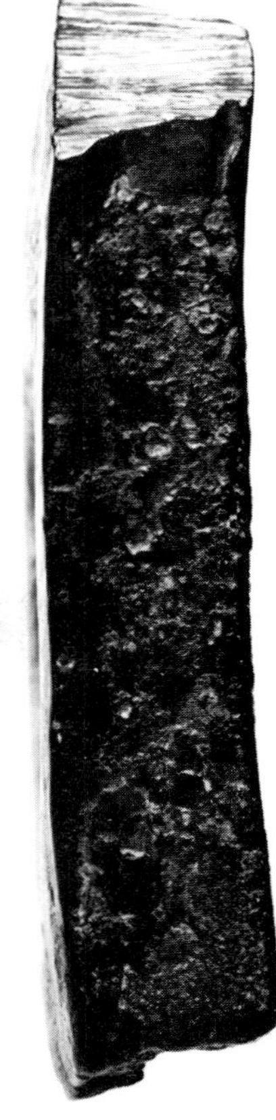

61. Matrix for Cuirass Pteryx

(first–second c. A.D.)

9159. Formerly Robinson Collection, acquired from Ritsos Collection. Bronze. L, 9.4 cm; w, 6.9 cm; th, 1.7 cm; cast ht, 6.9 cm; w, 6.7 cm. Smooth vertical sides; rough beneath. Lower right edge of underside sliced away in modern times.

Cast

U-shaped field described by two parallel ridges enclosing a row of raised knobs. Within this frame is a frontal lion-griffin head. Large eyes with pronounced eyelids; open muzzle with lolling tongue. Muscles of face rendered as schematic, symmetrical bulges. Upright, pointed ears. Ridges for whiskers and mane. Pair of S-shaped horns curve upward from midpoint of hairline.

Bibliography: D. M. Robinson, in *Classical Studies Presented to Edward Capps* (Princeton, 1936), 306–13; E. R. Williams, *AJA* 81 (1977), 233–35.

A relief made by hammering a bronze sheet into this matrix would have been used to decorate one of the many pteryges, or flaps, that formed part of the cuirass of a Roman soldier. The upper torso would have been covered by a leather or bronze muscle cuirass; beneath the waist extended a short skirt of flaps that were either attached directly to the cuirass or possibly formed part of an undertunic, which functioned as a lining for the cuirass.[1] The type of semi-circular pteryx represented in our matrix first appeared in the fourth century on Greek cuirasses that had two rows of such flaps.[2] During the Hellenistic period, leather straps replaced the flaps in popularity, but semi-circular pteryges returned to fashion under Augustus and again in the Trajanic-Hadrianic period, often in combination with either straps or pteryges of other shapes.[3]

The lion-griffin was not an uncommon motif on Roman cuirasses, since the apotropaic connotation was naturally appealing.[4] The closest parallels to our representation appear on Campanian reliefs of the Augustan period and among the lion-head waterspouts that were applied to the Temple of Zeus at Olympia during the first century B.C.[5]

It is unclear whether a relief from our matrix belonged to an actual cuirass or to a statue. In the former case the backing would have been of leather or possibly bronze, and the relief would have been riveted in place. If the relief belonged to a statue, the appliqué could have been riveted or soldered in position.

Although most matrices were made by cutting directly into the bronze, the smooth and fluid surface of our example suggests that it may have been made by fashioning in intaglio a wax model that was subsequently cast in bronze.

1. H. Russell Robinson, *The Armour of Imperial Rome* (London, 1975), 149.
2. K. Stemmer, *Untersuchungen zur Typologie: Chronologie und Ikonographie der Panzerstatuen* (Berlin, 1978), 140–41. See review article by D. E. E. and F. S. Kleiner, *AJA* 83 (1979): 367–68.
3. E. R. Williams, *AJA* 81 (1977): 234 n. 4.
4. Ibid., 235 n. 11; Stemmer, *Untersuchungen zur Typologie,* 163–64.
5. E. R. Williams, *AJA* 81 (1977), 235.

62. Statuette of Hephaestos

(ca. second c. A.D.)

412. Purchased in Rome or Naples in 1906–9. Bronze. Ht, 7.9 cm; w between hands, 5.4 cm. Right hand broken off. Toes of right foot broken off or not cast.

Stands with left leg relaxed. Arms extended with object in upturned palm of left hand. Wears short-sleeved, belted tunic (exomis) extending to knees and fastened only on left shoulder. Bearded head gazes to his right, with curly hair surmounted by wreath and pilos. Incised circle for nipple; pupils punched.

Bibliography: Letter from Wilson to Buckler, March 17, 1907, in JHU archives, box 51, Office of the President; S. Reinach, *Répertoire de la statuaire grecque et romaine* (Paris, 1906–10), vol. 4, 26.2; F. Brommer, *Hephaistos* (Mainz, 1978), 212, pl. 21.2 (Type I. 2).

Brommer has demonstrated that our statuette fairly accurately reflects a lost statue of Hephaestos that was made between 421/0 and 416/5 B.C. for the temple of Hephaestos in Athens.[1] The statue is usually attributed to Alcamenes, who is accredited by Cicero with an image of Hephaestos.[2] Brommer believes that the most reliable reflections of the artist's work are the Vatican Herm, a statue in Ostia, and a gem in Berlin, and on the basis of these monuments he restores Alcamenes' statue as a bearded figure who stood with left leg relaxed, a hammer in the lowered right hand, and tongs in the lowered left hand.[3] Brommer proposes that the god wore a pilos and an exomis fastened only on the left shoulder, in the manner of our statuette. Harrison[4] and Karousou[5] agree on most of these points but postulate that the god's left hand was upraised and held a torch, in the manner suggested by several bronze statuettes[6] of the deity.

Although Alcamenes' statue established what would become Hephaestos's traditional representation, the deity had actually appeared in Attic vasepainting from the second quarter of the sixth century[7] and was depicted with pilos[8] and tongs[9] soon after 500 B.C. The wreath our figurine wears alludes to this vasepainting tradition, since Hephaestos wears a wreath in scenes depicting his return to Olympos; this wreath is derived from the ivy wreath that Dionysos wears in vasepaintings that chronicle his own return.[10]

The worship of Hephaestos was established in Italy during the Republican period and was there assimilated with the cults of Vulcanus and Sethlans.[13] Hephaestos enjoyed his greatest popularity during the Roman Empire, in volcanic areas[14] and in metalworking centers, such as Gaul and southeast Germany.[15] The god was also popular in Rome and in Ostia, where he was regarded as protector of the storeroom.[16]

About fifty small bronze statuettes of Hephaestos are known, ranging in height from 8 to 20 cm.[11] Most of the examples are Roman and come from Italy, Gaul, and Germany. The figurines are remarkably similar and are clearly derived from a single prototype. Our own example should probably be dated in the second century A.D., since the treatment of the locks of hair on the forehead and in the coils of beard can be compared with Hadrianic and Antonine representations of Serapis.[12]

1. F. Brommer, *Hephaistos* (Mainz, 1978), 75–90.
2. Cicero, *Nat. D.* 130. See Brommer, *Hephaistos,* 75.
3. Brommer, *Hephaistos,* 75–90, especially 85–87.
4. E. B. Harrison, *AJA* 81 (1977):146–50, and 140, fig. 2.
5. S. Papaspyridi-Karousou, *AthMitt* 69 (1954):67–76, especially 74.
6. See M. Robertson's review of Brommer [*AJA* 84 (1980): 103–5] and Brommer, *Hephaistos,* 56.
7. Brommer, *Hephaistos,* 32.
8. Ibid., 32, 148.
9. Ibid., 154.
10. Ibid., 145.
11. Ibid., 53–59.
12. See discussions of items nos. 63 and 130. Note that Brommer (*Hephaistos,* 53) dates Schimmel and Decelea statuettes to second century A.D.
13. Brommer, *Hephaistos,* 168.
14. Ibid., in Lipari, Aetna, Pozzuoli.
15. Ibid., 179–80; Boucher, *Bronzes romains,* 117, no. 182; S. Boucher, *Recherches sur les bronzes figurés de Gaule pré-romaine et romaine,* in *Bibliothèque des Écoles françaises d'Athènes et de Rome* 228 (1976):146; P. Lebel, *Catalogue des collections archéologiques de Besançon V: Les bronzes figurés* (Paris, 1959 and 1961), 27, no. 41, pl. XXIV.
16. Brommer, 172.

63. Bust of Serapis

(second c. A.D.)

K 51. Kemper Simpson Collection. Bronze. Ht, 15.5 cm; w, 15.3 cm. Missing back of shoulders, curls at nape, all of modius above its toros base. Tip of nose and curls on forehead broken away. Cracked across neck. No evidence for attachment beneath.

Draped bust, including shoulders and upper arms, of male dressed in chiton with mantle draped over outstretched left arm. Full beard and curly hair to shoulders. Eyes gaze upward, with punched pupils just beneath upper eyelid. Grooved circle defines contour of iris. Silver over all of eyeball except pupil.

Bibliography: E. R. Williams, *BABesch* 52–53 (1977–78):201–7.

This bust probably belonged to the household shrine of a fairly well-to-do devotee of Serapis, a deity who was a fusion of the Egyptian god Osiris with a Hellenic god, such as Zeus.[1] The cult of Serapis evolved in Egypt during the fourth century B.C., but enjoyed its greatest popularity during Roman times.

The traditional representation of the god was inspired from the cult statue, which the Greek sculptor Bryaxis fashioned in Alexandria, probably in the third century B.C. The appearance of this statue has been reconstructed by Hornbostel following a thorough study of the many surviving representations of the deity.[2] Our bust proves to be a surprisingly accurate copy, faithfully reproducing from the original work the extended left arm, the configuration of drapery folds, the two vertical columns of curls over the chin, and (broken away) the five locks of hair, which fell vertically down over the forehead.

Our bust can be confidently ascribed to Alexandria and can be dated within the second half of the second century A.D. The upward gaze of the eyes, with their punched pupils, and the plastic treatment of the beard, with its restless mass of curls, are mid-Antonine in style. The accuracy of our piece is characteristic of representations worked in Alexandria under Antoninus Pius and Marcus Aurelius, at a time when Serapis was enjoying a tremendous following and when the

refurbishment of the cult statue by Hadrian was stimulating demand for small-scale representations.

The horizontal ridge across the neck of our figure is clearly the seam along which the wax model was assembled before casting. The head itself was probably made in two molds, with the join falling along the juncture where the tousled curls framing the face meet the smoother locks that cling closely to the back of the skull. Because the surface of the interior follows the contours of the exterior, even to the indentations for the facial features, we can conclude that the wax was pressed into a mold in the indirect method of lost wax casting, a process that by this time had been employed for many centuries by Egyptian metalworkers.

The Hopkins bust compares closely with several contemporary bronze busts of Serapis, which as a group testify to the popularity of the deity and to the skill of Alexandrian metalworkers during the second century A.D.

1. See E. R. Williams, *BABesch* 52–53 (1977–78):201–7 for the full publication of this piece.

2. Ibid., 201 n. 2.

64. Statuette of Isis-Aphrodite

(A.D. 150–200)

K 49. Kemper Simpson Collection. Bronze. Ht, 30 cm; w between arms, 15.5 cm. Left foot restored and small areas added on right thigh and below knees. Cracks around neck, across right knee, above left knee. Missing are upper section of headdress, inlaid eyes, and disc of mirror in right hand.

Nude maiden stands on right leg with left leg relaxed. Elbows bent, with arms extended to each side at breast level. Head turned slightly to her left. Hair center-parted and brushed to sides, with knot at nape and two long locks brought forward over each shoulder. She wears a stephane engraved with a band of incised leaves beneath a ray pattern; originally the stephane was surmounted by five regularly spaced attachments. She wears armlets incised with oblique grooves, and ball or pear-shaped earrings. Her necklace consists of a broad cord decorated with incised X's; suspended from cord are nine oval or diamond-shaped amulets, the central one being the largest. Necklace dips to V in back. Outstretched index finger and thumb of right hand touch. Remaining fingers are wrapped around a handle beneath a horizontal bar, surely for a mirror. Fingers of left hand are wrapped around stem of a lotus blossom, on which infant Harpocrates sits. He holds a cornucopia in his left hand and raises his right index finger to his mouth. His headdress takes form of sun disc.

Bibliography: E. R. Williams, *JARCE*, 16 (1979):93–100.

This statuette represents a syncretic deity who assimilates the Egyptian goddess Isis with the Greek divinity Aphrodite. Although Isis and Aphrodite first became thoroughly conflated during the Hellenistic period, this syncretic divinity enjoyed particular popularity in Egypt and Syria during Roman times, when the goddess came to be associated primarily with fertility and childbirth.[1] The Hopkins example, which can be dated on stylistic grounds to the second half of the second century A.D., was surely intended for the private shrine of a fairly prosperous household, probably in Egypt.

The Hopkins statuette belongs with several other examples that date from the first to the third centuries A.D.[2] The group has several distinctive features, including the large size, averaging 30–43 cm, elaborate headdress or stephane, and amuletic necklace. Also characteristic are the gesture of the arms, the presence of attributes in the hands, and the position of the fingers, with thumb extended to the outstretched forefinger.

It is clear that the appearance of these figurines was highly influenced by two traditional Hellenistic types. The first type is a standing nude Isis-Aphrodite, who holds either a piece of fruit between outstretched forefinger and thumb or occasionally a mirror. She often wears an elaborate floral crown, which, as we know from the account of Apuleius, was closely associated with Isis. The second type that influenced the appearance of our maiden shows Isis, again standing but now draped, holding in her outstretched hand a figure of Harpocrates squatting on a lotus leaf.

Distinctive to the Roman versions are the inlaid eyes and the elaborate necklaces, which are well documented in the cult of Isis.[3] Individual amulets were associated with Isis in her identity as protector of fertility and childbirth, and a necklace of amulets appears on Egyptian votive terracotta figurines that depict women, and occasionally Isis, squatting in childbirth.

Radiographs of the Hopkins statuette indicate that the figure was cast as a single piece, with the exclusion of the attributes in each hand. Head and arms to the armlets are solid, with torso and legs hollow. Ob-

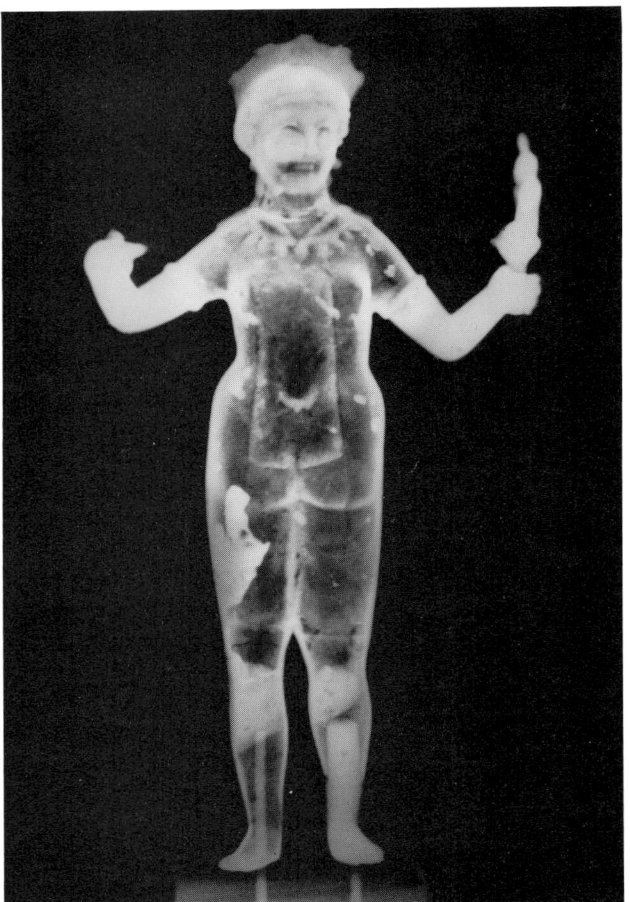

Radiograph

servation of the neck and arm area indicates that the wax models for the arms and for the head and neck were made by pressing wax into piece molds. The wax models were assembled for casting along seams that were subsequently concealed by armlets and necklace. The legs were also separately fashioned from wax and then joined to a wax model of the torso, probably across the knees.

The radiograph also revealed a rectangular area in the center of the torso that is either hollow or still filled with core material. The rectilinear contours of the core area, which do not echo the contours of the statue's exterior, indicate that the wax was pressed or poured into piece molds for the front and back of the torso. The excess wax was then cut away, leaving a trough into which the clay core material was pressed or poured. The final step in fashioning the wax model was the addition of details, such as the armlets, necklace, and attachments to the stephane. The fully assembled wax model was then cast in bronze, after which the separately cast bronze mirror and lotus leaf were soldered or welded in place.

1. See full publication in E. R. Williams, *JARCE* 16 (1979):93–100.

2. Other examples not included in my earlier publication are a statuette in the Princeton Art Museum (purchased 1957 from Adolph Loewi; ht, 30.5 cm) and one in the Barnes Foundation, Merion, Pennsylvania. I owe these references to F. Jones.

3. For a recent discussion of the crescent-shaped amulet, which appears on several statuettes of the Hopkins type, see A. Witteveen, *BMusArt* 6 (1974):69–70.

65. Head of Athlete

(second–fourth c. A.D.)

427. Purchased in Rome or Naples in 1906–9. Lead. Ht, 4.2 cm; depth from forehead to curl, 3.3 cm; l, 1.3 cm. Hollow, cast in two molds, with seam down center of nose. Open beneath.

Male frontal head with closely cropped hair in short tufts. On top of head is long lock, which hangs down back of head. Tufts over chin for beard. Large ears and eyes, protruding nose, thick lips, long neck.

Identical examples, as well as a few beardless versions, are in the Bibliothèque National,[1] Dresden,[2] Carlsruhe,[3] Berlin,[4] Warsaw,[5] and Rome.[6] The example in Dresden was found in Rome and two of those in Karlsruhe also have Italian provenance, in one case Apulia.

The tuft of hair at the crown of the head has been described as the cirrus in vertice, a hairstyle that was worn by professional athletes and slaves.[7] That identification is supported by the bulbous nose and thick lips, which characterize the eastern Mediterranean or African people who served the Romans as gladiators and slaves. The explanation would also account for our figure's distorted ear, an occupational hazard of an athletic career. It has been suggested that the cirrus in vertice is derived from the closely cropped hairstyle that slaves wore,[8] although it is possible that the lock originally carried a religious connotation.[9]

The lead heads were carelessly made in curiously flat molds, which were joined along a seam that distorts the facial features. Since the base of the neck is not broken away, and since no heads have been found attached to bodies, it is certain that the heads are complete in themselves. Gassowski suggests that the pieces are inexpensive votive offerings that were dedicated by athletes in their palaestras.[10]

Since most representations of the cirrus in vertice appear on monuments from the second and third centuries A.D., it is likely that the heads were made during this period, certainly in Italy, but possibly elsewhere as well.[11]

Similar heads, with the same features and hairstyles, are depicted on Roman appliqués and unguent jars (balsamaria) that have been found in a number of Roman sites, especially in Gaul, Germany, and Belgium.[12] These balsamaria are frequently found in graves together with strigils, an association that suggests that the balsamaria were used in the palaestra or the baths, establishments that were frequented by athletes and slaves, who would logically be figured on the containers.[13] The balsamaria have been dated to the first through fourth centuries A.D., and are thus approximately contemporary with the lead heads.

1. E. Babelon and J. Blanchet, *Catalogue des bronzes antiques de la Bibliothèque National* (Paris, 1895), 450, nos. 1036–39.

2. G. Treu, *AA* (1889):174.

3. K. Schumacher, *Beschreibung der Sammlung antiker Bronzen* (Karlsruhe, 1890), 174, nos. 923 a and b.

4. See note 2.

5. B. Gassowski, in *Mélànges offerts à Kazimierz Michalowski* (Warsaw, 1966), 421; K. Majewski, *Archeologia* 14 (1963):102.

6. See note 2.

7. S. Boucher, *Recherches sur les bronzes figurés de Gaule pré-romaine et romaine*, in *Bibliothèque des Écoles françaises d'Athènes et de Rome* 228 (1976):187; J. Schwartz, *Latomus* 22 (1963):472–77; Gassowski, *Mélànges* 421–27; A. Leibendgut, *Die römischen Bronzen der Schweiz II: Avenches* (Mainz, 1976), 55, pl. 42, no. 35, probably representing a mime actor or slave.

8. F. von Bissing, *ÖJh* 15 (1912):79–80.

9. V. von Gonzenbach, *Untersuchungen zu den Knabenweihen* (Bonn, 1957), 105–28.

10. Gassowski, *Mélànges*, 427.

11. Ibid., 427.

12. Boucher, *Recherches*, 186–87; Boucher, *Latomus* 32 (1973): 804; J. Schwartz, *Latomus* 22 (1963):472–77; J. Faider Feytmans, *Les Bronzes romains de Belgique* (Mainz, 1979), 127, no. 223, pl. 91; K. Majewski, *Archeologia* 14 (1963):95–126, especially no. 18; J. Balty, *RGZM* 20 (1973):261–64.

13. Ibid., 264.

Terracottas

CYPRIOT

66. Base Ring Ware Bull

(1400–1230 B.C.)

9012. Provenance unknown. L, 18.2 cm; ht, 12.5 cm; diam pour hole, 2 cm. Tips of horns broken away. Vessel mold-made in two halves, with seam down middle of back from nose to tail.

Cylindrical body and tubular legs; pierced muzzle. Eyes are pellets set within narrow coils for lids. Small petal ears beneath upright horns. At back of neck is cylindrical pour hole, behind which rises strap handle. Vertical ridge down haunch for tail. Decoration in white paint consisting of white stripe from nose to tail and numerous curved stripes branching off from it. Legs reserved.

The pierced muzzle and the pour hole identify the vessel as an askos, which was probably used for libations or dedication. Vessels of the Hopkins type were made in Cyprus from ca. 1400–1230 B.C. and belong to a class of pottery known as Base Ring Ware I, II, and III.[1] About one hundred fifty examples of these bull vessels are known, and most of those with secure provenances come from tombs[2] in sites including Limassol,[3] Kourion,[4] Enkomi,[5] and Angastina.[6] At least one example was exported to Ialysos on Rhodes.[7] The painted patterns vary somewhat and may consist of alternately wavy and vertical lines[8] or pinebranch patterns.[9]

This type of askos has its origin in the early Cypriot period, when bull heads were applied to vessels that were roughly shaped to approximate the bodies of bulls.[10]

The bull askoi of Base Ring Ware are to be distinguished from contemporary bull figurines that differ in form and decoration.[11]

1. P. Astro°bm, *The Swedish Cyprus Expedition: The Late Cypriote Bronze Age,* vol. 4, pt. 1C (Lund, 1972), 191–94; A. Brown and H. Catling, *OpusAth* 13 (1980):112–13, no. 49, fig. 42; E. Sjoqvist, *Problems of the Late Cypriote Bronze Age* (Stockholm, 1940), 34–43; H. W. Catling, *RDAC 1976* (Nicosia, 1976), 71–72.

2. Catling, *RDAC 1976,* 72. See also A. Kozloff, ed., in *Animals in Ancient Art from the Leo Mildenberg Collection* (Cleveland, 1980), 84, no. 67.

3. V. Karageorghis, *BCH* 102 (1978):892, fig. 33.

4. Catling, *RDAC 1976,* 72.

5. H. G. Buchholz and V. Karageorghis, *Prehistoric Greece and Cyprus* (London, 1973), 162, no. 1726.

6. V. Karageorghis *AA* (1963):529, fig. 13.

7. V. Karageorghis, *The Archaeology of Cyprus: Recent Developments* (Park Ridge, 1975), 93.

8. M. Yon, *Manuel de céramique chypriote* (Lyons, 1976), 93–94, fig. 31 b.

9. Buchholz and Karageorghis, *Prehistoric Greece,* 162, no. 1726.

10. See Yon, *Manuel,* 93; V. Karageorghis, *Treasures of Cyprus: Smithsonian* (1976–78), no. 29; Buchholz and Karageorghis, *Prehistoric Greece,* 146, no. 1522.

11. Catling, *RDAC 1976,* 68–71.

Terracottas

GREEK

67. Sima Fragment from Acropolis

(ca. 510 B.C.)

1974. Collection Baltimore Society AIA. Max l, 12 cm; ht, 11.2 cm; th, 4.5 cm. Base and left edge intact; other edges broken. Red and black ornament on front; underside painted red.

Against a black background is a volute and palmette scheme, reserved except for details in red. From viewer's left: right half of inverted seven-petal palmette; base of palmette red within narrow reserved border. To right is inverted twenty-five-petal palmette with similarly treated base. Between the palmettes is a volute wound in four loops, each enclosing a red disc within a reserved circle. Between loops is a three-petal palmette having a red base, and a red rhomboid with reserved border. Beginning of another series of loops visible at right.

This fragment belonged to the gable of a late archaic building on the Athenian Acropolis. Our piece comes from the lower half of an ovolo sima, which was classified by Buschor as a raking sima (no. X).[1] It is clear from undamaged sections that the pattern on our fragment was repeated in mirror reverse on the upper half of the sima.

Several fragments have been recovered from this entablature. A sima painted with a slightly different pattern belonged to the gable at the opposite end,[2] and the running sima,[3] antefixes,[4] and acroteria[5] were decorated with other variations on the scheme. The ornament finds its closest parallels on late archaic red-figure vases, especially those painted by Euphronios.[6] The parallels with vasepainting, as well as the profiles of the simas, indicate that the building was constructed or refurbished around 515–510 B.C. with some of the most lavish architectural terracottas of its age.

The original size of the building can be computed from the large quantity of surviving architectural fragments. Buschor recognized fifteen sections of sima X, and since each section had a length of about 62 cm, it appears that each gable was over 9m long.[7] Buschor also identified twenty-seven antefixes belonging to one of two types[8] and twenty-three acroteria.[9] From this material he estimated that the building must have been 100 ft long, or a hekatompedon.[10]

The structure probably stood to the south of the Parthenon, where most of the fragments were found. The signs of burning on many of the pieces indicate that the building was destroyed in the Persian invasion of 480 B.C.

1. E. Buschor, *Die Tondächer der Akropolis I: Simen* (Berlin, 1929), 20–33, and 22, fig. 23; T. Weigand, *Die archaische Poros-Architektur der Akropolis zu Athen* (Cassel/Leipzig, 1904), 185, no. 4; E. Douglas van Buren, *Greek Fictile Revetments in the Archaic Period* (London, 1926), pl. XI, figs. 32, 35.

2. Sima XI. Buschor (*Tondächer I,* 23–24) believed that this sima is more lavish than no. X and therefore must have decorated the front. However, the patterns are about the same in degree of detail.

3. Running sima type XIII (Buschor, *Tondächer I,* 27–33).

4. E. Buschor, *Die Tondächer der Akropolis II: Stirnziegel* (Berlin, 1933), 45–46, antefix type XII.

5. Ibid., 63–65, acroteria type II.

6. D. von Bothmer *AA* (1976):485–512.

7. Buschor, *Tondächer I,* 20–23, 30.

8. Buschor, *Tondächer II,* 45.

9. Ibid., 63–64.

10. Ibid., 64.

68. Peplophoros

(450–400 B.C.)

9087. Provenance unknown. Ht, 34.5 cm; ht base, 4.8 cm. Back unmodeled, with large rectangular opening extending from chest to feet. Open beneath. Extensive remains of thick, white slip overlaid with red paint on open, right edge of peplos, bottom half of kolpos, top of hair, base of polos. Two horizontal red bands across vertical front of base, one along upper edge, other one-third distance from top. Mended from many pieces, with upper section of polos broken away.

Maiden stands with right leg relaxed, arms at side, fingers grasping folds of drapery. She wears belted peplos, which falls over left supporting leg in regularly spaced folds. Hair is brushed back from face and falls in soft horizontal waves to shoulders.

Our maiden exemplifies a Boeotian type of figurine that first appeared in mid-fifth-century graves at Halae.[1] The type is derived from an Attic type that had been created a short time before.[2] The principal differences are in the treatment of the head. Maidens of the Attic type have a short hairstyle and a low stephane or no headdress at all. In contrast, the Boeotian version wears shoulder-length hair and a high polos. On our example the polos is damaged, but on surviving examples we find that the back of the polos had a vertical extension in the shape of a rectangle with an undulating upper edge.[3] This extension was probably inspired by the similar configuration of the crown of Lower Egypt.[4] The polos itself, however, is a Hittite headdress, which in archaic Greek art is worn by goddesses purely as ornament. By the fifth century the polos has taken on associations with death or marriage.[5] Goldman suggested that the headdress would be appropriate to Aphrodite,[6] but it is also possible that these Boeotian maidens allude only to the deceased person with whom the figurine was buried.

The Attic and Boeotian types differ in one more respect. On the Attic type the left leg supports the body, but in the Boeotian type, the left leg is relaxed. Since our maiden conforms to the Attic type, it is possible that our Boeotian koroplast used an Attic mold for the body or made the body mold by impressing an Attic figurine. He could then have paired the body with a head of Boeotian type.

Figurines of the Hopkins type continued to be made in Boeotia through the fifth century[7] and although most examples come from Boeotia, several were found in Argos.[8] Our piece shows the technical features characteristic of Boeotian terracottas of the second half of the fifth century and early fourth century: the large, rectangular back vent,[9] slip,[10] and horizontal bands painted across the base.[11]

1. F. Winter, *Die Typen der figürlichen Terrakotten, Die antiken Terrakotten,* ed. R. Kekule von Stradonitz vol. III.1 (Berlin, 1903), 62.4; H. J. Holzhausen, *Böotische Terrakottatypen des 5 und 4 Jahrhunderts vor Christus* (Bonn, 1972), 17–21; H. Goldman, *Hesperia* 11 (1942):388, Group D, Type II–a–6, pl. XI; Besques, vol. 1, 91, nos. C48, C49, pl. LXIV; B. Schmaltz, *Terrakotten aus dem Kabirenheiligtum bei Theban* (Berlin, 1974), 174, no. 286, pl. 23; Higgins, 218, no. 815, pl. III; R. A. Higgins, *Greek Terracottas* (London, 1967), 78, pl. 33c.

2. F. Poulsen, *ActaArch* 8 (1937):53–55. Poulsen discusses the Boeotian type on 74 and 77, fig. 48. Besques, vol. 1, 82, no. C 2, pl. LV. See also P. N. Ure, *Aryballoi and Figurines from Rhitsona in Boeotia* (Cambridge, 1934), 73, no. 138–8, pl. XX.

3. V. Müller, *Der Polos: Die griechische Götterkrone* (Berlin, 1915), 41.

4. Goldman, *Hesperia* 11 (1942):386.

5. Müller, *Der Polos,* 51, 71, 76–77, 82, 85.

6. Goldman, *Hesperia* 11 (1942):377.

7. Schmaltz, *Terrakotten,* 109, dated before 450 B.C.; *Deltion* 3 (1917):237–38, fig. 170, from a Theban tomb of the end of the fifth century.

8. Schmaltz, *Terrakotten,* 109.

9. Higgins, 204; Higgins, *Terracottas,* 77.

10. Goldman, *Hesperia* 11 (1942):371.

11. Ibid., 372. Similar painted bands appear on another example, in J. Sieveking, *Die Terrakotten der Sammlung Loeb I* (Munich, 1916), 15–16, pl. 21.

69. Aphrodite

(early fourth c. B.C.)

K 75. Kemper Simpson Collection. Ht, 25.6 cm; ht base, 3 cm; l base, 6.5 cm; w base, 4.5 cm; ht vent hole, 15.2 cm. Smooth, unmolded back with rectangular vent hole. Open beneath. Slip over surface. Intact.

Maiden stands on left leg with right leg relaxed. Mantle is draped around hips and legs, with left hand holding folds and tray of fruits at genitals. Rest of mantle is brought behind back and over top of head, with right hand lifting folds beside left ear. Short curly hair center-parted and brushed off face. Oval spool base.

Our figurine represents a modification of a Boeotian type that has been found in Thespiae,[1] Lake Copais,[2] and in a grave of the first half of the fourth century at Halae.[3] The vertical folds of drapery between the legs and the concentric catenary folds over the left supporting leg are reminiscent of figures from the Erechtheum frieze[4] of the late fifth century, and of the Venus Genetrix,[5] which is thought to be based upon a contemporary work.

On the Boeotian examples the head is frontal and the right hand fondles the long locks that fall to the shoulders. On our figurine the head is inclined and the short hair is brushed back over the ears, while the right hand now appears to draw the mantle over the head. The gesture has become meaningless, however, since the smooth arc that frames the head cannot possibly be the continuation of the mantle, but is most comparable to the diadem found on Attic heads of Aphrodite and Nike of the late fifth and early fourth centuries.[6] It is apparent, then, that the Attic koroplast substituted an Attic head into the Boeotian type, thereby altering the function of the gesture and the arrangement of the drapery.

Characteristic of late fifth-century Attic figurines of the pre-Tanagran stage are the smooth, unmodeled back and the rectangular vent.[7] The spool base also appears on contemporary Attic figurine vases.[8]

1. Breitenstein, 33, no. 297, pl. 34.

2. Higgins, 230, no. 864, pl. 123.

3. H. Goldman and F. Jones, *Hesperia* 11 (1942):405, Group F, no. V–e–3, pl. XXI.

4. P. N. Boulter, *Antike Plastik* 10 (1970):7–28; 9, no. 1077, pl. 3, and 12, no. 1071, pl. 11.

5. W. Fuchs, *Der Skulptur der Griechen* (Munich, 1969):209, fig. 224.

6. M. Trumpf-Lyritzaki, *Griechische Figurenvasen* (Bonn, 1969), 7, no. 10, pl. 3, and 60, nos. 163–64, pl. 23; E. R. Williams, *Hesperia* 47 (1978):379–81, nos. 1, 2, 8, pl. 91.

7. D. B. Thompson, *AJA* 70 (1966):52, and *Hesperia* 21 (1952):130–32.

8. Trumpf-Lyritzaki, *Griechische Figurenvasen*, 115.

70. Dancer

(ca. 350 B.C.)

K 74. Kemper Simpson Collection. Ht, 23.2 cm; h base, 3 cm; l base, 7.7 cm; depth base, 5.8 cm. Back unmodeled, with rectangular vent extending from behind breast to feet. Open beneath. Much white slip remains on figure and front of base. Intact.

Maiden wearing chiton, visible only at ankles, and himation, which envelops body and is wrapped around head. She steps forward with left leg advanced and uplifted, right arm at side. Left hand holds folds of drapery at left hip. Hair center-parted and brushed back from face over ears. Stepped oval base.

This type of himation-draped dancer first appears in Attica and Boeotia in the beginning of the fourth century,[1] and is probably based upon the figure of a dancing nymph on a contemporary Attic relief.[2] The terracotta figurines vary among themselves in dress and gesture. The head may be uncovered[3] or more tightly wrapped in the folds of the himation.[4] Occasionally the elbows are sharply bent and the right hand is brought to the right shoulder.[5] In examples dating from the third century, the head turns back toward the left shoulder,[6] exhibiting a torsion that becomes more emphatic in versions of the second to first centuries B.C.[7]

The Hopkins figurine was probably made in an older mold, since many of the folds are faint, and the lower passages of chiton and himation have been carelessly reworked by hand. The stiff, halolike configuration of the mantle around the head is probably an adaptation of the more softly draped arrangement of the original type.

In Hellenistic times the himation-draped dancer sometimes assumed the identity of the personification of winter and, especially in the Roman period, enjoyed a long-lived popularity as one of the four seasons, who carried connotations of rebirth and renewal.[8]

1. Besques, vol. 3, 2; D. B. Thompson, *AJA* 70 (1966):57, 62.
2. T. Leslie Shear, *OpusRom* 9 (1973):183–91. See also J. N. Svoronos, *Das Athener National Museum* (Athens, 1908), 577, no. 1879, pl. XCVII; W. Fuchs, *Die Vorbilder der neuattischen Reliefs, JdI-EH* 20 (1959):20–41.
3. Hornbostel, 152, no. 126.
4. Besques, vol. 1, 92, no. C54, pl. LXV and III; 2, no. D4, pl. 1.
5. H. Goldman, *Excavations at Eutresis in Boeotia* (Cambridge, 1931), 260, no. 2, fig. 318; 261, no. 6, fig. 318.
6. Ibid., 261, no. 2, fig. 317.
7. E. Töpperwein, *Terrakotten von Pergamon: Pergamenische Forschungen* 3 (1976):44, 212, no. 164, pl. 25.
8. G. M. A. Hanfmann, *The Season Sarcophagus in Dumbarton Oaks*, vol. 2 (Cambridge, 1951), 113–14, 137–38, 185–92. See also entry for item no. 92.

71. Head of Silenos

(late fourth–third c. B.C.)

K 90. Kemper Simpson Collection. Ht, 5 cm; w base of neck, 2.6 cm; depth from front to back at base of neck, 3 cm. Broken off across neck.

Bald head, wrapped in fillet, with beard and flowing mustache. Head inclined to right; eyes cast downward. Pointed ears, furrowed forehead, bushy brows contorted in frown. Snub nose.

Although the drawn brows and downcast glance suggest a contemplative and even troubled spirit, the pointed ears and the festive taenia identify our figure as a Silenos. The pensive Silenos is first encountered during the last half of the fourth century, when the mythical being had become closely associated with Socrates. Richter suggests that Plato's comparison of Socrates to the Silenos inspired an early fourth-century portrait[1] which was soon replaced in popularity by a portrait commissioned from Lysippos about 350 B.C.[2] The Lysippan portrait presented Socrates as a thoughtful teacher and made only minimal allusions to a Silenos—in the snub nose, small eyes, and full beard.[3] We know that this Lysippan interpretation in turn influenced the traditional representation of the Silenos, who was henceforth presented as a wise old man of philosophic bent.

The new type of Silenos first appeared in masks[4] and statuettes in the last half of the fourth century. The statuettes may depict the Silenos with hand upraised in instruction[5] or with the child Dionysos in his arms.[6] Our head can be most closely compared to terracottas of the fourth–third centuries B.C.,[7] and to the face of the Silenos on the Derveni krater of about the third quarter of the fourth century.[8] By the late Hellenistic period, the assimilation of Silenos and philosopher was so complete that the Silenos was often portrayed with human ears (see no. 14), thereby eliminating the last distinction between human and hybrid and leaving only the context or degree of exaggeration in the features to establish the identity.

1. Plato, *Symp.* 215a; Xenophon, *Symp.* v.5–7; G. M. A. Richter, *The Portraits of the Greeks*, vol. 1 (London, 1965), 35, and 109–12, Type A; Bieber, *Sculpture*, 45–46.

2. Diogenes Laertius II.43; Richter, *Portraits*, 109–10, and 112–15, Type B.

3. Bieber, *Sculpture*, 46–47.

4. C. Weickert, in *Festschrift für James Loeb* (Munich, 1930), 109, pl. XV.

5. O. W. Muscarella, *Ancient Art: The Norbert Schimmel Collection* (Mainz, 1974), no. 48, from Centuripe; K. Schefold, *AntK* 2 (1959):24, pl. 13.

6. Besques, vol. 2, 80, pl. 97d, second century, from Myrina; B. Schmaltz [*Terrakotten aus dem Kabirenheiligtum bei Theben* (Berlin, 1974), 32] points out that the many Silenos heads in the Kabirenheiligtum must indicate an association between the Kabiri and Dionysos.

7. D. B. Thompson, *Hesperia* 26 (1957):111, 115–19, 127, pl. 35, no. 6, from a cistern with pottery before 300 B.C.; Schmaltz, *Terrakotten*, 152, no. 56, pl. 3, dated on 31 between 350 and 300 B.C. Also compare U. Liepmann, *Griechische Terrakotten, Bronzen, Skulpturen, Kestner Museums: Hannover* (Hannover, 1975), 92, no. 99, dated third century and Weickert, *Festschrift*, of late fourth or early third century.

8. K. Schefold, *AntK* 22 (1979), pl. 34; M. Andronikos, *The Greek Museums* (New Rochelle, 1975), 279.

72. Terracotta Grotesque Head

(fourth–third c. B.C.)

K 88. Kemper Simpson Collection. Ht, 8.5 cm; diam base neck, 4 cm. Closed beneath; solid; intact.

Male head with short curly hair beneath wreath. Furrowed forehead with arching brows; flaring nostrils; wide mouth with thick, slightly parted lips.

The exaggerated features link our piece with several so-called grotesques, figurines that are caricatures of deformed or normal individuals.[1] These figurines first appeared in the fourth century and became especially popular in Asia Minor and Egypt during the Hellenistic period.[2] It is believed that the type was partially inspired by the mime, a theatrical form that parodied everyday life, in which the actors were unmasked but were probably distinguished by exaggerated facial expressions.[3] The solidity and quality of our head, as well as the fact that it does not belong to a figurine, suggest that it may have been an archetype from which molds were made.[4]

1. A. de Ridder, *Catalogue collection de Clerq*, vol. 6 (Paris, 1909), 103, no. 202, and 112, no. 221, pl. VI. J. Vogt, *Die griechisch-ägyptische Sammlung Ernst von Sieglin II.2 Terrakotten* (Leipzig, 1924), 146, no. 2, pl. LIX; 163; see also 146, no. 1, pl. LIX and 162, no. 1, pl. LXXII.
2. G. Chase, *Classical Studies Presented to Edward Capps* (Princeton, 1936),58–60; R. A. Higgins, *Greek Terracottas* (London, 1967), 112; S. Unge, *Medelhausmuseet Bulletin* 11 (1976):12–17.
3. See discussion of item no. 80 and especially M. Bieber, *AJA* 17 (1913):149–56, as well as Bieber, *Theater*, 106, 248–49.
4. I owe this suggestion to R. Nicholls.

73. Antefix of Hermes

(fourth c. B.C.)

1792. Collection Baltimore Society AIA, formerly Helbig Collection. Ht, 18 cm; w, 19 cm. Broken off behind; piece missing from petasos; chin chipped.

Square field with curving top. Frontal face, with wavy, flowing hair beneath petasos. Iris incised. Furrowed brow and parted lips.

Bibliography: Furtwängler, *ND*, 252, no. 6; D. M. Robinson, *AJA* 27 (1923):20–21, fig. 23.

The petasos identifies the face as that of Hermes, the deity associated with travel, commerce, and the journey of souls to the underworld. Our antefix belongs to a class of head antefixes that share a common shape, size, and style. Other types include a Silen,[1] a Medusa,[2] a face in Phrygian cap,[3] a woman in topknot (see no. 74), a horned head with necklace that has been identified as Pan or Io,[4] and a winged head with a lion-scalp who has been termed Herakles, Omphale, Perseus, or Bendis.[5] I know of no other example of a face of Hermes, and such rarity may indicate that the face has been reworked from another similar type, perhaps that of Medusa.

Most of these antefixes have been found in Tarentum,[6] where they were probably made; occasionally they were exported to other cities, such as Gela,[7] and Agrigentum.[8] Since some examples from these latter sites are made of local clay, it appears that an imported antefix or mold was occasionally used by a local artisan to produce a second generation of antefixes.

Within this class of antefixes there is significant variation in the handling of hair and features, indicating that the series was made over a period of time, probably beginning in the late fifth century. Our example's flying hair, protruding brow, and parted lips invite comparison with coin types of the middle and second half of the fourth century.[9]

1. L. Bernabò Brea, *NSc* 7, 1 (1940):476.
2. Higgins, 370, no. 1365, pl. 192.
3. D. M. Robinson, *AJA* 27 (1923):19, fig. 24.
4. Poulsen, 24, no. 35, pl. XVIII; Higgins, 370, no. 1364, pl. 191.
5. Breitenstein, 42, no. 377, pl. 45; Higgins, 370, no. 1363, pl. 191; P. Orlandini, *NSc* 8, 14 (1960):171, fig. 9; L. Bernabò Brea *NSc* 7, 1 (1940):476–77, fig. 44.
6. Bernabò Brea *NSc* 7, 1 (1940), fig. 44; see also note 2.
7. P. Orlandini, *NSc* 8, 14 (1960):171, fig. 9.
8. Ibid., 171.
9. Early example in Hornbostel, 148, no. 120. C. Kraay, *Greek Coins* (New York, 1966); compare no. 468, pl. 148 (Larissa, ca. 350 B.C.) and no. 660, pl. 191 (Lycia, ca. 360 B.C.) with no. 122, pl. 44 (Syracuse, ca. 400 B.C.).

74. Antefix of Woman

(fourth–third c. B.C.)

1791. Collection Baltimore Society AIA, formerly Helbig Collection. Ht, 19 cm; w, 18 cm; th, 2.5 cm. Part of circular back survives.

Female head within elliptical field. Hair tied with fillet into topknot at crown. Ends of fillet and wavy locks flow out to sides. Disc earrings; incised iris and punched pupil; Venus rings. Beginning of garment's neckline.

Bibliography: Furtwängler, *ND*, 252, no. 6; D. M. Robinson, *AJA* 27 (1923):19–20, fig. 21.

This antefix is another example of the class that was discussed in the previous entry. Close parallels, possibly from the same mold, have been found in Tarentum.[1] An antefix of the same type but with a more controlled hair arrangement, indicating an earlier date, has been assigned to the second quarter of the fourth century.[2] Our example's deep-set eyes, broad bridge of the nose, and fleshy Venus rings are best paralleled in sculpture from a Tarentine naiskos of the second half of the fourth century and first half of the third century.[3]

1. Higgins, 370, no. 1366, pl. 192, from Taras; P. Wuilleumier, *Tarente* (Paris, 1939), 429, pl. XXXIX.6.
2. Hornbostel, 148, no. 120.
3. J. Carter, *AJA* 74 (1970):131, pl. 31.

75. Figurine of Maiden

(ca. 300 B.C.)

HT 7. Helen Tanzer Collection. Ht, 17.6 cm; w behind elbows, 4.8 cm; ht base, 2.1 cm. Lower section of back with base broken away. White slip over most of figure.

Woman stands on right leg with left knee bent. Right arm bent at elbow with hand behind waist. Left hand rests on left breast. Over a chiton is a himation draped over upper torso to mid-thigh. Ends are wrapped around left forearm and hang down left side. Himation conceals forehead and hair. Small hat on back of head beneath larger brimmed hat, which was made separately.

Terracotta figurines that are described as Tanagran are primarily characterized by their subjects, which are usually human and often draped women and children. Although the term Tanagran is derived from a site in Boeotia where the first examples were discovered, it is likely that the class originated in Athens between ca. 350 and 335 B.C.[1]

During the first half of the fourth century, the Attic koroplastic industry underwent a major transformation as terracotta figurines ceased to be regarded as votive offerings and began to be appreciated as miniature sculpture to be enjoyed in the home.[2] The changing role of the medium was undoubtedly a result of the contemporary appeal of small-scale bronze figurines whose crispness and detailed workmanship were emulated by koroplasts. Another factor was the popularity of Old and Middle Comedy, whose parodies of everyday life stimulated a demand for statuettes of theatrical characters.[3]

During the transitional or pre-Tanagran years from ca. 400–350 B.C., many figurines of draped women were made in Attic workshops, including the prototype of our maiden.[4] Despite the common pose, however, there is a significant difference between pre-Tanagran examples of our type and the Tanagran versions that appear after ca. 335 B.C. In contrast to the flat unmodeled backs of pre-Tanagran figurines, the true Tanagras have a carefully modeled back, which may be mold-made or fashioned by hand. The back of a Tanagra figurine may have no vent hole, or, if the figurine stands upon a plaque base, a small vent hole.[5]

Soon after their evolution in Athens between 350 and 335 B.C., figurines of the Tanagran type were exported to Boeotia, where they were locally imitated. Our figurine is of Boeotian manufacture, although she is closely linked both in pose and style with contemporary Attic examples of about 300 B.C.[6] Typical Boeotian features are the long rectangular vent hole[7] and the high base, in contrast to the plaque base commonly found on Attic figurines of this period.[8] Another characteristically Boeotian feature is the thick, glossy slip, which obscures both the delicately worked folds of drapery and the facial features.[9] Despite the thick slip, however, it is apparent that the modeling is fairly crisp, thereby indicating that the Hopkins figurine is probably a first-generation piece, from a mold impressed from a handmodeled archetype. However, the artist of our figurine was apparently dissatisfied with the small hat that was included in the mold and consequently added his own handmade and more emphatic version above it.

Figurines of the Tanagran class continued to be made throughout the Hellenistic period all over the Greek world, especially in Alexandria and southern Italy. Traditional types were revised to conform to contemporary fashion in several ways. The artist could model a new archetype by hand or he could rework a figurine still soft from its mold and then make a new mold from the resulting image. Another method was to impress an existing figurine and then rework the representation within the negative surface of the mold. Figurines made by the latter two methods use derivative molds and are therefore classified as belonging to a second generation. These figurines can be recognized because they are smaller and usually less crisp in detail than their first-generation forebears.[10]

1. D. B. Thompson, *AJA* 70 (1966):52–63, especially 52–53.
2. D. B. Thompson, *Hesperia* 21 (1952):116–58. See evidence of this transitional period in dump with lower date of 320–300 B.C. (p. 122).
3. D. B. Thompson, *AJA* 70 (1966):53–58.
4. G. Kleiner, *Tanagrafiguren, JdI-EH* 15 (1942):53 n. 2 & 3; A. Köster, *Die griechischen Terrakotten* (Berlin, 1926), pl. 40.
5. D. B. Thompson, *AJA* 70 (1966):52–53; D. B. Thompson, *Hesperia* 21 (1952):130.
6. Kleiner, *Tanagrafiguren,* 53, pl. 8a (Athens 4471). See Besques, vol. 3, 22, no. D103, pl. 24d; and E. Breccia, *Catalogue général des antiquités égyptiennes, Musée du Alexandrie: La necropoli di Sciatbi* (Cairo, 1912), 120, no. 379, pl. LXIV.
7. Higgins, 204; D. B. Thompson, *AJA* 70 (1966):53.
8. Thompson, *AJA* 70 (1966):52; D. B. Thompson, *Hesperia* 21 (1952):123, 130; R. A. Higgins, *Greek Terracottas* (London, 1977), 77.
9. Higgins, 204.
10. R. V. Nicholls, *BSA* 47 (1952):217–26.

76. Figurine of Maiden

(ca. 300–275 B.C.)

K 76. Kemper Simpson Collection. Ht, 17.9 cm; w behind waist, 7.5 cm; max w at feet, 7.1 cm; max depth at feet, 4.1 cm; diam vent hole, 2.5 cm. Head missing; modern dowel in neck.

Maiden stands on left leg with right leg relaxed. Left elbow bent, with hand resting behind hip. Right elbow bent, with hand above right breast. She wears chiton beneath himation, which covers most of legs and both arms except for right hand. Ends of himation fall down left side.

The maiden is an example of the so-called Sophocles type, which takes its name from a Roman copy of a lost statue of Sophocles, which is believed to have been made about 330 B.C. for the Lycurgan refurbishment of the Theater of Dionysos in Athens.[1] The type was much imitated and reworked and enjoyed an enduring popularity in the Roman world for portraits of draped men in the Roman pallium.

Our figure exemplifies a modification and simplification that became a popular type among terracotta figurines.[2] The relaxed and supporting legs have been reversed, thereby allowing the relaxed protruding knee to emphasize the long groups of folds that originate at the left hip. At the same time the drapery folds hanging from the left hip completely conceal the supporting leg. New features are the horizontal folds extending from the right elbow across the waist and the two groups of folds that curve from the right elbow over the right thigh.

The closest parallels to our maiden are dated in the end of the fourth century and the first part of the third century.[3] Later versions of the type[4] are more hipshot and the right arm is more vertical, thereby increasing the two-dimensional effect. Plasticity is further lost in the later figurines by the way the folds along the left side of the body completely obscure its contour. Another change lies in the handling of the drapery. On our figurine there is a marked contrast between the plastic groups of continuous folds and the smooth surfaces. These differences of texture are minimized on later examples, where a multitude of broken folds agitate the surface.

On the Hopkins maiden, the blurred effect of the larger groups of folds can probably be attributed to a worn mold. It is likely then that our figurine was made sometime during the third century in a mold that was fabricated near 300 BC.

1. M. Bieber, *Ancient Copies* (New York, 1977), 130, fig. 581; B. Neutsch, *Studien zur vortanagräisch-attischen Koroplastik, JdI-EH* 17 (1952):30; G. Kleiner, *Tanagrafiguren, JdI-EH* 15 (1942):95–98, 123.
2. E. Breccia, *Terrecotte figurate greche e greco-egizie del Museo di Alessandria: Monuments de l'Égypte gréco-romaine,* vol. 2, fasc. 1 (Bergamo, 1930), 27, nos. 1, 4, 6–9, pls. A, H, M, IX, LIV.
3. Poulsen, 24–25, no. 37, pl. XIX; Besques, vol. 3, 5, no. D51, pl. 12, dated 330–320; Kleiner, *Tanagrafiguren,* 95–96, 104, pls. 5b, d, dated 325–300.
4. Ibid., 96, 105, pl. 5c (London, C263), dated 300–250; Breccia, *Terrecotte figurate,* 27, pl. D2, no. 5, dated by Kleiner (96, 104) to 300–275 B.C.; and Breccia, 27, no. 3, pl. H.1.

77. Figurine of Maiden

(ca. 200 B.C.)

K 72. Kemper Simpson Collection. Ht, 27.7 cm; max w behind waist, 9 cm; diam vent hole, 2 cm; base, 10 cm × 6.2 cm. Broken across neck, with modern dowel.

Woman stands on left leg with right knee bent and foot placed behind her and to the side. Over her chiton she wears a himation, which is brought over the right shoulder and left arm with the ends hanging down the left side. Both arms are concealed by drapery folds; her left arm is at her side, while her right arm is bent at the elbow with the hand placed just above the right breast.

Our figurine exemplifies a type that derives from a pair of statues that survive only in ancient copies, the best known of which are the Large and Small Women of Herculaneum, after whom the types take their name. The original statues are thought to have represented Demeter and Kore and to have been made in the late fourth century under Praxitelean inspiration.[1] Both statues enjoyed a substantial popularity in the following centuries, and often, as here, inspired conflated versions. Our figurine is reminiscent of the Large Herculaneum Woman in the gesture of the right arm, which is bent and brought just above the right breast. She recalls the Small Herculaneum Woman in the way her left leg supports the body while the right leg is relaxed.

Similar to both Herculaneum types is the draping of the himation over the right shoulder with the ends brought over the left arm. Unique to the terracotta type, however, is the simplification of the folds and the way the fabric is pulled tautly in continuous ridges over the front of the torso, thereby flattening the form and obscuring the contours of the right forearm. The result is a lack of plasticity and an emphasis on the triangular patterns described by the passages of drapery between the elbows, hands, and knee.

Terracottas of the type of our figurine are fairly common, both in mainland Greece and in the west.[2] An example from Herakleia Minoa of the first half of the third century[3] is probably earlier, since our figure's himation has a weightier, more constraining quality over the right arm, and the fabric over the abdomen and right hip forms isolated mannered passages that fragment the surface. A close parallel to our maiden is a Sicilian figurine of ca. 250–200,[4] on which we also see a similar elongation of the body, with very narrow shoulders, broad hips, and long thighs.[5] Particularly noteworthy on our figurine is the transparency of the fabric over the abdomen, thereby revealing the vertically corrugated folds of the underlying chiton in a manner that foreshadows second-century examples.[6] The large size suggests that the figurine is a product of southern Italy, where the type was known from about 300 B.C.[7]

1. M. Bieber, *Ancient Copies* (New York, 1977), 148–62, figs. 664–65, 668–69; G. Kleiner, *Tanagrafiguren, JdI-EH* 15 (1942):107.

2. Kleiner, *Tanagrafiguren,* 16, 25, 90, 108, pls. 6.6; 7; 9c,d,f; 21a.

3. M. Bell, *OpusRom* 9 (1973):88–89, fig. 7.

4. Compare E. Langlotz and M. Hirmer, *Ancient Greek Sculpture from South Italy and Sicily* (New York, 1965), 299–300, pl. 152, dated 100 B.C. by Bell (see note 3), 87, 90–92, fig. 2, dated 250–200 B.C.

5. See D. B. Thompson, *Ptolemaic Oinochoai and Portraits in Faience: Aspects of the Ruler Cult* (Oxford, 1973), 112–16.

6. Kleiner, *Tanagrafiguren,* 112, pl. 19e,f; Bell *OpusRom* 9 (1973):87, 92–94, fig. 4; D. B. Thompson, *AJA* 54 (1950): 371—85.

7. Bell, *OpusRom* 9 (1973):88 n. 13, from a tomb in Tarentum.

78. Figurine of Maiden

(second c. B.C.)

K 73. Kemper Simpson Collection. Ht, 27.7 cm; w behind waist, 9 cm; diam vent hole, 2.8 cm; w base, 8 cm; depth base, 6.3 cm; ht base, 3 cm. Intact.

Woman stands on right leg with left relaxed. Left elbow bent with hand across waist; right elbow bent with hand behind hip. Over chiton is himation draped over right shoulder, passing between the breasts, and covering body

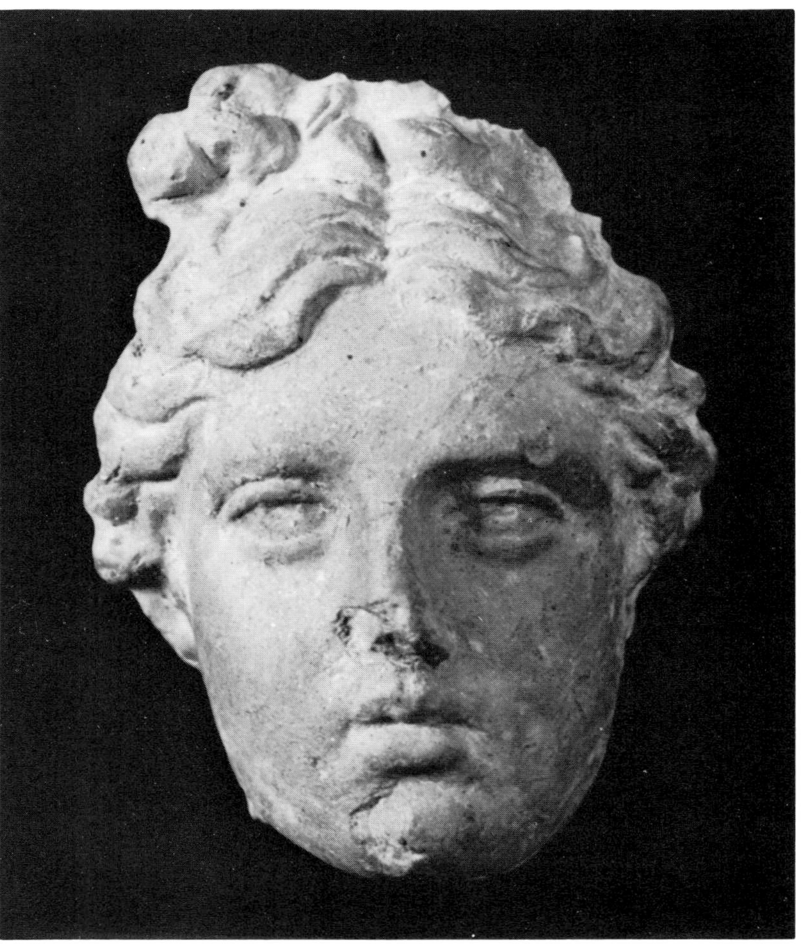

to the knees. Maiden, gazing to her right, has a long neck with Venus rings. Hair is arranged in stippled melon hairstyle with bun at crown and braids around forehead; fabric added at crown hangs behind head. Stepped rectangular base.

The maiden stands in the same pose as that of the Boeotian maiden (no. 75). However, the effect has dramatically changed. The figure is larger and the proportions are elongated, especially in the area between hip and thigh. The horizontal placement of the left forearm and the cascade of drapery falling vertically down her right side heighten the two-dimensional effect. In contrast to the arrangement of drapery on the earlier figure (no. 75), the himation here passes between the breasts, thereby dividing them. Also having a partitioning effect are the horizontal lower edge of the himation and the V-shaped folds outlining the genitals.

The lengthened proportions and divisive nature of the fabric, coupled with the exaggerated thrust of the right hip and the sagging lines of the drapery folds (especially those to the right knee), suggest a date in the second century.[1] The lack of plasticity in the upper edge of the mantle and the mechanically furrowed valleys in the lower part of the chiton indicate a worn mold that was halfheartedly reworked.

1. E. Langlotz and M. Hirmer, *Ancient Greek Sculpture from South Italy and Sicily* (New York, 1965), pls. 151–52.

79. Female Head

(second–first c. B.C.)

42.58. Brooklyn Museum Gift. Ht, 6.6 cm; w, 4.9 cm. Back concave. Broken across neck. Chin chipped; top of hair broken away.

Wavy hair parted in middle and brushed over ears; ends tied in knot at crown. Disc earrings. Incised contour of iris; punched pupils set just beneath upper lids. Full lips, slightly open.

Many of the terracotta figurines made in Smyrna were small-scale renderings of major sculpture and betray their debt to statuary in their large size (up to 80 cm in height), occasional gilding, delicacy of modeling, and the incisions of iris and pupil.[1] Our piece reflects Praxitelean inspiration in the oval face, triangular forehead, almond-shaped eyes, and soft bow lips. The hairstyle is a more elaborate version of that worn by the Aphrodite of Cnidos, here with the ends brought up from the nape to the crown. Several parallels for our head exist, a few possibly from the same mold, others representing a degenerated treatment of the same type, perhaps from as late as the second century A.D.[2] The handling of our example assigns it to the second century B.C., to which figurines of comparable style, also with pierced pupils, have been dated.[3]

1. A. Delhaye-Cahen, *L'Antiquité classique* 38 (1969):394, no. 1, pl. I; 401, no. 5, pl. V; and 404, no. 7, pl. VII. Besques, vol. 3, 190.

2. Delhaye-Cahen, 399, 406–7, no. 4, pl. IV; Poulsen (39, no. 76, pl. XLIII) and P. G. Leyenaar-Plaisier [*Les terres cuites grecques et romaines: Catalogue de la collection du Musée National des antiquités à Leiden* (Leiden, 1979), 162, no. 367, pl. 61] date the head in the second century A.D., but Delhaye-Cahen (404) dates it to the first century B.C.

3. Besques, vol. 3, 199 and 202, no. D1506, pl. 283c; J. Sieveking, *Die Terrakotten der Sammlung Loeb II* (Munich, 1916), 49–50, pl. 108. Compare heads from Smyrna, which Sieveking dates by their hairstyles to periods of Claudius and Trajan (49–50, pl. 108).

80. Infant Herakles with Snakes

(first c. B.C.–A.D.)

9200. Provenance unknown. Ht, 12 cm; ht head, 3.6 cm; w between legs, 7 cm. Hard-baked reddish clay. Broken away are left arm, right leg, most of left leg except for part of thigh and lower leg. Mended across right upper arm, but wrist and right hand missing. Black glaze across joins where left arm and right leg attached. Other spots of black glaze on underside of left leg where shin would have rested on base. Figurine mold-made with modeled back, no vent. Left thigh and torso are hollow. Extensively retouched after molding and before firing.

Nude stocky male kneels with thighs widespread, left thigh pressing upon left lower leg, which was slightly elevated above right thigh. Torso presses upon left side; right arm is uplifted with elbow bent; left arm was held close to side. Head, perched above a very short neck, is directed downward. Ridged forehead, arched eyebrows, open mouth. Short curly locks of hair.

Bibliography: E. R. Williams, *Hesperia* 51 (1982):357–64.

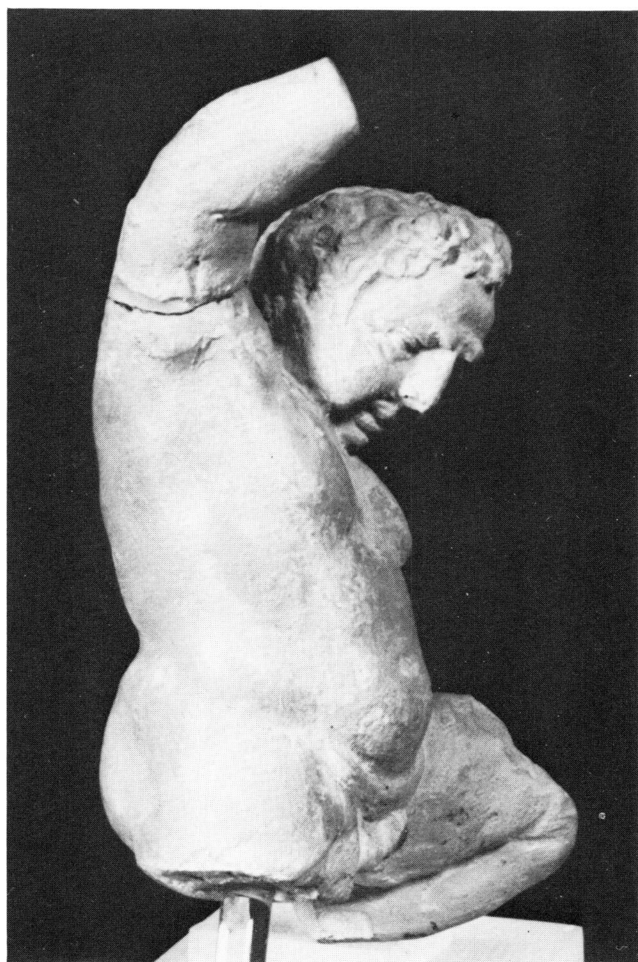

This figurine represents one of the more familiar episodes in the adventures of Herakles. Although his ostensible father was the mortal Amphitryon, Herakles was actually the son of Zeus. To test or to reveal the child's true parentage, Hera or Amphitryon sent snakes to attack Herakles and his twin brother Iphicles as they lay sleeping.[1] The terror of the helpless Iphicles was obvious proof of that child's mortal nature; Herakles, however, was undaunted and skillfully crushed the snakes, therewith revealing his divine birth.

The Hopkins figurine exemplifies the admirable quality of the terracottas made in Smyrna between the early third century B.C., when the city was refounded by Lysimachus, and 178 A.D., when the city was destroyed by earthquake. Distinctive technical features of terracottas from Smyrna are the reddish, hard-baked clay and the extensive reworking by hand. The Hopkins statuette contributes another characteristic: the use of black glaze as an adhesive, a practice first attested in Athens during the second century B.C. Terracottas from Smyrna can be dated only by stylistic comparison with securely dated figurines from other sites; in this instance, the pose and facial expression of our Herakles find their closest parallels among representations of mime actors made in the first century B.C. and first century A.D.

Although a pictorial tradition of Herakles' snaky drama is attested as early as the fifth century B.C., our figurine is certainly based upon a Hellenistic sculpture that is most clearly reflected in Roman copies in the Uffizi and Hermitage, as well as in a figure on a pillar from the Hadrianic baths in Aphrodisias. Since the composition and style of this type compare closely with figures on the Pergamon Altar (ca. 180–160 B.C.), it is likely that the prototype of our piece was created during the second century B.C.

1. See full publication of E. R. Williams, *Hesperia* 51 (1982):357–64.

Terracottas

ETRUSCAN AND ITALIC

81. Mold for Gorgon Antefix

(late sixth c. B.C.)

9201. Baltimore Society AIA, formerly Helbig Collection. "Capua." Ht, 33 cm; w, 35 cm; th, 4–7 cm. Broken across top and down right side. Section of semicylindrical cover tile remains in place behind.

Cast

Gorgon head with five shell curls on each side of a central part, which continues down to the nose as a pronounced ridge. Two beaded locks fall from behind each ear to shoulders. Fourteen flame-shaped locks are suspended from jaw as beard. Open mouth with gaping tongue between four tusks. Beneath head is projecting taenia and, in lower relief, a broad fascia. Head is enclosed by a thin band winding into volutes at base, a half-round molding and a shell frame.

Bibliography: Robinson, *AJA* 27 (1923):1–7, figs. 1–2.

This mold and the following four antefixes are said to have come from Capua, a city located in the region of Campania south of Rome. This area came under Etruscan domination around 650 B.C.[1] and enjoyed a period of exceptional prosperity during the sixth century. Soon after the Etruscan defeat at Cumae in 474, however, Campania began to drift out of Etruscan control and between 450 and 400 was lost to the Samnites.[2]

Capua had two religious centers, one of which was a temple to Diana Tifatina,[3] which has yielded only a few architectural fragments dating from 550–500. The much larger sanctuary of Fondo Patturelli was in existence by 550, but its most prosperous phase is dated around 500 B.C.[4] This latter complex was probably dedicated to Juno, or possibly Jupiter, who was equally honored on Capuan coinage. The sanctuary was excavated between 1845 and 1873 and yielded many architectural fragments, which were subsequently dispersed among a number of museums. Several types of antefixes were identified, including a gorgon and a female head, both of which are represented by examples at Hopkins. Other types include a palmette, Herakles and the Nemean lion, and Eos and Cephalos.[5] Each type admitted variants, and there are as many as seven versions of the gorgon type

The artists who produced the Capuan antefixes were primarily influenced by koroplasts at Cumae and Pithecusa, who were themselves inspired by Corinthian and Ionian workshops.[6] The shell of concave tongues is thought to be a Capuan contribution that soon came into great favor in Etruscan centers, e.g., Veii.[7]

Campanian antefixes were very much admired in ancient Italy. Replicas made in the same molds have been found in several sites in southern Italy, at Satricum, and at Caere in Etruria.[8] There is, however, no evidence for the export of Campanian molds,[9] although it is possible that an imported cast could have been used as the archetype for a second generation of locally manufactured antefixes.[10]

The closest parallel for our mold is an antefix from Capua.[11]

1. M. Frederiksen, in *Italy Before the Romans*, ed. D. Ridgway (New York, 1979), 298, 305.

2. A Boëthius, *Etruscan and Early Roman Architecture* (New York, 1978), 33; J. Heurgon, *Recherches sur l'histoire, la religion et la civilisation de Capoue préromaine, Bibliothèque des Écoles françaises d'Athènes et de Rome*, no. 154 (Paris, 1942), 81–82; Brendel, 256.

3. Heurgon, *Recherches*, 298–329.

4. Heurgon, *Recherches*, 330–92, especially 344, 362, 368; M. Frederiksen (see note 1), 300.

5. Heurgon, *Recherches*, 347, 348, 353, 360, pl. 4.

6. Frederiksen (see note 1), 300–301.

7. R. J. Riis, *Tyrrhenika* (Copenhagen, 1941), 185; E. Richardson, *The Etruscans* (Chicago, 1964), 100.

8. Boëthius (*Architecture*, 36) dates the temple of Mater Matuta at Satricum to ca. 500; Frederiksen (see note 1), 301.

9. Frederiksen, 301.

10. See discussion of generations in E. Jastrow, *OpusArch* 2 (1941):1–28.

11. Robinson, *AJA* 27 (1923), 6, fig. 5 (Berlin 7154); which is the same as H. Koch, *Dachterrakotten aus Campanien* (Berlin, 1912), 36, pl. VI.4.

82. Gorgon Antefix

(late sixth c. B.C.)

9202. Baltimore Society AIA, formerly Helbig Collection. Ht, 33 cm; w, 33 cm; th, 3.5 cm. Right side of fascia broken away, as is most of back.

Shell frame of fifteen tongues encloses half-round molding and band winding into a volute at each side. Hair rendered as eight ringlets with shell tips on either side of central part. Extended tongue beneath seven upper teeth flanked by tusks. Two pelleted locks extend from behind each ear to shoulders. Seventeen flame-shaped locks of beard around jawline. Shoulders below curving neckline are slightly raised; fascia beneath slightly recessed.

Border of tongues and bands on half-round molding colored alternately red and purple. Eyes of volute purple; horizontal lines across half-round molding above volutes are red. Hair purple; ears red. Features purple except for red mouth and tongue. Locks of beard alternately red and purple. Red on neckline; wavy line beneath dots. Meander on fascia has red band enclosing purple blocks.

Bibliography: Robinson, *AJA* 27 (1923):9–12, fig. 7.

This and the following four entries are antefixes, or ornamental and apotropaic additions to the roofline of a temple. The semi-cylindrical extension behind the painted unit rested directly upon the eave tile at the edge of the roof.[1]

The closest parallels to this antefix are from Capua[2] and Caere,[3] and there are similar examples from Satricum.[4] The antefix from Caere is believed to have been made around 500–490 B.C., which is also the probable date of our piece.

1. A. Boëthius, *Etruscan and Early Roman Architecture* (New York, 1978), 57 and fig. 47.

2. H. Koch, *Dachterrakotten aus Campanien* (Berlin, 1912), 33, pl. V.6. See also Spinazzola, pl. 10.1. A final example is Robinson, *AJA* 27 (1923):9, fig. 8, in Berlin (no. 7237).

3. E. Douglas van Buren, *Figurative Terra-cotta Revetments in Etruria and Latium* (New York, 1921), 6, pl. II, fig. 2 (Florence no. 72997); which is the same as R. Vighi, *StEtr* 5 (1931):119 and 120, pl. XI.3, where it is dated to 500–490 in the second period of phase II. See also A. Andrén, *Architectural Terracottas from Etrusco-Italic Temples* (Lund, and Leipzig, 1939), 34, no. II.12, pl. 10:32.

4. Andrén, *Terracottas*, 467, no. II.5, and pl. 144:502 (type II.5), which is the same as van Buren, *Terra-cotta Revetments*, pl. II.1. See also Mrs. S. A. Strong, *JRS* 4 (1914):167–68, pl. 26, no. 1, from the temple of Mater Matuta.

83. Gorgon Antefix

(ca. 500 B.C.)

9203. Baltimore Society AIA, formerly Helbig Collection. "Capua." Ht, 16.5 cm; w, 28 cm; av th, 2.5 cm. Shell broken away along top and right side. Cover tile broken away behind. Black on eyebrows, eyelids, pupil.

Hair is center-parted and brushed smoothly to each side. Eyes elongate to a point at outer corners. Protruding tongue and two upper front teeth are enclosed by four tusks, on other side of which are four upper and lower teeth on each side. Shell behind.

Bibliography: D. M. Robinson, *AJA* 27 (1923):7–9, fig. 6.

This antefix is an early example of the type that represents a gorgon head within a shell. Noteworthy is the absence both of intermediary members between hair and shell and of a taenia and fascia beneath. The hair does not yet exhibit the shell curls and beaded locks that distinguish later versions. The closest parallel is an antefix from Capua, which differs from our own example in having larger tusks and eyebrows in higher relief.[1]

1. H. Koch, *Dachterrakotten aus Campanien* (Berlin, 1912), 38, pl. VII.2 of class B.

1. Spinazzola, pl. 11, probably from the same mold. Also similar is H. Koch, *Dachterrakotten aus Campanien* (Berlin, 1912), 41, type 4, pl. VIII.1, but, versus Robinson, *AJA* 27 (1923):17, probably not from same mold. See P. J. Riis [*From the Collection of the Ny Carlsberg Glyptothek II* (Copenhagen, 1939), 141, 142, fig. 2], who dates the type to the first third of the sixth century.

2. A. Andrén, *Architectural Terracottas from Etrusco-Italic Temples* (Lund and Leipzig, 1939), 467, no. II.6, pl. 144:503–4; which is the same as E. Douglas van Buren, *Figurative Terra-cotta Revetments in Etruria and Latium* (New York, 1921), 20, pl. XIII, fig. 2. Van Buren notes that three sizes of this type have been identified. See also antefix said to be from Etruria in van Buren, 20, pl. XIII, fig. 3.

84. Female Head Antefix

(ca. 500 B.C.)

9204. Baltimore Society AIA, formerly Helbig Collection. "Capua." Ht, 34.3 cm; w, 34 cm. Intact.

Within a sixteen-tongued frame is a half-round molding, then a band terminating in a volute at each side. Female head in high relief; garment very low relief. Hair center-parted, with wavy strands brushed behind each ear; two long, straight, pelleted locks fall from behind each ear to shoulder. Disc earrings. Curving neckline of dress; beneath is narrow taenia above broader fascia in lower relief.

Border of tongues and bands on half-round molding alternately outlined in red and purple. Volutes have purple eyes and red borders. Maiden has purple hair. Red outlines contours of ears and of disc earrings. Two red necklaces: a semicircle crossed by short lines above a wavy line with row of discs beneath. Features purple except for red lips. Garment rendered as two solid-purple triangles enclosing a reserved area containing a purple triangle flanked by dots enclosing swastika. Bands alternating red and purple on taenia and for meander on fascia.

Bibliography: D. M. Robinson, *AJA* 27 (1923):16–18, fig. 18.

The closest parallels come from Capua;[1] similar examples were found in Satricum.[2]

85. Female Head Antefix

(ca. 500 B.C.)

9205. Baltimore Society AIA, formerly Helbig Collection. "Capua." Ht, 36 cm; w, 3.3 cm. Volutes and lotus broken away on right side, as is shell over head. Part of cover tile survives. Red on background behind lotus and along edges of stalks. Red on stephane and diadem; black hair. Red and black meander on fascia.

Female head enclosed by stalks rising from round blossom with raised center. Each stalk flanked by stem with drooping lotus blossom. Head wears stephane surmounted by diadem with volute tips. Center-parted hair brushed smoothly to sides behind ears; two beaded locks fall to shoulders. Neckline completely unmodeled. Below is narrow raised taenia above broader fascia in lower relief.

Bibliography: D. M. Robinson, *AJA* 27 (1923):14–15, fig. 15.

In its undamaged state, this antefix had an arc of shells between the stalks above the head. A similar antefix from Capua[1] has a more advanced treatment of eyes and mouth. A related type was found in Cumae.[2]

1. Spinazzola, pl. 11. The type is closest to H. Koch, *Dachterracotten aus Campanien* (Berlin, 1912), 55, pl. XII.2, which Robinson [*AJA* 27 (1923):14] believed was from the same mold. See also P. J. Riis, *From the Collections of Ny Carlsberg Glyptothek II* (Copenhagen, 1939), 141, 142, fig. 3, dated 575–550 B.C.

2. L. Scatozza, *Klearchos* 13 (1971), 73–74, no. 674, fig. 19.

86. Antefix with Mistress of Wild Beasts

(fourth c. B.C.)

383. Purchased in Rome or Naples in 1906–9. "Palestrina." Ht, 31 cm; max w, 22 cm; max th, 16 cm. Heads and forepaws of animals broken off, as is female's body above waist. Most of cover tile broken away behind. Red on paryphe, edge of hem, and shoes. Across fascia is white band between red bands.

Female stands frontally, heels touching and toes turned out to each side. Broad central paryphe overlies longer stepped panels beneath; both hem edge and overfold at hip level fall in schematic patterns. Felines stand on hind legs with near leg advanced, tails curving up between legs, extended forelegs resting on maiden's sides. Fascia beneath.

The mistress of wild beasts first appeared on Campanian antefixes in the sixth and fifth centuries.[1] The theme was introduced into Etruria and Latium in the fourth century, and there it continued in fashion into the first century B.C. These later antefixes are of two types. In that represented by the Hopkins example, the goddess is winged only at the shoulders and wears a long apoptygma to midthigh. On each side of her is a feline standing on its hind legs with one of its forepaws against the woman's leg and the other one in her hand.[2]

Antefixes of the Hopkins type have been found in a number of sites in Latium and in Etruria.[3] An especially close parallel comes from Ardea and belonged to a group of architectural terracottas that were applied to the temple during the fourth century.[4] The Ardea antefixes also include a variant,[5] in which the toes of the maiden's feet point to the front and are almost concealed by the broad folds of her garment, which lacks our figure's paryphe and patterned lower hemline. The felines crouch on their haunches, their forepaws clasping the grapes that she holds in each hand.

A second example of this variant comes from Palestrina, where the Hopkins antefix was reputedly discovered.[6] The excavators concluded that the antefixes alternated with ones representing winged males in Phrygian caps, a type known from Civita Castellana and Capua.[7] If the provenance of the Hopkins piece is correct, our antefix probably came from the same structure and thus should be dated within the fourth century.

1. P. J. Riis, *Tyrrhenika* (Copenhagen, 1941), 12–13; A. Andrén, *Architectural Terracottas from Etrusco-Italic Temples* (Lund and Leipzig, 1940), ccxxix.

2. Andrén, *Terracottas,* ccxxx. On the second type the goddess stands frontally but with her feet in right profile. Three pairs of wings rise from her shoulders, ankles, and below the overfold at her waist. Two felines stand at either side of her waist, their hind legs resting on the wings, the forelegs upon her breast. See Andrén, ccxxix, and pl. 97:352.

3. Ibid., ccxxx; Riis, *Tyrrhenika,* 12–13, 37, 39, 41–42.

4. Andrén, *Terracottas,* 438, 442, 447, no. II.8, pl. 135. See also A. Andrén, *Terrecotte di Ardea: Corolla Archeologica* (Lund, 1932), 107, no. A19, pl. II, fig. 2; E. Stefani, *NSc* 7, 5–6 (1944–45):102, fig. 29b.

5. Stefani, 102, fig. 30.

6. D. Vaglieri, *NSc* 5, 4 (1907):300, fig. 19.

7. Andrén, *Terracottas,* ccxxx.

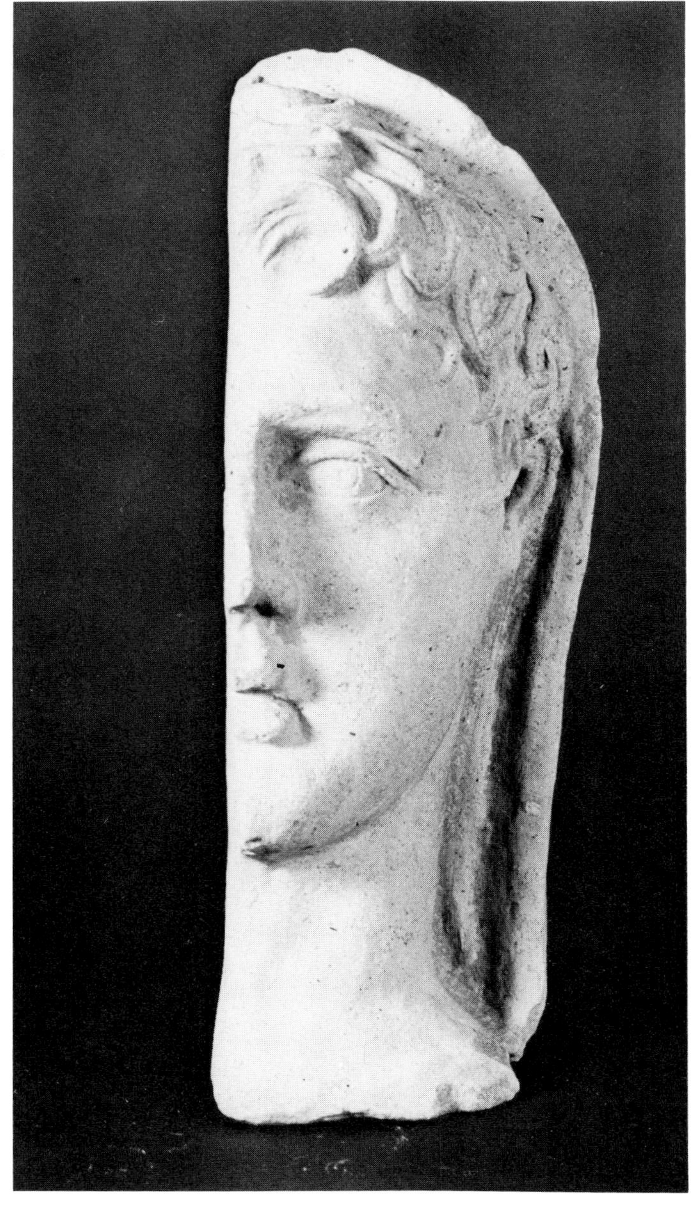

87. Half Votive Head

(300–250 B.C.)

1805. Baltimore Society AIA. Ht, 31 cm; w base, 11.8 cm. Diam vent hole in center of back is 4 cm. Open beneath. Flat side curves smoothly into unmolded back. Intact.

Left side of male head with short curly hair beneath a mantle, which is draped over top and back of head. Incised iris and punched pupil.

Bibliography: D. M. Robinson, *AJA* 27 (1923):21–22, 340, fig. 26.

Large, even lifesize terracotta heads,[1] full face or in either profile, have been found in a number of sites, including Caere,[2] Rome,[3] Capua,[4] and Narce.[5] Most of the heads are male, although female examples are known from Caere, Veii, and Capua.[6] Usually the heads are draped for sacrifice, a feature that would be appropriate to the use of these objects as votive gifts. Most examples have been dated on stylistic grounds between the fourth and first centuries B.C.[7]

The heads are mold-made but occasionally show reworking, probably added to introduce individual features. Our example has not been retouched but clearly belongs to a type inspired by Lysippan works, such as those reflected in the Apoxyomenos and the Azara Herm.[8] Particularly similar are the short curls with cowlick, the small eye, fleshy brow, and the short, full lips. Comparable votive heads are found in the Schloss Fasanerie[9] and the Chesterman Collection[10]

1. For a full study of the type, see G. Hafner, *RömMitt* 73 (1966):29–52; and *RömMitt* 72 (1965):41–61.

2. R. Mengarelli, *StEtr* 9 (1935):91–94, pls. XIX–XXI; E. Richardson, *MAAR* 26 (1960):378, no. 3, fig. 93, from Cosa; D. M. Robinson, *AJA* 27 (1923):21, fig. 27, from Veii.

3. L. G. LoGuzzo, *Il deposito votivo dall'Esquilino detto di Minervo Medica* (Rome, 1978), 90, pl. XXXV.

4. M. Bonghi Jovino, *Terrecotte votive: Capua preromana* vol. 1 (Florence, 1963), 23–24; Brendel, 393–94.

5. Breitenstein, 85, no. 803, pl. 102.

6. Hornbostel, 141, no. 112; Mengarelli, *StEtr* 9 (1935):91, pl. XIX.2; Hafner, *RömMitt* 72 (1965):41–61; Bonghi Jovino, *Terrecotte,* 23.

7. Hafner, *RömMitt* 73 (1966):35, 50. R. Blatter [*AntK* 3 (1960):41–42] compares a head with a first-century B.C. portrait of Drusus.

8. *The Search for Alexander: An Exhibition* (New York, 1980), 99, no. 3; C. Havelock, *Hellenistic Art,* 2d ed. (New York, 1981), 119, no. 80.

9. See H. von Heintze, *Die antiken Porträts in Schloss Fasanerie bei Fulda* (Mainz, 1968), 2, no. 2, pls. 6, 7, 100, 104.

10. J. Chesterman, *Classical Terracotta Figurines* (Woodstock, 1975), 70, fig. 80.

88. Cinerary Urn with Echetlos

(second–first c. B.C.)

9185. Probably purchased in Rome or Naples in 1906–9. Urn: l, 35 cm; ht, 21.8 cm; depth, 17.3 cm. Lid: l, 33 cm; ht, 12.5 cm. Slip over surface and extensive color over front. Intact.

Scene completely enframed by smooth border. In center is male seen from behind, nude except for roll of red fabric around waist with end over left thigh. He lunges forward on left leg, his hands supporting a long plowshare, which he thrusts at the neck of a crouching opponent. This figure faces front, weight on left knee, right leg extended to side. He carries a shield over left shoulder and a sword in uplifted right hand. He wears a helmet and cuirass above a chiton. Behind him stands a warrior with blue shield in left hand and sword in right hand, wearing a helmet, short pink tunic, and pink and blue mantle billowing out behind. At viewer's far right is a warrior moving to his right, head turned back with upraised right arm, red shield covering body, cloak hanging behind.

Lid

Figure draped in mantle lies on left side, legs bent. Head rests on two pillows, right elbow bent, with right hand on pillow beneath chin.

This urn belongs to a type of terracotta cinerary urn that was made in Chiusi.[1] The urns are distinguished by the recumbent or semi-reclining figure on the lid and by the mythological relief on the front of the urn itself. Examples with reliefs identical to our own have been found in Chiusi or bear inscriptions referring to individuals who are otherwise documented in the Chiusi area.[2]

Our scene is a common one.[3] The nude male with plowshare is generally believed to be the Athenian hero Echetlos, who arose out of the ground at Marathon to protect his fellow countrymen during the Persian attack in 490.[4] The battle was the subject of a painting executed in the 460's by Mikon for the Stoa

Poikile in Athens (Paus. 1.15.3, 1.32.5) and it is surely this much-copied work that provided the prototype for the urn's figure. Harrison, following Robert, suggested that the warrior behind Echetlos was also derived from the Marathon painting and represents Epizelos, the Athenian who continued to fight valiantly although blinded by a vision; Epizelos is thought to have been depicted in the painting as we see him here, with hand upraised to his face.[5]

The appearance of these mythical Attic heroes on Etruscan urns is explained by the Etruscan tendency, apparent as early as the fourth century, to emphasize allegorical connotations of traditional myths.[6] Understandably, the patriotic zeal of Echetlos had particular appeal.[7]

The reliefs for the urns were produced in molds that were made either from a hand-modeled archetype or by taking an impression from another mold-made relief. Because a terracotta shrinks 10%–20% between generations (from relief to mold to relief), the reliefs on the urns vary widely in size.[8] They also vary in composition. We occasionally find a dentil molding on the Echetlos urns[9] or, as on our own example, none at all. Some reliefs show a fifth figure, a female, to the far left of the scene.[10] Because urns with this fifth individual are larger than the others, and because the five-person composition is more symmetrically balanced than the four-figure group of the Hopkins type, it is likely that reliefs like our own are an abbreviated version of the more complex type. Our relief was probably made in a mold that had been impressed from a reworking of the more complex scene.

Urns like our own were placed in large, many-roomed tombs that were used over several generations. For this reason the urns cannot be dated by their burial contexts alone. Stylistically, the reliefs compare closely with those on alabaster ash urns that were made in Volterra from the third century, with marked production in the second century and in the beginning of the first century B.C.[11]

1. F. Boitani et al., *Etruscan Cities* (New York, 1975), 57; Brendel, 422. See also note 2 below.

2. Thimme, *StEtr* 25 (1957):149–50, fig. 23; G. Körte and E. Brunn, *I Rilievi della urne etrusche III* (Berlin, 1890), 5–16, fig. 3 on p. 11; A. Minto, *NSc* 6, 12 (1936):400, fig. 1; R. Noll, *StEtr* 9 (1935):308–9, pl. XLIII; G. M. A. Richter, *Handbook of the Etruscan Collection* (New York, 1940), 49–50, 56–57, fig. 143.

3. E. Harrison, *AJA* 76 (1972):367, pl. 78, fig. 18; A. Andrén, *Medelhausmuseet Bulletin* 5 (1969):39–43, who adds others; Andrén, *OpusArch* 5 (1948):81, no. 204, pl. XXXVII.

4. Harrison, *AJA* 76 (1972):367–68, but see Körte and Brunn, *Rilievi*, 5–16.

5. Harrison, *AJA* 76 (1972):367–68.

6. Brendel, 353.

7. Ibid., 380.

8. E. Jastrow, *OpusArch* 2 (1941):1–2.

9. A. Andrén, *OpusArch* 5 (1948):81, no. 204, pl. XXXVII.

10. *EAA* III, fig. 254; Körte and Brunn, *Rilievi*, vol. 3, pl. VII.

11. I. Krauskopf, *Der thebanische Sagenkreis und andere griechische Sagen in der etruskischen Kunst* (Heidelberg, 1974), 49, 87 n. 318.

89. Cinerary Urn with Eteocles and Polyneices

(second c. B.C.)

312. Purchased in Rome or Naples in 1906–9. Urn: l, 38.2 cm; ht, 27 cm; av depth, 17.6 cm. Lid: l, 43.5 cm; ht, 13 cm.

Lid

Figure draped in mantle reclines on left side, legs drawn up. Head rests on pillow; left arm bent with hand at chin. Size and staining of surface indicate that lid is alien.

Body

At top and bottom is narrow smooth band enclosing a row of tongues in low relief. At each side is vertically grooved pilaster with horizontal ribs for capital and base. In center of scene is warrior in right profile wearing blue crested helmet; red chiton; red, green, and blue cuirass; and red mantle. He lunges forward on left leg, his extended right arm, presumably with dagger, directed at throat of his opponent, while the left hand grasps the rim of the other's shield. His own shield lies beside his left leg; between his legs is the yellow and red helmet of his victim. Adversary is shown crouching on right knee, his left leg outstretched behind him, his right arm extended and holding dagger directed at the other's stomach. His left arm is upraised and bears a green shield. He wears a blue muscle cuirass above a red chiton. Symmetrically flanking the two figures is a pair of winged Vanths, who move away holding a torch with red tip in the outside hands, with the inner arms outstretched toward the center. Each wears red boots and a red and green garment to the knee that is cross-girded between the breasts and belted twice, below the breasts and at the waist, where there is an overfold. Dark blue background. Remains of inscription painted in dark red retrograde across top band.

The battle of the brothers Eteocles and Polyneices appears frequently on both alabaster and terracotta funerary urns from Chiusi.[1] Eteocles and Polyneices, who were the sons of Oedipus, agreed to alternate the administration of Thebes, but when Eteocles refused to give way to his brother, Polyneices attacked the city, precipitating a duel in which the brothers killed each other. The subject is depicted frequently in Etruscan art from the beginning of the fifth century[2] and it appears on sarcophagi from the end of the fourth century, beginning with the well-known example from the François tomb (330–300 B.C.).[3]

We know that the artistic tradition of the conflict originates in archaic Greek art because Pausanias (5.19.6) tells us that on the Cypselos chest, Eteocles was shown killing a kneeling Polyneices.[4] A major work of the fifth or fourth century may have served as the prototype for our scene, since on the sarcophagus from the François tomb the composition echoes the description in Euripides' *Phoenissae* (1404ff.), where Eteocles is said to have thrust his sword into the fallen Polyneices, who in turn directed his sword upward into his brother's torso. The more immediate predecessors for the scene on our urn are represented

by two stone sarcophagi of the early third century now in Tarquinia and London.[5]

As is typical with Etruscan terracotta urns, several variations of this composition and combination of moldings are known. Our two Vanths are substitutions for the two warriors[6] who appear on the earliest examples from the beginning of the third century. On urns from the end of the series, the shield of the crouching Eteocles is omitted and that of Polyneices is transformed into drapery. Occasionally we find that a fallen warrior or Oedipus with a companion has been added.[7] Because our relief retains the shield as well as the moldings and pilaster, it probably dates to not long after the beginning of the series, in the later third or first part of the second century B.C.

1. I. Krauskopf, *Der thebanische Sagenkreis und andere griechische Sagen in der etruskischen Kunst* (Mainz, 1974), 53–60; H. Möbius, *RömMitt* 73 (1966):68–69, pls. 30, 31; G. Körte, *I Rilievi della urne etrusche II* (Berlin, 1890), 32–56; J. Thimme, *StEtr* 23 (1954):87, 90, fig. 38; V. Poulsen, *Etruskische Kunst* (Königstein im Taunus, 1969), 21, 87; F. Boitani et al., *Etruscan Cities* (New York, 1975), 58; A. Kharsekin, *StEtr* 26 (1958):270, fig. 4; D. Levi, *NSc* 6, 4 (1928):60, 61, 73, figs. 3, 4, 11.

2. Krauskopf, *Der thebanische Sagenkreis*, 61; R. Hampe and E. Simon, *Griechische Sagen in der frühen etruskischen Kunst* (Mainz, 1964), 18–28.

3. Krauskopf, *Der thebanische Sagenkreis*, 53.

4. Paus. 5.19.6. See Hampe and Simon, *Griechische Sagen*, 23.

5. Krauskopf, *Der thebanische Sagenkreis*, 54–55.

6. Ibid., 54.

7. Ibid., 54.

90. Lid of Cinerary Urn

(second c. B.C.)

9193. Probably purchased in Rome or Naples in 1906–9. L, 47.8 cm; w, 25.5 cm; ht, 35.5 cm; ht base, 1.8 cm. Traces of white slip. Intact.

Woman reclines on left side with knees bent and legs drawn up. Her left forearm is supported by two pillows; her left index finger is extended and the rest of the fingers curled under. Right elbow bent with right hand drawing folds of mantle to left shoulder. Head turns to left and upward. She wears mantle wrapped completely around body and head, exposing only left hand, the face, and some of the hair, which is drawn back from forehead and bound in knot at nape.

The lids of Etruscan stone and terracotta sarcophagi and urns traditionally depicted the deceased in a recumbent position, as a sleeper, a banqueter, or a sleeping symposiast.[1] Our maiden belongs to Brendel's type III,[2] in which the deceased is a fully awake banqueter whose left side is supported by pillows so that the upper torso is almost vertical.

Although this type of reclining figure first appeared before the middle of the fourth century, our example is somewhat later. The body has the elongation, broad hips, and long thighs in fashion in the second century B.C., and her rubbery and inorganic construction compares well with figures on other Etruscan lids of this period.[3] The gesture of the right hand and the handling of the drapery have been inspired by contemporary Hellenistic statues and terracotta figurines. The face follows a Hellenistic interpretation of a Lysippan type, wherein the underbrow area is fleshy, the cheeks full, and lips short.

1. Brendel, 387–92.
2. Ibid., 391–92.
3. Brendel, 421, fig. 321 (dated 150–100 B.C.), and 423, fig. 322 of ca. 150 B.C.

Terracottas

ROMAN

91. Campanian Relief with Nereid

(first c. B.C.–first c. A.D.)

374. Purchased in Rome or Naples in 1906–9. L, 22.5 cm; ht, 20 cm; th, 2.2 cm. Broken across top and sides. Surface worn.

A nereid seen from behind reclines on the back of a sea horse or hippocamp (having a horse torso and forelegs, a fish tail), who moves to the viewer's left. Her left hand clasps his chest; her right arm is not shown. She is nude except for drapery folds over her right thigh and left upper arm. In the foreground and moving in the same direction is a small wingless Eros riding astride a dolphin, his right uplifted hand about to plunge a trident into a squid. A mantle fastened at his neck blows out behind. Undulating background indicates waves.

Campanian plaques are terracotta reliefs that were made in Italy from the middle of the first century B.C. well into the second century A.D., enjoying their greatest popularity in the first quarter of the first century A.D.[1] The reliefs have their antecedents in the architectural friezes that decorated Etruscan temples; however, Campanian reliefs were primarily applied to the rooflines of baths, theaters, and private homes. The reliefs are often described as neo-Attic, in reference to those products of Greek and Italian workshops from the first century B.C. to second century A.D. that freely copy or adapt earlier Greek works.[2]

The Hopkins relief bears a typical neo-Attic representation, the type of which is known to us from fragments in London and Paris.[3] The Hopkins relief is of special significance because it is the only example that preserves intact the figure of Eros. The composition on our relief is probably an earlier version than that on the relief in Paris because the space in front of our horse's head is unfilled, whereas on the Louvre relief that area is occupied by an Eros who flies toward the nereid.

The reliefs in London and Paris preserve the rest of the original composition. Advancing toward our group was another hippocamp or sea horse bearing a nereid seated sideways, her torso facing front. Her uplifted right arm held the end of her mantle, which billowed out around her head. At her knee was another Eros swimming beside her.

The nereid was traditionally seated sideways upon a dolphin and may first have been introduced to the hippocamp on the east pediment of the Parthenon as the mount of Amphitrite.[4] This composition may be reflected in the group of nymph and hippocamp on a late fifth-century or early fourth-century mosaic from Olynthos.[5] The group reappears on a pier from the Artemis temple in Ephesos[6] and surely formed part of the renowned marine thiasos of Scopas.[7]

One of the first appearances of the nereid seen from behind as she reclines on the back of a hippocamp is on a marble Rhodian vase of the late fourth century.[8] The fully reclining nude nereid seen from behind did not appear before the second century, when she was paired with a marine dragon or ketos on a pyxis lid from Canosa.[9] Other nereids in similar poses are mounted on marine centaurs and ketoi on the San Spirito marble basin of about the early first century B.C.[10]

Eros became associated with the dolphin through his mother Aphrodite, who was said to have been carried by a dolphin to Cyprus.[11] Although he rides on a dolphin as early as the fifth century, the motif is not common before the late fourth century when he also accepts other mounts, such as a triton, on a mosaic from Olympia of ca. 300 B.C.[12] or a hippocamp and sea lion, on reliefs from Thermopylae of the third century.[13] Our figure can best be compared to the figure of Eros, mounted on a dolphin and carrying a trident, seen on the Conservatori sandal, which Lattimore dates to the first century B.C.[14]

1. A Borbein, *Campanareliefs: Typologische und stilkritische Untersuchungen, RömMitt-EH* 14 (Heidelberg, 1968), 14–21, 28–29.

2. B. Ridgway, *The Severe Style in Greek Sculpture* (Princeton, 1970), 110; W. Fuchs, *Die Vorbilder der neuattischen Reliefs, JdI-EH* 20 (1959), 1–5.

3. Borbein, *Campanareliefs*, 41, pl. 8.2. The London relief is in H. von Rohden and H. Winnefeld, *Architektonische römische Tonreliefs der Kaiserzeit, Die antiken Terrakotten*, ed. R. Kekule von Stradonitz, vol. IV.2. (Berlin, 1911), 284, pl. LXXXVIII. The Paris relief is p. 302, pl. CXXXIII. A similar fragment in Basel bears a related composition of a nereid on a dolphin. See K. Schefold, *Essays in Memory of Karl Lehmann* (New York, 1964), 279–82.

4. S. Lattimore, *The Marine Thiasos in Greek Sculpture* (Los Angeles, 1976), 28; E. B. Harrison, *AJA* 71 (1967):39.

5. Lattimore, *Marine Thiasos*, 29.

6. Ibid., 52, pl. XXI, fig. 26.

7. Ibid., 13–18; Pliny, *N.H.* 36.26.

8. Ibid., 30, pl. VII, fig. 8.

9. E. Langlotz and M. Hirmer, *Ancient Greek Sculpture of South Italy and Sicily* (New York, 1965), 70, 249, pl. XX.

10. Lattimore, *Marine Thiasos*, 18, pls. V–VI, figs. 6–7.

11. Nonnus Panopolitanos, *Dionysiaca*, Bk. 13, lines 439–43.

12. Lattimore, *Marine Thiasos*, 31.

13. Ibid., 33–35, pls. X–XI, figs. 14–16.

14. Ibid., 35–37, pls. XII, XIII, figs. 17–18.

92. Campanian Relief with Winter

(first c. B.C.–first c. A.D.)

317. Probably purchased in Rome or Naples in 1906–9. Max ht, 14.5 cm; w, 13.7 cm; th, 3.5 cm. Broken all around.

Maiden in right profile strides forward with weight on advanced left leg. Right arm extended behind right hip with hand gripping left rear leg of dangling boar. Left hand supports staff, which rests on shoulder; from the tip of the staff behind maiden's shoulder hangs a hare. Figure wears a short-sleeved garment with overfold to thigh; mantle draped over shoulders with folds hanging down behind and concealing left arm and hand. Following her is a draped figure holding a staff. Plain band beneath.

The boar, hare, and enveloping mantle identify the maiden as the personification of winter. On undamaged examples of the type, the figure wears a cap and carries birds suspended from the front end of her staff.[1] Preceding her are her sisters, spring, summer, and fall. Although the four maidens are often depicted on Campanian plaques by themselves, they also appear in representations of the marriage procession of Peleus and Thetis. In this latter composition the maidens are accompanied by Herakles carrying the bull and by Hermes.[2] Our fragment probably belonged to the latter scene, since the figure with staff following winter cannot be spring, who typically carries a vessel and goat.

The prototype upon which the figure of our maiden and of her sisters is based is still undetermined; however, its prominence is attested by the frequent appearance of these figures on Arretine pottery, glazed ware from the eastern Mediterranean, and gems.[3] On the Campanian plaques the rendering of the figures exemplifies the neo-Attic style of the first century B.C. and A.D.,[4] in the slenderness of the forms, the metallically crisp relief, and the misunderstanding of the garment (whose front and back hems fall in front of the legs).

Several elements in the representation indicate a specifically Roman adaptation of the motifs. The figure of spring leads the procession, thereby reflecting the order of seasons in the Roman year.[5] Also noteworthy is the fact that in addition to carrying symbols of seasonal bounty in the traditional manner of the Greek Horae, the maidens on the Campanian plaques are engaged in agricultural activities, a feature that we

know characterized the late Roman Republican calendars.[6]

Campanian reliefs depicting the seasons were made from the late first century B.C. into the late first century or early second century A.D.[7] Although it is difficult to date our fragment more closely, the clarity of the impression indicates that the relief was made in a fresh mold and thus probably dates from the beginning or middle of the series.

1. H. von Rohden and H. Winnefeld, *Die architektonische römische Tonreliefs des Kaiserzeit; Die antiken Terrakotten* IV.2 (Berlin, 1911), 262, 288, pls. XLVII, XCVIII; Breitenstein, 90, no. 860, pl. 111; G. Hanfmann, *The Season Sarcophagus in Dumbarton Oaks* (Cambridge, 1951), vol. 1, 131–41.

2. Rohden and Winnefeld, *Tonreliefs des Kaiserzeit*, 262, pl. XLVII; Hanfmann, *Season Sarcophagus*, 131.

3. Ibid., 131–32, 140.

4. A. Borbein, *Campanareliefs: Typologische und stilkritische Untersuchungen. RömMitt-EH* 14 (Heidelberg, 1968), 25–17, 35–36. See W. Fuchs, *Die Vorbilder der neuattischen Reliefs, JdI-EH*, 20 (1959), 164–83. See Hanfmann, *Season Sarcophagus*, vol. 1, 132.

5. R. Hinks, *Myth and Allegory in Ancient Art* (London, 1939), 46; Hanfmann, *Season Sarcophagus*, vol. 2, 141.

6. Hanfmann, *Season Sarcophagus*, vol. 2, 132, 222.

7. Ibid., vol. 1, 131–32; vol. 2, 141.

93. Campanian Antefix with Nike

(late first c. B.C.–first c. A.D.)

1196. Probably purchased in Rome or Naples in 1906–9. Ht, 23.2 cm; w, 20 cm; th, 2.5 cm. Broken off behind. Face of nike and front of globe chipped.

Winged nike moves to her right, but with torso and face frontal. Over her left shoulder she carries a trophy, which is supported by her lowered left hand and raised right hand. Trophy consists of pole, cuirass, crested helmet, two spears, and two shields. Nike has short curly hair, incised iris, and punched pupil. She wears a belted peplos and mantle, the folds of which blow out to either side. She stands upon a globe, which is flanked by two horned capricorns (goat-fish) seen in profile. Beneath, as groundline, is fascia 2.5 cm high. Antefix has undulating upper contour accented by an echoing groove just inside edge.

The representation on this antefix is a well-known type[1] that combines traditional motifs into a new composition that is distinctively Augustan.

The Nike carrying a trophy appeared for the first time on the catafalque of Alexander (ca. 323 B.C.).[2] Soon afterward, the motif was seen on Seleucid coins[3]

and was later adopted by Augustus for a series of coins he issued following his victory at Actium in 31 B.C.[4]

The globe had appeared beneath Nike's feet since the Hellenistic period, as seen, for example, in a third-century B.C. tomb painting from Gnathia.[5] Although the motif was not prominent in Roman Republican art, Pompey associated himself with it[6] and Julius Caesar issued coins with Venus holding a Nike and resting her shield upon a globe.[7] It was Augustus who promulgated the composition of a Nike on a globe by employing it as a device on a series of coins that he issued after his triumph at Actium (31 B.C.). Although it has been suggested that the coin types reproduce a Greek statue that Augustus brought from Tarentum to the Curia Julia following his victory,[8] this last conclusion is not without difficulty, since the Curia statue was dedicated in 29 B.C., two years after the beginning of the coin series; furthermore, the figures on the coins are not consistent in type, sometimes appearing with, sometimes without, a trophy.[9]

The capricorn is the birth or conception symbol of Augustus.[10] Before Actium the motif played only a minor role in Augustan propaganda, but following Actium the capricorn was frequently seen, appearing, for example, on a series of coins issued in 28–27 B.C.[11]

The composition of the Hopkins antefix can thus be seen as a specifically Augustan combination of motifs. Picard has shown that the trophy originated in the Greek world as an apotropaic battlefield and grave monument. In the Hellenistic period the trophy became the personal monument of the conquering leader, carrying connotations of the leader's patron deity as well as of the goddess Tuxe. At first, the Romans regarded the trophy as the actual image of the favoring deity with whom the felicitas of the general was so closely linked. Under Julius Caesar this identification was modified and the trophy was seen to symbolize the personification of Caesar's own felicitas. Finally, under Augustus, the trophy was considered to be the embodiment of Augustus's own genius.[12]

Hölscher points out that under Augustus's predecessors, Nike, or Victoria, almost exclusively connotated military success, but that Augustus preferred to stress the security and peace attained by those conquests.[13] Although the Curial Nike was intended to evoke directly the Actium victory, the figure of Nike was soon detached from a military association. On a series of coins from 11–10 B.C., a globe is surmounted by a quietly seated Nike, significantly unaccompanied by a trophy or other military accouterments.[14] Our scene probably also bears a generalized, nonmilitary message, a formal salute to Augustus for the widespread stability and prosperity that he established.

The Hopkins antefix is related to several other types of antefix, all of which are probably earlier than our own. On one type the Nike appears in front of a palmette without a globe, but holds two capricorns by the tail.[15] A second type is almost identical to our own, but lacks a globe.[16] A final type represents a trophy upon a prow flanked by dolphins and is undoubtedly a more direct allusion to the battle at Actium.[17]

Examples of the Hopkins type of antefix have been found in Ostia, together with antefixes depicting Magna Mater; probably both groups of antefixes belonged to the same building.[18] The type was popular and continued to be made into the second century A.D.[19]

1. Breitenstein, 98, no. 932, pl. 128; T. Hölscher, *RGZM* 12 (1965):52, pl. 16.4.

2. C. Picard, *Les trophées romains, Bibliothèque des Écoles françaises d'Athènes et de Rome* 87 (Paris, 1957):47, 53.

3. Ibid., 53.

4. T. Hölscher, *Victoria Romana* (Mainz, 1967), 8.

5. Ibid., 15, pl. 3.

6. Ibid., 22–23.

7. Hölscher, *RGZM* 12 (1965):12.

8. Picard, *Les trophées*, 140, 259, 262–65; Hölscher, *Victoria Romana*, 6–7.

9. Hölscher, *Victoria Romana*, 6, 9, 38–39.

10. T. Hölscher, *RGZM* 12 (1965):62, 71ff.

11. Ibid., 64–65.

12. Picard, *Les trophées*, 27, 58, 97, 124, 159, 169, 181, 185, 225, 227, 310–11.

13. Hölscher, *Victoria Romana*, 163.

14. Ibid., 17.

15. Hölscher, *RGZM* 12 (1965):59, pls. 15–16.

16. Poulsen, 50, no. 111, pl. LXIV.

17. Picard, *Les trophées*, 256–57, 269, pl. XI.

18. Hölscher, *RGZM* 12 (1965):70; I. Jucker, *Museum Helveticum* 16 (1959):58–68; D. Vaglieri, *NSc* 5, 9 (1912):438, fig. 2.

19. Hölscher, *RGZM* 12 (1965):61.

94. Seated Doll

(late first–early second c. A.D.)

HT 787. Helen Tanzer Collection. Ht, 21.7 cm; w across buttocks, 4.5 cm; w across arms and back, 7.8 cm. Arms attached by modern wire, but fabric and scale suggest that they are original.

Nude female seated with legs together. Arms, attached by modern wire, have elbows bent and hands at side with palms facing and fingers extended. Bracelet on right upper arm. Hair center-parted in melon hairstyle with four sections on each side of part. Rising from crown is stack of five braids on either side of part, with small oval ornament in depression. Rudimentary modeling of fingers and toes.

Nude terracotta standing dolls with jointed arms and legs were made as early as the archaic period.[1] The finer examples may have been dressed and dedicated as votive offerings, while the simpler versions served as toys.[2] These dolls are thought to represent divinities, such as Aphrodite, Athena, Demeter, and Hera, or simply anonymous dancing votaries.[3]

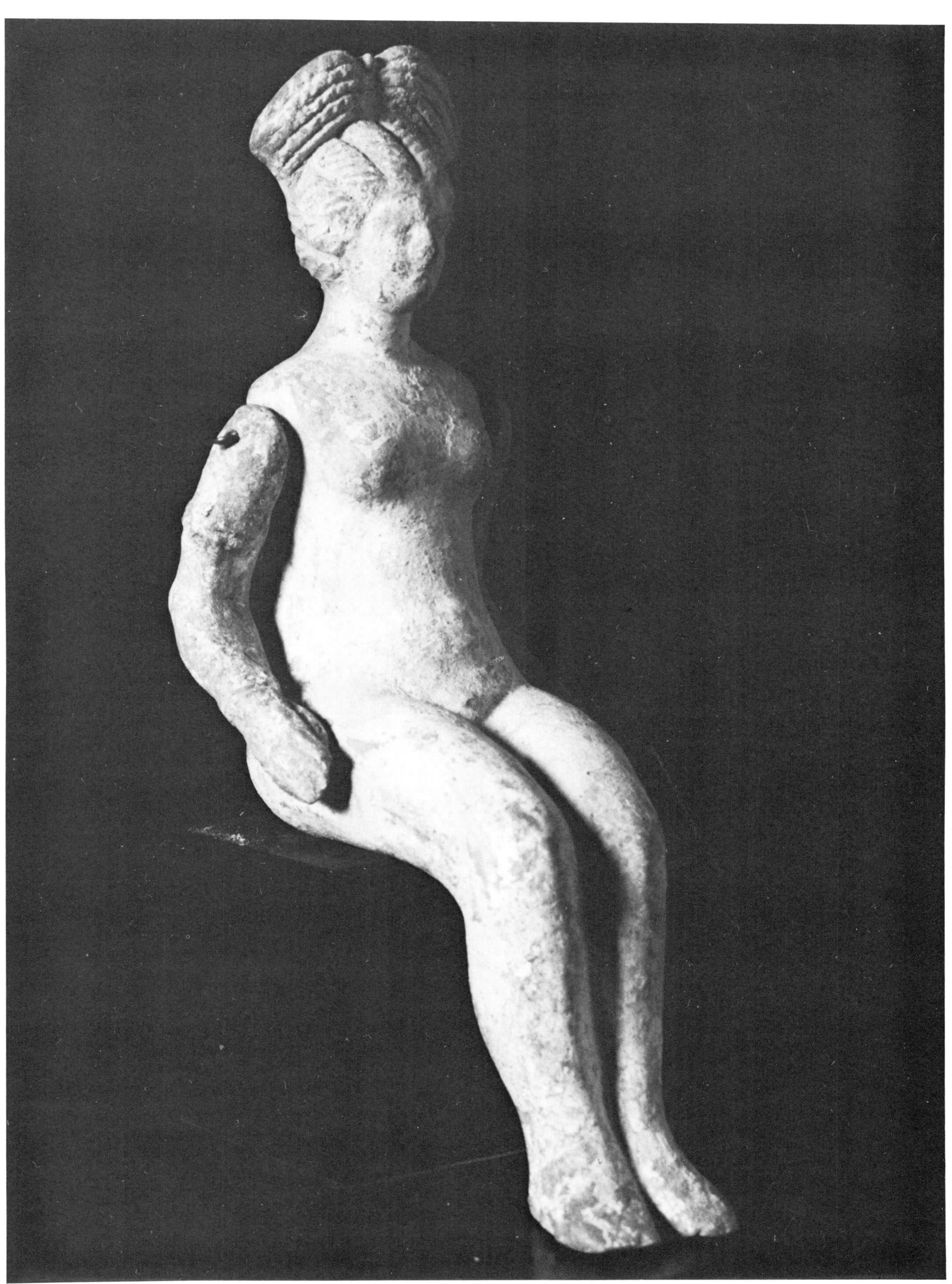

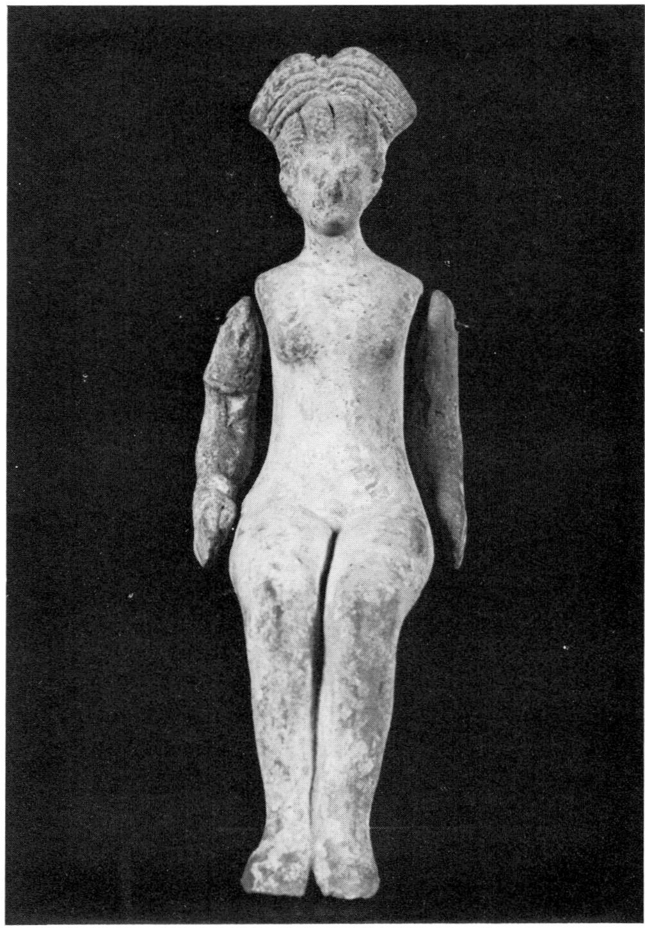

During the fifth century a seated type of doll was introduced who has immovable legs. The arms can be jointed[4] or fixed, with either both hands resting on the thighs, or one hand on thigh and one on breast.[5] Beginning in the Hellenistic period, some of these dolls wore elaborate hairstyles, cothurnoi, and ornate breast jewelry. The headdresses often include emblems of Isis,[6] thereby identifying the figures as representations of the syncretic deity Isis-Aphrodite,[7] and probably also the oriental Aphrodite-Astarte.[8] Some examples from the late Hellenistic period are dressed.[9]

The majority of the Hellenistic seated dolls, however, are nude and unadorned except for the occasional elaborate hairstyle, earrings, and wreath or diadem. These nude dolls served primarily as dedicatory offerings, grave gifts, and private possessions,[10] and enjoyed a lasting popularity well into Roman times in Greece, Asia Minor, Egypt, and southern Italy. While continuing to represent Aphrodite or Hera, they were probably also regarded either as sacred prostitutes in the cult of Artemis or the Great Mother, or, from their similarity to the more ornate dolls, Isis-Aphrodite.[11] In the Roman period figurines were occasionally modernized by reworking the hairstyle.[12] Thus our figure wears the melon arrangement of the Hellenistic period, but the braided locks at the crown, although reminiscent of some Hellenistic hairstyles,[13] most closely resemble Flavian and Trajanic fashions.[14]

1. K. Elderkin, *AJA* 34 (1930):455–79; J. Dörig, *AntK* 1 (1958):41–52.

2. Elderkin, *AJA* 34 (1930):456.

3. Thompson, *Troy*, 89.

4. A. Andrén, *OpusArch* 5 (1948):61–64, no. 31; Elderkin, *AJA* 34 (1930):468–71; Dörig, *AntK* 1 (1958):47–51.

5. Andrén, *OpusArch* 5 (1948):62; E. Töpperwein, *Terrakotten von Pergamon; Pergamenische Forschungen*, 3 (1976):57.

6. A. Laumonier, *Exploration archéologique de Délos 23; Les figurines de terre cuite* (Paris, 1956), 144–45, no. 382, pl. 42, especially 143ff; Töpperwein, *Terrakotten*, 59, 217, no. 236, pl. 38. See review by D. B. Thompson, *AJA* 83 (1979):117–18.

7. Töpperwein, *Terrakotten*, 57. See J. Sieveking, *Die Terrakotten der Sammlung Loeb*, vol. 2 (Munich, 1916), 52–53, pl. 110.

8. Töpperwein, *Terrakotten*, 57 n. 227; W. van Ingen, *Figurines from Seleucia on the Tigris* (Ann Arbor, 1939), 18–20; Thompson, *Troy* 90.

9. D. Burr, *Terra-cottas from Myrina* (Vienna, 1934), 29–30, nos. 1, 3, pl. I.

10. Töpperwein, *Terrakotten*, 56.

11. Besques, vol. 2, 11; D. B. Thompson, *AJA* 83 (1979):117–18; Thompson, *Troy*, 90–91.

12. W. Weber, *Die ägyptische griechischen Terrakotten* (Berlin, 1914), 222, no. 388, pl. 35 and 224, no. 391, pl. 35; Hornbostel, 165, no. 142.

13. P. Leyenaar-Plaisier, *Les terres cuites grecques et romaines: Catalogue de la collection du Musée National des antiquités à Leiden* (Leiden, 1979), 167, no. 381, pl. 63.

14. Besques, vol. 3, 211, no. E98, pl. 292n, o, of ca. 90–100 A.D.

95. Head of Isis-Aphrodite

(second c. A.D.)

HT 782. Helen Tanzer Collection. "Near Smyrna." Terracotta. Ht, 8.9 cm; w, 7.7 cm. Intact.

Frontal female head wears melon hairstyle consisting of five sections on either side of central part. Part continues down center back of head with hair brushed to each side. At crown of head is large flower with circular center. Behind it is a wreath comprised of four braids that overlap at crown. The back of the wreath is treated as a coil. Holes in ears. Venus ring. Broad, squat nose; short, full lips.

This head belongs to a group of terracotta heads[1] that are distinguished by their smooth undersides, indicating that the heads were never intended for attachment to bodies. The heads are also characterized by the elaborate hairstyles and head ornaments, which often include braids and floral garlands. Usually, the earlobes are pierced for earrings, which are invariably missing and were probably of metal. Examples of these heads have been found in Egypt, especially in the Fayoum,[2] and in Asia Minor, particularly around Tarsus.[3] The heads have been dated primarily by the hairstyles, which echo fashions from the first to third centuries A.D.[4] Our particular version of the melon hairstyle can be compared with portraits of the younger Faustina (161–178 A.D.),[5] wife of Marcus Aurelius, and with portraits of Julia Domna.[6] The round face, fleshy cheeks, and short, full lips are also characteristic of portraits of the later second century A.D.

Because some examples wear the disc or horns as a headdress,[7] these heads have been identified as representations of Isis. Similar ornaments also appear on contemporary bronze and terracotta figurines whose poses and gestures are those traditionally linked with Aphrodite;[8] for this reason, the figurines have been identified as representations of the syncretic deity Isis-Aphrodite. Considering the popularity of this goddess in Egypt and the eastern Mediterranean from late Hellenistic through the Roman times,[9] it is very likely that heads of the Hopkins type also depict Isis-Aphrodite.

Because Isis was considered a deity of life and love, she was naturally linked with blossoms, which, Apuleius tells us, played an important part in her cultic ceremonies.[10] We also know that ornament was important to the goddess, who is addressed in the Oxyrhynchus Litany as the "diadem of life"[11] and who was presented with diadems and jewelry in her cult at Philae.[12] Still another association was with locks of hair, both because Isis was said to have dedicated a lock to her husband Osiris[13] and because Berenice dedicated a lock to Euergetes at his departure for the Syrian Wars in 175 B.C.[14]

Since several of the terracotta heads are pierced on top for suspension, it is likely that they served as votives or amulets.[15] This latter function is especially appropriate to Isis, who was regarded as a deity of magic and who is associated with amulets[16] in connection with her special realm of childbirth.[17]

Both the elaborate headdress and the link with amulets and childbirth relate the Hopkins head to several other terracotta Isis types. Foremost among these are the so-called Brides of Death, which are large figurines who stand with feet together and hands at their sides.[18] They are nude except for necklaces, breast ornaments, and lavish headdresses. Although they were formerly thought to be concubines, it is now agreed that the figurines are statuettes of Isis that carry connotations of Aphrodite and Hathor. Examples have been found in both houses and tombs dating from the first to the third centuries A.D.; the contexts suggest that the figurines were used in private cult and as grave offerings.[19]

Floral headresses and necklaces of amulets are also worn by three other terracotta types. One of these represents Isis as an orante, standing with hands uplifted.[20] Another related type presents Isis in her association with Boubastis, protector of childbirth; these figurines are shown standing frontally while lifting their garments to expose their genitals.[21] A further type associates Isis with another goddess of childbirth, Baubo; these nude maidens squat with legs drawn up and spread wide apart, while their hands clasp the genitals in an obvious allusion to childbirth.[22]

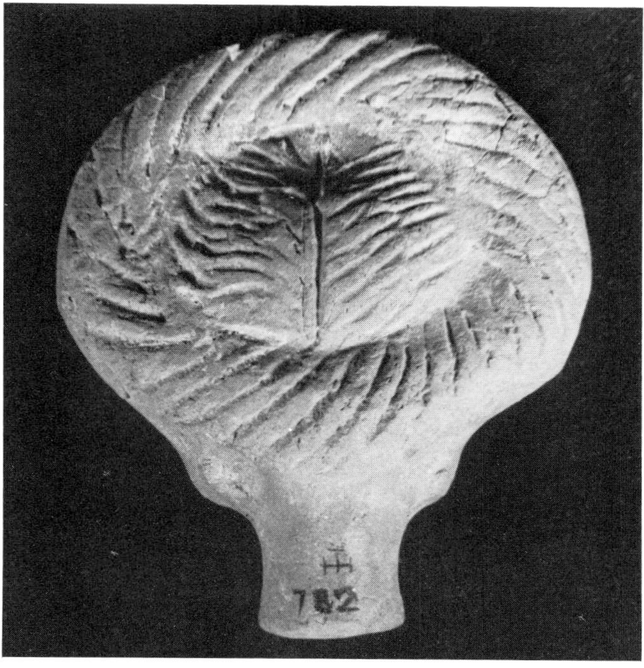

1. P. Perdrizet, *Les terres cuites grecques d'Égypte de la collection Fouquet* (Paris, 1921), 8, no. 19, pl. IX; F. Dunand, *Le culte d'Isis dans le bassin oriental de la Méditerranée, vol. 3: Le culte d'Isis en Asie Mineure* (Leiden, 1973), pl. III, from Tarsus; H. Philipp, *Terrakotten aus Ägypten im ägyptischen Museum Berlin* (Berlin, 1972), 25, no. 25, fig. 23; P. Graindor, *Terres cuites de l'Égypte gréco-romaine* (Antwerp, 1939), 34, 116–17, 120–21, nos. 41–43, pl. XVI; M. Mogensen, *La Glyptothèque Ny Carlsberg: La collection égyptienne* (Copenhagen, 1930), 40–41; C. M. Kaufmann, *Graeco-ägyptische Koroplastik* (Leipzig and Cairo, 1915), 141–42, pl. 52; W. Wijngaarden, *De Grieks-Egyptische Terracotta's in het Rijksmuseum van Oudheden* (Leiden, 1958), 26–27, nos. 83, 85–86, pl. 19.

2. W. Weber, *Die ägyptisch-griechischen Terrakotten* (Berlin, 1914), 222, no. 388, pl. 35; 224, no. 391, pl. 35. Graindor, *Terres cuites*, 118.

3. Dunand, *Le culte d'Isis en Asie Mineure*, pl. III; Graindor, *Terres cuites*, 118 n. 2, from Smyrna.

4. Weber, *Terrakotten*, 217; Perdrizet, *Les terres cuites*, 7–8, pl. IX; Phillipp, *Terrakotten*, 25, 29.

5. M. Wegner, *Das römische Herrscherbild, II.4: Die Herrscherbildnisse in antoninischer Zeit* (Berlin, 1939), 48, 53–54, pl. 36; J. Inan and E. Rosenbaum, *Roman and Early Byzantine Portrait Sculpture in Asia Minor* (London, 1966), 77, no. 46, pls. XXVIII–XXIX; A. Hekler, *Greek and Roman Portraits* (London, 1912), pl. 284b, of Lucilla.

6. H. von Heintze, *Die antiken Porträts in Schloss Fasanerie bei Fulda* (Mainz, 1968), 64, no. 43, pls. 71, 127, 128; C. C. Vermeule, *Roman Imperial Art in Greece and Asia Minor* (Cambridge, 1968), 304, fig. 158.

7. Mogensen, *La Glyptothèque*, 40, no. 232, pl. 39.

8. F. Dunand, *Le culte d'Isis dans le bassin oriental de la Méditerranée, I: Le culte d'Isis et les Ptolémées* (Leiden, 1973), pl. XX.2.

9. Ibid., 81–83.

10. Ibid., 197–98; Apuleius, *Met.*, Bk. XI, 3.5.

11. Perdrizet, *Les terres cuites*, 7; B. Grenfell and A. Hunt, *The Oxyrhynchus Papyri* (London, 1898–1972), pt. XI (1915), 190–220, no. 1380, lines 139–40, 193–94.

12. Dunand, *Le culte d'Isis et Ptolémées*, 201.

13. Ibid., 38.

14. Ibid., 38. For the association between Isis and the wives of Egyptian kings, see 34ff.

15. Kaufmann, *Koroplastik*, 142; Graindor, *Terres cuites*, 116, nos. 41, 42, pl. XVI.

16. Graindor, *Terres cuites*, 110, no. 38, pl. XV; Plutarch, *Mor., De Is. et Os.*, 377b–c, 378b. See also entry for item no. 64 and C. Bonner, *Studies in Magical Amulets* (Ann Arbor, 1950), 24, 40.

17. Dunand, *Le culte d'Isis et Ptolémées*, 25. See also Williams, *JARCE* 16 (1979):98.

18. Perdrizet, *Les terres cuites*, 1–4, nos. 1–8, pls. II–IV; Weber, *Terrakotten*, 132–33, nos. 200, 201, pls. 20, 21; Philipp, *Terrakotten*, 9; W. Deonna, *RA* 20 (1924):127–29, nos. 138–42; F. Dunand, *Religion populaire en Égypte romaine: Les terres cuite isiaques de Musée du Caire* (Leiden, 1979), 68–69 and 183–84, nos. 52–54.

19. Perdrizet, *Les terres cuites*, 4; Dunand, *Le culte d'Isis et Ptolémées*, 82–83; Graindor, *Terres cuites*, 42.

20. Perdrizet, *Les terres cuites*, 122; Weber, *Terrakotten*, 147, nos. 217–18, pl. 22.

21. Dunand, *Le culte d'Isis et Ptolémées*, 85.

22. Graindor, *Terres cuites*, 105, no. 33, pl. XIII; 106, no. 34, pl. XIII and 100, no. 30, pl. XII.

96. Savings Bank

(second–third c. A.D.)

395. Purchased in Rome or Naples in 1906–9. Ht, 12.5 cm; base l, 10 cm; w, 9 cm; w coin slot, 3.6 cm. Moldmade in two pieces. Intact.

Bank has beehive shape.

Obverse

Beneath coin slot is aediculum consisting of two spiral columns without capitals supporting a pediment having cable pattern along roofline and patera within tympanum. Standing on grooved base in front of aediculum is Mercury, wearing short-sleeved, belted tunic, boots, and winged cap. He holds a caduceus in his left hand, a money bag in his right hand; there is a lamb at his right knee. Groundline indicated by three horizontal grooves.

Reverse

Thirteen tongues radiate from apex. Bounded above and below by three horizontal grooves is mark of maker (BASAUGU) stamped in rectangle between two vertical rows of stamped dot-and-circle motifs. At top and bottom of rectangle are two oblique grooves.

Bibliography: Mentioned in letter from Wilson to Buckler, March 17, 1907; R.V..D. Magoffin, *Alumni Magazine* 4 (1915–16), fig. 4; D.M. Robinson, *AJA* 28 (1924):239–50; Graeven, *JdI* 16 (1901):182, as part of Saulini collection, appearing in *Catalogue des objets antiques recueilles par M. le. chev. Louis Saulini vente à Rome 26 avril, 1899*, no. 352, pl. III; M. Cheilik, *AJA* 67 (1963):70–71.

About twenty examples of the beehive form of savings bank are known,[1] bearing reliefs of Mercury, Fortuna, Venus, and a charioteer. The figures usually stand within an aediculum having two or four columns. Although early examples of this type may still date within the first century A.D., the flat frontality of our figure and the twisted column shafts without capitals suggest a date at least in the second century. A similar example from Ostia was found in a context of the time of Commodus.[2]

The stamp on the reverse of our bank, BASAUGU, is an abbreviation of the genitive form of the name of the potter, with the words *ex officina* ("from the workshop") understood.[3] The abbreviation may stand for Bassienus, Bassenius, or Passienus Augurinus.[4] The stamp appears on at least one other bank of beehive shape.[5]

The beehive form is one of several types of Roman savings banks, which were also made in the shapes of a chest, or *arca*,[6] of a pot,[7] or of a lamp body whose disc is decorated with a relief.[8] We know that all of these types of banks were made within the same

workshops because identical representations, possibly from the same molds, are found on banks of both beehive and lamp form.[9]

The stamps on the reverses of the banks tell us that the banks were also made in the same workshops that manufactured clay lamps. It is not surprising, then, that both lamps and banks of beehive or lamp form share the same representations.[10]

Roman savings banks have been found in graves of children and maidens.[11] We also know that, like lamps, they were exchanged as New Year's gifts.[12] Thus a bank of lamp form in Rome bears the same relief, a Victory and inscribed New Year's blessing, as a lamp in the British Museum.[13] The appearance of Fortuna and Mercury on the beehive banks is also appropriate to a gift of goodwill.

The most intriguing aspect of the beehive banks is their shape. It has been suggested that the form was derived from the similar shape of the Mycenaean tholos tombs.[14] It is indeed logical that the beehive's connotation of a repository[15] was strengthened both by the memory of the wealthy Mycenaean burials in structures of similar appearance and by the ancient custom of storing valuables in underground chambers.[16] By Roman times the association between the beehive shape and a treasury was well established. Pausanias (9.38.2–3) refers to the Mycenaean tholos tombs as *thesauroi*, 'treasuries,' and Varro described the beehive-shaped omphalos at Delphi as having the shape of a treasury (*thesauri specie*).[17] Unfortunately, we do not yet know what word the Romans used for their beehive savings banks nor whether there existed a Greek savings bank of beehive shape that served as a prototype for the Roman form.

1. H. Graeven, *JdI* 16 (1901):160–89; D.M. Robinson, *AJA* 28 (1924):244–50; Breitenstein, 100, no. 956, pl. 132; P. Mingaz-

zini, *Catalogo dei vasi della collezione Augusto Castellani* (Rome, 1971), 341, no. 919, pl. CCXLVII.1 (Mercury) and 344, no. 920, pl. CCXLVII.2 (Fortuna). Mingazzini adds others; he seems to have confused the Hopkins bank from the Saulini Collection with the Columbia example, which is said to be from the Ferroni Collection but which may have belonged to Alessandro Castellani, if Mingazzini's own no. 919 did not.

2. D. Vaglieri, *NSc* 5, 10 (1913):470, fig. 1 (with a Victory) and Mingazzini, Catalogo, 343.

3. H. Walters, *Catalogue of the Greek and Roman Lamps in the British Museum* (London, 1914), XXXIV.

4. Robinson, *AJA* 28 (1924):247–48; S.M. Cheilik, *AJA* 67 (1963):70–71.

5. Breitenstein, 100, no. 956, pl. 132 (BAS AVGV), and probably Graeven, *JdI* 16 (1901):181, figs. 25, 26; Robinson, *AJA* 28 (1924):248.

6. Robinson, *AJA* 28 (1924):239–40, fig. 1; Graeven, *JdI* 16 (1901):168, figs. 6, 7.

7. Robinson, *AJA* 28 (1924):240–41, fig. 2; Graeven, *JdI* 16 (1901):170, figs. 8–10.

8. Robinson, *AJA* 28 (1924):242–44, fig. 3; Graeven, *JdI* 16 (1901):178–81. Hermes, Mercury, and Fortuna appear on banks of lamp form.

9. Graeven, *JdI* 16 (1901):179, figs. 22, 23, and 180, fig. 24.

10. Cheilik, *AJA* 67 (1963):71; Walters, *Catalogue*, 177, no. 1180, pl. XXXIII. For lamps with same stamp, see Walters, *Catalogue*, nos. 1067, 1070, 1166, and 1167. See also H. Menzel, *Antike Lampen* (Mainz, 1969), 7.

11. Mingazzini, *Catalogo*, 342.

12. Menzel, *Antike Lampen*, 7.

13. Robinson, *AJA* 28 (1924):242, which is the same as Graeven, *JdI* 16 (1901):178, fig. 21.

14. Robinson, *AJA* 28 (1924):248–50; J. Harrison, *Themis* (Cambridge, 1927), 400. See also *RE Supplement* 7, 1224–227.

15. See Aristophanes, *Wasps*, line 241.

16. Mingazzini, *Catalogo*, 342–43.

17. *de Ling Lat*, Bk. 7, line 17. See also Mingazzini (*Catalogo*, 342) and Cheilik [*AJA* 67 (1973):71]. Chelik sees a connection between the omphalos and the lararium.

97. Terracotta Head Vase of Man with Cap

(second–fourth c. A.D.)

K 89. Kemper Simpson Collection. Ht, 7.3 cm; diam base of neck, 2.7 cm. Tip of peaked cap broken away. Base of handle behind head survives. Closed beneath.

Male head wears peaked cap with rolled brim. Large round eyes, bulbous nose, broad mouth.

Our head belongs to one of several types of figurine or head vases that were popular in the Hellenistic and Roman period.[1] The type represented by our example consists of a neck and head surmounted by a spout with a vertical handle behind. Although the type may have been made in Asia Minor,[2] the closest parallels are of Greco-Egyptian fabric. A head vase from Hadra[3] has the same round face, large eyes, bulbous nose, and peaked cap, but a more sensitive modeling that indicates an earlier date. Our vase is surely Roman, since close comparison can be made with the peaked-cap head vases in Copenhagen[4] and the Ashmolean,[5] the latter dated to the fifth and sixth centuries A.D. Also late and of the same type is a head vase from Memphis.[6]

The features suggest that the subject is from the eastern Mediterranean or Africa; his peaked cap may indicate that he is a slave[7] or an actor in the mime.[8]

1. Other types are: A) complete figure, spout with conical mouth [in M. Chehab, *Bulletin du musée de Beyrouth* 10 (1951–52):20; 11 (1953–54):pls. VI, VII]; B) a head or bust with cylindrical spout and ring handle [E. Breccia, *Terrecotte figurate greche e greco-egizie del Museo di Alessandria: Monuments de l'Égypte gréco-romaine* II, fasc. 1 (Bergamo, 1930), pl. XXIX.7, 9; pl. XXX.2–3, etc.; also, M. Mogensen, *La Glyptothèque Ny Carlsberg; La collection égyptienne* (Copenhagen, 1930), 51, no. 361, pl. L]; C) figure surmounted by high ring handle [Breccia *Terrecotte figurate*, pl. XXIX.4]; and D) head alone with tubular spout [W. Wijngaarden, *De Grieks-Egyptische Terracotta's in het Rijksmuseum van Oudheden* (Leiden, 1958), 20, no. 64, pl. XIII; also, Mogensen, *Glyptothèque*, 51, nos. 359 and 363, pl. L].

2. J. Sieveking, *Die Terrakotten der Sammlung Loeb* (Munich, 1916), 64.

3. Breccia, *Terrecotte figurate*, 68, no. 408, pls. XXIX.6 and LVII.5.

4. V. Schmidt, *De Graesk-Aegyptiske Terrakotter I: Ny Carlsberg Glyptothek* (Copenhagen, 1911), 84, fig. 151, pl. LII.

5. Ashmolean E9. 1963. I am indebted to R. Nicholls for this parallel and his suggestions.

6. W.M.F. Petrie, *Meydum and Memphis*, vol. 3 (London, 1910), 46, no. 170, pl. XLIV.

7. P. Perdrizet, *Les terres cuites grecques d'Égypte de la collection Fouquet* (Paris, 1921), 163, nos. 465, 466, pl. CXII.

8. M. Bieber, *AJA* 17 (1913):152–53.

Pottery

GREEK

98. Boeotian Trefoil Oinochoe

(750–720 B.C.)

K 116. Kemper Simpson Collection. Ht, 22.5 cm; diam foot, 9.6 cm; max diam mouth, 8.2 cm. Intact.

Glaze orange-brown. Solid glazed neck. Principal zone of decoration in panel opposite handle on shoulder, bounded beneath by three horizontal lines. Long-legged bird stands in right profile beneath a zigzag. In front of him is four-spoked wheel with short strokes radiating outward from circumference and with circle enclosing dot between each spoke. Beneath this panel are six vertical lines, alternately wavy and straight. Each side of body occupied by seven concentric circles. Strap handle has wavy line down center and a line down each side continuing across its base above long-legged bird in right profile. Horizontal band encircles foot of vase.

This jug exemplifies the heavily Atticizing character of late geometric Boeotian vasepainting.[1] The class to which our vase belongs was produced in the Oinochoe Workshop in Thebes[2] and was inspired by Attic oinochoai of the Concentric Circle group, which are dated by Coldstream between 750 and 720 B.C.[3] The Attic vases have been found only in Attica and bear motifs associated with contests, such as tripods, double axes, and horses; for this reason it is suggested that these Attic oinochoai served primarily as prizes.[4] In contrast, we can conclude that the Boeotian oinochoai were primarily funerary because the wavy bands on the handles surely echo the plastic snakes on Boeotian vessels that were destined for burial.[5]

The Boeotian oinochoai reflect their Attic prototypes both in the shape and in the technique, whereby brown paint is applied directly to the surface without slip.[6] Most of the decorative scheme is also similar: the solid glazed neck, the concentric circles on each side of the body, and the horizontal band around the foot. In the panel scene on the shoulder, however, the Boeotian artist introduces horizontal zigzags and crosshatched triangles, which are often detached on other Boeotian examples of this same class.[7] And, in contrast to the striding Attic birds, the Boeotian counterparts are stationary and long-legged.[8] On the Attic vases, beneath the panel there is a series of horizontal lines, but on the Boeotian jugs they are replaced by straight or wavy vertical lines, which are possibly derived from Corinthian vasepainting.[9] On the basis of the profiles and the painted snakes on the handles, the Boeotian oinochoai are thought to be contemporary with their Attic counterparts and thus also to date to the period 750 to 720 B.C.[10]

The ultimate origin of the shape and the concentric circles lies in Cypriot Ware, Bichrome IV,[11] and possibly in Mycenaean pottery. Perhaps also of Cypriot inspiration are the double axes that appear on the Attic examples.[12]

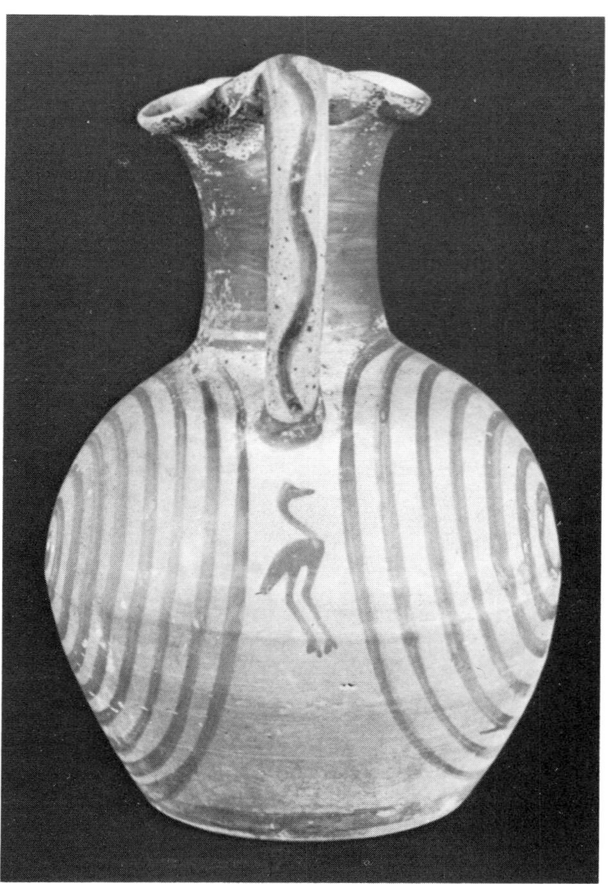

1. J. N. Coldstream, *Greek Geometric Pottery* (Leiden, 1968), 196–211.

2. A. Ruckert, "Frühe Keramik böotiens," *AntK Beihept* 10 (1976):17, 41–44, 59–60.

3. Coldstream, *Pottery*, 74–76, 330–31, LG Ib 750–735 and LG IIa 735–720.

4 V. Karageorghis, *The Archaeology of Cyprus: Recent Developments* (Park Ridge, 1975), 172.

5. J. N. Coldstream, *Geometric Greece* (New York, 1977), 201.

6. Ruckert, "Frühe Keramik," 17, 59.

7. Coldstream, *Pottery*, 210.

8. Ruckert, "Frühe Keramik," 43.

9. F. Canciani, *JdI* 80 (1965):68.

10. Ruckert, "Frühe Keramik," 17, 41, 43–44, I 750–735 and II 735–720.

11. Karageorghis, *Archaeology of Cyprus*, 172.

12. Ibid., 172–73.

99. Black-Figure Amphora with Herakles and Amazons

(550–500 B.C.)

60.55.2. Baltimore Museum of Art, formerly Robinson Collection, from Barden Collection of Hamberg. "Gela." Ht, 54.2 cm; diam mouth, 34.4 cm; diam foot, 20.8 cm. Dull black glaze, chipped. Intact.

Upper surface of rim reserved. Reserved ring molding between body and foot. Neck glazed inside to depth of 3.6 cm.

Side A

Figures stand on glazed groundline. Herakles moves to his left, with left leg upraised. He wears chiton beneath lion-skin, with scalp brought up over head, paws tied at neck, tail flying out behind. Bow-case over shoulder, scabbard at waist. His right hand holds a dagger, which he is about to thrust at his opponent, while his left hand is hidden by her shield. She is moving away from Herakles, with her legs in right profile, her left leg advanced. She turns back to Herakles, her right arm uplifted with a spear, her head and crested helmet in left profile, and over her left arm a shield with emblem of serpent and ball. She wears a chiton beneath a muscle cuirass, which is shown frontally, and an animal skin. On either side of the pair are two Amazons, each in crested helmet, short chiton, and cloak, with shield and spear. Devices on shields are, from left: pellets, bull's head (?), disc, tripod.

Added red: eyes, cloaks, shield rims of all Amazons. 1 and 2: skirt, 3: lion-skin, 4: skirt, 5: plume of helmet, 6: panels in skirt.

Added white: flesh of Amazons, devices of shields, dots in borders below helmet plumes, lion tusks, Herakles' baldric, sections of plumes on helmets of 2 and 5.

Side B

Figures stand on glazed groundline. Dionysos, in center in right profile, wears a himation and ivy wreath and carries kantharos in uplifted left hand. Four vine branches wind away from shoulder. Flanking him on each side is maenad with long hair and wreath, wearing a long chiton with incised crosses at waist and incised dotted border at neckline. Maenad facing Dionysos wears short jacket. Nude satyr seen in profile at each side of scene.

Added red: panels in skirts, dots at waist, centers of eyes, curls of maenads, leaves of ivy wreaths. Added white: flesh of maenads.

Lotus and palmette above picture on side A. Chain of lotus buds above picture on side B. Rays around base. Two red lines around neck and two more below each picture (one line above rays, one around foot).

Bibliography: CVA, USA fasc. 4, Robinson fasc. 1, 43–44, pls. XXV.2, XXVI, XXVII; D. von Bothmer, *Amazons in Greek Art* (Oxford, 1957), 57, no. 183, pl. 45.3; *Heldensage*[3], 13, no. 17.

The uninterrupted profile of neck and shoulder classifies the form of this amphora as Type B, examples of which are commonly found among black-figure vases of the second half of the sixth century. The amphorae are usually ornamented with a ray pattern around the foot and ivy or lotus patterns above the pictures, which commonly portray mythological battles or Dionysiac revelry.

The obverse of our amphora illustrates a popular myth, the representations of which have been thoroughly examined by von Bothmer. Our composition belongs within Bothmer's category C, examples of which first appeared after 550 B.C. and depict an unassisted Herakles in combat with three or more Amazons.[1] Our scene belongs in subsection gamma,[2] because the retreating Amazon directly behind Herakles is dressed as a hoplite and glances behind her as she flees. Our representation is also related to compositions of subsection alpha,[3] where there is only a single Amazon behind Herakles, but one with the pose and gesture of the Amazon who stands at the viewer's far left side of our panel.

Typical of representations of Herakles and the Amazons after 550 are Herakles' choice of club or sword rather than spear,[4] and the use of the Attic helmet with oblong or L-shaped cheekpieces.[5] Both the position of Herakles' left arm behind the shield[6] and the gesture of the right sword arm[7] are paralleled in other representatives of this conflict.

1. D. von Bothmer, *Amazons in Greek Art* (Oxford, 1957), 30.
2. Ibid., 56.
3. Ibid., 53.
4. Ibid., 31.
5. Ibid., 33, 59.
6. Ibid., pls. 30.1 and 39.1.
7. Ibid., pl. 41.4.

100. Nikosthenic Amphora

(540–530 B.C.)

B 64. Baltimore Society AIA, formerly Helbig Collection. Ht, 30 cm; max w across handles, 20.9 cm; diam at rim, 11.3 cm; diam of foot, 10.1 cm. Mended from several pieces, with part of lip and neck restored.

Ray pattern around rim. Inside neck are three glazed bands of varying heights separated by reserved strips. Strap handles have central vertical line flanked by bands of rays. On each side of neck is a combat between two pairs of boxers shown in profile. Added red on hair. Beneath foot of boxers on side A is signature:

NIKOSΘ[E]NESMEΓOIESEN.

Beneath neck, principal zone of decoration lies between two raised ridges around center of body and consists of double row of ivy leaves. Above is band of tongues above rightward key pattern. Beneath are bands of: tongue, rays, reserved zigzag upon a glazed background, and rays. Between body and foot is glazed ridge with incised groove on either side. Foot has echinus shape, with vertical side reserved.

Bibliography: Furtwängler, *ND*, 252, no. 2; D. M. Robinson, *AJA* 26 (1922):54–58; J. C. Hoppin, *A Handbook of Greek Black-Figured Vases* (Paris, 1924), 179; CVA/USA fasc. 4. Robinson fasc. 1, 43, pls. XXIV.2, XXV.1; *ABV*, 220, no. 336.

Soon after 550 B.C., the Attic potter Nikosthenes[1] created a distinctive Attic version of a type of Etruscan bucchero amphora that originated in Caere (see item no. 125). He retained the wide lip, strap handles, and ridges around the body, but he substituted black-figure decoration for the relief ornament on the Etruscan prototype. All of the one hundred or more surviving Nikosthenic amphorae that have a provenance are said to come from Caere; therefore, it appears that the Attic version was made specifically for the city where the prototype originated.

Most of the Nikosthenic amphorae are signed by Nikosthenes as potter or shopowner, but none bears the signature of a painter. Beazley believed that all the amphorae were painted by a single hand, whom he called Painter N. More recently it has been proposed that we broaden this designation to the Group of Nikosthenes, since it is plausible that several artists, including apprentices, participated in the decoration of the vases.[2]

The Hopkins vase is typical of Nikosthenic amphorae both in the patterns and the representations of boxers.[3] The shape, with the pronounced spherical body, is somewhat unusual, although Beazley noted that the echinus foot appears in the "B" Torlonia group assigned to the early years of Nikosthenes' career, about 550 B.C.[4] It does indeed seem that the Hopkins example belongs among the early or middle phases, since the later amphorae, made around 520 B.C., have a more elongated neck and tapering body, and a greater simplicity of ornament that compares closely with decorative patterns employed on other black-figure vases of the last third of the sixth century.[5]

The workshop of the potter Nikosthenes was certainly one of the larger and more innovative Attic studios between 550 and 510 B.C. The Six technique may have originated here, as may have the practice of applying a white-ground background to black-figure ware. The shop certainly introduced the kyathos, which was inspired by an Etruscan shape. Prominent painters, such as Oltos, Psiax, Epiktetos, and the Theseus Painter, are thought to have been associated with this establishment.[6]

1. For Nikosthenes, *ABV* 216–23 and *Paralipomena*, 108–9; Boardman, *Black Figure*, 64; M. Eisman, *GettyMusJ* 1 (1974):43–54.

2. Eisman, *GettyMusJ* 1 (1974):48.

3. Ibid., 45. Our vase is no. 2 in the list of boxing scenes in footnote 18.

4. *ABV*, 220.

5. Eisman [*GettyMusJ* 1 (1974):52 no. 48] believes that the latest amphorae date from about 515. Boardman [*Black Figure*, 64] thinks that the workshop was active to about 510 B.C.

6. Boardman, *Black Figure*, 64; Eisman, *GettyMusJ* 1 (1974):48–49.

101. Fragment from Kylix by Oltos

(ca. 520 B.C.)

B 1. Baltimore Society AIA, formerly Hartwig Collection. Max ht, 5 cm; max l, 7.7 cm. Part of exterior decoration of kylix with upper edge belonging to original rim.

Maenad moves to her right; torso frontal, head in left profile. She wears chiton, himation fastened over right shoulder, and panther skin knotted at throat. Her left elbow is bent, with a pine branch in left hand. Her hair is drawn behind the ears, bent up at nape, and fastened to back of head with fillet. Disc earrings, bracelet on left wrist. Behind her are the extended fingers of a right hand.

Relief contour throughout. Dilute glaze for mouth and inner line of ear. Added purple for fillet, leaves, bracelet. Hairline incised.

Bibliography: Philippart, 50; D. M. Robinson, *AJA* 21 (1917): 167, fig. 7; Beazley, *VA*, 7, 12, no. 51; Hoppin, *II*, 261, no. 47c; Beazley, *AttV* 17, no. 70; J. D. Beazley, *Campana Fragments in Florence* (London, 1933), pl. X; CVA USA fasc. 6, Robinson fasc. 2, 11, pl. I.1; *ARV*², 59, no. 55.

This fragment arrived at the university as part of the restored sections of the kylix by the Pistoxenos Painter (no. 115). Subsequently, Beazley recognized the Hopkins piece to be part of the exterior of a kylix to which fragments in Florence, Heidelberg, Braunschweig, Bowdoin, and the Villa Giulia also belong (see *above*, Beazley pl. X).[1] The maenad on our segment formed part of a procession of satyrs and maenads whose counterparts on the opposite side are a fleeing girl and two men. In the tondo was a representation of Pegasus, together with the signature of Kachrylion, the prominent Attic potter for whom Phintias (see no. 102) and the Kiss Painter (see no. 105) may also have worked.[2]

Oltos was one of the most skilled early artists of red-figure vasepainting.[3] He signed two cups and is accredited with over one hundred fifty vessels in all. Although he primarily painted kylixes, he also worked on amphorae, psykters, stamnoi, and a kyathos. He was employed by the best potters of his age, including Kachrylion, Nikosthenes, Pamphaios, and Hischylos.[4]

The artist's distinctive style can be recognized in the stumpy bodies and the square heads with long noses and narrow, elongated eyes. Also characteristic is the patterning of the extended figures. Oltos's use of relief line was extensive and particularly skilled.

1. For Oltos, see J. D. Beazley, *JHS* 58 (1938):267; Boardman, *Red Figure*, 56–57; *ARV*², 53–67; *Paralipomena*, 326–28; J. Beazley, *Campana Fragments in Florence* (London, 1933), 7, pls. I.21, 23; X. The Bowdoin fragment appears in D. Buitron, *Attic Vase Painting in New England Collections*. *Fogg Art Museum* (Cambridge, 1972), 69, no. 30.

2. Bloesch, 45–50.

3. E. Finkenstaedt, *AJA* 72 (1968): 383, pl. 129.

4. Bloesch, 31, 33, 45–50, 64; *ARV*², 53.

102. Kylix by Phintias

(520–510 B.C.)

B 4. Baltimore Society AIA, formerly Hartwig Collection. Ht, 7 cm; diam with handles, 25 cm; diam rim, 18.5 cm; diam foot, 7.4 cm. Mended from many pieces.

Tondo is bordered by narrow reserved band. Youth stands in right profile, a mantle thrown over his left shoulder, exposing only right shoulder and breast. Vine wreath in hair. He has just arisen from a stool and leans forward with both arms outstretched, money bag in left hand, fingers of right hand extended, staff leaning against left shoulder. In front of him are a skyphos, amphora set in a stand, and a kylix resting in rim of amphora. Inscribed in field:

ΦIN[TI]AΣ·EΛPAΦΣEN+AIPIAΣ KAVOΣ

Relief contour throughout, except at hairline. Dilute glaze for inner markings and for fuzz on cheeks. Added red for wreath, cord on money bag, lettering. Incised hairline.

Bibliography: Hartwig, *RömMitt* 2 (1887):169, no. VIII; K. Wernicke, *Der griechischen Vasen mit Lieblingsnamen* (Halle, 1889), 54, no. 2; H. S. Jones, *JHS* 12 (1891):372–73; Hartwig, *Meisterschalen*, 172, pl. XVII.1; J. Harrison and D. MacColl, *Greek Vase Paintings* (London, 1894), 18; Furtwängler, *ND*, 251–52, no. 1; E. Pottier, *Douris and The Painters of Greek Vases* (London, 1909), fig. 5; G. Perrot, *Histoire de l'art dans l'antiquité* (1882–1914), vol. 10, 464, fig. 265; J. C. Hoppin, *Euthymides and His Fellows* (Cambridge, 1917), 99–102; Beazley, *VA*, 28; Hoppin, *II*, 355, no. 2; E. Pfuhl, *Malerei und Zeichnung der*

Griechen (Munich, 1923), vol. 1, 441, and vol. 3, 119, fig. 384; G. M. A. Richter, *The Craft of Athenian Pottery* (New Haven, 1923), 81–82, no. 5, fig. 85; Beazley, *AttV*, 57, no. 2; Phillippart, 50; P. Cloche, *Les classes, les métiers, le trafic* (Paris, 1931), 51, pl. XXXII; CVA USA fasc. 6, Robinson fasc. 2, 12–13, pls. II.1, III.2; L. Schnitzler, *Griechische Vasen* (Freiburg, 1948), pl. 39; B. Sparkes and Lucy Talcott, *Pots and Pans of Classical Athens* (Princeton, 1958), fig. 12; M. L. Bernhard, *Greckie Malarstwo Wazowe* (Warsaw, 1966), fig. 86; *ARV*², 24, no. 14.

Phintias belonged to the Pioneer group of red-figure painters, who began work in the time of the Andokides Painter and continued into the late sixth century. About seventeen vases of a variety of shapes have been attributed to Phintias, seven of which, including this one, he signed as painter.[1]

Phintias betrays his heritage from black figure in his use of incision rather than reserve line to delineate the hairline. Also typical of early red figure is Phintias's reliance on relief line, rather than dilute glaze, for interior markings, and his penchant for the stacked pleats and swallowtails seen in contemporary sculpture. Figures painted by Phintias can be recognized by the length and pronounced curve of the eye, and by the almost concave profile of the nose. Other characteristic features are the animated contour of the hair and the long fingers and feet.[2]

Bloesch suggested that many of the vases that Phintias painted were supplied by the prominent potter Kachrylion, who also fashioned pieces for the Kiss Painter.[3] Our kylix would indeed seem to be associated with Kachrylion, since the bulge above the foot recalls Kachrylion's distinctive treatment of Type-C cups having a plain lip.[4] The tall, slender stem and shallow bowl indicate that our cup is later than an example in Boston that is signed by Kachrylion.[5]

Besides being a painter, Phintias was also a potter. He signed as potter one cup of Type-B shape and two aryballoi,[6] and several more cups have been attributed to him.[7] Recent study of the style of the painting and the profiles of the vases attributed to Phintias has determined that Phintias worked in the same studio with Euthymides and the Dikaios Painter, and that he trained several prominent artists, including Kleophrades and the Berlin Painter, for whom Phintias may have fashioned several cups.[8]

1. *ARV*², 22–26; *Paralipomena*, 323, 507, 509; Boardman, *Red Figure*, 30–32.

2. Simon, 97, pls. 98–101; G. Pinney, *AJA* 85 (1981):151; C. M. Cardon, *AJA* 83 (1979):172.

3. Simon, 97–98, pls. 98–101; *ARV*², 25, nos. 1–3.

4. Bloesch, 119–22 and 120, nos. 1–4. Type-C kylixes are characterized by a flat plate foot and a bulge in the stem. Occasionally the lip is offset.

5. Boston 95.33. Bloesch, 119, no. 1. I owe this comparison to Sally Roberts.

6. *ARV*², 25. Cup is Athens 1628. Bloesch, 61.

7. *ARV*², 178, nos. 1–6; G. Pinney, *AJA* 85 (1981):155, 157.

8. M. Robertson [*AJA* 62 (1958):57, 62, 64] attributes Athens 1628 to the Berlin Painter. G. Pinney [*AJA* 85 (1981):146, 155–58] discusses the relationship between the Berlin Painter and Hermokrates, whom she believes to be identical with the Salting Painter.

103. Kylix by Epiktetos

(520–510 B.C.)

B 3. Baltimore Society AIA, formerly Hartwig Collection. "Chiusi." Ht, 14.1 cm; diam rim, 32.8 cm; diam foot, 12.7 cm. Mended from many pieces. Foot is ancient but does not belong. A few parts along rim restored (before acquisition) with segments of another ancient kylix.

Tondo is bordered by narrow reserved band. Wreathed satyr reclines on a couch, which is indicated by narrow reserved band (fragments imprecisely assembled give inaccurate effect of bent line). His back is supported by a pillow decorated with three black bands crossed by two close-set lines. His legs are bent and upraised, with feet pressed against edge of tondo. With both hands and upraised right knee he raises pointed amphora to his lips. Inscribed beneath couch and in field above satyr's head:

ΕΓΙΚΤΕΤΟΣ ΕΛΡΑΦΣΕΝ

Relief contour throughout except for reserved contour of beard. Dilute glaze for inner markings. Added red for tail, wreath, lettering. Incised contour of hair at crown and nape.

Bibliography: P. Hartwig, *RömMitt* 2 (1887):167, no. 1; P. Hartwig, *JdI* 6 (1891):250–57, pl. V; P. Hartwig, *JdI* 7 (1892): 118; J. E. Harrison and D. S. MacColl, *Greek Vase Paintings* (London, 1894), pl. IX.1; Beazley, *VA*, 14–16, fig. 7; Hoppin, *I*, 301, no. 2; Beazley, *AttV*, 26, no. 20; Philippart, 50; W. Kraiker, *JdI* 44 (1929):177, no. 33; CVA USA fasc. 6, Robinson fasc. 2, 11–12, pls. I.3, II.3; D. K. Hill, *JWalt* 1 (1938):29, fig. 6; E. Buschor, *Satyrtänze und frühes Drama* (Munich, 1943), fig. 42; *ARV*², 75, no. 56.

Epiktetos was a prominent early red-figure painter who specialized in cups.[1] He signed his name on forty vases and is accredited with sixty more, many of which are signed only with "*egraphsen*." Epiktetos also worked as a potter. He signed one vase as both potter and painter,[2] and he wrote only "*epoiesen*" on other vases that we know he both potted and painted.[3]

Epiktetos worked for a number of potters, including Andocides, Nikosthenes, and Hischylos, for whom he painted bilingual cups. In his later years, Epiktetos painted for Pistoxenos, Pamphaios, and Python, and he undoubtedly came into contact with artists of the early fifth century, such as Douris (see nos. 108, 114) and Makron (see no. 112).[4]

Epiktetos displays influence from black-figure vase-painting in his use of incision along the contour of the hair, but, in contrast to Phintias and other painters of

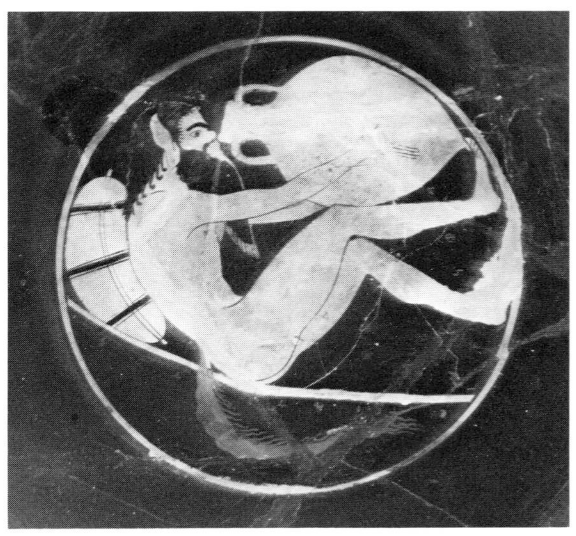

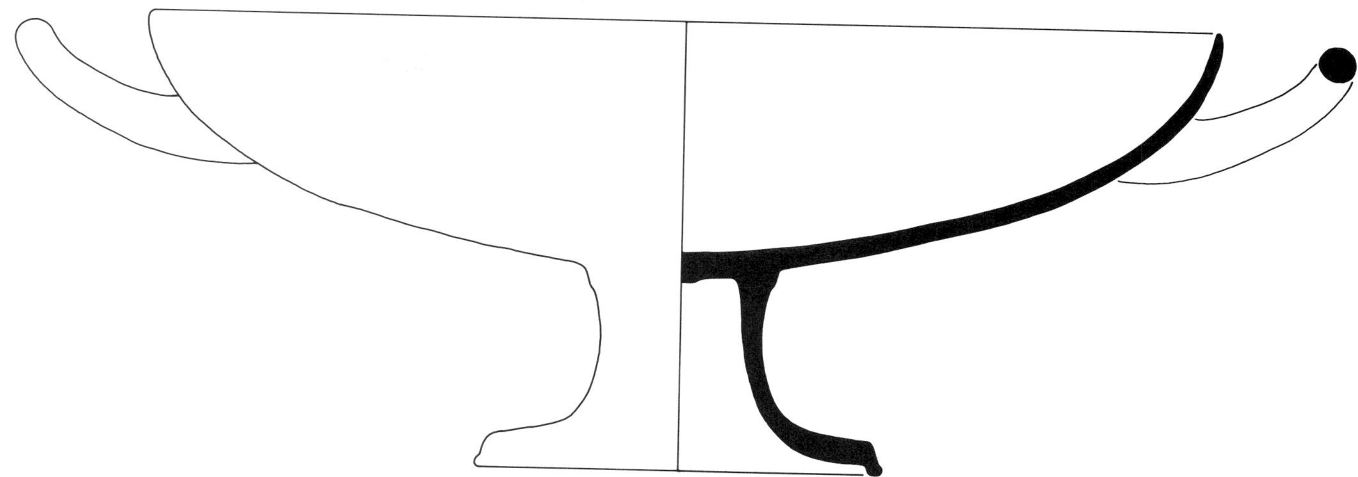

the Pioneer Group, Epiktetos prefers the newer dilute glaze, rather than relief line, for the interiors of his figures. He is especially admired for the excellence of his tondo compositions, of which our example is a good illustration. The scene displays a sensitive balance of light and dark and an admirable skill in the handling of the satyr, who, as the cup is rotated, appears to stand and lean over the amphora.[5] Also noteworthy is the skillful draughtsmanship of the face.

Our cup is probably an early work, since the proportions of the satyr are slender,[6] the use of red is generous,[7] and the profile of bowl and stem can be compared with those on cups by the potter Hischylos,[8] with whom Epiktetos was associated early in his career. A later version of the same scene appeared on a kylix once in Rome; that cup was said by Beazley to be in the manner of Epiktetos and possibly by the artist himself.[9]

1. *ARV*[2], 70–79; *Paralipomena*, 328–29; Boardman, *Red Figure*, 57–59; J. D. Beazley, *JHS* 58 (1938):267.

2. *ARV*[2], 78 no. 102 (Athens Acr. 6, a plate).

3. He also signed one vase, which he both potted and painted, with the word "*egraphsen*" (*ARV*[2], 76, no. 78). Another bears the words "*egraphsen*" and "*epoiesen*" (*ARV*[2], 73, no. 31).

4. Ibid., 70; M. Robertson, *JHS* 85 (1965):100; Boardman, *Red Figure*, 59.

5. Beazley [*JHS* 58 (1938):267] notes that the vertical axis of a tondo composition is rarely at right angles with the handles.

6. D. Buitron, *Attic Vase Painting in New England Collections: Fogg Art Museum* (Cambridge, 1972), 72.

7. Simon, 96, pls. 96–97.

8. Bloesch, 31–35; see also M. Robertson, *JHS* 85 (1965):99–100.

9. *ARV*[2] 80, no. 15.

104. Kylix Fragment by Epiktetos

(ca. 500 B.C.)

B 2. Baltimore Society AIA, formerly Hartwig Collection. "Chiusi." Greatest dimension, 15.5 cm; diam tondo, 9.5 cm. Broken all around. Includes part of stem. Surface worn.

Tondo is bordered by narrow reserved band. Beardless youth wearing red wreath strides forward in right profile, his knees bent, his right leg advanced. His outstretched right hand grasps a wineskin; his left hand supports a staff over his left shoulder, from the end of which hangs his cloak. Inscribed in red lettering in field:

ΕΓΟΙΕ≶ΕΝ

Relief contour throughout. Incised hairline.

Bibliography: P. Hartwig, *RömMitt* 2 (1887):169, no. X; P. Hartwig, *JHS* 12 (1891):347, fig c; A. E. Pottier, *MonPiot* 20 (1913):144, fig. 18; Beazley, *VA*, 19; Beazley, *BSR* 11 (1929):16 n. 3; W. Kraiker, *JdI* 44 (1919):194, no. ,2; CVA USA fasc. 6, Robinson fasc. 2, 11, pl. I; *ARV*[2], 76, no. 75.

This fragment bears the word "*epoiesen*," which we know Epiktetos inscribed on vases that he both potted and painted.[1] Typical of later archaic painting are the greater slimness and elasticity of the thighs, the attempt at a three-quarter view with the left shoulder advanced, and the refined profile of the face. Characteristic of Epiktetos are the skillful composition, with the pose and scale of the youth perfectly adjusted to the field and with the animation of the stride in harmony with the curving frame. The incised hairline contrasts with the reserved line in use among contemporary artists.

1. *ARV*[2], 70.

105. Kylix by the Kiss Painter

(ca. 500 B.C.)

B 5. Baltimore Society AIA, formerly Hartwig Collection. "Chiusi." Ht, 11 cm; diam with handles, 38.7 cm; diam rim, 30.7 cm; diam foot, 11.1 cm. Mended from many pieces.

Interior

Standing on exergue is bearded male facing front. His weight is on his right leg; his left knee is bent with foot behind him. He wears a mantle brought over his left shoulder, exposing right shoulder and chest. Right hand on hip; left arm extended, with hand holding end of staff. His head, seen in right profile, wears an ivy wreath. Facing him is a nude youth wearing a laurel wreath, legs in left profile, torso three-quarters turned to front. He stands on a two-stepped starting block and holds an aryballos and sponge in left hand. In field are aryballos and sponge suspended from nail. An upended pick is set in ground in front of base. Inscribed in field, second word retrograde:

ΛΕΑΛΡΟ≶ΚΑΛΟ≶

Tondo is bordered by reserved band.

Exterior, Side A

Striding youth with mantle draped over shoulders carries skyphos in left hand and staff supporting oinochoe in right. Inscribed in field above tip of staff: E. Youth approaches a large-column krater, on the other side of which is a nude youth with himation over shoulders. Inscribed in field beneath figures:

ΚΑΛΟ≶

Rest of scene consists of one striding nude youth and another in draped himation.

Exterior, Side B

Standing bearded male extends left hand to approaching youth, who carries skyphos in extended right hand, staff in left. Both figures are nude, with mantles draped over shoulders. Remainder of scene consists of beardless youth in right profile, nude except for mantle over shoulders, playing flutes. In front of him is maiden, of

Interior

whom only a part of pleated chiton and mantle survives. Inscribed in field above all four figures:

ΕΠ]ΙΔΡΟΜΟΣ [Κ]ΑΛΟΣ

Relief contour throughout interior and exterior, except for some feet on exterior. Hairline reserved at forehead and nape and incised at crown. Dilute glaze for inner markings. Added red: interior—wreath, javelin loop, string and wristband of aryballoi, nail securing one aryballos, lettering; exterior—lettering. Graffito on underside of foot.

ト上

Bibliography: K. Wernicke, *AZ* 43 (1885):255, no. 16, pl. 19.2; P. Hartwig, *RömMitt* 2 (1887):167, no. 2; K. Wernicke, *Die griechischen Vasen mit Lieblingsnamen* (Halle, 1889):41, no. 20; Hartwig, *Meisterschalen*, 39–43, figs. 5a–b; Klein, *LI*, 75, no. 20, fig. 15; Beazley, *VA*, 22; Hoppin, *I*, 176, no. 20; K. Elderkin, *HSCP* 35 (1924):119, no. 2; Beazley, *AttV*, 54, no. 3; A. Raubitschek, *Hesperia* 8 (1939):162; M. Guarducci, *Annuario, NS* 3–4 (1941–42), 132; CVA USA fasc. 6, Robinson fasc. 2, 13–14, pls. V, VI.1; *ARV*², 177, no. 3.

The Kiss Painter is known from only five cups. He takes his name from the affectionate scenes on the tondos of kylixes in Berlin and New York.[1] All but one of the cups has a komos scene on the exterior. The Baltimore vase is the only inscribed example and bears within the tondo the well-known love name Leagros, which appears on a number of black-figure vases of about this date.[2] The inscription on the exterior, *epidromos kalos*, praises the delights of athletic pursuits.

The profile of the vase resembles those of kylixes by the potter Kachrylion, to whom this cup has been attributed.[3] Kachrylion also fashioned the kylix to which our fragment by Oltos (no. 101) belonged, and possibly made the cup that was decorated by Phintias (no. 102).

The scene in the tondo takes place in a palaestra, where youths trained in the various sports whose equipment is depicted here: the casting of the javelin, the broad jump (for which a pick was used to measure distances), and the foot race, which made use of a starting gate, a block of which is probably shown here.[4] The aryballos contained the olive oil that athletes applied with a sponge before exercising.

The advances made by vasepainters of about 500 B.C. can be seen in the foreshortened frontal leg of the trainer in the tondo and the three-quarter positions of the youthful torsos on the tondo and exterior. Also typical of vasepainting from the end of the sixth century is the use of dilute glaze for interior mark-

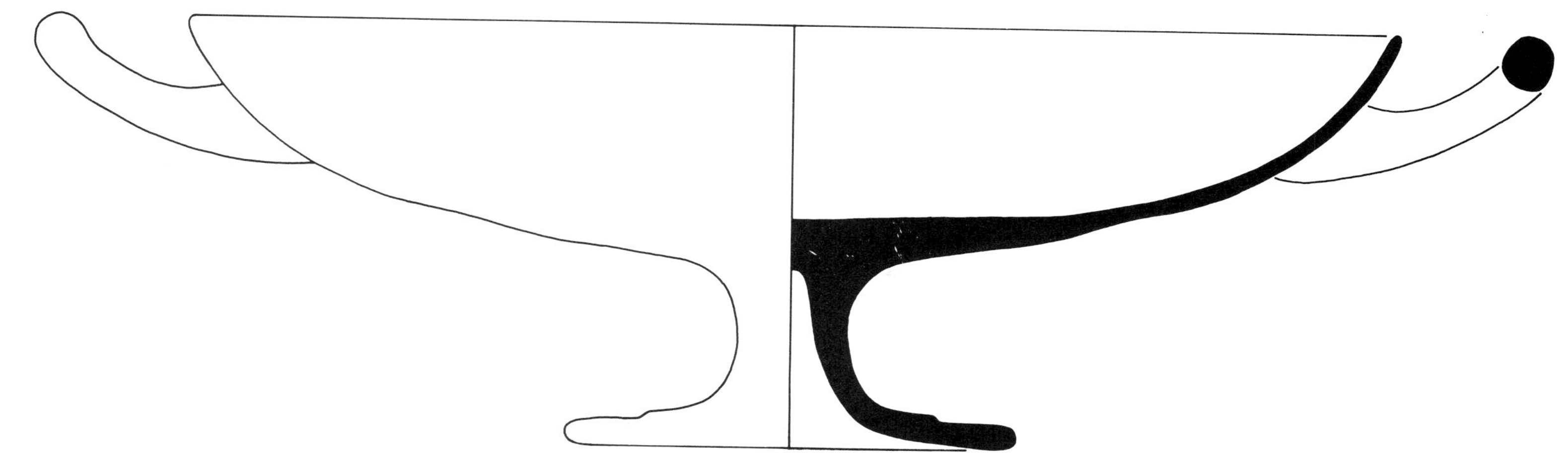

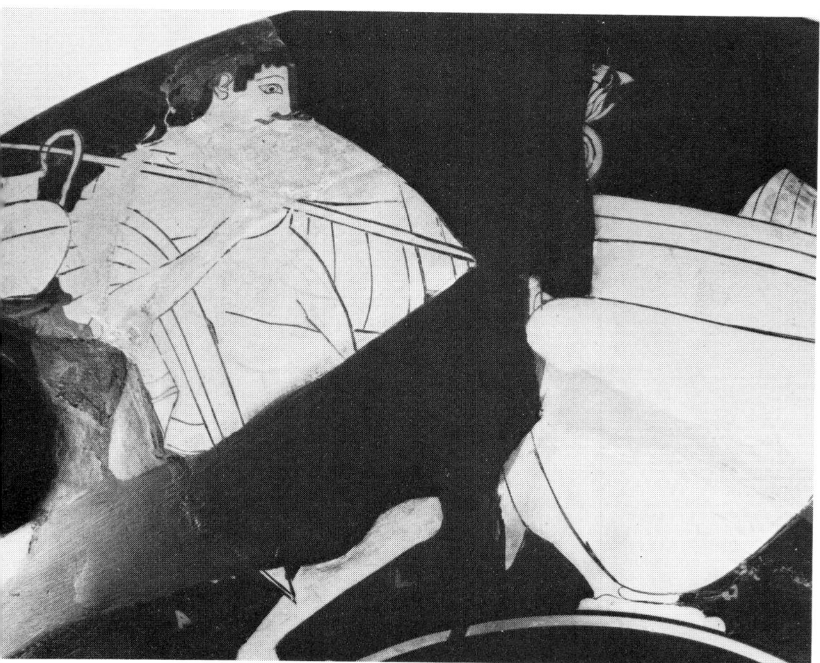

Exterior, *side A*

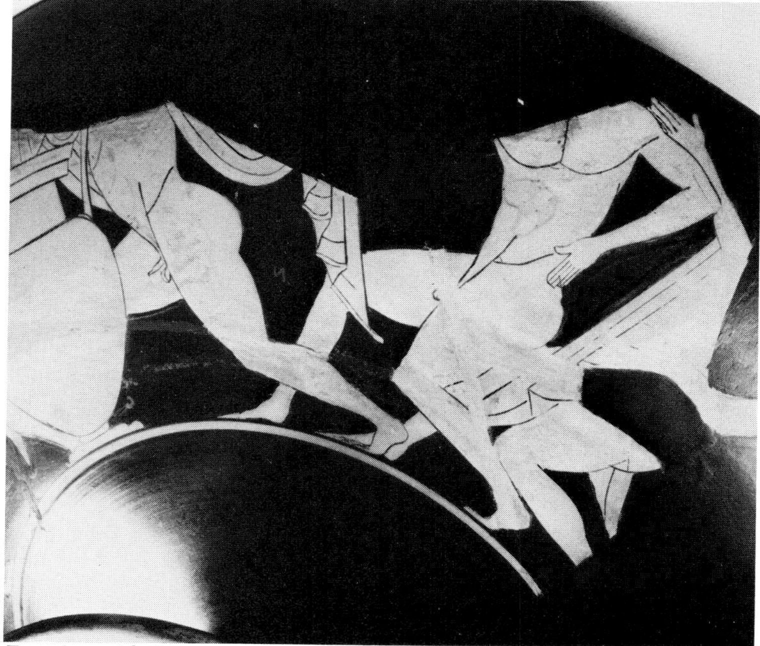

Exterior, *side A*

Exterior, *side B*

ings. The large bodies with protruding buttocks and the expanses of flesh and drapery uninterrupted by detail recall the similar broad style of the contemporary Euthymides.[5]

The graffito on the underside of the foot is one of several examples that are found on many vases dating between ca. 550 and 500 B.C. These markings are believed to have been applied to vases intended for export, especially to Etruria, and to signify prices and other commercial information relating to the sale of the vessels.[6]

1. *ARV*², 177–78 (no. 1 [177] is in Berlin, no. 2 [177] is in New York); *Paralipomena*, 339; J. Beazley, *JHS* 58 (1938):267.
2. Boardman, *Black Figure*, 110.
3. G. Nicole, *RA* 5, 3–4 (1916):396; Hoppin, *I*, 176, no. 20; see also Bloesch, 45–50.
4. H. A. Harris, *Sport in Greece and Rome* (Ithaca, 1972), 27–29. Alternate interpretation proposed by A. E. Raubitschek [*Hesperia* 8 (1939):161–63].
5. Simon, 101, pls. 112–15.
6. Boardman, *Black Figure*, 202–3; A. W. Johnston, *Trademarks on Greek Vases* (Warminster, 1979), 6–8, 12.

106. Lekythos in Six Technique

(ca. 500 B.C.)

9022. Ht, 18.9 cm; diam mouth, 4 cm; diam foot, 5 cm. Mended from many pieces, with parts of handle and rim restored.

Rim and inside of neck glazed. Glazed handle, with underside reserved. On shoulder is chain of lotus buds, with stalks linking every three buds; band of tongues above.

Body

Satyr strides in right profile, left leg advanced. Right outstretched hand grasps right wrist of a maenad, while left arm is outstretched toward her genitals. Maenad advances in left profile, left leg advanced and both arms outstretched. Contour and interior markings of satyr incised. Delicate incisions for maenad's eye, brow, hairline, arms, back left leg, and back of right thigh. Interior of maenad was painted white.

Two red lines above scene; one red line beneath figures as groundline. Foot in two degrees, glazed except for reserved side of top step and underside.

In Six technique the background is in black glaze, like the background in red-figure vasepainting, but the artist works the figures either by incising their contours through the black glaze or by applying white, red, or brown paint on top of the glaze before the vase is fired.[1] The painter may, as in the case with our maenad, render a figure entirely or mostly in color, using incision only for details. Alternately, he may work a figure like our satyr in "outline Six," wherein all of the figure is incised and no color is added.[2]

The Six technique originated during the first half of the sixth century, but at first was employed only for parts of figures. Not until around 530 B.C., in the experimental atmosphere that stimulated the introduction of red-figure vasepainting, did Nikosthenes and Psiax first work entire vases in Six technique.[3] In the later sixth century the technique was most popular in the workshops of the Sappho[4] and Diosphos Painters,[5] artists who were influenced, and perhaps trained, by the Edinburgh Painter. The Sappho and Diosphos Painters were primarily black-figure artists who painted a variety of shapes but specialized in lekythoi, which they executed in Six technique as well as in black-figure and white-ground. The Diosphos Painter is credited with over thirty-six lekythoi; the Sappho Painter is assigned only eleven lekythoi and one hydria.

Our vase is best paralleled by work of the Sappho Painter. Although both the Sappho and the Diosphos Painters used lekythoi of the DL type, those of the Sappho Painter have the shallow mouths and squat, full bodies with tapering profiles of the Hopkins vase, in contrast to the deeper mouths and straight-sided cylinders preferred by the Diosphos Painter.[6] The stalks in the bud patterns of the Sappho Painter generally skip two buds, as on our example, while those of the Diosphos Painter usually skip only one, but oc-

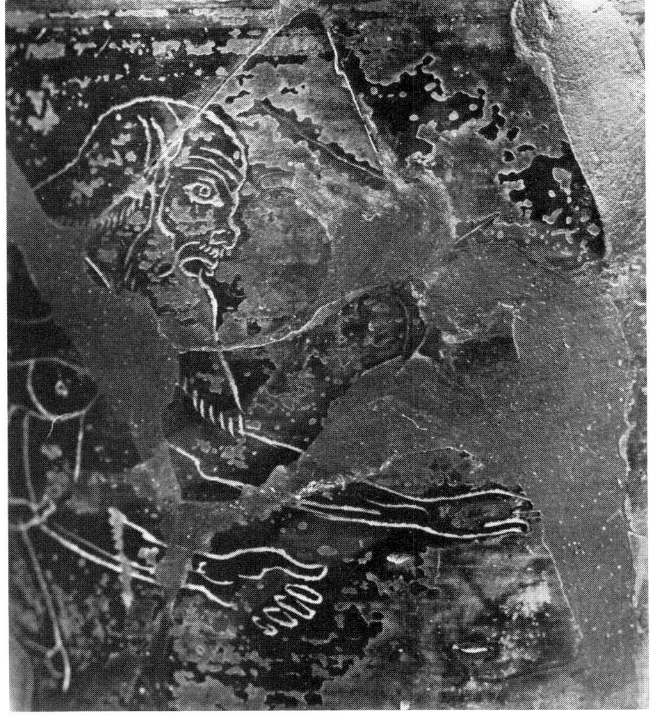

casionally two, and sometimes add white dots between the buds.[7] The Six lekythoi of both painters have a red line beneath the scene, but the Sappho Painter almost always applies two red lines above, as on our vessel, while the Diosphos Painter may employ a checker or key pattern.[8] While the Diosphos Painter often relies upon incision alone, the Sappho Painter also executes elements of his representation in added white.[9] Our vase is especially similar to a lekythos by the Sappho Painter in New York on which a satyr, worked entirely by incision, crouches amid an amphora, serpent, and rocks, all of which are rendered in white.[10]

On the Hopkins vase the incisions for the maenad are so much lighter and more delicate than those for the satyr that they could not have been intended to be seen through the white paint and thus must be preliminary incisions intended as guidelines for the artist. On this lekythos the artist carefully respected these sketches in his final application of color, but on other Six vases the preliminary incisions are often disregarded.[11]

The Sappho Painter used Six technique early in his career, and certainly the heavy thighs and strict profile of the satyr support a date for our vase of ca. 500 B.C.

1. Boardman, *Black Figure*, 178; J. Six, *Gazette Archéologique* 13 (1888):193–294; *ABL*, 106ff.; P. E. Corbett, *JHS* 85 (1965):24; D. Kurtz, *Athenian White Lekythoi* (Oxford, 1975), 116–19.

2. Ibid., 116, 119.

3. Boardman, *Black Figure*, 178.

4. *ABV*, 507–8; *ABL*, 94–130, 227–28; *Paralipomena*, 246–48.

5. *ABV*, 508–11; *ABL*, 94–130, 235–36; *Paralipomena*, 248–50. To the examples listed by Beazley, add: Hornbostel, 298, no. 258; Kurtz, *White Lekythoi*, pl. 6.4 in Columbia, Missouri. Another, surely by one of these two painters, is discussed by D. von Bothmer in *Festschrift für Frank Brommer* (Mainz, 1977), 61, pl. 19 (NY 67.11.22).

6. Kurtz, *White Lekythoi*, 80.

7. *ABL*, 94.

8. Ibid., 95.

9. Kurtz, *White Lekythoi*, 119.

10. *ABL*, 228, no. 43, which is the same as *Bulletin of the Metropolitan Museum of Art* (1930):136, fig. 4. (17.8 cm; NY 23.160.87).

11. P. Corbett, *JHS* 85 (1965):16–28, especially 24–25.

107. Black-Figure Neck Amphora by the Michigan Painter

(ca. 500 B.C.)

9260. Ht, 21.5 cm; diam rim, 11.4 cm; diam body, 14.2 cm; diam foot, 7.5 cm. Mended from many pieces.

Upper surface of rim reserved; neck glazed inside. Glazed triple handles with undersides reserved. Profiled ridge separating neck from body; ring molding between body and foot. Both ridge and molding are painted red.

Side A

Glazed groundline. A bull in left profile collapses beneath the attack of two lions. In field above is inscription *ISIS*. Added red for dots in lions' manes and for streams of blood under mouth and claws.

Side B

Two bulls drink from vessel between them. Vines above their heads wind from base of handles.

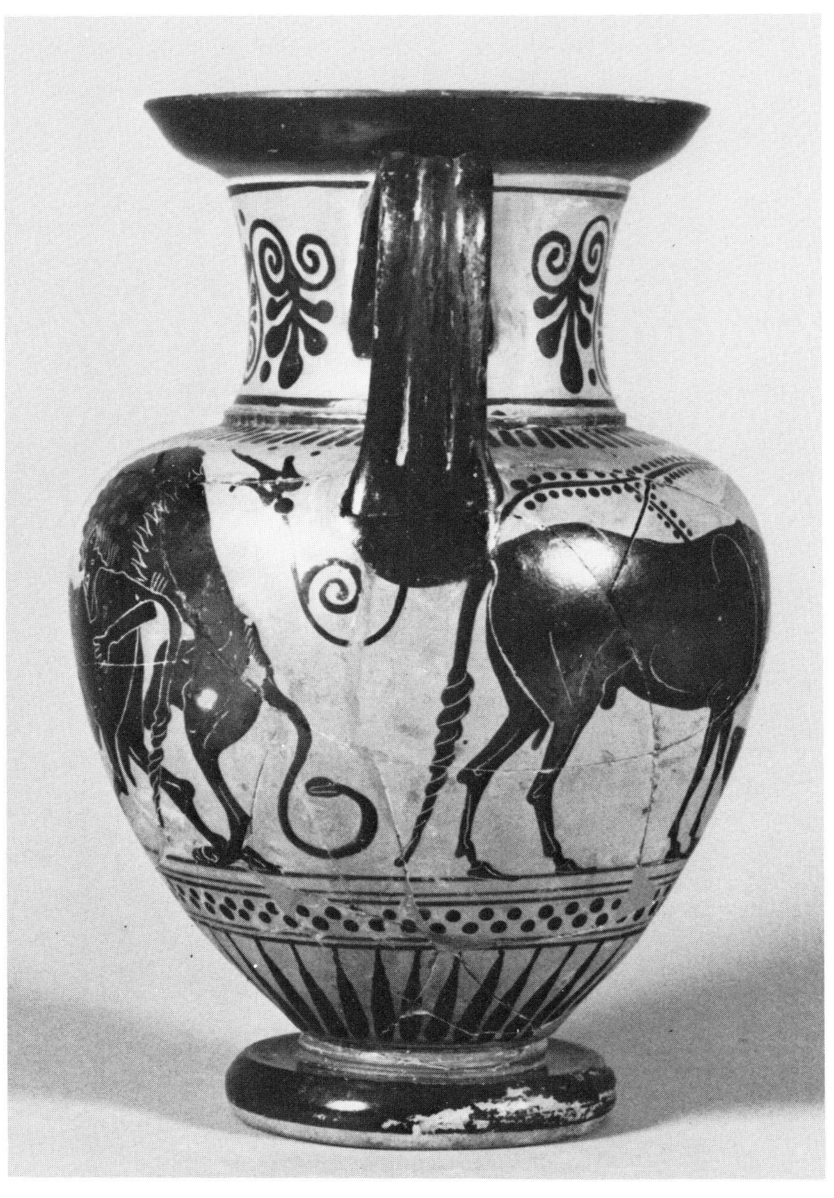

Neck

Framed by a line above and a line beneath are three palmettes. The central seven-petal palmette is upright, the flanking five-petal palmettes are suspended. Two dots flank the middle leaf of the central palmette and two more dots lie on the inner sides of the middle leaves of the side palmettes.

Band of black tongues above picture. Beneath picture is a line, then two staggered rows of dots, double lines, rays. Foot glazed except for bottom of sides and underside. Below handles are volutes terminating in triple lotuses. Beneath foot is dipinto.

This vase is the work of the Michigan Painter, whom Beazley later recognized to be identical with the Painter of Brussels R 312, an artist of the Dot-Band Class who was active in the late sixth century.[1] The painter principally worked on small neck amphorae, but he also painted larger neck amphorae, Panathenaic amphorae, stamnoi, and at least one oinochoe.

On the necks of the small amphorae we find two

another example in Boulogne[7] (Boulogne no. 13), and of komos or Dionysiac figures, who appear on amphorae in Michigan[8] and Chicago[9].

The Michigan Painter was content with a limited repertory of motifs. The bull on the Hopkins vase is almost identical with the one defeated by Herakles on the amphora in London and is clearly inspired by black-figure representations of the Cretan bull in combat with Herakles.[10] The reverses are particularly redundant, and usually feature dancing figures. The two women on the reverse of the Michigan amphora are almost identical with those on the reverses of the vases in Boulogne 85 and London, except for their gestures and details like the addition of castanets. The two youths flanking the woman on the obverse of the Michigan vase are re-

distinct palmette patterns. In the scheme on our example and on those vases originally attributed to the Painter of Brussels R 312, the central seven-petal palmette is upright and enclosed by four dots, while the flanking palmettes are suspended and have five petals each. These later palmettes can also be seen in the ornament under the handles of Brussels R 312. On amphorae formerly assigned to the Michigan Painter, the central seven-petal palmette is suspended and there are no dots, while the flanking upright palmettes have five or seven petals.

On his small neck amphorae, the Michigan Painter favors the heroic themes popular in the late sixth century, such as the Labors of Herakles (on examples in London[2] and Maplewood[3], of Ajax and Achilles (on vases in Brussels[4] and Lucerne[5]), and of Peleus and Thetis (on an amphora in Boulogne[6] [Boulogne no. 85]). He is also fond of Hermes, whom we find on

placed by satyrs on the reverse of the amphora in Chicago and by women on the reverse of the example in Boulogne.

The signature characteristics of the painter were pointed out by Philippaki:[11] the stacked arcs for the knees, the emphatic engraved arcs delineating the upper contour of the beard, and the description of the eye by means of a circle set between short horizontal lines. Typical of his treatment of animals are the four gashes for the ribs, the preponderance of wrinkles under the neck and behind the forelegs, and the presence of one or two arcs on the shoulder [e.g., on our bull, on the bull on the amphora in London, and on the horse on the reverse of the vase in Maplewood]. On his human figures we often find two horizontal lines for the mouth, a large shock of hair above the forehead, and an emphatically beaked nose. The collarbone is described by a long incision terminating in

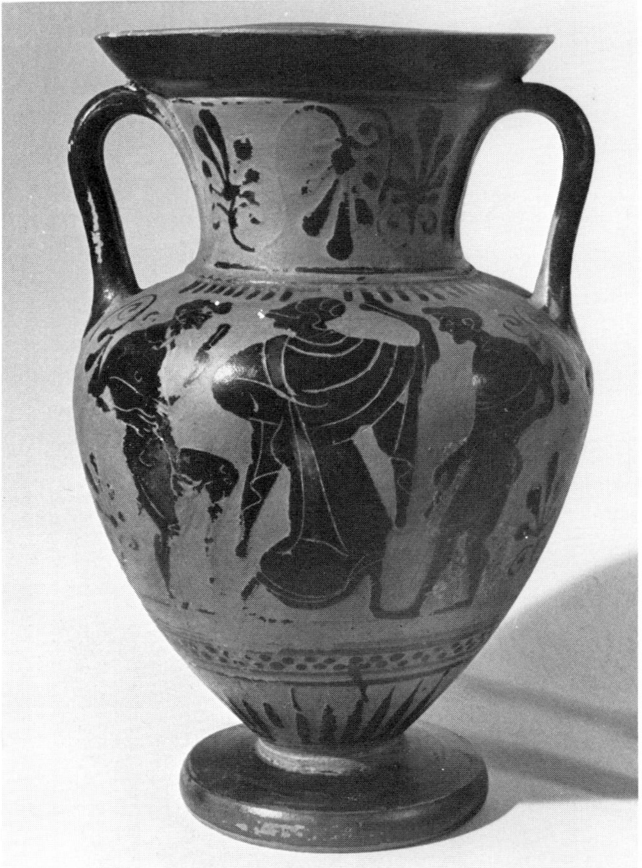

Michigan 2599, *obverse*

Michigan 2599, *reverse*

an arc, and the ribs are delineated by a cluster of lines.

To the vases assembled by Beazley we can add a further example that was recently on the art market in Freiburg.[12] The neck pattern on that amphora is identical to the one on the Hopkins vase. On the obverse we find Herakles fighting Nereus, a subject compatible with this artist's known affinity for that hero. The composition and much of the detail in the scene compare closely with the representation of Peleus and Thetis on the amphora in Boulogne 85. On the reverse of the Freiburg vase, the woman flanked by two armed warriors can be compared with the scene on the reverse of the Brussels amphora, where two warriors are shown in combat. Finally, the Freiburg figures exhibit the jutting chin, nose, and back of the head familiar in other works from the hand of this artist.

The scene on the obverse of the Hopkins vase is a familiar one in Attic sculpture of the last half of the sixth century. Pedimental groups representing one or two lions in triumph over a fallen bull have been assigned to the Hekatompedon and to the Peisistratid temple on the Acropolis. Another pedimental group was found in the Agora.[13]

The dipinto on the underside of the foot is of the type classified by Johnston as 32Av. The same mark appears on two oinochoai in Boston by the Chicago Painter. Those vases are said to come from Gela, a provenance that supports Johnston's contention that dipinti bore commercial information relevant to the export of the vessels.[14]

1. The Michigan Painter is discussed in *ABV*, 343–44. For the Dot-Band class, recognized by the dot band beneath the scene and by the ornament on the neck, see *ABV*, 483, and *Paralipomena*, 220–21. The Painter of Brussels R 312 is discussed in *ABV*, 483. The artists are identified in *Paralipomena*, 221, with other additions on 157. See also B. Philippaki, *The Attic Stamnos* (Oxford, 1967), 22.

2. London, British Museum Inv. no. B 277 (Herakles and the Bull), *ABV*, 343, no. 8, which is the same as *CVA* GB fasc. 5, BM fasc.4, pl. 70.

3. Maplewood (Herakles and Antaeus) is the same as *Paralipomena*, 157, no. 9 quarter.

4. Brussels, Musées royaux d'Art et d'histoire, R 312, *ABV*, 483, no. 1, is the same as *Paralipomena*, 157, no. 9 bis, which is the same as *CVA* Belgium fasc. 1, Brussels fasc. 1, 3, pl. 9.1. See S. Woodford, *AJA* 84 (1980):37, no. G.1.

5. Lucerne, art market, which is the same as *Paralipomena*, 157, no. 9 ter. See S. Woodford, *AJA* 84 (1980):37, no. G.3.

6. Musée des beaux-arts et d'archéologie, Boulogne, Inv. no. 85-B, *ABV*, 483, no. 3 is the same as *Paralipomena*, 157, no. 9^{6}.

7. Boulogne, 13-A, *ABV*, 483, no. 4 is the same as *Paralipomena*, 157, no. 9^{7}.

8. Kelsey Museum of Ancient and Medieval Archaeology, Univ. of Michigan, 2599, *ABV*, 344, no. 9 is the same as *CVA* USA fasc. 3, Michigan fasc. 1, 30, pl. XIV.3.

9. Art Institute of Chicago, 1889.97, *ABV*, 483, no. 2 is the same as *Paralipomena*, 157, no. 9^{5}.

10. See H. A. Shapiro, *Art, Myth and Culture: Greek Vases from Southern Collections* (New Orleans, 1981), 64, no. 23.

11. Philippaki, *Attic Stamnos*, 22.

12. Galerie Günter Puhze, Stadtstrasse 28, D-7800 Freiburg.

13. For the Hekatompedon, see B. S. Ridgway, *The Archaic Style in Greek Sculpture* (Princeton, 1977), 199. The Peisistratid temple is discussed on 205–8, and the Agora pediment on 210. Still another group is divided between Athens and New York (210).

14. A Johnston, *Trademarks on Greek Vases* (Warminster, 1979), 85–86; D. von Bothmer, review of Johnston in *AJA* 85 (1981): 353.

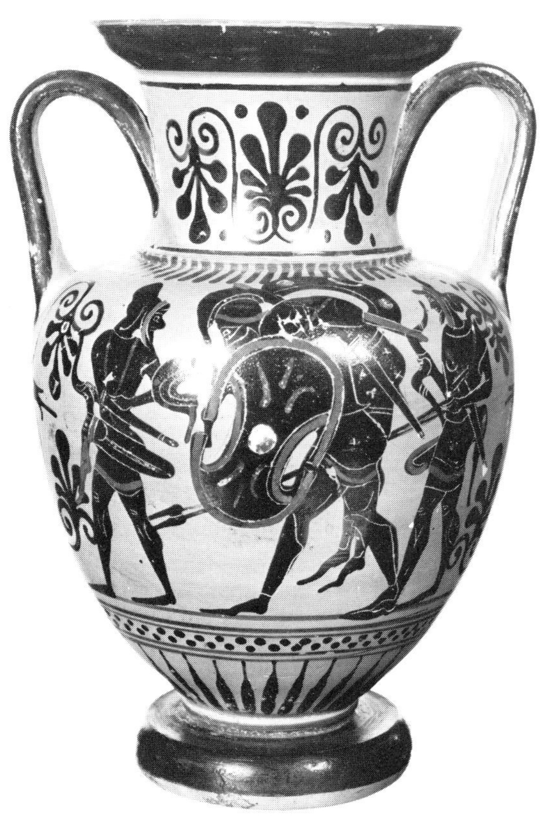

Brussels R 312, *obverse*

Brussels R 312, *side*

Brussels R 312, *reverse*

Brussels R 312, *side*

London B 277, *obverse*

London B 277, *reverse*

Maplewood, *obverse*

Maplewood, *reverse*

Boulogne 85, *obverse*

Boulogne 85, *reverse*

Boulogne 13, *obverse*

Boulogne 13, *reverse*

Freiburg, *obverse*

Freiburg, *reverse*

Chicago 1889.97, *obverse*

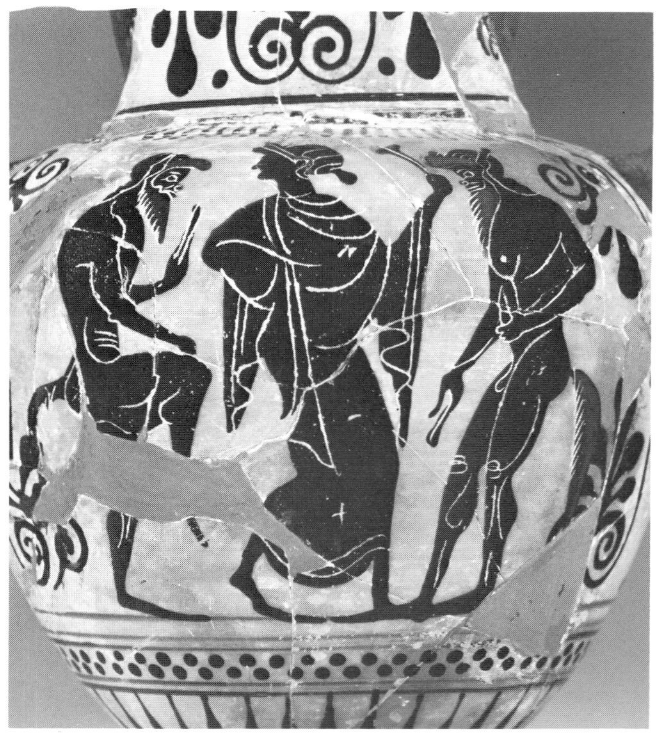

Chicago 1889.97, *reverse*

108. Kylix by Douris

(500–490 B.C.)

B 8. Baltimore Society AIA, formerly Hartwig Collection. "Chiusi." Ht, 9.5 cm; diam with handles, 30.4 cm; diam of rim, 23.2 cm; diam foot, 9.6 cm. Mended.

Two warriors in left profile step on left leg, right leg extended, right arm upraised with spear. Male in foreground wears chiton, cuirass with star on shoulder lappet, greaves, and crested Corinthian helmet with upraised cheekpieces and dot band at base of crest. Over his left arm is shield with dotted rim and emblem consisting of left profile of lion head. Scythian companion wears tight-fitting, long-sleeved, long-legged garment alternating black and reserved bands; on top is sleeveless pleated tunic. He wears a Phrygian cap with two lappets by left ear; open gorytos hangs at left side. Both warriors are barefoot. Inscribed in field:

+ΑΙΡΕΣΤΡΑΤΟΣ ΚΑΛΟΣ

Relief contour throughout, except for underside of toes of left feet and reserved outline of Scythian's hair. Dilute glaze for folds of Scythian's tunic. Added purple for pads under greaves and lettering. Border consists of rightward meander.

Bibliography: P. Hartwig, *RömMitt* 2 (1887):168, no. 5; Hartwig, *Meisterschalen*, 212, pl. 22.2; Klein, *LI*, 99, no. 10; Furtwängler, *ND*, 251–52, no. 1; Beazley, *VA*, 97, no. 7; Hoppin, *I*, 277, no. 45; Beazley, *AttV*, 200, no. 14; Philippart, 50; CVA USA fasc. 6, Robinson fasc. 2, 15–16, pl. XI; *ARV*^{2}, 442, no. 215.

Douris, one of the most prominent of all red-figure painters, was active during the first three decades of the fifth century.[1] He signed forty vases and has been assigned about two hundred fifty more. Most of these pieces are cups, but Douris worked on other shapes as well, both in white ground and red figure. He was also a competent potter and signed one kantharos in Brussels as both potter and painter.[2] Despite his familiarity with the potter's wheel, Douris preferred to paint vessels fashioned by Python,[3] and, as a young artist, by Euphronios, for whom Onesimos also worked.[4]

Beazley divided the painting career of Douris into four periods and assigned our cup to the first phase, dating about 500–490 B.C..[5] In these years Douris's style was still in a formative stage, and his admiration

for Chairestratos, as demonstrated by the inscriptions, steadfast.

The picture in the tondo shows a hoplite accompanied by a member of the Scythian tribe, which lived to the north of Greece. Scythians served as archers in the Athenian army from about 530 B.C. to the end of the sixth century, but after this date the Persians, who had by now acquired control of Scythia, curtailed emigration to Athens,[6] and the few Scythians who did settle in Athens were primarily employed as policemen. For this reason representations of Scythian warriors after 500 B.C. were based on memory rather than observation, and, not surprisingly, the depictions are often inaccurate. For example, the striped garment our Scythian wears appeared on representations of Scythians from about 510 B.C. and thus is probably a reliable rendition of the actual dress,[7] but the chiton and spear are surely artistic license. On the other hand, Douris has correctly coupled the Scythian with a hoplite; we know that hoplites traditionally advanced under cover of Scythian arrows.[8] Douris portrayed Scythians on three later vases of his third and fourth periods, and these depictions are, not unexpectedly, even less accurate.[9]

The lion head on the hoplite's shield is a common image in Achaemenian art, especially among gold appliqués, or bracteae.[10] The motif first appears in Attic vasepainting at the end of the sixth century, undoubtedly as a result of increased contact with the Persian world, which erupted in the invasions of 490 and 480 B.C.[11]

1. *ARV*², 425–51; J. D. Beazley, *JHS* 58 (1938):267; *Paralipomena*, 374–76; O. W. Muscarella, *Ancient Art: The Norbert Schimmel Collection* (Mainz, 1974), no. 59, potting attributed to Euphronios; Dörig, no. 205; Boardman, *Red Figure*, 137–39.

2. *ARV*², 425, and 445, no. 256.

3. Ibid., 426–27; Bloesch, 96–101.

4. Bloesch, 70.

5. *ARV*², 425–26.

6. M. Vos, *Scythian Archers in Archaic Attic Vase-Painting* (Groningen, 1963), 60, 68, 87.

7. Ibid., 12, 40, 51, 81; K. Schauenburg, *AthMitt* 90 (1975): 107, 111.

8. Vos, *Scythian Archers*, 72–73.

9. *ARV*² 432, no. 55, and 433, no. 63, from period 3. No. 130 (p. 438) is from period 4. For this last, see K. Schauenburg, *AthMitt* 90 (1975):111.

10. R. Ghirshman, *Persia from the Origins to Alexander the Great* (London, 1964), 380–81, 439, nos. 553–55.

11. See a lion head as shield device on kylix by the Foundry Painter (ca. 495 B.C.) in *Münzen und Medaillen* 13 (1961):84, no. 159, pl. 51.

109. Lekythos by the Athena Painter

(ca. 490 B.C.)

60.55.1 Baltimore Museum of Art from Robinson Collection. "Gela." Ht, 31.8 cm; diam, 12.6 cm; diam foot, 8.5 cm. Crack across lower part of body. Surface chipped.

Neck glazed inside. On shoulder is band of five nine-petal palmettes with central one inverted, others upright and angled toward handle. Dots flank base and topmost petal of each palmette. Above is band of tongues beneath red line. Glazed handle with underside reserved.

Body

Youth in right profile astride a dolphin extends right arm with phiale toward a satyr who crouches on a rock, right knee drawn up, right arm extended with oinochoe in right hand. Vine tendrils grow from rock. Behind satyr are another youth and dolphin seen in right profile. Added white for bellies of dolphins, lines on rock, flowers on satyr's oinochoe.

Above picture is band of zigzag between two pairs of bounding lines. Red line beneath scene and another between body and foot.

Bibliography: *ABL*, 255, no. 14; CVA USA fasc. 4, Robinson fasc. 1, 51, pl. XXXVII.

The Athena Painter[1] was one of a number of artists who continued to work in black figure long after many of his contemporaries had taken up the new red-figure technique. The artist was trained in the workshop of the Edinburgh Painter, together with a colleague of similar style, the Theseus Painter. The Athena Painter began work around 490 B.C. and devoted himself primarily to oinochoai and lekythoi. His lekythoi resemble those of the Edinburgh Painter in their standard shape, with straight outline and toros foot, and in the shoulder pattern, which consists of five palmettes amid dots. Our lekythos dates from the early years of the artist's career, before he painted the neck black, enclosed his row of bars within black lines, and added a tendril with bud to the palmettes on either side of the handle. Still later lekythoi are often in white ground.

The Athena Painter treated a variety of subjects, usually active scenes, and on his early vases he often depicted riders, satyrs, and silens.[2] His figures do not stand upon a groundline, in the traditional manner, but instead upon two red lines directly beneath the scene or upon the black field.[3] Characteristic features of the artist's work are the oval heads, the incised outline at the top of the beard and hair, and the reverse E pattern for the kneecap.[4] Typical of the date at which the painter was working is the inaccurate depiction of the dolphin's flukes, which are here set vertically instead of horizontally.[5]

The subject of our vase has been variously described as Arion.[6] Taras,[7] or Theseus.[8] The last identification is especially appealing since both Bacchylides (*Dithy* 16, 97–100) and Hyginus (*Poet. Astr.* II.5) tell us that Theseus rode a dolphin on his visit to

the Nereids or to Amphitrite. Beazley believed that the second rider was merely one of the repeat figures that characterize late black-figure lekythoi, and he suggested that the satyr, with whom Theseus is occasionally shown, was derived from a satyr play.[9] The satyr's presence in this scene would not be inappropriate, since there was a traditional connection between wine and the sea, and consequently between dolphins and Dionysiac figures, such as satyrs.[10]

Haspels, followed by Beazley, tentatively suggested that the Athena Painter was identical with a red-figure artist, the Bowdoin Painter.[11] The lekythoi attributed to the latter artist are similar in shape to those of the Athena Painter (BL) and exhibit the Athena Painter's distinctive innovations, which consist of the black neck, outlined bars, and black-figure palmettes with added tendril and bud. Should the identification be correct, the career of this artist extended into the second half of the fifth century.

1. *ABV*, 522–25; *Paralipomena*, 260–62; *ABL*, 147–65, 254–58; D. Kurtz, *Athenian White Lekythoi* (Oxford, 1975), 14–16; Boardman, *Black Figure*, 148. To these add Hornbostel, 292, no. 254, and Dörig, nos. 210–11.

2. *ABL*, 254–55.

3. Ibid., 148.

4. Ibid., 148–49; Boardman, *Black Figure*, 48.

5. E. B. Stebbins, *The Dolphin in the Literature and Art of Greece and Rome* (Menasha, Wisconsin, 1919), 6, 9, 16.

6. Robinson, CVA USA fasc. 6, Robinson fasc. 2, 27. See J. D. Beazley, *JHS* 58 (1938):268.

7. See J. D. Beazley, *JHS* 54 (1934):90.

8. See *ABL*, 151, and CVA USA fasc. 6, Robinson fasc. 2, 27.

9. J. D. Beazley, *JHS* 58 (1938):268 and *JHS* 54 (1934):90.

10. M. Davies, in *Athens Comes of Age: From Solon to Salamis* (Princeton, 1978), 72–81. Our vase is discussed on 78.

11. *ABL*, 157; Beazley, *ARV*², 677; Kurtz, *White Lekythoi*, 16.

110. Kylix of the Proto-Panaetian Group

(ca. 490 B.C.)

B 6. Baltimore Society AIA, formerly Hartwig Collection. "Chiusi." Ht, 8 cm; diam with handles, 26.6 cm; diam rim, 20 cm; diam foot, 7.8 cm. Mended from many pieces.

Tondo is bordered by narrow reserved band. Satyr seated to his left on wineskin, torso three-quarters frontal. Left knee is raised, with lower leg extended; right knee is bent, with lower leg drawn back. Elbow bent with left hand uplifted over head. Right hand in front of chest; fingers of both hands outstretched. Head is turned back in left profile and wears fillet with long ends hanging down over torso. Inscribed in field:

ΓΑΝΑΙΤΙΟΣ ΚΑ[V]ΟΣ

inscribed on wineskin:

Κ[Α]VΟΣ.

Relief contour throughout, except for reserved outline of beard and incised contour of back of head. Dilute glaze for interior markings. Added red for fillet and lettering.

Bibliography: W. Klein, *Euphronios* (Vienna, 1886), 278; P. Hartwig, *RömMitt* 2 (1887):167, no. 3; P. Hartwig, *Meisterschalen*, 448, pl. 44.1; Klein, *LI*, 107, no. 4; Furtwängler, *ND*, 251–52, no. 1; D. M. Robinson, *AJA* 21 (1917):87; Beazley, *VA*, 87; Hoppin, *I*, 421, no. 36; Beazley, *AttV*, 167, no. 14; Philippart, 50; CVA USA fasc. 6, Robinson fasc. 2, 14, pl. VII; *ARV*[2], 316, no. 7.

It was Furtwängler who first suggested that the Panaitios Painter was really the youthful Onesimos.[1] This identification was endorsed by Beazley in his revised edition of *ARV*, where the vases previously assigned to the two artists were grouped as the work of the single painter Onesimos.[2] Beazley listed our vase as one of nine cups that he believed were "specially akin" to the early work of Onesimos and perhaps

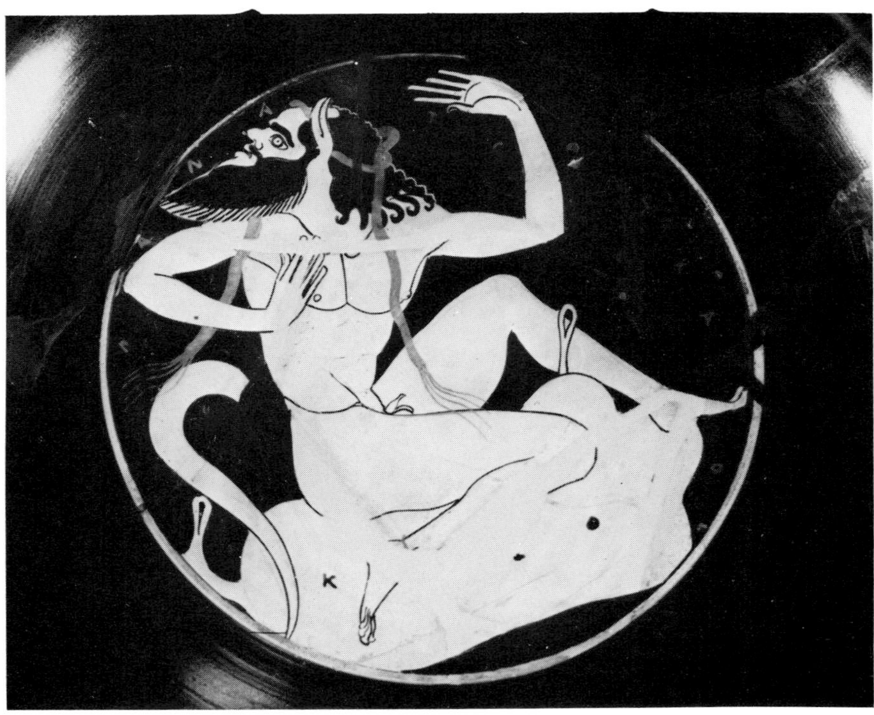

from his own hand.[3] Hence Beazley termed this group "Proto-Panaetian."

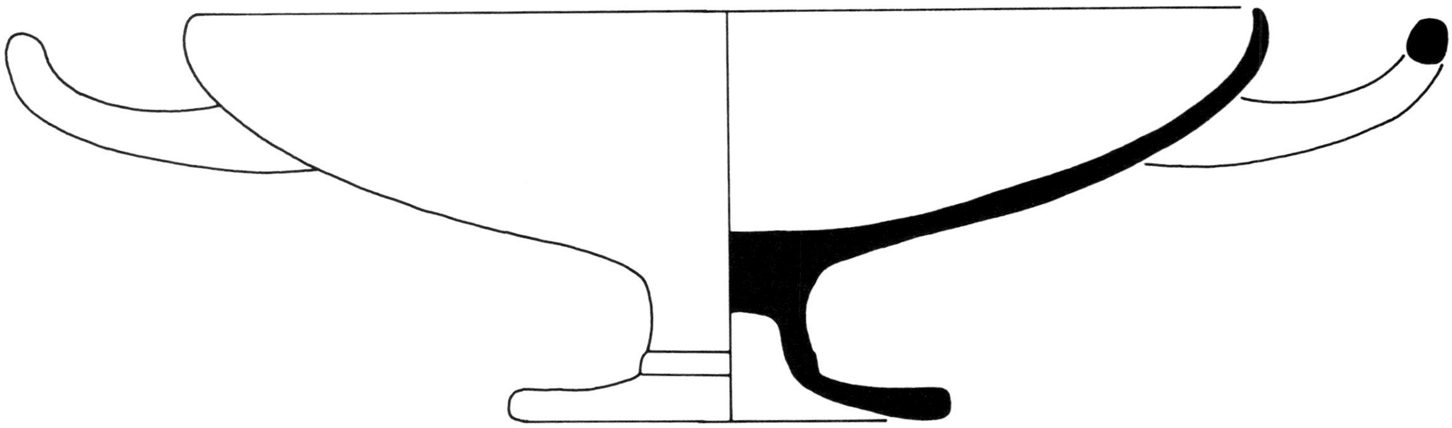

Onesimos was a prolific and skilled painter who specialized in cups, which were often supplied to him by the renowned potter and painter Euphronios. Onesimos's style is distinguished by the overall mastery of draughtsmanship, and particularly by his elegant patterns of elongated fingers and tails.[4]

The motif of the satyr astride a wineskin appears frequently in Attic vasepainting, as does the similar image of a satyr riding a dolphin. Davies reminds us of the traditional association of wine and the sea,[5] and certainly this animated figure would have bobbed in a lively manner once this cup was filled with wine and jostled by an eager symposiast.

1. *FR*, vol. 2, 134.

2. *ARV*², 313–31; *Paralipomena*, 358–61; Boardman, *Red Figure*, 133–34.

3. *ARV*², 314–16. Add: Hornbostal, 307, no. 263, and 310, no. 264.

4. S. Buluç, *AJA* 70 (1966):369–70.

5. M. Davies, in *Athens Comes of Age: From Solon to Salamis* (Princeton, 1978), 79.

111. Kylix by the Antiphon Painter
(490–480 B.C.)

B 11. Baltimore Society AIA, formerly Hartwig Collection. "Cervetri." Ht, 9.3 cm; diam with handles, 30.7 cm; diam rim, 24 cm; diam foot, 8 cm. Mended from many pieces. Foot is ancient but may not belong. (Top of foot and base of stem were filed for close fit.)

Interior

Standing youth in left profile wears fillet and mantle, which expose only top of head and face. Left arm at hip; right arm raised to chest. In field before him are a sponge, strigil, aryballos. Inscribed in field on either side of youth:

ΗΟ ΓΑΙϟ ΚΑ⋁Ο[ϟ].

Tondo is bordered by leftward meander between reserved bands.

Exterior, Side A

Pankration scene. Standing at left is youth in right profile wearing a mantle that exposes only top of head and eyes. Right hand beneath folds is uplifted to conceal most of face. Fillet indicated by reserved band between relief lines. Hanging in field in front of youth are weights and bag. Suspended nearby are strigil, sponge, and bag. In center are two wrestling youths, the victor crouching with left knee drawn up, torso frontal, right arm upraised. Left hand is placed over mouth of opponent, who lies on his back, left hand extended over head, right forearm uplifted, legs in air. Approaching them is a trainer wearing mantle over left shoulder and holding staff in outstretched right hand. Head in left profile wearing taenia.

Relief contour throughout, except beneath feet and incised hairlines. Dilute glaze for inner markings and lettering. Added purple for fillets of youth on tondo and of two figures with staffs on A and B. Vertical edge of foot reserved with black line around lower edge.

Exterior, Side B

Palaestra scene. Standing in right profile is trainer wearing fillet and mantle draped over left shoulder, exposing right shoulder and arm. Staff in left hand; right arm with rod in hand is extended to pair of wrestlers, one of

Side A

whom is almost entirely missing except for right foot. Opponent is shown in left profile, with back in three-quarter view, elbows bent with hands extended.

Bibliography: P. Hartwig, *RömMitt* 2 (1887):168, no. VI; Hartwig, *Meisterschalen*, 575ff, pl. 64; Furtwängler, *ND*, 251–52, no. 1; E. N. Gardiner, *Greek Athletic Sports and Festivals* (London, 1910), 437; G. Perrot, *Histoire de l'art dans l'antiquité*, vol. 10 (Paris, 1882–1914), 629, fig. 350; Beazley, *VA*, 111; Hoppin, *II*, 166, no. 1; Beazley, *AttV*, 232, no. 26; Philippart, 51; E. N. Gardiner. *Athletics of the Ancient World* (Oxford, 1930), 214, fig. 189; CVA USA fasc. 6, Robinson fasc. 2, 18–19, pls. XVII, XVIII.1; E. Buschor, *Griechische Vasen* (Munich, 1940), 153, fig. 172; *ARV*^{2}, 340, no. 65.

The Antiphon Painter is credited with almost one hundred cups, most of which have exterior as well as tondo decoration.[1] The painter prefers genre scenes, either very active ones involving athletes and hunters, or quiet figures like the youth in our tondo. His inscriptions are general words of praise (e.g., "the boy is beautiful," as on our own vase), or refer to specific individuals, such as Antiphon, for whom the painter is

Side B

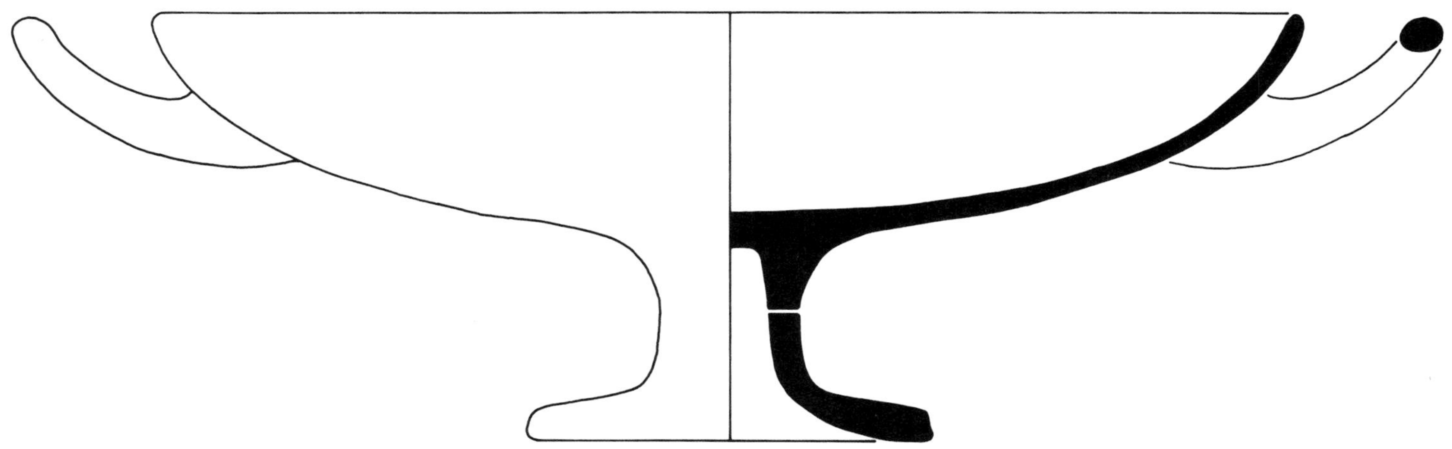

named.[2] Other youths who are complimented include Lysis,[3] Aristarchos,[4] and Nikostratos.[5] The Antiphon Painter worked for several potters, especially Euphronios, who provided vases for Onesimos and Douris.[6] Our artist also decorated vases for the potter Python, for whom Epiktetos and Douris also worked.[7]

The style of the Antiphon Painter is representative of early fifth-century vasepainting in the rounded, prominent jaws, the garments, which fall with few folds, and the three-quarter and back views, which are not always completely successful. The painter's style is close to that of the early or proto-Panaetian phase of Onesimos and can be recognized by the even, almost monotonous spacing of the folds, the drapery pulled tightly over the arms and grasped by the fists, and the black borders just above the hems of the garments.

On our cup, the scenes in the tondo and on the exterior represent a palaestra where youths trained in wrestling and in the pankration.[8] Side A illustrates the beginning of the encounter, which continues on side B, where the trainer gesticulates at the contestants. The sponges, strigil, and aryballos were used for applying oil before exercising and for removing it afterward.

1. *ARV*[2], 335–41; Beazley, *JHS* 58 (1938):267; *Paralipomena*, 361–62; Boardman, *Red Figure*, 135; Hornbostel, 312, no. 266.

2. *ARV*[2], 335, no. 1

3. *ARV*[2], 336, no. 10; 338, no. 39; 339, nos. 52, 60.

4. *ARV*[2], 336, no. 16, which is the same as D. K. Hill, *JWalt* 23 (1960):16, 24. See also *Paralipomena*, 362, in Schimmel Collection.

5. *ARV*[2], 337, no. 26.

6. *ARV*[2], 336, nos. 10, 14, 18; 337, no. 25; 339, no. 57; 340, nos. 63, 73; 341, nos. 77, 88. Bloesch, 71, 79, 80.

7. *ARV*[2], 340, no. 71. See also *ARV*[2], 1646 and *Paralipomena*, 361.

8. H. A. Harris, *Greek Athletes and Athletics* (London, 1964), 105–9.

112. Kylix by Makron with Dionysiac Scene

(490–480 B.C.)

B 10. Baltimore Society AIA, formerly Hartwig Collection. "Caere." Ht, 12.5 cm; diam with handles, 39 cm; diam rim, 29 cm; diam foot, 11.1 cm. Mended from many pieces. Surface abraded.

Interior

On exergue, dancing to their right, are two maenads in girded chitons with overfolds, necklaces, bare feet. Maiden in advance stands with weight on frontal left leg, right leg bent and in left profile, thyrsos in right hand. She glances back at her companion, with her head in right profile, long hair bound in fillet and knotted at tip. Her companion steps forth with right leg extended, left knee bent, torso frontal. Upraised right hand holds small branch. Left hand at hip holds end of thyrsos. Head in left profile, with hair gathered up at nape and bound in fillet. Tondo is bordered by leftward meander.

Side A

Goat beneath handle follows maenad standing in right profile holding torches. In front of her is another maenad, also in right profile, carrying kithara. Approaching them is Dionysos, who is standing in left profile and is wearing ivy wreath and chiton beneath mantle draped over left shoulder and around waist. He carries a kantharos in upraised right hand, a vine with two grape bunches in left. Behind him are a maenad with castanets, another in right profile blowing double flute, and a final frontal maenad with castanets. All maenads wear chitons and mantles except for end maenad with castanets, who wears chiton only. Sketch lines visible beside head of maenad blowing flute.

Side B

Beneath handle is lotus and palmette scheme. Four pairs of satyrs and maenads clad only in chitons and wreaths or fillets: satyr carrying maenad; maenad with thyrsos repelling satyr in fawnskin, maenad resisting satyr with thyrsos; dancing satyr and maenads.

Side A

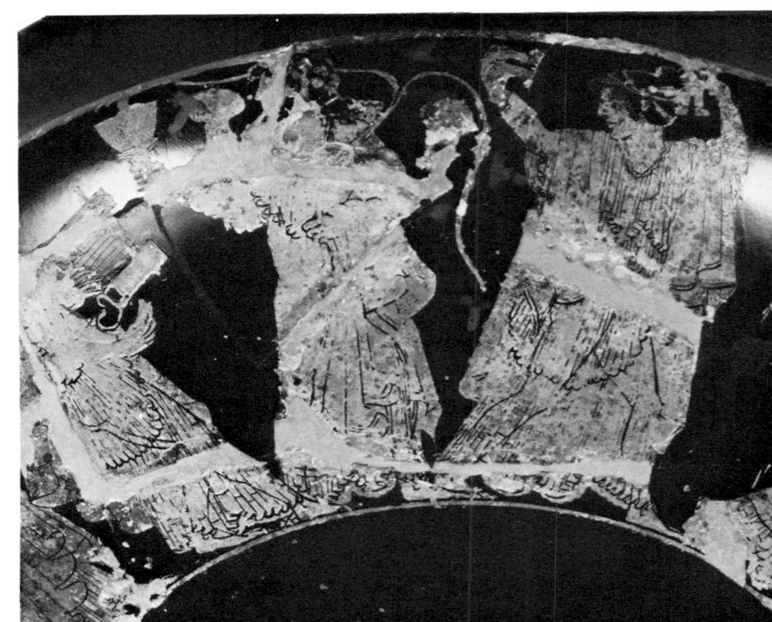

Side B

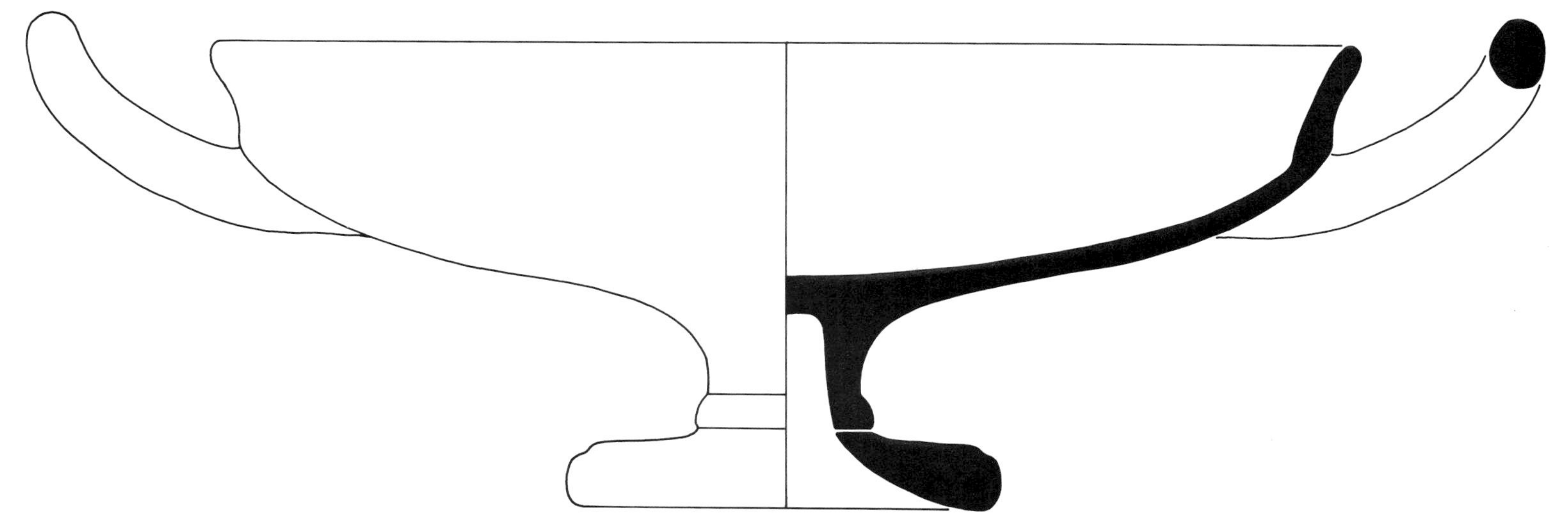

Relief contour throughout, except for reserved hairline. Added red for vine leaves and some wreaths. Reserved line beneath scene; reserved line above scene except at handles.

Bibliography: P. Hartwig, *RömMitt* 2 (1887):168, no. VII; Hartwig, *Meisterschalen*, 289–94, pls. 30.3 and 31; Furtwängler, *ND*, 251–52, no. 1, *FR*, vol. 1, 237; Beazley, *VA*, 101, 103, no. 28; Hoppin, *II*, 96, no. 43; Beazley, *AttV*, 214, no. 35; P. Jacobsthal, *Ornamente griechischer Vasen* (Berlin, 1927), 132; L. Lawler, *MAAR* 6 (1927), pls. XIX.1, XX.4; Philippart, 50–51; CVA USA fasc. 6, Robinson fasc. 2, 17–18, pls. XV, XVI.1; *ARV*², 463, no. 51.

Makron was a prolific painter; almost three hundred fifty vases are attributed to him.[1] He primarily painted cups, but he also worked on skyphoi, plates, aryballoi, askoi, and at least one pyxis. He signed only one vase, a skyphos in Boston that also bears the signature of Hieron the potter.[2] We know that Hieron and Makron had a particularly close association, since thirty-one vases that bear the signature of Hieron have been attributed to Makron; occasionally, however, Hieron fashioned vases for other artists.[3] Our cup has the unusual shape of Type C, which is characterized by an offset lip, a bulge in the stem, and a flat, platelike foot.[4]

Makron has a penchant for komos scenes involving numerous animated figures with objects in uplifted hands. The maenads usually wear closely pleated chitons with billowing overfolds and carry thyrsoi. The ornamental motifs under the handles vary greatly.[5]

Makron did not rely heavily on his sketch lines, but often disregarded those delineating the drapery or the head, as can be seen in the figure of the maenad in the middle of side A.[6]

1. *ARV*², 458–81; J. D. Beazley, *JHS* 58 (1938):267; *Paralipomena*, 377–79; Boardman, *Red Figure*, 140. Add: A. Ashmead and K. Phillips, *AJA* 70 (1966):366–68; C. Boulter, CVA USA fasc. 17, Toledo fasc. 1, 34, pls. 53–54.
2. *ARV*², 458, no. 1, and perhaps 479, no. 336.
3. Bloesch, 91–96; *ARV*², 481–82.
4. Bloesch, 111, and 132, nos. 17–19.
5. Ashmead and Phillips, *AJA* 70 (1966):366–68. Ours is especially close to Simon, pl. 169, which is the same as *ARV*², 462, no. 48.
6. R. DePuma, *AJA* 72 (1968):152–54.

Side B

113. Neck Amphora by the Harrow Painter

(ca. 480 B.C.)

B 13. Baltimore Society AIA, formerly Hartwig Collection. "Tarentum." Ht, 39 cm; diam mouth, 16.1 cm; diam foot, 11 cm. Mended from many pieces, with handles and most of rim restored in plaster. Foot is ancient but may not belong. Alien lid with which vase was first published is now at the University of Mississippi.

Scenes on both sides are unframed, with figures standing on narrow bands as groundlines.

Side A

Silenos strides forward in right profile, hands bound behind back. Following him is a bearded hunter who looks back, head in left profile. Hunter wears boots, short chiton that has a black border at neckline and hem, and petasos hanging behind neck. Right hand holds two spears; left hand hold ends of the thongs that wrap Silenos's wrists. To the hunter's left is hunting dog.

Relief contour line throughout. Relief line for drapery detail, top of boots, thongs. Hair outlined in reserve. Dilute glaze for inner details of body, neck and sleeve of chiton. Added purple for petasos cord, thongs of Silenos.

Side B

Bearded Midas stands three-quarters left, face in left profile. He wears a pleated chiton beneath himation, carries staff in upraised right hand. Some relief contours. Hair and beard outlined in reserve. Dilute glaze for inner details of chiton.

Tongues above each picture, terminating beneath handles. Graffito on shoulder.

Bibliography: Furtwängler, *ND*, 252, no. 3; J. D. Beazley, *JHS* 36 (1916):133, no. 30; Beazley, *VA*, 56; Hoppin, *II*, 3, no. 3; Beazley, *AttV*, 120, no. 40; CVA, USA fasc. 6, Robinson fasc. 2, 25, pls. XXIX, XXX; F. Brommer, *AA* (1941):40, no. 4, and 44, fig. 6; *Ancient Art in American Private Collections* (Cambridge, 1954), no. 278, pl. LXXXIII; *ARV*[2], 73, no. 22; F. Brommer, *Heldensage*[3], 535, no. B4.

When Dionysos was passing through Asia Minor, Silenos, a human-equine member of the entourage, wandered away and was captured by a hunter who brought the captive to King Midas.[1] The king returned Silenos to Dionysos, and the grateful deity agreed as a reward to grant Midas's wish that everything he touched be turned to gold. Midas soon discovered, however, that all food and drink became golden, too, and thus he appealed to Dionysos to re-

Side A

move the magic touch. The god instructed Midas to wash in the river Pactolus, which henceforth became renowned for its gold-bearing sands.

This adventure of Midas was first seen on Chiote and Spartan vases of the mid-sixth century.[2] Around the year 500 B.C. the subject appeared in Attic vase-painting, where it remained popular for the next one hundred fifty years.[3] Artists depicted several different moments in the tale, including the capture of Silenos in Midas's garden, his abduction to King Midas, and his presentation before the king. Not before the fifth century do we find Midas depicted in oriental dress,[4] and after 450 B.C. he wears the ass ears that he acquired by unwisely voting against Apollo in a musical competition.[5]

The Harrow Painter is known for almost one hundred large vases, of which half are amphorae and column craters.[6] The profile of the body of the Baltimore example compares most closely with those of the artist's neck amphorae with twisted handles, and for this reason twisted handles have been restored on our vessel.[7]

The Harrow Painter was most comfortable with genre subjects, but on his amphorae he occasionally turned to mythological and especially Dionysiac themes. His style was inspired primarily by that of the Berlin Painter, whose influence is apparent in the use of one or two quietly standing figures on each side of the amphora, and in the tendency to distribute figures from a single scene on both sides of the vase. The Harrow Painter falls short of the Berlin Painter, however, both in draughtsmanship and in the ability to endow a scene with emotional content. Our painter also has a tendency to repeat his figures, especially the older man draped in a mantle.[8]

The graffito on the shoulder of the vessel was applied after the vase was fired. Although most graffiti are thought to carry a commercial meaning, the unusual position of this mark may denote ownership or dedication.[9] The lettering is Etruscan or possibly Oscan.[10]

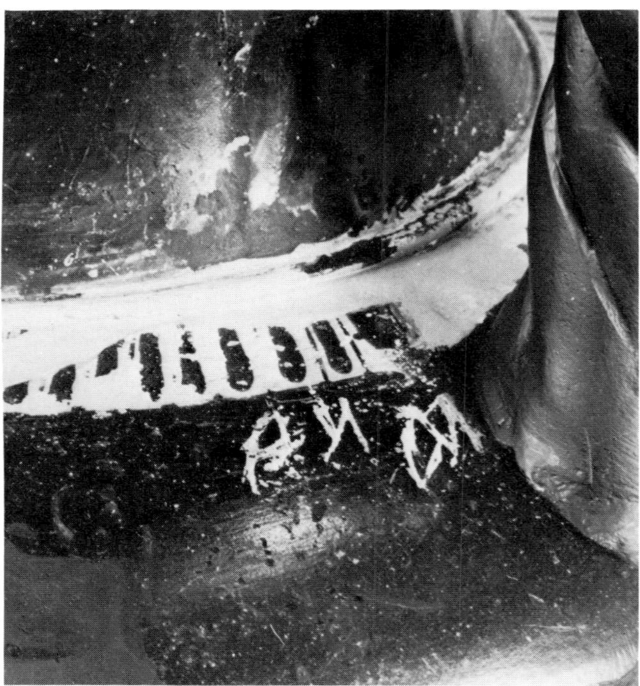

1. Herodotus 8.138; Xenophon *An.*, I.2.13. See F. Brommer, *AA* (1941):36.

2. F. Brommer, *AntK Beiheft* 7 (1970):55–57.

3. F. Brommer, *AA* (1941):43.

4. F. Brommer, *AntK Beiheft* 7 (1970):56.

5. Ibid., 56; Brommer, *AA* (1941):43; Ovid *Met.* 11.153ff.; Hyginus *Fab.* 191.1.

6. *ARV*^{2}, 272–77; *Paralipomena*, 353–54, with note on alien lid, which is in Mississippi, not Cambridge. J. D. Beazley, *JHS* 58 (1938):267–68.

7. Our vase is especially similar to *ARV*^{2}, 272, no. 6, upon which the restoration of our vase is based. I thank very much D. von Bothmer, who provided photographs and advice. Through no fault of his, the handles of our restoration are not quite correctly proportioned.

8. *ARV*^{2}, 272, no. 8, which is the same as *Münzen und Medaillen* 40 (December 13, 1969):60, no. 100, pl. 41. *ARV*^{2}, 273, no. 19 bis, is the same as *Münzen und Medaillen* 13 (May 1961): 89, no. 165, pl. 55.

9. Boardman, *Black Figure*, 202; A. Johnston, *Trademarks on Greek Vases* (Warminster, 1979), 5, 6, 8.

10. I owe this suggestion to A. Johnston.

114. Kylix by Douris

(480–470 B.C.)

B 9. Baltimore Society AIA, formerly Hartwig Collection. "Chiusi." Ht, 9.5 cm; diam with handles, 30 cm; diam rim, 22.5 cm; diam foot, 8.7 cm. Mended.

Standing on exergue is a bearded male bending over a whip top, his supporting right leg frontal, his left leg in left profile. In the hand of his upraised right arm is a stick, on which there are three strings. His left hand rests on his left knee. His torso is largely concealed by his chlamys, which is fastened on his right shoulder. His head is in right profile and he wears a petasos. In field below his right elbow is a floral motif. On other side of top is youth whose torso faces three-quarters front, legs in left profile, right arm extended, left hand on hip. Mantle draped over body and back of head, exposing only right shoulder and arm. Fillet. In field above his head is a floral motif. Inscribed in field:

KAVOS + H

Relief contour throughout, except for reserved hairline. Dilute glaze for some inner markings. Added red for strings of stick and lettering. Border consists of rightward meander.

Bibliography: P. Hartwig, *RömMitt* 2 (1887):169, no. 9; Hartwig, *Meisterschalen*, 657–59, pl. 72.2; Furtwängler, *ND*, 251–52, no. 1; P. Wolters, *MJb* 8 (1913):89, fig. 7; Beazley, *VA*, 97; Hoppin, *I*, 277, no. 46; Beazley, *AttV*, 208, no. 119; Philippart, 50; CVA USA fasc. 6, Robinson fasc. 2, 16, pl. XII; W. Zschietzschmann, *Hellas und Rom* (Tübingen, 1959), pl. 181.2; *ARV*², 445, no. 251; D. Gould, *Expedition* 22 (1980):44, fig. 4.

The petasos and chlamys suggest that the top-spinner is Hermes, and this identification is confirmed by vases in Florence[1] and Tübingen[2] on which Hermes, outfitted with kerykeion and winged sandals, is engaged in spinning a top. Beazley[3] suggests that, after receiving the whip from Apollo (*Hymn to Hermes*, 497), Hermes invented the whip top, although other types of tops subsequently evolved.[4] We are perhaps to imagine that the god is in the palaestra, an area sa-

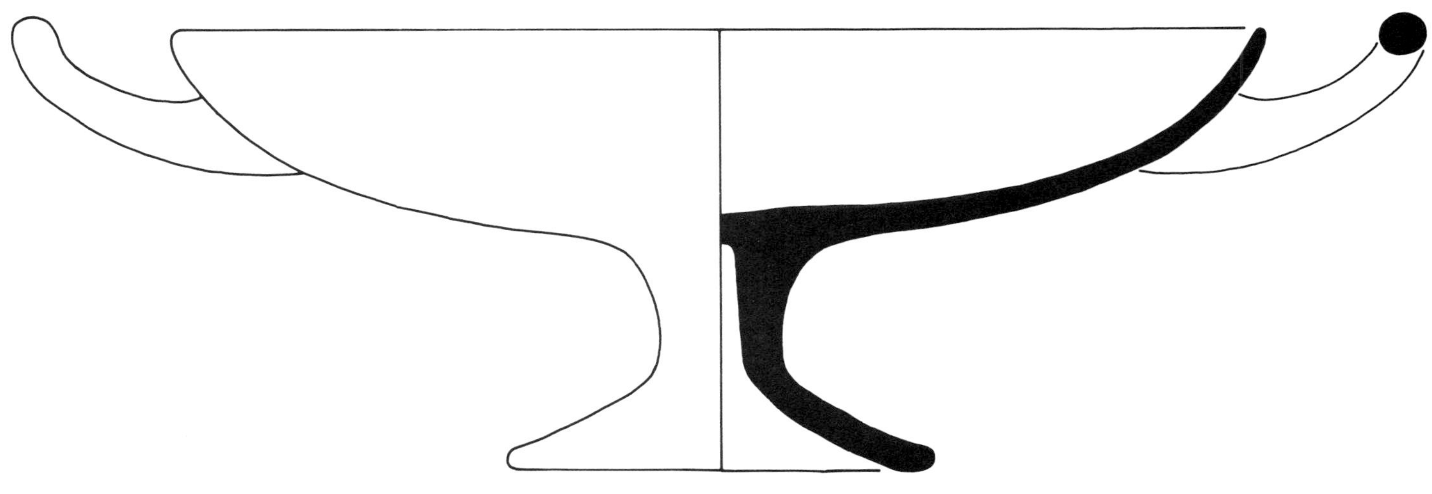

cred to Hermes and an association that accounts for the deity's special rapport with youth.[5]

This cup belongs to Douris's late period,[6] when the stopt meander was common, the drawing was delicate, and the small figures were well contained within the circular field. At this time Douris was working primarily for the potter Python.

1. CVA Italy fasc. 38, Florence fasc. 4, 6–7, pl. 124.2, which is the same as *ARV*², no. 113, p. 377. Also J. D. Beazley, *JHS* 58 (1938):267. For Hermes in traveler's attire, see P. Zanker, *Wandel der Hermesgestalt in der attische Vasenmalerei*, in *Antiquitas*, vol. 2 (Bonn, 1965), 115–116.

2. C. Watzinger, *Griechische Vasen in Tübingen* (Reutlingen, 1924), 44, no. E78, pl. 25.

3. Beazley, *JHS* 58 (1938):267.

4. D. Gould, *Expedition* 22 (1980):43–47. Our vase is on p. 44, fig. 4.

5. Zanker, *Wandel der Hermesgestalt*, 94, 99.

6. *ARV*², 425–27.

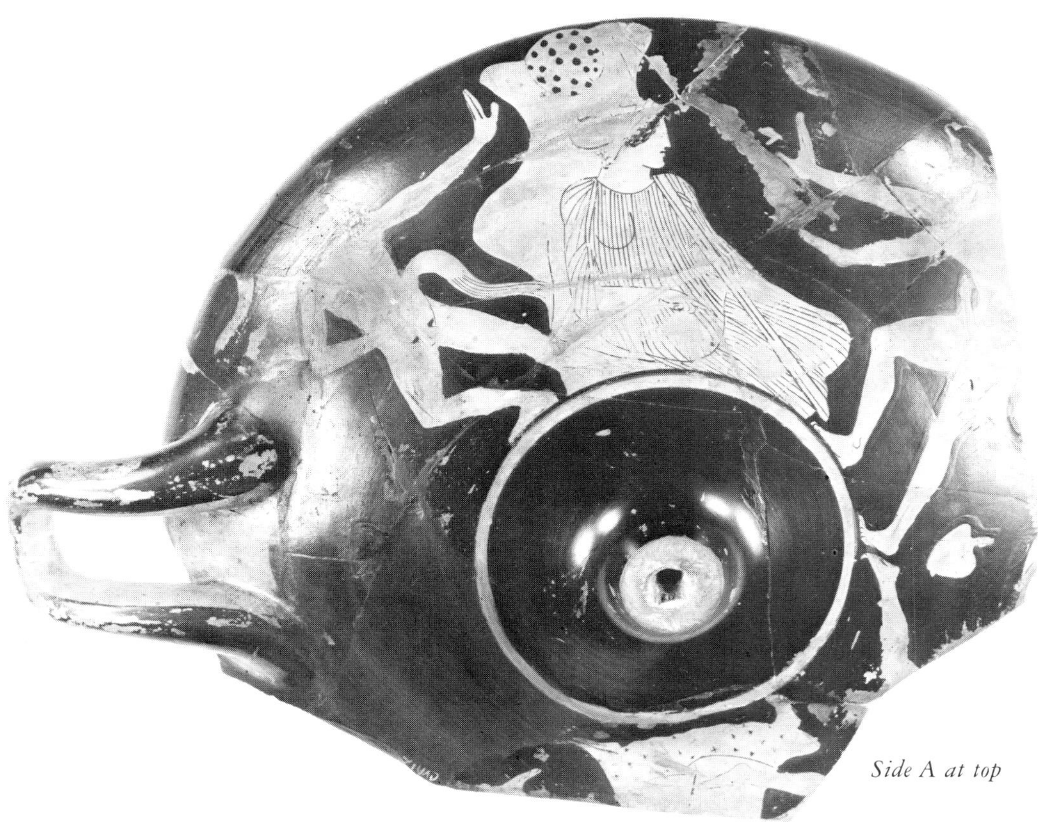

Side A at top

115. Kylix in the Manner of the Pistoxenus Painter

(ca. 460 B.C.)

B 12. Baltimore Society AIA, formerly Hartwig Collection. Max dimension, 24 cm; diam tondo, 14.3 cm. Mended from a number of pieces, with large sections and stem missing.

Interior

Bearded satyr dances in left profile, weight on left leg, with right leg raised. Right arm extended. Left hand holds a panther skin behind back; feet of skin brought forward over shoulder. Drinking horn in field before left foot. Tondo is bordered by leftward meander between reserved bands.

Side A

Maenad dressed in chiton with overfold and sakkos reclines to her left against a rock, with legs drawn up and thyrsos resting against left shoulder. She looks to her left at an approaching bearded satyr, shown in left profile with arms outstretched. Drinking horn in field between figures. Behind maenad is another bearded satyr standing frontally with right knee bent, left leg extended out behind him. Right hand grasps phallus, left arm extended toward maenad. Drinking horn in field behind him. Relief contour. Dilute glaze for hair, beard, some drapery folds.

Side B

Left leg of satyr running toward maenad, of whom only the lower part draped in chiton survives. To her left is hand or tail of another satyr. Dilute glaze for chiton. Ivy leaf under handles.

Bibliography: D. M. Robinson, *AJA* 21 (1917):160–68; J. D. Beazley, *Campana Fragments in Florence* (London, 1933), no. 42, pl. 16; CVA USA fasc. 6, Robinson fasc. 2, 20, pl. XXI.1; *ARV*², 865, no. 2.

Beazley determined that fragments in Florence belong to side B, which also depicts a Dionysiac scene[1] in which a maenad is turning toward a satyr approaching from her right; behind her is another satyr who runs away.

The Pistoxenus Painter is accredited with over thirty vases, most of which are cups.[2] His best work is in white ground, of which only a handful of examples are known. Both Pistoxenus and Euphronios are known to have supplied pots for him.

This vase was acquired in a restored state that incorporated the fragment by Oltos (no. 101).

1. *ARV*², 865, no. 2; J. D. Beazley, *Campana Fragments in Florence* (London, 1933), 16, no. 42.
2. *ARV*², 859–63.

Side A

116. Bell Krater by the Christie Painter

(ca. 440 B.C.)

51.486. Baltimore Museum of Art, from collection of Saidie May, purchased from J. Brummer. "Attica." Ht, 37 cm; diam rim, 32.5 cm; diam foot, 17.8 cm. Intact.

Side A

Striding winged Eos in right profile, left leg advanced, arms extended. She wears chiton with belted overfold; hair gathered at nape and surmounted by diadem with ornament executed in pellets of clay. In front of her and moving away is Cephalos, left leg advanced, head turned back in left profile. He wears chlamys fastened on right shoulder, laurel wreath, petasos hanging behind neck, and laced sandals. He carries two spears in his right hand. Behind Eos and moving away from her is similarly attired youth, grazing back at Eos, with his head in right profile. Inscribed in field above hand of Eos:

K]AΛΛE

Relief contour for face, back of neck, edge of wings of Eos, faces, and spears of youths. Relief line for drapery folds. Dilute glaze for ends of hair, borders of garments, thongs of boots, details on wings. Added white for ornament on diadem, laurel wreath, lettering. Reserved hairline.

Side B

Standing youth seen in right profile leans on staff and faces two other youths standing in left profile. All are draped in himatia and wear fillets; central youth also leans on staff. In field are halteres and bag. Added white for cords of bag and fillets. Reserved hairlines.

Beneath pictures is band of meander alternating with dotted cross-square; reserved band beneath. Leftward laurel wreath between reserved bands encircles vase above pictures. Band of tongues around base of handles. Reserved groove at juncture of body and foot.

Bibliography: *CVA* USA fasc. 6, Robinson fasc. 2, 32–33, pl. XLV; *ARV*², 1048, no. 27; S. Kaempf-Dimitriadou, *AntK Beiheft* 11 (1979):85, no. 110; F. Brommer, *Göttersagen in Vasenlisten* (Marburg, 1980), 24, no. 49.

About fifty vases have been attributed to the Christie Painter, of which twenty-five are bell kraters, the rest being calyx kraters, stamnoi, pelikai, and hydriai.[1] Common to many of these vases are a meander and saltire border and a representation of three standing youths on the reverse.[2]

The Christie Painter favors Dionysiac themes and lively mythological scenes, such as Amazonomachies. On our vase, Eos, the goddess of dawn, is eagerly

Side B

pursuing the Attic hunter Cephalos; according to some traditions, the offspring of that union will be Phaethon.[3] The Christie Painter took up the subject a second time on a bell krater (now in Genoa) on which Eos again advances to her left, but now hastens to embrace a youth with a lyre.[4] That figure is Tithonos, who requested from the deity eternal life but forgot to ask for eternal youth. As Tithonos grew older and less attractive, Eos enclosed him in a chamber, where according to some traditions he was transformed into a cicado.[5] Behind Eos is a youth identical to the figure retreating from Eos on the Hopkins vase. The youth on the Genoa krater has been identified as Cephalos and the scene has been described as a conflation of the two romantic episodes.[6] On the Hopkins vase, the retreating hunter is probably only a nameless, decorative pendant to Cephalos and typical of the unrelated bystanders who often appear in contemporary representations of the myth.[7]

The subjects of Eos and Tithonos and of Eos and Cephalos were very popular in late sixth- and early fifth-century vasepainting. The striking similarities between the representations suggest that the vasepaintings were inspired by a single pictorial prototype.[8]

The Christie Painter exercised a tremendous influence on a contemporary early Lucanian painter, the Pisticci Painter, who imitated the ornament and style of the Attic artist and even depicted the myth of Eos and Tithonos on at least three vases. The similarities between the two painters are so extensive that it is possible that the Pisticci Painter was trained in Athens and was even Greek.[9]

1. *ARV*², 1046–49; *Paralipomena*, 444, 517; J. D. Beazley, *JHS* 58 (1938):268; Hornbostel, 335, no. 286.

2. D. Buitron, *Attic Vase Paintings in New England Collections: Fogg Art Museum* (Cambridge, 1972), 128, no. 71, which is the same as *ARV*², 1047, no. 20; Hornbostel, 335, no. 286.

3. S. Kaempf-Dimitriadou, *AntK Beiheft* 11 (1979):17, 61 n. 94; *Theogony* 986ff.; Pausanias 1.3.1.

4. *ARV*², 1048, no. 28, which is the same as Genoa 1216; *CVA* Italy fasc. 19, Genoa fasc. 1, 6, pl. 9.

5. *Odyssey* 5.1; *Hom Hymn Aphrodite* 218; Hellanicos frag. 140 Jacoby.

6. *CVA* Genoa fasc. 1, 6, pl. 9.

7. Kaempf-Dimitriadou, *AntK Beiheft* 11 (1979):18.

8. See late archaic metope from Selinus [R. R. Holloway, *Influences and Styles in the Late Archaic and Early Classical Greek Sculpture of Sicily and Magna Graecia* (Louvain, 1975), 19, 22]. Kaempf-Dimitriadou, *AntK Beiheft* 11 (1979):16–21; A. D. Trendall, *The Red Figure Vases of Lucania, Campania and Sicily* (Oxford, 1967), 16.

9. Trendall, *Red Figure Vases*, 9; Trendall, *South Italian Vase Painting* (London, 1966), 16; B. MacDonald, *AJA* 85 (1981): 160.

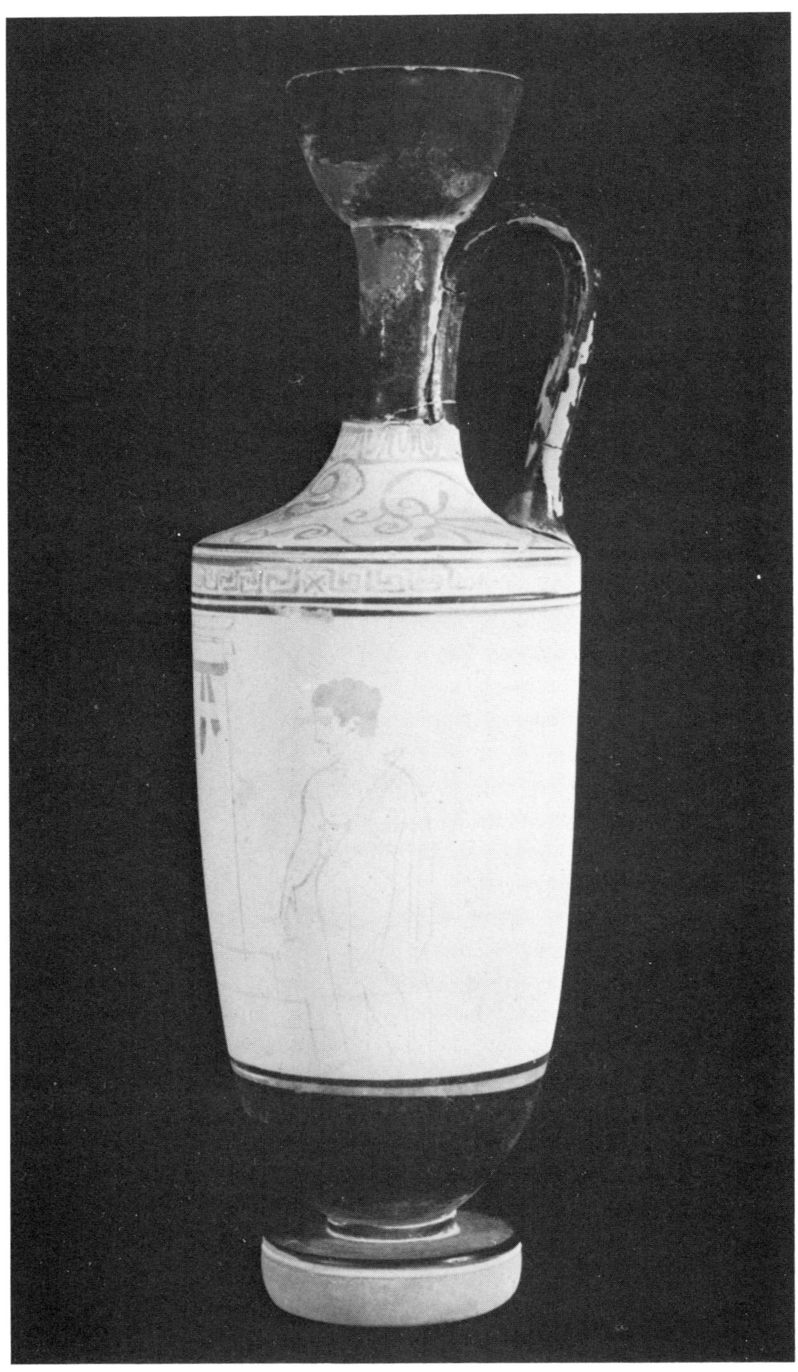

117. White-Ground Lekythos

(440–420 B.C.)

41.134. (P.4015 on underside of foot.) Baltimore Museum of Art, gift of Blanche Adler, purchased in 1926 from Joseph Brummer. Ht, 24.6 cm; diam mouth, 4.6 cm; diam foot, 4.8 cm. Handle is probably not original.

Color of figure scene and ornament fired red. Maiden in right profile holds object (now missing) in both hands. The color of her garment has faded, leaving only her nude body. She stands before a grave stele wrapped with taenia and surmounting stepped base. On other side of stele is youth, standing frontally, head in left profile. He wears a himation, which is draped over his body, exposing his right shoulder and breast.

Upper surface of lip reserved. On neck is tongue pattern between single lines. On shoulder is scheme of three five-petal palmettes entwined in volutes. Central palmette is inverted, other two are turned toward handle. Above picture is meander in groups of three, alternately leftward and rightward, separated by saltire squares. Two lines above and beneath. Single line under picture.

The white-ground technique developed in Athens at the end of the sixth century B.C. The artist outlined his figures upon a field of white slip before firing the vase. After the vessel was removed from the kiln, matte colors were applied, but because this paint was not baked onto the vase, the colors have often faded or vanished.[1]

From its early years, the technique was applied to lekythoi, but it was only in the second quarter of the fifth century that white-ground lekythoi regularly depicted funerary subjects and became primarily associated with the grave.[2] The vessels were used to hold libations of olive oil and were placed as offerings at the base of the grave stele or were buried with the deceased.[3]

In the middle of the fifth century the Achilles Painter dispensed with the relief line heretofore used for outlining the figures and introduced the softer matte paint that would become almost canonical on later lekythoi like ours. Our vase is surely the product of the Bird Group, a large workshop that was active in the 430's and 420's under the leadership of the Bird Painter,[4] and in which the Painter of Munich 2335 may also have worked. The palmette ornament on the neck of our lekythos is characteristic of vases by this latter artist, as is the emotional note conveyed by the sharply downturned head of the maiden.[5] We might also compare examples by the Bird Painter[6] and by another colleague, the Carlsberg Painter.[7]

1. D. Kurtz, *Athenian White Lekythoi* (Oxford, 1975), XX.

2. Ibid., XIX; J. Boardman and D. Kurtz, *Greek Burial Customs* (Ithaca, 1971), 102–5.

3. Kurtz, *White Lekythoi*, XIX; J. D. Beazley, *Attic White Lekythoi* (London, 1938), 5.

4. *ARV*[2], 1231–235; 1687–688; *Paralipomena*, 467; Kurtz, *Athenian White Lekythoi*, 52–55. His palmettes are IIa.

5. *ARV*[2], 1168–169, 1685, 1703, 1707; *Paralipomena*, 458–59; Kurtz, *Athenian White Lekythoi*, 55–56. His palmettes are also IIa. See also F. Felton, *AthMitt* 91 (1976):94, no. 28, pl. 29 and 94, no. 29, pl. 30.

6. *ARV*[2], 1232, no. 10. I owe this and the following comparison to D. Kurtz.

7. Ibid., 1235, no. 10.

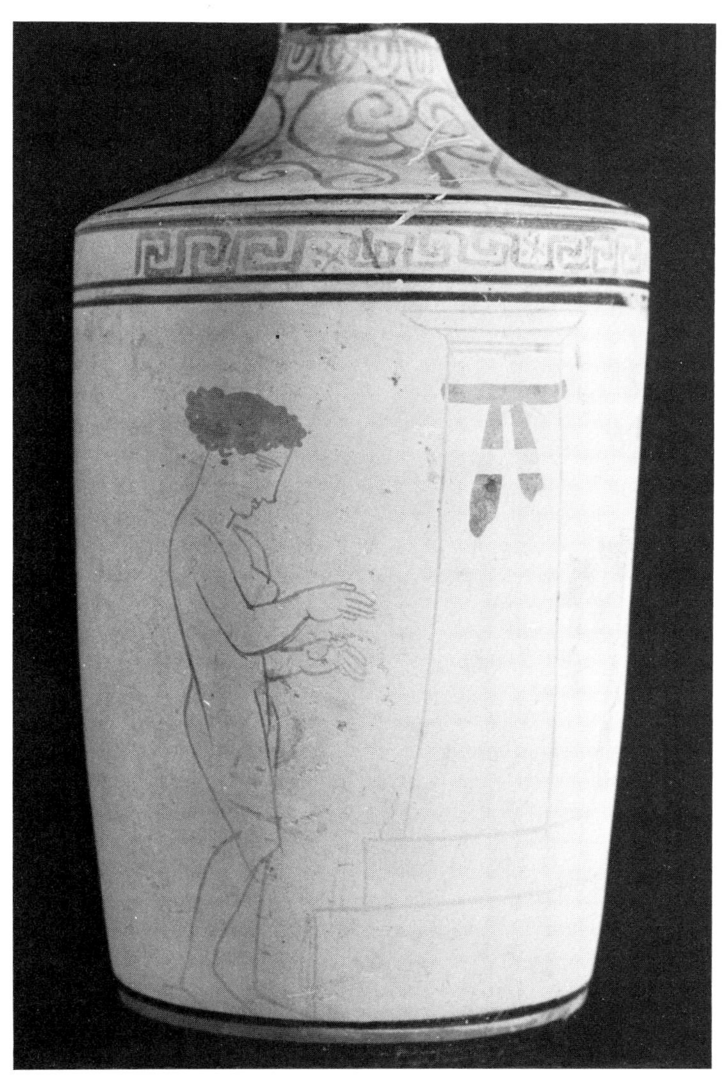

118. White-Ground Lekythos

(440–420 B.C.)

41.133. (P.2468 on underside of foot.) Baltimore Museum of Art, gift of Blanche Adler. Ht, 28.7 cm; diam mouth, 5.8 cm; diam foot, 5.2 cm. Chipped all over.

Color of figure scene and ornament fired red. Nude maiden, seen in right profile, carries a duck in her extended hands and approaches a grave stele on stepped base. On other side of stele is youth in left profile with right arm extended. He is draped in a red cloak.

Upper surface of lip reserved. On shoulder beneath single line is palmette scheme of three five-petal palmettes entwined in volutes. Central palmette inverted, other two turned toward handle. Upper border of picture consists of meander grouped in threes, alternately leftward and rightward, separated by saltire squares. Two lines above and beneath. Single line under picture.

Like the previous example, this lekythos can also be attributed to an artist of the Bird Group, a workshop headed by the Bird Painter, whose work this vessel particularly recalls, both in the configuration of the palmette pattern and in the less emphatic poignancy of the representation.[1] In contrast to the maiden on the preceding vase, the figure on our example has more delicate features, with a shorter face and a more subtly rounded profile of the nose.[2]

1. *ARV*², 1231–235; *Paralipomena*, 467; D. Kurtz, *Athenian White Lekythoi* (Oxford, 1957), 52–55. Compare *ARV*², 1233, no. 23, a comparison I owe to D. Kurtz.

2. See *ARV*², 1687–688, and *Paralipomena*, 467, for his late and fine style. See also F. Felton, *AthMitt* 91 (1976):99–100.

Side A

119. Bell Krater by Hoppin Painter

(ca. 380–350 B.C.)

9286. Robinson Collection. "Tarentum." Ht, 34.8 cm; diam rim, 38 cm; diam foot, 19 cm. Intact.

Side A

Three figures run in left profile. In front is bearded nude male with pail in left hand, torch in uplifted right hand, and cloak over shoulders. In center is woman dressed in chiton with overfold, her right hand uplifted, her left hand holding a tympanum. Behind her is nude youth carrying jug in right hand. His mantle is flung over the left arm and hand, in which he holds a spear. Relief contour for some details. Band of wave pattern above figures.

Side B

Bearded youth with short, curly hair stands in right profile and addresses two youths who turn toward him. All figures are enveloped in long mantles to ankles. Youth in center holds staff in right hand; in field behind his head is reserved disc.

Figures on both sides stand on narrow reserved band above band of leftward meander that terminates below handles in dotted cross-square, from which rises a scroll motif. Above pictures is leftward laurel band between reserved bands. Zone of tongues around roots of handles.

Bibliography: Furtwängler, *ND.* 252, no. 4; *CVA* USA fasc. 7, Robinson fasc. 3, 27, pl. XIX; A. D. Trendall, *Frühitaliotisch Vasen* (Leipzig, 1938), 26 n. 41; A. Cambitoglou and A. D. Trendall, *Apulian Red Figure Vase-Painters of the Plain Style* (Rutland, Vermont, 1961), 56, no. 2.

Side B

Side A, detail

This krater is one of eleven vases attributed to the Hoppin Painter, who with five colleagues formed the Hoppin Group, painting in the Plain Apulian style.[1] The workshop was located in Tarentum and was active between about 380 and 350 B.C. The Hoppin Painter was probably trained by artists of the school of the Tarporley Painter (400–380 B.C.), a disciple of the Sisyphos Painter, who originated both the Plain and the Ornate Styles.

The Hoppin Painter worked mostly on bell kraters, although he also painted one pelike and one calyx krater. His vases are recognized by their tall, slim figures with flying drapery, the wrapped heads of the women, and the youths with white fillets and himatia draped over their arms.[2] The three figures on the reverse of our vase also appear on vases by the artist in Lecce[3] and Cambridge.[4] The style of the Hoppin Painter is especially close to that of the Lecce Painter,[5] who was active at about the same time, the second quarter of the fourth century.

1. A. D. Trendall, *South Italian Vase Painting* (London, 1966), 20; A. Cambitoglou and A. D. Trendall, *Apulian Red Figure Vase-Painters of the Plain Style* (Rutland, Vermont, 1961), 55–56. Our vase is p. 56, no. 2.
2. Cambitoglou and Trendall, *Vase-Painters*, 55.
3. Ibid., 56, no. 3, and Lecce 620, *CVA* Italy fasc. 6, Lecce fasc. 2, pl. 12.
4. Cambitoglou and Trendall, *Vase-Painters*, 56, no. 1.
5. Ibid., 62.

120. South Italian Squat Lekythos

(ca. 350–325 B.C.)

42.70. Brooklyn Museum Gift. "Apulia, near Capua." Ht, 31.7 cm; diam rim, 9.2 cm; diam foot, 13.1 cm. Mended and restored. Deposit over surface.

Youth seated in left profile turns his head to gaze behind him. He is nude except for mantle draped across waist and legs. He holds a staff in his outstretched right hand. Behind him is draped standing maiden, turning to her left. In front of her is Dionysos, seated three-quarters to his right with nude torso, mantle draped over legs. In his right hand he holds a thyrsos. He turns his head to glance back at a standing female in left profile who holds a thyrsos in her right hand. Extensive use of added white.

Tongues around lower half of neck; band of wave pattern on shoulder above reserved band. Figures stand on white band enclosed by black bounding lines. Beneath is band of wave pattern beneath dotted white line, then white and black bands. At back is seventeen-petal palmette amid scrolls.

Bibliography: A. D. Trendall, *The Red Figured Vases of Lucania, Campania and Sicily* (Oxford, 1967), 480, no. 282, pl. 185.

This vase was identified by Trendall as a product of the LNO Painter, who worked in the Cumaean shop of the CA Painter during the third quarter of the fourth century.[1] Trendall points out that the LNA Painter was influenced by the Orvieto and CC Subgroups (Cumae A) within the CA workshop, as well as by another subgroup, the Apulianizing Group (340–320 B.C.), best represented by the Ivy Leaf Painter (Cumae A II).

The Hopkins vase is characteristic of Cumaean painting in its generous use of white, yellow, and red paint, and its spiky stephanai. Distinctive of the LNO Painter are the tall headdresses on the women and the quiet groupings of standing and seated figures with multiple attributes.

1. A. D. Trendall, *The Red Figured Vases of Lucania, Campania and Sicily* (Oxford, 1967). Our vase is 480, no. 282, pl. 185. See discussion on 479–83.

Pottery

ETRUSCAN AND ITALIC

121. Impasto Jug

(eighth c. B.C.)

9248. Ht, 11.7 cm; diam rim, 6.5 cm; diam foot, 5.4 cm. Mended with part of neck restored in plaster.

Handmade. Brown, burnished surface. Spherical body tapers to rim with slightly flaring lip. Short, conical foot. Tubular handle set vertically. On neck are two bands of six incised grooves, one band beneath lip, other at base of neck. On body is band of zigzag comprised of eight grooves. All grooves filled with white substance.

Bibliography: *CVA*, USA fasc. 7, Robinson fasc. 3, 47, pl. 35.1.

The Early Iron Age civilization of eighth-century Italy is believed to have resulted from the assimilation of Indo-European Apennine inhabitants of the Bronze Age with Indo-European invaders of the eleventh century.[1] In the center of the country, this civilization is usually designated Villanovan and is partially characterized by coarse and often handmade impasto pottery.[2] Our vase compares with counterparts from Sala Consalina,[3] and Caere,[4] but is distinctive in the abbreviated neck, raised foot, and position of the handle, which is attached at the lip instead of the shoulder.

1. Brendel, 18–19; Hencken, *Peabody*, 469.
2. Brendel, 23; A. Boëthius, *Etruscan and Early Roman Architecture* (New York, 1978), 19–21.
3. Boëthius, *Architecture*, 19, 23, and 26, fig. 14, for an example from tomb 63 in Sala Consalina.
4. I. Pohl, 16, fig. 12, and 184, fig. 159, from graves dated from 720–690 B.C. (p. 300).

122. Capenate Plate

(ca. 650–600 B.C.)

269. Purchased in Rome or Naples in 1906–9. "Leprignano." Diam, 22 cm; ht, 2.6 cm. Mended from several pieces.

Coarse, brown clay, burnished. Flat plate with upturned rim, ring foot. Spaced at 2-cm intervals around rim are groups of six to eight transversely incised grooves. Incised decoration on exterior consists of four waterbirds striding in right profile; interiors hatched, long zigzag crests streaming from heads. Within ring foot is incised circle enclosing two bands of four and five incised lines crossing at a right angle.

Bibliography: *CVA* USA fasc. 7 Robinson fasc. 3, 47, pl. 34.1.

The provenance of this plate is the Faliscan area around Capena, located to the south and east of Etruria.[1] Although the Capenates were distinct from the Etruscans, they were strongly influenced by the southern Etruscan centers of Veii and Caere.

The coarse fabric and incised ornament of this plate are characteristic of Capenate impasto. Similar incised, elongated birds appear singly or in procession on a number of vases from Leprignano.[2] The birds and the shape of our plate can also be compared with those on the red-on-white bird plates of Italo-Archaic Decorated Ware, which was probably produced principally in Caere during the last half of the seventh century,[3] with local variants in Veii[4] and Narce.[5] Incised waterbirds also appear on late impasto and early bucchero ware from Etruria[6] and on contemporary vessels from Narce.[7] The waterbird was originally a Greek motif that was introduced from Cyprus and the Cyclades into Etruria by the late eighth century.[8]

1. See L. Holland, "The Faliscans," *PAAR* 5 (1925):1–3.
2. B. M. Felletti Maj, *CVA* Italy fasc. 21, Pigorini fasc. 1, pls. 5.8, 6.2, 6.3, 7.7, 10.6 from Contrada S. Martino.
3. E. Rystedt, *Medelhausmuseet Bulletin* 11 (1976):50–54.
4. J. Palm, *OpusArch* 7 (1952):65, no. 4, pl. XX, from Vacarreccia tomb 9.
5. J. Davison, *Seven Italic Tomb Groups from Narce*, in *Dissertazioni di etruscologia e antichità italiche pubblicata a cura dell' Istituto di Studi etruschi ed italici* (Florence, 1972), 41, no. 13 of tomb V, burial B, pl. V.d.
6. Rystedt, *Medalhausmuseet Bulletin* 11 (1976):53.
7. Dohan, 55, no. 5, pl. XXX, and no. 6, pl. XXXI; 56, no. 9, pl. XXX, all from tomb 1.
8. Brendel, 26, 37, and 437 n. 17.

123. Capenate Stemmed Plate

(ca. 630–600 B.C.)

9250. Ht, 10 cm; diam rim, 18 cm. Mended from many pieces and restored in plaster.

Chesnut brown, burnished impasto. Concave bowl with circular depressed center and high narrow stem. Incised ornament on interior. Immediately encircling the undecorated center are two concentric circles enclosing zigzag. This is surmounted by garland comprised of six floral units alternating with six birds, seen in right profile with wings outspread. Interiors of floral units and of birds filled with incised lines.

Bibliography: *CVA* USA fasc. 7, Robinson fasc. 3, 47, pl. 34.2.

Characteristic of Capenate ware of the second half of the seventh century is the polished, thin, brown impasto, in which the stemmed plate is a common form.[1] Capenate impasto is often incised with orientalizing imagery, especially vegetal units comprised of scrolls and blossoms interspersed with birds and hybrid beings, such as winged horses and griffins.[2]

The ultimate origin for the floral imagery is Phoenician and Cypriot ware, especially Bichrome IV, Cypro-Archaic I of the seventh century.[3] The more immediate inspiration for our vase, however, lies in contemporary Etruscan vessels in metal and early bucchero.[4] It is interesting to observe how the Etruscan and Capenate artists transformed the volutes beneath

the palmettes into the beaked bird heads so frequently encountered in Villanovan art.[5] Our vase can be distinguished from Etruscan treatments by the insistent interior incision and by the unnaturalistic birds, with their symmetrically spread wings.

1. L. Holland, *PAAR* 5 (1925):95, 108.
2. Ibid., 102–4, pl. IV, fig. 18; A. Mura, *Medelhausmeet Bulletin* 4 (1964):42–48; *CVA* Denmark fasc. 5, Copenhagen fasc. 5, 155, nos. 1, 6, pl. 199; *CVA* Italy fasc. 21, Pigorini fasc. 1, pls. 2.9, 3.5, 4.1.2, 5.9; G. M. A. Richter, *Handbook of the Etruscan Collection* (New York, 1940), 4, fig. 11. Compare H. Roberts, *ActaArch* 45 (1974):86–90 and 89, fig. 73, from tomb no. IV, in Capena, dated 575–550 B.C.
3. V. Karageorghis, *JdI* 80 (1965):1–17.
4. Brendel, 81–82, fig. 51, and 445 n. 12, 13.
5. Ibid., 37; *CVA* Italy fasc. 21, Pigorini fasc. 1, pl. 2.9.

124. Faliscan Vase Carrier with Bowl

(ca. 625–600 B.C.)

42.5. Brooklyn Museum Gift. "Chamber tomb at Narce." Vase carrier: ht, 28.5 cm; diam mouth, 20 cm; diam base, 16 cm. Bowl: ht, 15 cm; diam mouth, 14 cm. Brown clay with red ornament over white slip. Chip missing from rim of bowl.

Vase Carrier (Hypokraterion)

Conical, wheelmade base; bulbous midsection, probably handmade. Shallow, flaring top, handmade with four incised circles around interior. Exterior decoration (top): band of zigzag above four horizontal lines. Midsection: band of zigzag above five horizontal lines. Base from above: bands of vertical zigzag, latticed hourglass separated by vertical lines, lattice pattern, solid hourglass separated by vertical lines. Tongues around foot.

Bowl (olla)

Wheelmade spherical bowl with flaring rim and four incised circles inside lip. Reserved neck. Around shoulder is solid band above four zones of latticed hourglass separated by vertical lines. Beneath are zones of lattice pattern, solid hourglass separated by vertical lines, lattice pattern. Rays beneath.

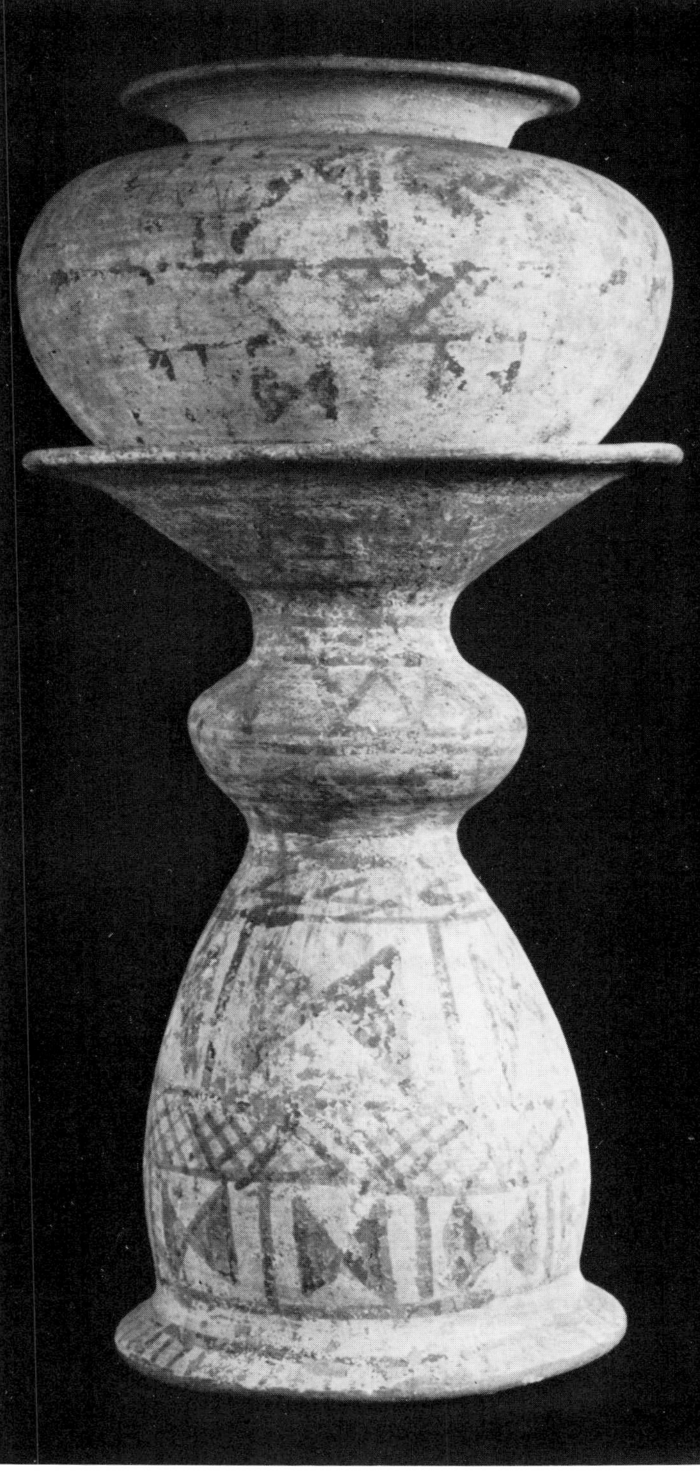

This vase is said to have come from Narce, which lies in the Faliscan territory east and south of Etruria.[1] The Faliscans spoke a Latin dialect and were linked with the Latin peoples, but they were heavily influenced by Etruscan culture, and especially by the nearby city of Veii.[2]

The hypokraterion, or vase carrier, served as a support for the bowl, or olla, and may occasionally have been set over the fire so that heat could be directly conveyed to the contents of the bowl above. The shape is probably derived from a type of bronze cauldron stand that was made in northern Syria, an example of which, dated to ca. 725–700 B.C., was found in the Bernardini tomb (ca. 630–600 B.C.).[3] The first Etruscan terracotta version comes from the Bocchoris tomb (ca. 670 B.C.),[4] and during the remainder of the seventh century the terracotta or impasto variety was especially popular in southern Etruria and in the neighboring Faliscan region.[5] Occasionally, carriers have been found without the bowls, evidence that suggests that the stands were combined with other vessels or that the upper section of the carrier itself served as a container.[6]

Impasto ware is a coarse fabric that is characterized by thick walls and a greyish brown color.[7] Vase carriers and bowls like our example were made in plain and incised impasto[8] as well as in painted versions with white decoration on red,[9] or, as here, red decoration on a white ground.[10]

Close parallels to the Hopkins example were found in tombs at Narce, which have been dated to the last decades of the seventh century.[11]

1. L. Holland, *PAAR* 5 (1925):1–3. I. Edlund, *The Iron Age and Etruscan Vases in the Olcott Collection at Columbia University, New York*, in *TAPA* 70, *pt. 1* (1980), 43.

2. J. Davison, *Seven Italic Tomb Groups from Narce, Dissertazioni di etruscologia e antichità italiche pubblicata a cura dell' Istituto di Studi etruschi ed italici* (Florence, 1972), 2.

3. Brendel, 444 n. 2; A. Rathje, in *Italy Before the Romans*, ed. D. Ridgway (New York, 1979), 158, 160; C. Curtis, *MAAR* 3 (1919), 77, no. 81, pls. 58–59. See bronze example from Regolini-Galassi tomb of ca. 650–630 in Brendel, 76, 444 n. 2, and L. Pareti, *La tomba Regolini-Galassi* (Rome, 1947), 304–5, no. 303, pl. XXXIX. See also Davison, *Seven Italic Tomb Groups*, 7.

4. Brendel, 444 n. 2.

5. Ibid., 444 n. 3; Holland, *PAAR* 5 (1925):87–91.

6. Brendel, 76.

7. Edlund, *Etruscan Vases*, 45; Brendel, 23.

8. G. M. A. Richter, *Handbook of the Etruscan Collection* (New York, 1940), 2–4; Edlund, *Etruscan Vases*, 23, 41, 49, no. 28, pl. 11; *CVA* Italy fasc. 21, Pigorini fasc. 1, pl. 5.1, from Contrada S. Martino.

9. A. Emilozzi, *La collezione Rossi Danielli nel Museo Civico di Viterbo* (Rome, 1974), 100, no. 27, pl. LIV; H. Roberts, *ActaArch* 45 (1974): 54, no. 4099, figs. 5–6.

10. *CVA* Italy fasc. 21, Pigorini fasc. 1, pl. 11.2, from Contrada S. Martino.

11. Davison, *Seven Italic Tomb Groups*, 55, pl. XII, from tomb XI. (Discussion of dating, 16, 27–31.) Dohan, 18 nos. 2, 3 from tomb 109F, pl. VIII; 24, nos. 1–3 from tomb 4F, pl. XII; 30, nos. 1–2 from tomb 42M, pl. XV; 64, no. 3 from tomb 2F, pl. XXXIV; 73, nos. 4 and 5 from tomb 64B, pl. XXXVIII. Roberts, *ActaArch* 45 (1974):54, no. 4099, figs. 5–6; 68, no. 4140, fig. 29; 77, no. 4161, and 75, fig. 47.

125. Bucchero Amphora with Openwork Handles

(ca. 575 B.C.)

42.3. Brooklyn Museum Gift. "Narce." Ht, 23 cm; diam mouth, 10.7 cm; diam with handles, 17 cm; diam foot, 7.9 cm; w each handle, 3.7 cm. Intact.

Nikosthenic form. Encircling body beneath handles are two concentric ridges, 2.4 cm apart and vertically notched. Strap handles *à jour*, each divided into two identical metopes with winged griffin striding vertically up handle to rim.

Bucchero pottery is an Etruscan wheelmade ware that was thoroughly blackened to the core by means of reduction and the combustion of carbon, probably from the wood used to fire the kiln.[1] The pottery is unpainted, but is often highly polished. The earliest bucchero was made in Caere around 675 B.C.,[2] and has been called *sottile*, after its distinctively thin walls. By 600 B.C. the fabric had become heavier and thicker, and hence is termed *pesante*. High-quality bucchero was made during the first half of the sixth century, but about 500 B.C. the fabric began to deteriorate, although the ware continued to be manufactured through the fifth century, mostly in small bowls and plates.[3]

The prototype for our amphora is an impasto strap-handled amphora that is squatter than our own and

has an incised double spiral on the belly. Rasmussen suggests that this vessel evolved in Narce and the Faliscan area around 700 B.C. and notes that examples have been found in tombs at Veii of the late eighth century.[4] This shape is one of the first to have been made in bucchero, around 675–650 B.C., surely in Caere.[5]

The Hopkins vase exemplifies the fully developed stage of a type that first appeared in Caere in about 575 B.C. and underwent a slight modification over the next quarter century.[6] The form is distinguished by the two horizontal ridges on the upper part of the body, and the handles, which are either *à jour*, as here, or bear stamped reliefs. The handles often portray griffins[7] or other orientalizing motifs, such as panthers.[8]

In the middle of the sixth century, the Attic potter Nikosthenes created his own, Nikosthenic, version of this shape (no. 100), after which both the Attic and Etruscan types are named. Almost all of the Attic Nikosthenic amphorae with a recorded provenance are said to come from Caere, and thus it appears that Nikosthenes manufactured his vases specifically for the city where the prototype originated.

1. T. B. Rasmussen, *Bucchero Pottery from Southern Etruria* (Cambridge, 1979), 2.

2. Ibid., 4.

3. Ibid., 159.

4. Ibid., 68, type 1; N. Ramage, *BSR* 3 (1970):20; T. Dohrn, *Studi in onore di Luisa Banti* (Rome, 1965), 144, pl. XXXVI; but see also Pohl, 299.

5. Rasmussen, *Bucchero Pottery*, 69; N. Ramage, *BSR* 38 (1970): 14, 50, fig. 12. Compare silver example from Regolini-Galassi tomb of ca. 650–630 B.C. in Brendel, 50, fig. 26. See also D. Strong, *Greek and Roman Gold and Silver Plate* (Ithaca, 1966), 63, pl. 10, and L. Pareti, *La tomba Regolini-Galassi* (Rome, 1947), 223, no. 164, pl. XVII.

6. Rasmussen, *Bucchero Pottery*, 74, type 1 g, pl. 6. See an inscribed fragment in E. Stefani, *NSc* 6, 6 (1930):317, no. 39, fig. 40, pl. 12a.

7. P. Mingazzini, *Catalogo dei vasi della collezione Augusto Castellani* (Rome, 1930), Vol. 1, 36, no. 125, pl. III; E. von Mercklin, *StEtr* 9 (1935):318, no. 16, pls. XLIV, XLVI.

8. Mingazzini, *Catologo*, 35, no 124, pls. III–IV. See discussion of Nikosthenes amphora (no. 100).

126. Bucchero Amphora

(ca. 560–530 B.C.)

42.7. Brooklyn Museum Gift. Ht, 15.5 cm; diam mouth, 7.4 cm; diam foot, 6 cm; w between handles, 15 cm; w each handle, 2.7 cm. Intact.

Long conical neck; strap handles from rim to top of shoulders. Low, flaring foot.

The prototype for our vase probably is the Etruscan biconical bronze urns of the late eighth century,[1] whose elongated necks were perpetuated in the one-handled bucchero jugs of the late seventh century.[2] The attenuated elegance of our vase and the mannered flare of the handles suggest a date somewhat later. Close parallels are in the Field Museum in Chicago and come from a tomb in Chiusi dated 560–530 B.C.[3]

1. Brendel, 29, fig. 8, from Tarquinia.
2. Ibid., 81, fig. 51.
3. R. DePuma, *Archaeology* 29 (1976):220–28, illustrated on 224.

127. Bucchero Stemmed Cup

(ca. 550–500 B.C.)

42.4. Brooklyn Museum Gift. "Chiusi." Ht, 15.8 cm; diam mouth, 13.6 cm; diam foot, 7.8 cm. Section of bowl restored.

Bowl has scalloped sides in six curving sections, tapering to narrow base, around which are three horizontal grooves. Conical stem has flaring foot with rounded edge. Around midpoint of stem are three grooved circles; two more grooved circles lie one-quarter the distance down from top of stem.

The chalice, or high-footed, fluted goblet, has its ultimate origin in a type of Near Eastern fluted vessel with a low and moderately tapering cup,[1] which the Etruscans elevated on a conical foot. Examples in bucchero were made in Caere soon after 650 B.C.[2] and an ivory version was placed in the Barberini tomb (630–600 B.C.).[3] In a more elaborate version, also of the second half of the seventh century and from Caere, four caryatids surround the foot and support the bowl.[4]

Several examples from Poggio Buco, dated between 625 and 550 B.C.,[5] illustrate a later step in the development. The cup is still low but is now scalloped, and the foot is attenuated and interrupted by ribbings and moldings. Our vase represents a still later phase,[6] when the bowl is deeper, the number of scallops reduced, and the foot returns to the smooth, elegant profile of the earliest examples. Stemmed cups like our own must have been made in Chiusi, where almost all bucchero was being produced at this time. The wide distribution of examples of this type is testimony to its popularity.

1. N. Ramage, *BSR* 38 (1970):8–9; Brendel, 60, 442 n. 22.
2. Brendel, 80, fig. 49.
3. Brendel, 60–61, fig. 35; C. Curtis, *MAAR* 5 (1925):29, no. 36, pl. 13.
4. Brendel, 79, fig. 48.
5. G. Matteucig, *Poggio Buco: The Necropolis of Statonia* (Berkeley, 1951), 51, no. 63, pl. XXI; 52, no. 64, pl. XXI from tomb G, suggested to be from Chiusi. G. Bartoloni, *La tombe da Poggio Buco nel Museo Archeologico di Firenze* (Florence, 1972), 75, 92–94, 107, nos. 66–69, from tomb VII.
6. See somewhat similar examples from Chiusi. A. Fairbanks, *Greek and Etruscan Vases in the Boston Museum of Fine Arts I* (Boston, 1928), 215, no. 635, pl. LXXXIV. I. Edlund, *The Iron Age and Etruscan Vases in the Olcott Collection at Columbia University, New York*, in *TAPA* 70, pt. 1 (1980):32, 44, no. 41, pl. 16, dated 550 B.C.

128. Duck Askos

(fourth c. B.C.)

9249. Ht, 16.5 cm; l, 23.5; cm; diam spout, 4 cm; diam foot, 5 cm. Mended from several pieces and restored in plaster. Duck perches on low ring base, has tapering tail, arched neck. Eye, jaw, and bill carefully modeled, with bill pierced for pouring. Strap handle attached between neck and cylindrical filler spout with flaring lip. Body moldmade, with spout, handle, head, and neck added separately.

Decoration in black and dilute brown glaze. Each side of body framed by two brown lines, which flank base of neck and spout and extend along breast and tail, skirting edge of foot. Within is flying nude, winged female. With both hands she holds a taenia with tasseled ends. She has short black hair forming point at nape, pyramidal earrings, necklace of black beads, shoes. Added white for pendants to necklace, for bracelets around upper arms and for anklets. Background behind her framed by band of black circles enclosing a field of brown concentric arcs. Beneath handle is vertical band of wave pattern adjoining vertical rows of black tongues. Over tail are striated feathers.

Head and neck of duck black. Reserved are necklace, white of eyes, and bill, over which are brown striated bands. On chest of duck are groups of concentric arcs beneath band of black circles encircling neck. Added in white is necklace of vertical pendants and another of white dots. Beneath handle are concentric arcs with reserved band. On top of tail are concentric arcs and black tongues. Raised edges of handle reserved, with flat central black band and underside reserved. On fill spout is band of black dots beneath rays. Around exterior of lip is band of tongues; row of dots within lip. Upper part of right foot reserved. Underside of foot has two concentric black bands.

Bibliography: Furtwängler, *ND*, 252, no. 5; *CVA* USA fasc. 7, Robinson fasc. 3, 50, pl. 38.2

This vase belongs to a group of duck askoi that share the same shape and repertory of ornament but vary in their figural representations.[1] Many of the vases, like our own, bear on each side a painted or relief nude figure, usually a woman. On other examples we find a painted profile of a female head on each side of the vase, and still other askoi have only a painted feather pattern.[2]

Among those vases with representations of flying females, the shape, vocabulary of pattern, and distribution of ornament remain remarkably consistent, thereby testifying to a mass production of these vessels without sacrificing an admirable degree of quality.

Our example is unusual only in the position of the spiral-and-tongue ornament. On our askos the black tongues lie directly beneath the spout, while on other examples the tongues are placed beneath the base of the handle, thereby allotting more space to the tail feathers.

The maiden is generally identified as a Lasa, an attendant of Turan with whom birds are also linked.[3] On various askoi of our group the Lasa may hold a taenia in both hands, as she does here, or in only one hand.[4] She may also hold an alabastron.[5]

These duck askoi have been attributed to Chiusi and bear the characteristic Chiusine features of a profusion of ornament and the use of concentric arcs and black circles.[6] Our Lasa closely resembles the nude maidens on Chiusine vases, who also wear necklaces of black beads and whose torsos have vertical lines down the midsection ending in concentric arcs at the base of the abdomen.[7] The Chiusine school of vase-painting commenced in the first half of the fourth century and continued for about a century.[8] Duck vases of our type were probably still made within the fourth century and reflect the contemporary enthusiasm for both nudity and Lasae.[9]

A somewhat later group of askoi differs markedly in shape, ornament, and figural motif, and has been attributed to southern Etruria and dated to the end of the fourth century and beginning of the third century.[10]

The pierced bill indicates that the duck was actually used as a container, perhaps for perfume.

1. *EVP*, 119–20. Ours is no. 7. M. del Chiaro, *RA NS* (1978, fasc. 1):27–38, *Bulletin of the Cleveland Museum* 63 (1976):108–15; *Medelhausmuseet Bulletin* 12 (1977):62–69.

2. del Chiaro, *RA NS* (1978, fasc. 1):27.

3. Brendel, 351 and 473 n. 35.

4. *EVP*, 119, no. 5; del Chiaro, *RA* (1978, fasc. 1):28, fig. 1 (Louvre H100).

5. *EVP*, 119, no. 6, which is the same as *NSc* 6, 3 (1927): pl. 13 (Ferrara T224).

6. C. Albizatti, *RömMitt* 30 (1915):129–54; *EVP*, 119–20; Brendel (350–51) suggests the place of manufacture may be Volterra. See M. Harari, *StEtr* 48 (1980):102.

7. S. Haynes, *Mitteilungen des deutschen archäologischen Instituts* 6 (1953):31–34.

8. Brendel, 343, 349–50.

9. Ibid., 335.

10. del Chiaro, *RA NS* (1978, fasc. 1):30–38, especially 38. Harari, *StEtr* 48 (1980):117.

Pottery

ROMAN

Side A

129. Oinophoros with Dioskouroi

(third–fourth c. A.D.)

228. Purchased in Rome or Naples in 1906–9. Ht, 24.7 cm; diam mouth, 5 to 6.3 cm; diam foot, 11.4 cm. Sections of neck and body restored in plaster. Cracked over front. Traces of burning.

Cylindrical amphora has sharply angled shoulder, cylindrical neck and mouth. Fillets between mouth and neck and between neck and shoulder. Tubular handles rise vertically from shoulder, then bend sharply to meet base of neck. Top and underside of handles smooth, with sides obliquely ribbed. On shoulder are tongues in relief. Body occupied by scenes in relief.

Side A

Flanked by vine tendrils and clusters of grapes is a nude youth standing on raised base. Torso frontal, weight on left leg, head on right profile, chlamys fastened on right shoulder and thrown back over left shoulder. Pilos over short curly hair; spear in right hand. Left hand holds reins of horse, whose right foreleg is raised and who wears bridle, breastplate, and saddle pad. Above horse's head is a six-pointed star.

Side B

Nearly identical representation in mirror reversal except that youth's hair is longer and more loosely waved; pilos is peaked; chlamys exposes left breast but folds conceal left upper arm. Beneath each handle is plain vertical band extending to smooth projecting ledge around foot. Encircling body above picture is ridge above groove.

Bibliography: D. M. Robinson, *AJA* 13 (1909):30–38; *CVA* USA fasc. 7, Robinson fasc. 3, 51, pl. 39.

This vase belongs to a class of pottery that was manufactured in a two-part mold and that bears relief decoration.[1] About eighty examples are known, mostly cylindrical amphorae, but also jugs, pelikai, olpides, and oinochoai. The representations belong to any of fifteen types. Some of the vases have been found in Greece, Egypt, Germany, and Africa, but the largest number come from Asia Minor.

The class of pottery takes its name from the inscription on the underside of the Hopkins amphora: *oinophoros* ("wine-carrier"). The word occurs in Persius (v.140), Juvenal (vi.426), and Horace (*Sat.* 1.6.109), but probably only as a generic term and not as a specific reference to our class of vessel.[2]

We know that in addition to their role as wine containers, vases of the Hopkins type also served as burial gifts,[3] and Heimberg suggests that the signs of burning on the Hopkins amphora resulted from a cremation fire.[4] The representations are appropriate both to burial and banqueting contexts, since the subjects belong to the Dionysiac world (satyrs and maenads) or depict figures connected with saving (Asclepius, Dioskouroi) or with death and the afterlife (Hermes, Leda, Aphrodite, and Eros).[5]

This class of pottery has been dated from the fourth century B.C.[6] to the fourth century A.D.,[7] but recently it has been shown that the earliest known contexts are of the first century A.D.[8] and that most examples belong to the third century A.D.[9] The Hopkins amphora was probably made in the third or fourth century A.D.,[10] although the motif of a Dioskouros beside a horse with uplifted foreleg can be found on coins and gems from as early as the second century B.C.[11] The Roman interest in mirror reversal is well documented from at least the first century B.C., but images of the

Side B

Dioskouroi are not frequently handled in this manner before the second century A.D.[12]

The concentration of findspots in Asia Minor and the presence of one example of the green glaze typical of Cnidos[13] suggest that some of the vases were made in that area or perhaps around Pergamon.[14] From here the vessels could have been exported to markets in the Aegean and mainland Greece, where many have been found. Another center of manufacture was probably Alexandria,[15] and related ware was made in another northern African workshop of the late third and early fourth centuries A.D.[16]

A subgroup of this class of pottery is comprised of head lagynoi, which are named for the grotesque heads on the necks of the vessels. This latter ware was made in Asia Minor from the second century A.D. and in Africa from the third century A.D.[17]

1. U. Hausmann, *AthMitt* 69–70 (1954–55):125. Ours is no. 1, pp. 133, 138. See also U. Haussmann, *AthMitt* 71 (1956):107–12; U. Heimberg, *JdI* 91 (1976):251–90. Ours is A1, p. 285.
2. Hausmann, *AthMitt* 69–70 (1954–55):133; H. A. Thompson, *Hesperia* 17 (1948):184 n. 85.
3. Heimberg, *JdI* 91 (1976):253 n. 13, 264.
4. Ibid., 264.
5. Ibid., 264.
6. See CVA Robinson 3, 51, pl. 39.
7. Heimberg, *JdI* 91 (1976):251–52, 266.
8. Ibid., 255 n. 16.
9. Ibid., 255, 276, 281.
10. Hausmann [*AthMitt* 69–70 (1954–55):138] dates the piece to the end of the second c. A.D. Heimberg [*JdI* 91 (1976):266] dates the Baltimore vase around 300–350 A.D.
11. Robinson [*AJA* 13 (1909):36 and CVA Robinson 3, 51, pl. 39] dates the Baltimore vase in the second c. B.C. See M. L. Vollenweider, *Catalogue raisonné des sceaux, cylindres, intailles and camées, Musée d'Art et d'Histoire de Genève*, vol. 2 (Mainz, 1979), 157, no. 158, pl. 54 (where she discusses a coin of 109 B.C.).
12. C. C. Vermeule, *Greek Sculpture and Roman Taste* (Ann Arbor, 1977), 5, 14, 36–38.
13. Hausmann, *AthMitt* 69–70 (1954–55):126.
14. O. Zeigenaus and G. de Luca, *Das Asklepieion: Altertümer von Pergamon XI.2* (Berlin, 1975), 109; Heimberg, *JdI* 91 (1976):255.
15. Hausmann, *AthMitt* 69–70 (1954–55):140–41; F. Courby, *Les vases grecs à reliefs* (Paris, 1922), 536.
16. J. W. Salomonson, *BABesch* 44 (1969):85–88.
17. Salomonson, *BABesch* 55 (1980):65–106.

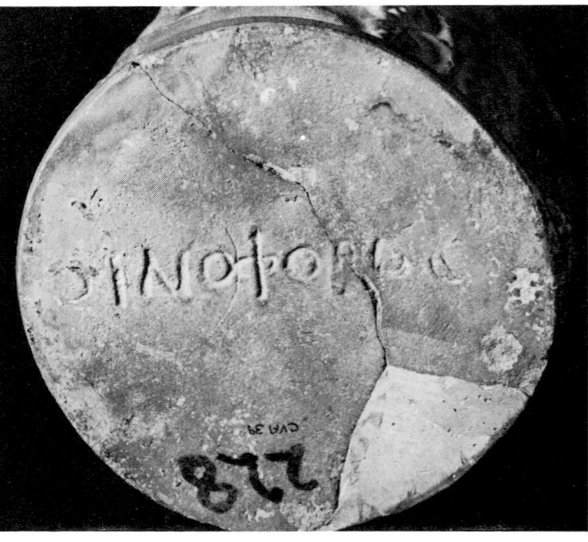

Plaster

ROMAN

Mold

Cast

130. Mold of Serapis

(second c. A.D.)

10,003. Plaster: ht, 9.6 cm; w at base, 7.5 cm; Cast: ht, 9 cm; w, 5.5 cm. Intact.

Mold has smooth, convex back. Cast: bearded god seated frontally on throne, feet on footstool, with right foot advanced. Left arm is bent at elbow, with hand upraised as if grasping end of staff. Right hand rests on head of dog. Wears sleeved tunic and himation draped over hips and legs, with ends brought over left shoulder. Curly locks of hair fall forward on brow; beard falls in two vertical clumps over chin. Modius on head. Throne extends almost to top of head; sides have curving profile. Left armrest terminates in phiale above floral vines.

Our mold was used to produce a terracotta relief representing Serapis, a deity whose cult evolved in Egypt during the fourth century B.C. but who enjoyed his greatest popularity in Roman times.

Our representation is a surprisingly accurate reflection of the great statue of Serapis, which was probably created in Alexandria during the third century. Hornbostel has concluded that the god was seated with his right hand resting on the head of the dog Cerberus, his left hand uplifted and supporting a staff. The god wore, as here, an ungirded, transparent, sleeved tunic, which fell in concentric V-shaped folds between the breasts and formed a triangular panel over the right shoulder. The mantle was brought over the left upper arm and across the lower torso. Five coiled locks of hair fell forward on the forehead and the curly locks of the beard were arranged in two vertical columns on the chin.[1] Both the handling of the beard and the accuracy of our representation suggest that the mold dates from the Antonine period, when the most faithful renderings of the statue were being made in Alexandria.[2] The accuracy of the copies was undoubtedly the result of a renewed focus on the statue after its restoration under Hadrian.[3]

A number of terracotta reliefs similar to our example are known, ranging in size from 8 to 18 cm.[4] Many comparable reliefs, representing a seated Isis with Harpocrates, also exist, a fact that suggests that the reliefs were made in pairs.[5] These reliefs were probably used in domestic cult, although some of the examples that are smaller than our own could also have served as appliqués, possibly on lamps.[6]

Although the terracotta reliefs of Serapis agree in essential features and are occasionally identical,[7] variations occur in details, such as the contour of the throne, the presence of the footstool, the decoration of the armrest, and the substitution of the figure of Horos or Harpocrates for that of Cerberus.[8] These differences are due to the different patrixes or archetypes from which the first-generation molds, such as the Hopkins one, were made.

Molds could also be made by taking impressions from other reliefs, which were occasionally worn. The derivative molds were then used to make second-generation reliefs which were smaller and less sharp than those that belong to the first generation. The lack of clarity in many of the surviving Serapis reliefs suggests that this latter technique was widespread, as would be expected during the second century A.D., when there was a tremendous demand for representations of the deity.[9]

By the second century B.C., plaster molds were being used by Athenian koroplasts,[10] who may have learned of the technique in Egypt, where many Hellenistic plaster casts have been found.[11] It is likely that our mold was also made in Egypt, both because similar plaster molds and reliefs of Serapis were found there[12] and because the accuracy of our representation suggests that the mold was made close to its prototype. Although Egypt manufactured many representations of Serapis,[13] many of which were undoubtedly exported, it is also possible that our mold was itself made for export and was used in a workshop outside Egypt to manufacture inexpensive casts.

1. Hornbostel, *Sarapis* (Leiden, 1973), 72ff., especially 72–91, 213, 216.

2. Ibid., 210, 248–49, 291–93.

3. Ibid., 209, 360.

4. P. Graindor, *Terres cuites de l'Égypte gréco-romaine* (Antwerp, 1939), 128, no. 47, pl. XVIII (8.5 cm); G. Faccenna, *RendPontAcc* 29 (1956–57):189, no. 11, pl. II; F. Dunand, *Religion populaire en Égypte romaine* (Leiden, 1979), 265–66, nos. 342–45, pls. CXIV–CXV. See also notes 7, 8, 12, and 13 below. Bronze examples are also known: see C. C. Edgar, *Catalogue général des antiquités égyptiennes du Musée du Caire: Greek Bronzes* (Cairo, 1904), 2, no. 27, 635, pl. 1.

5. W. Weber, *Die ägyptisch-griechischen Terrakotten* (Berlin, 1914), 47, no. 17, pl. 2; Dunand, *Religion populaire*, 165–66, nos. 1–4; W. D. van Wijngaarden, *De Grieks-Egyptisch Terracottas in het Rijksmuseum van Oudheden* (Leipzig, 1958), 3, no. 7, pl. II; Besques, Vol. 3, 67, no. D 419, pl. 89c (ht, 8.7 cm).

6. Wijngaarden, *Terracottas*, 3, no. 7, pl. II.

7. M. Mogensen, *La Glyptothèque Ny Carlsberg, La collection égyptienne* (Copenhagen, 1930), no. 202, pl. XXXV.1; J. Vogt, *Die griechisch-ägyptische Sammlung Ernst von Sieglin II.2. Terrakotten* (Leipzig, 1924), 85–88, pls. III, IV.

8. Weber, *Terrakotten*, 30, no. 7, pl. 1; Hornbostel, 169, no. 147.

9. Hornbostel, *Sarapis*, 112, 209–10, 255–57, 386–88.

10. D. B. Thompson, *Hesperia* 34 (1965):35–36. See also D. B. Thompson, *Hesperia* 32 (1963):277.

11. O. Rubensohn, *Hellenistiches Silbergerät in antiken Gipsabgüssen* (Berlin, 1911), reportedly from Memphis.

12. C. C. Edgar, *Catalogue général des antiquités égyptiennes du Musée du Caire: Greek Moulds* (Cairo, 1903), no. 32,001, pls. 1 and XXXII.

13. C. M. Kaufman, *Graeco-ägyptische Koroplastik* (Leipzig and Cairo, 1915), 40, nos. 64, 66, pl. 13; E. Breccia, *Terrecotte figurate greche e greco-egizie del Museo di Alessandria: Monuments de l'Égypte gréco-romaine* II, fasc. 1 (Bergamo, 1930), 54, no. 252, pl. XXI.

131. Mummy Mask

(ca. 350–400 A.D.)

HT 241. Helen Tanzer Collection. "Near Luxor." Plaster. Ht, 17.3 cm; neck opening, 14.1 cm; depth from chin to nape, 17.8 cm. Eyeballs cracked; broken around neck; cracked across hairline. Hollow; open beneath. Inlaid iris and pupil of painted glass. Brown paint on hair; peachy pink on eyelids, nose, mouth, ears, and jawline.

Very little modeling of features. Eyes gaze upward with upper contour of iris just beneath upper lid. Short, thin lips. Locks of hair are indicated by grooves radiating from face to nape. At back of head is a braid terminating in corkscrew knot.

Bibliography: G. Grimm, *Die römische Mumienmasken aus Ägypten* (Wiesbaden, 1974), 91, no. 1, pl. 107.

As early as the Fifth and Sixth Dynasties (ca. 2500–2200 B.C.), the linen wrappings over a mummy's face were strengthened with plaster, modeled with facial features, and then painted.[1] By the First Intermediate Period these representations had evolved into plaster anthropoid mummy cases.[2] Many centuries later, in the first century A.D., the practice was revived and a modeled stucco head and bust were placed upon the mummy, which was otherwise wrapped in the traditional manner.

Stucco busts like our own were made in Egypt from the first to the fourth centuries A.D., disappearing only after the Edict of Theodosius in 391 A.D.[3] The masks were particularly common in Alexandria[4] and in Middle Egypt around Antinoopolis.[5] In the Fayoum the busts were never as popular as the painted portraits on wooden panels[6] that were also introduced in the first century A.D.

A typical bust consisted of a plaster or stucco head and a flat rectangle of stucco or wood, which was placed on the chest of the mummy and painted with the jewelry, dress, and hands of the deceased. On the earliest examples the heads are only in low relief, but by about 200 A.D. the heads were worked completely in the round.[7] In these later examples the face and back of the head were made in molds, which were

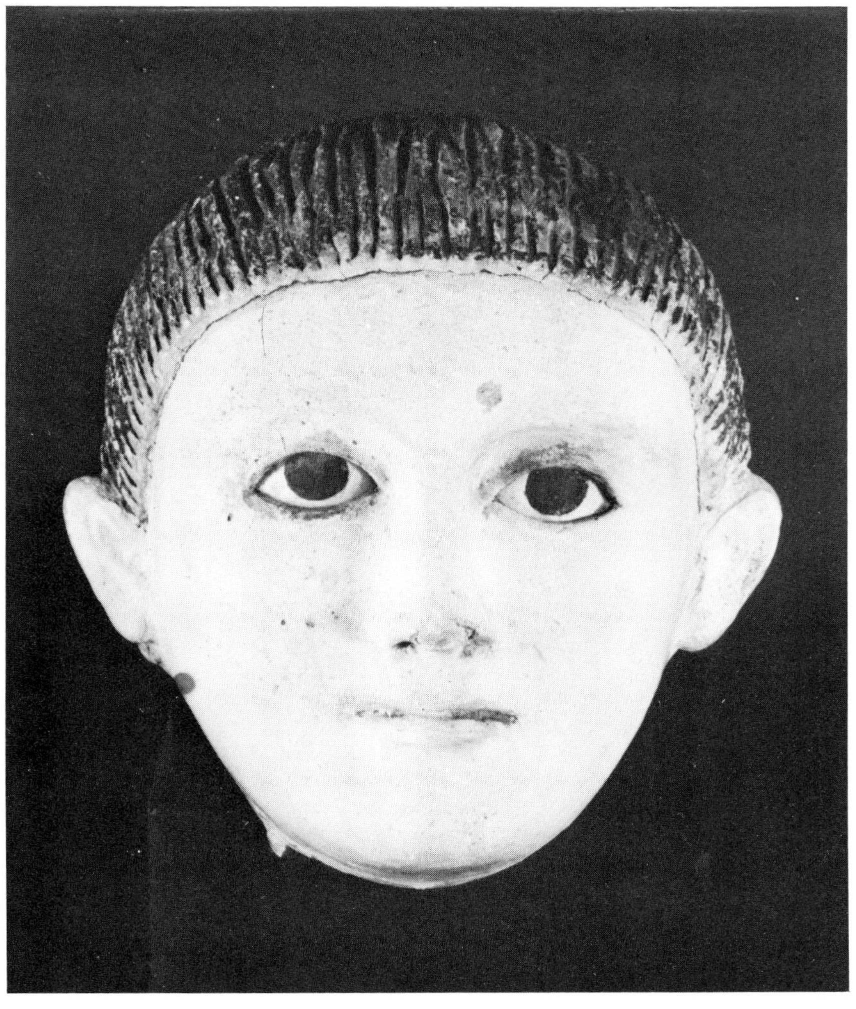

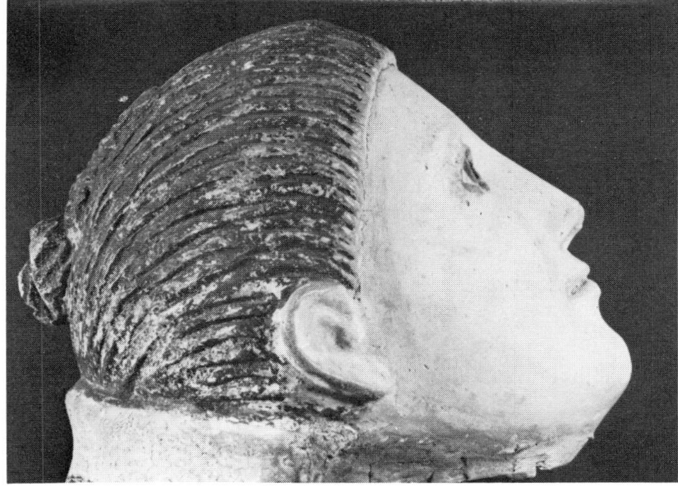

used interchangeably for males and females. The ears and hair were then added by hand.[8] The eyes were made several different ways, usually combining limestone and glass.[9]

The heads often wear hairstyles earlier in date than would be expected from the burial contexts. The explanation may lie in the distance of provincial Egypt from fashion centers like Rome;[10] it is also possible that the heads were executed during the lifetime of the deceased,[11] as was customary with the painted Fayoum portraits. Our face displays the geometric symmetry, unmodeled features, short, thin lips, and upward stare of Roman portraiture of the late fourth century A.D.[12]

1. W. Stevenson Smith, *The Art and Architecture of Ancient Egypt*, 2d ed. rev. (New York, 1981), 107, fig. 102.

2. Ibid., 61.

3. G. Grimm, *Die römischen Mumienmasken aus Ägypten* (Wiesbaden, 1974), 104, 106; K. Parlasca, *Mumienporträts und verwandte Denkmäler* (Wiesbaden, 1966), 99–100. Others are in C. C. Edgar, *Catalogue général des antiquités égyptiennes du Musée du Caire: Graeco-Egyptian Coffins, Masks and Portraits* (Cairo, 1905), II–X, pls. VII–IX.

4. Grimm, *Mumienmasken*, 14.

5. Ibid., 14, 102; Parlasca, *Mumienporträts*, 40, 41.

6. See B. Ridgway, *Museum of Art, Rhode Island School of Design. Classical Sculpture* (Providence, 1972), 23, no. 5.

7. Grimm, *Mumienmasken*, 105.

8. Ibid., 15–16, 103.

9. Ibid., 18.

10. Parlasca (*Mumienporträts*, 117, 149–50) points out that Antinoopolis was founded in 130 A.D. but that some hairstyles on the masks are Claudian in style.

11. Ibid., 75.

12. Grimm, *Mumienmasken*, 91. Grimm (92) points out that Luxor is a commonly cited, but almost invariably inaccurate, provenance. See a late example in G. Grimm, *Kunst der ptolemäer und römerzeit im ägyptische Museum Kairo* (Mainz, 1975), 25, no. 55, pl. 94.

Gems

GREEK AND ETRUSCAN

132. Black Steatite Lentoid

(seventh–sixth c. B.C.)

9227. Diam, 1 cm. Pierced along horizontal axis for stringing.

Cast: two identical birds, one upside down and above the other. Each is in right profile with head inverted. Fine ridges along body and wings. Two vertical ridges flank birds.

This gem is characteristic of seals from the Cyclades and especially Melos of the later seventh and early sixth centuries B.C.[1] The motif has parallels in contemporary orientalizing vasepainting, where we often find animals with heads inverted or paired in a similar symmetrical composition.[2]

Both the lentoid shape and many of the devices of Cycladic gems compare closely with Minoan-Mycenaean gems and thereby suggest that either random finds of the earlier stones or long-cherished heirlooms stimulated the revival of gem carving that took place in the islands during the archaic period.[3] From the ninth century to the beginning of the sixth century, artists worked primarily with ivory or soft stones like steatite or serpentine, which could be carved with simple tools. By the middle of the sixth century, however, artists had turned to harder stones like carnelian, which required more sophisticated instruments, such as the drill. It has been suggested that this tool was made of iron but that the actual cutting was performed by a powder, such as corundum, which the tip of the drill pressed into the stone.[4] The finest carving of both the hard and the soft stones during the archaic period comes from East Greece, and in the sixth century, from Etruria, where many Greek craftsmen emigrated.[5]

Gems were used to make wax or clay impressions, which served as identifying signatures on objects and written documents. The motifs often had protective connotations and thereby safeguarded both the impressed object and the owner of the gem, who probably wore his seal on a string around the neck.

1. J. Boardman and M. L. Vollenweider, *Catalogue of the Engraved Gems and Finger Rings I. Greek and Etruscan* (Oxford, 1978), 1; G. Richter, *Catalogue of Engraved Gems: Greek, Etruscan, and Roman* (Rome, 1956), 3, no. 11, pl. II, and 12, no. 12; Boardman, *GGFR*, 118–22.
2. W. Schuchhardt, *Greek Art* (New York, 1972), 21–22, no. 7. A geometric example is in J. Benson, *Horse, Bird and Man. The Origins of Greek Painting* (Amherst, 1970), 61, pl. XVII, fig. 2.
3. E. Zwierlein-Diehl, *Antike Gemmen in deutschen Sammlungen. Band II. Staatliche Museen preussischer Kulturbesitz: Antikenabteilung Berlin* (Munich, 1969), 25, no. 6.a, pl. 2; Benson, *Horse, Bird and Man*, 61, 107–15, 117, 121, pl. XVII, fig. 1; Richter, *Catalogue of Engraved Gems*, 3.
4. Richter, *Catalogue of Engraved Gems*, xxii–xxiii. J. Boardman, *Archaic Greek Gems* (London, 1968), 169–72.
5. Boardman and Vollenweider, *Catalogue*, 12.

133. Etruscan Carnelian Scarab with Hermes Psychopompos

(later fifth–fourth c. B.C.)

HT 889. Helen Tanzer Collection. Carnelian. L, 1.6 cm; w, 1.2 cm; ht, 0.9 cm. Pierced lengthwise.

Thorax has hatched border. Four arcs define border of elytra (wing-cases). V-winglets striated. Forelegs stippled. First set of hindlegs hatched. Vertical border of sides carefully hatched.

Cast: within hatched border is bearded Hermes, nude except for winged cap. He stands in right profile with left leg advanced, leaning forward. He holds inverted caduceus (*kērykeion*), his left hand around its base and his right hand around its tip.

During the last half of the sixth century, Etruscan workshops, probably employing Greek craftsmen, began to produce scarabs. These Etruscan examples, which are usually of carnelian, can be recognized by their careful carving, the highly polished surfaces, and the decorative treatment of the wings.[1] The finest examples, among which our own can be placed, date from the later sixth to the early fourth centuries. Later examples, carved from around 350 B.C. to the end of scarab production about 200 B.C., are worked

in a simple globolo style characterized by concave depressions made by the ball drill and by grooves with little detail.[2] Because these globolo scarabs have been found over much of central Italy, it is believed many of them were made in workshops outside Etruria.[3]

Close parallels to the Hopkins scarab are provided by examples of the later fifth and early fourth centuries, which also exhibit similarly striated winglets and carefully hatched borders. Scarabs of this date also combine careful modeling of the nude male torso with cursory treatment of details, such as face and hair, thereby foreshadowing the globolo style.[4]

The device on the Hopkins example represents Hermes in his role as *psychopompos* ("leader of souls"). The deity was regarded as the conveyor of souls to the underworld, but he could also be associated with their return—in, for example, the tradition of Persephone.[5] It is in the latter role that we see Hermes here, calling forth the deceased as he directs his caduceus over the ground. The composition first appears on Etruscan scarabs of the early fourth century,[6] and by the second half of the fourth century is adopted on Etruscan oval ringstones, with convex base and a flat, carved surface.[7] Beneath the caduceus on these stones is a head[8] or half a torso.[9] It has been suggested that the theme was inspired by the Orphic Pythagorean cult in southern Italy and that the motif represents a conflation of images of Etruscan oracular figures, such as Tages, who was also depicted arising from the ground.[10]

1. J. Boardman and M. L. Vollenweider, *Catalogue of the Engraved Gems and Finger Rings I. Greek and Etruscan* (Oxford, 1978), 48; M. Maaskant-Kleinbrink, *Classification of Ancient Engraved Gems* (Leiden, 1975), 70; J. Boardman, *Archaic Greek Gems* (London, 1968), 13–16.

2. P. Zazoff, *Etruskische Skarabäen* (Mainz, 1968), 118, 141; W. Martini, "Die Etruskische Ringsteinglyptik," *RömMitt-EH* 18 (1971):27–28.

3. Boardman and Vollenweider, *Catalogue*, 48; Martini, *RömMitt-EH* 18 (1971):78–79.

4. See Boardman and Vollenweider, *Catalogue*, 51, 56, no. 215, fig. 10, pl. XXXVI; 52, 56, no. 219, fig. 10, pl. XXXVII; 53, 56, no. 225, fig. 10, pl. XXXVIII.

5. P. A. Zanker, *Wandel der Hermesgestalt in der attische Vasenmalerei*, in *Antiquitas*, vol. 2 (Bonn, 1965), 104.

6. Martini, *RömMitt-EH* 18 (1971):33–34; A. Furtwängler, *Die antiken Gemmen* (Leipzig, 1900), vol. 3, 202–3, 253–56. See G. Lippold, *Gemmen und Kameen des Altertums und der Neuzeit* (Stuttgart, n.d.), no. 4, pl. X.

7. Martini, *RömMitt-EH* 18 (1971):33, 127, 159. Martini points out (on 19, 46) that the motifs and styles of these fourth-century ringstones are closely influenced by those of scarabs of the late fifth and early fourth centuries. The motif continues on later ringstones. E. Brandt and E. Schmidt, *Antike Gemmen in deutschen Sammlungen: Munich I.2* (Munich, 1970), 32, no. 724, pl. 84. M. Schlüter et al., *Antike Gemmen in deutschen Sammlungen: Hannover-Hamburg IV* (Wiesbaden, 1975), 32, nos. 60, 61, pl. 19.

8. Martini, *RömMitt-EH* 18 (1971):133, no. 22, pl. 7.1.

9. Ibid., 133, nos. 20–21, pl. 6.

10. Ibid., 34, 42–45. Furtwängler, *Gemmen*, 253.

134. Ringstone with Palaestra Scene

(second–first c. B.C.)

9228. L, 11 cm; ht, 1.2 cm; w, 0.9 cm. Green agate. Oval ringstone carved on a very convex face, which curves down directly to flat base. Part of youth's face, left shoulder, and arm chipped away. Another chip missing from left edge.

Cast: nude youth with short curly hair stands in right profile, weight on right leg, with left leg relaxed and foot slightly advanced. Right hand pushes strigil down upper part of extended left arm. In front of youth is amphora containing palm branch. Behind youth is bearded herm on tapering pillar and square base. Narrow ridge for groundline.

The Hellenistic ringstone is descended from the scaraboid of the sixth century, an oval stone with a shape similar to the scarab but without the beetle motif on the curved back. On the early scaraboids of the sixth and fifth centuries, the carved surface is usually the flat one, although the curved back may be carved instead of, or together with, the flat side.[1] During the fourth century the popularity of the scaraboid is overshadowed by the ringstone with carved convex face.[2] By the end of the century the ringstone is made in a number of shapes, varying in the degree of curvature and in the angle at which the edges meet. Variations also exist in the form of the uncarved back, which can be flat, convex, or concave.[3] Especially popular in the Hellenistic period is the oval ringstone with pronounced convex face, worked in a variety of colored stones.[4]

The prototype of our youth is the Apoxyomenos, from whom, however, our version differs in the position of the strigil on top of the arm and in the advanced position of the relaxed left leg, a pose that is familiar from late Hellenistic statues, such as the Aphrodite of Melos. The youth is depicted just after an athletic victory, to which the traditional prizes of the amphora and palm bear witness. The palm was associated with Apollo as early as the seventh century, when votive palms were dedicated to him as Delos.[5] In vasepainting of the second half of the sixth century the palm appears in contexts (such as the struggle of Herakles with the Nemean lion) that identify the branch as a symbol of victory.[6] By the end of the fifth century, if not earlier, palms were awarded to victors at Delos, Nemea, and Olympia.[7] The Herm behind the youth probably locates the scene in the palaestra, where Hermes as god of athletics was especially honored.

Similar scenes appear on several other ringstones where the Herm is omitted,[8] or where the youth holds discus and palm branch beside a Herm.[9]

1. Boardman, *GGFR*, 139–40, 191–92; J. Boardman and M. L. Vollenweider, *Catalogue of the Engraved Gems and Finger Rings I. Greek and Etruscan* (Oxford, 1978), 23.
2. Boardman, *GGFR*, 206.
3. Boardman and Vollenweider, *Catalogue*, 72–73, 113.
4. Boardman, *GGFR*, 359–61, 376; J. Boardman, *Intaglios and Rings* (London, 1975), 19.
5. C. Picard, *Les trophées romain*, in *Bibliothèque des Écoles françaises d'Athènes et de Rome* 187 (1957):62–63.
6. J. F. Miller, *AJA* 84 (1980):223–24.
7. Picard, *Les trophées*, 62 (Delos).
8. A. Furtwängler, *Die antiken Gemmen*, vol. 2 (Leipzig, 1900), 212–13, no. 19, pl. XLIV.
9. Ibid., 213, no. 22, pl. XLIV.

Gems

ROMAN

135. Carnelian Ringstone with Actor and Mask

(first c. B.C.–A.D.)

9222. Carnelian. L, 10 cm; ht, 1.1 cm; w, 0.9 cm. Intact.

Oval ringstone with two flat surfaces: obverse has beveled edge. Cast: right profile of male head with mustache and a beard of short clumps of hair. On top of his head he wears a male mask with similar mustache and beard. Mask has short hair brushed back off forehead; coil of hair and two ringlets beneath.

The oval carnelian ringstone with two flat surfaces was popular from Hellenistic through Roman times. The motif of the actor's head with mask pushed back to the crown is fairly common on gems and glass pastes of the second century B.C. to first century A.D.[1] The delicate features of our face and mask as well as the long, pointed nose suggest a date for the Hopkins gem in the late first century B.C. or early first century A.D.[2] The image has an ironic note, as the features and beard of the actor are almost identical to those of the mask.

On other gems from this period we may see two or three masks worn on the top or back of an actor's head.[3] We also find composites of two or more theatrical masks by themselves.[4] Other gems show fantastic assemblages, termed *grylloi*, comprised of animal protomes combined with masks, one of which is usually that of a satyr.[5]

1. A. Furtwängler, *Die antiken Gemmen* (Leipzig, 1900), vol. 2, 133, no. 76, pl. XXVI; M. Maaskant-Kleinbrink, *Catalogue of the Engraved Gems in the Royal Coin Cabinet, The Hague* (Wiesbaden, 1978), 246, no. 647, pl. 114 and 167, no. 323, pl. 64; E. Brandt and E. Schmidt, *Antiken Gemmen in deutschen Sammlungen I.2* (Munich, 1970), 193, nos. 1863 and 1864, pl. 168; M. Schlüter et al., *Antike Gemmen in deutschen Sammlungen IV, Hannover-Hamburg* (Wiesbaden, 1975), 138, no. 642, pl. 83; M. L. Vollenweider, *Catalogue raisonné des sceaux, cylindres, intailles et camées: Musée d'art et d'histoire de Genève* (Geneva, 1976), vol. 2, 334, no. 370, pl. 106 and 338, no. 376, pl. 107; Boardman, *GGFR*, 302, pl. 800.

2. See Vollenweider, *Catalogue*, 195, no. 205, pl. 62.

3. Brandt and Schmidt, *Antiken Gemmen*, I.3 (Munich, 1972), 22, no. 2225, pl. 194; G. Lippold, *Gemmen und Kammen des Altertums and der Neuzeit* (Stuttgart, n.d.), nos. 10–13, pl. LXI.

4. Furtwängler, *Gemmen*, vol. 2, 133, no. 76, pl. XXVI; Vollenweider, *Catalogue*, 332, no. 367, pl. 106.

5. Brandt and Schmidt, *Antiken Gemmen*, I.1 (Munich, 1968), 90, no. 503, pl. 54 and 90, no. 507, pl. 55; Vollenweider, *Catalogue*, 344, no. 384, pl. 108.

136. Oval Carnelian Ring with Personification of Africa

(first c. B.C.–first c. A.D.)

9234. Bronze ring with carnelian ringstone. Ht ring, 2.1 cm; total ht stone, 1.5 cm; w stone, 1.2 cm. Intact.

Flat bronze ring inset with oval ringstone carved on convex surface. Cast: right profile of female head, including neckline of garment. She wears an elephant scalp as headdress; the trunk rises above her forehead, and the ears fall over the back of the head. Her own hair is visible at the side of the face, extending to the bottom of the neck. Large prominent eye.

Among the gem shapes fashionable in the Hellenistic and Roman periods is the oval ringstone with a convex surface. It was often set, as here, so that it protrudes from a flat bronze ring with a broad shoulder.[1]

The elephant-scalp headdress was first worn by the deified Alexander on coins of Ptolemy I (323–318 B.C.),[2] Seleucus (ca. 312 B.C.),[3] and Agathocles (ca. 306 B.C.).[4] The scalp is that of the small-eared Indian elephant, and it rests upon the horns of Ammon. None of Alexander's successors assumed this headdress, which reappeared only on coin portraits of Demetrius of Bactria, issued about 200 B.C.[5]

The elephant scalp had a greater popularity as a headdress for women. On the coins of Juba I of Mauretania (ca. 50 B.C.),[6] and on the coins of contemporary Roman generals resisting Caesar in Africa,[7] the personification of Africa wears the scalp of the large-eared African elephant. After Caesar's victory at Thapsus in 46 B.C., this motif appeared on coins of Caesar's supporters, surely in reference to the province Africa Nova organized from Juba I's Numidian lands.[8] The figure of Africa is again shown wearing this headdress in a painting of the Abandonment of Dido from the House of Meleager.[9]

Many representations of a female in a large-eared elephant scalp survive from the late Hellenistic and early Roman period. Best known, perhaps, is the head on the Boscoreale plate,[10] but there also exist several appliqués,[11] paintings,[12] and gems,[13] all of which have been variously described as Africa or Alexandria. This last identification is dubious, however, since, as Babelon points out, Alexandria never appears on coins wearing the scalp.[14] There is also no strong evidence to support an identification as Libya.[15]

Our gem compares closely in style with gems of the late second and first centuries B.C.,[16] where we also find the same prominent eye, broad surface of the cheek, and fleshy neck. The features of our gem are closely paralleled on the coins depicting Africa issued by M. Eppius (47–46 B.C.)[17] and Juba I,[18] of ca. 50 B.C. It would seem that the figure on our gem has been copied from one of the coins, since the locks of hair and the beginning of the neckline are faithfully rendered, although the elephant tusks beneath the upraised trunk are simplified and possibly omitted, and the ears are so schematized that they designate neither the Indian nor African variety of elephant.

1. J. Boardman and M. L. Vollenweider, *Catalogue of the Engraved Gems and Finger Rings I. Greek and Etruscan* (Oxford, 1978), 74–75.

2. H. Sauer, *Festschrift Eugen V. Mercklin* (Waldsassen, 1964), 155. E. Babelon [*Arethuse* I (1923):95–107] dated the Ptolemaic coins between 312 and 306 B.C.

3. Ibid., 97–98, dated following the battle of 312 B.C. at Gaza.

4. Ibid., 101–2, dated the coins before 306 B.C.

5. Ibid., 103. See also a series of bronze appliqués in Sauer, *Festschrift*, 154–62.

6. Babelon, *Arethuse* I (1923):103 and pl. 19.9.

7. E. A. Sydenham, *The Coinage of the Roman Republic* (London, 1952), 175, no. 1051, pl. 28, and 171, no 1028, pl. 27; Babelon, *Arethuse* I (1923):104, pl. 19.3.

8. Ibid., pl. 19.8 and Sydenham, *Coinage*, 188, no. 1154; 187, no. 1153, pl. 29; 212, no. 1355. See also *OCD*, s.v. "Africa."

9. L. Richardson, *MAAR* 23 (1955):141, pl. XLI.

10. A. de Villefosse, *MonPiot* 5 (1899):39–43, pl. I as Alexandria. Sauer, 158. Babelon, *Arethuse* I (1923):104–5 identified the figure as Africa, but P. Perdrizet [*Bronzes grecs d'Égypte de la collection Fouquet* (Paris, 1911), 40] and V. Spinazzola [*Pompeii alla luce degli scavi nuovi di Via dell'Abbondanza* (Rome, 1953), 156, fig. 194] identify her as Alexandria.

11. Perdrizet, *Bronzes grecs*, 39, no. 64, pl. XXXIV. Spinazzola, *Pompeii*, 157, fig. 195 (as Alexandria). C. C. Edgar, *Catalogue général des antiquités égyptiennes du Musée du Caire: Greek Bronzes* (Cairo, 1904), VI and 55, nos. 27, 843–27, 844, pl. XVII; 72, no. 27, 923; 91, no. 32, 372, as Alexandria. Sauer, *Festschrift*, 159, pl. 55.2, as Africa.

12. Spinazzola, *Pompeii*, 156, fig. 193 from House II.II.5, as Alexandria.

13. E. Brandt and E. Schmidt, *Antike Gemmen in deutschen Sammlungen 1.2* (Munich, 1970), 66, no. 945, pl. 108, as Africa, and G. Lippold, *Gemmen and Kameen des Altertums und der Neuzeit* (Stuttgart, n.d.), pl. CXXXII.1, as Africa. Babelon, *Arethuse* I (1923):95, fig. 24 and 105, pl. 19.7.

14. Ibid., 102, 104.

15. Libya is the term the Greeks used for Africa. A personification of Libya in corkscrew curls is on an inscribed relief from Cyrene, and coins of that city depict a female head wearing similar ringlets [see F. Cumont, *MonPiot* 32 (1932):42, 49]. For this reason female heads in ringlets and elephant scalp have been identified as Libya (see Brandt and Schmidt, *Antike Gemmen*, 181, no. 1773, pl. 162).

16. Boardman and Vollenweider, 207, no. 217, pl. 64.

17. Sydenham, *Coinage*, 175, no. 1051, pl. 28; Babelon, *Arethuse* I (1923):104, pl. 19.3.

18. Babelon, *Arethuse* I (1923):103, pl. 19.9.

Mosaic

ROMAN

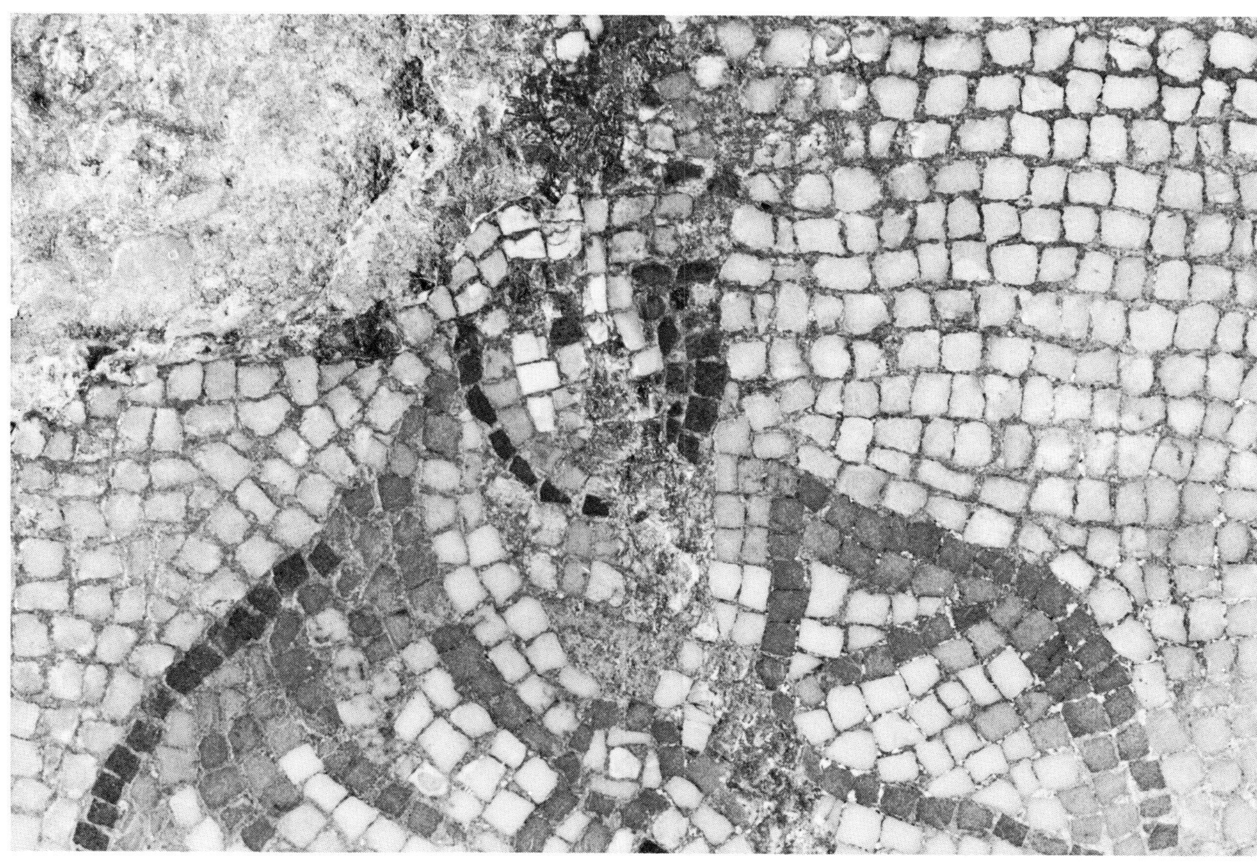

137. Emblema Mosaic with Rural Scene

(fourth c. A.D.)

9188. Limestone tray. W, 38.2 cm; ht, 39.5 cm; depth, 1.3 to 2.5 cm; th of border, 1.5 cm. Individual tessera, 0.4 cm sq. Mended from twelve pieces with areas missing. Worked largely in shades of grey, brown, and red against grey background.

Single limestone block was hollowed out, leaving a narrow rim on all four sides. Tesserae were set into the tray flush with surface. Three rows of black tesserae enframe scene. Grazing upon a beige meadow of brown and grey grassy clumps and red flowers is a grey donkey in left profile. He wears a grey and yellow saddle-pad beneath a brown woven wicker basket that is secured by a breastplate. Emerging from top of basket are brown vessels, red flowers, and a bird. Donkey's bridle consists of red noseband, browband, and a strap passing between eyes and ears. Yellow discs at juncture of straps. Behind animal's head and holding the reins is a man standing frontally, head turned three-quarters to his left. He wears a short grey tunic beneath a brown mantle draped over both shoulders and fastened in front. Cap with upturned rim. In front of donkey's haunch stands a small boy in left profile wearing a brown sleeved tunic with legs exposed. Boy is gathering red flowers into a brown basket, which he holds in his left hand together with a duck.

Our mosaic is an emblema, a separately made picture panel that was inserted into a floor mosaic, the rest of which would have been worked in the same or larger sized tesserae in a nonfigural pattern. The use of the hollowed stone tray or tile enabled the emblema to be transported long distances from the workshops, although we know that many were also made close to their final destination. The emblema technique was in use by about 200 B.C.[1] and is best known from the examples in Pompeii of about 100 B.C. by Dioskurides of Samos.[2] In the eastern Mediterranean the technique was not common after 100 A.D.[3] and in Italy it was employed only occasionally through the Roman period.[4] It is in Africa that the technique flourished from the first to the fourth centuries A.D.,[5] particularly in Tripolitania around Zliten.

On the Hopkins mosaic many of the forms, such as the donkey's neck and the man's leg, have been worked by juxtaposing rows of radically different colored tesserae, thereby creating a striated and flat effect that is underscored by the man's dangling feet. Similarly without substance are the geometrically shaped faces, which are expressionless except for the heavy, dark brows and large, staring eyes. The glances are the only links between the figures, who are otherwise unrelated by pose or gesture. The artist's primary emphasis was on the detailed patterns of drapery and baskets. The closest parallels to this style are found on mosaics from Hippo Regius[6] and Piazza Armerina,[7] which are attributed to Carthaginian craftsmen working in the first half of the fourth century. Also comparable is the Dominus Julius mosaic from Carthage of the late fourth century, where there is a similar handling of basket, cap, and grassy terrain.[8] It is likely, therefore, that our mosaic was made during the fourth century, perhaps in North Africa, but possibly in Sicily or southern Italy, where African influence was strong.[9]

Both the pastoral setting of our scene and the composition—comprised of two figures, an animal, and rural bounty—invite comparison with mosaics of the calendar tradition.[10] A calendar floor mosaic is generally composed of several square or rectangular scenes, each of which depicts a rural activity or attribute of a single month or season. Occasionally, each scene is worked as an emblema. It is believed that these calendar mosaics are based upon lost Roman rural calendars that evolved in the first century A.D., when scenes of the Roman agricultural cycle were introduced into the Greek liturgical calendar.[11] Since no early example of these Roman calendars survives, their appearance must be reconstructed from later manuscripts[12] or from the calendar mosaics, which date from the second through fourth centuries.

Our mosaic departs from the calendar tradition because the scene is not representative of any specific season or month. Whereas the dead birds and fruits suggest autumn or winter,[13] the gathering of flowers is appropriate to spring.[14] It would seem then that, like many late African examples, our mosaic is only a general rural composition inspired by the calendar tradition. One might compare it to the fourth-century mosaic depicting the estate of Dominus Julius, where, within a single setting, four vignettes portray the master and mistress in rural activities representative of each season.

1. The Sophilos mosaic [K. Dunbabin, *The Mosaics of Roman North Africa* (Oxford, 1978), 3].

2 J. Charbonneaux, *Hellenistic Art* (New York, 1973), 140–41, figs. 139–40.

3. Dunbabin, *Mosaics*, 4.

4. M. Blake, *MAAR* 17 (1940):101–5. R. P. Hinks, *Catalogue of The Greek Etruscan Roman Paintings and Mosaics in the British Museum* (London, 1933), 65, pl. 25.

5. Dunbabin, *Mosaics*, 17–18, 23, 29, 137–38. F. Baraite, *Mosaiques romaines et paléo-chrétiennes du Musée du Louvre* (Paris, 1978), 49, no. 13.

6. Dunbabin, *Mosaics*, 55, 238–39, pl. 29.

7. Ibid., 53–54, 198–212, pls. 198–201. W. Dorigo, *Late Roman Painting* (London, 1970), 156–57, 180 (of the Carnage Master).

8. Dunbabin, *Mosaics*, 118–19, pl. 109. D. Parrish, *AJA* 83 (1979):279–85.

9. Dunbabin, *Mosaics*, 212.

10. Best known is the mosaic from St. Romain en Gal. See H. Stern, *Gallia* 9 (1951):21–30; J. Webster, *The Labors of the Months* (Chicago, 1938), 123–24; Dunbabin, *Mosaics*, 109–11.

11. G. Hanfmann, *The Season Sarcophagus in Dumbarton Oaks I* (Cambridge, 1951), 222; Dunbabin, *Mosaics*, 111; D. Levi, *Art Bulletin* 23 (1941):277.

12. H. Stern, *Le calendrier de 354* in *Bibliothèque archéologique et historique*, no. 55 (Paris, 1953); D. Levi, *Art Bulletin* 23 (1941):251–91.

13. Hanfmann, *The Season Sarcophagus*, 64; Stern, *Le calendrier de 354*, 245–47, 263, 292.

14. Levi, *Art Bulletin* 23 (1941):261; Stern, *Le calendrier de 354*, 249.